SECTION 6 PRODUCTION STRATEGIES

SECTION 7 HUMAN RESOURCES

SECTION 8 COMMUNICATIONS

SECTION 9 BUSINESS IN ITS ENVIRONMENT

Preface

The fourth edition of this book retains all the features which has made it the market leader since it was first published in 1988, but it now includes many new items.

It continues to use an enquiry-based approach which is designed to encourage students to think and act like businessmen and businesswomen from the start by actively participating in a great variety of realistic situations, ranging from one-person businesses, through small companies, to multinationals.

The format of the book remains substantially the same with each double-page unit starting off with stimulus material about an essential business situation or problem which is invariably presented in the form of a case study. Students' comprehension is tested in carefully-graded **study points** before they are asked to solve the problem or come to a decision.

The text provides a many-faceted view of the topic under examination. It is broken up into convenient sections, with important points or concepts carefully explained in simple language to increase accessibility for the widest range of students. For the same reason, many full colour charts, diagrams and illustrations are also included. **Key terms**, which form an essential part of preparation for the examination, are highlighted in the text and then separately defined in alphabetical order on each right-hand page. Simple **checkpoints** test the students' basic understanding of the text and, occasionally, lead on to further activities.

The book is divided into nine colour-coded sections. Each unit is self-contained. To provide for the greatest flexibility in use, the units contain cross-references to earlier and later units to make it easy for teachers to take any path through the book they prefer. There is a comprehensive index with emboldened references to all the key terms.

There are also many new features.

Case studies There are many more case studies. Sometimes there are two in one unit, and there are further case studies in a new section of the book. Most of them are sourced direct from the internet which often provides more authentic and revealing material than newspaper cuttings.

Online links There are online links throughout the book to internet sources on which the case studies are based. These links make it easy for students and teachers to obtain additional information or to carry out further online research into the topic.

Revision and exam practice One important new feature is the 19 revision and exam practice sections, located at logical points throughout the book. These contain more case studies to provide additional practice in using business skills; review points and extended questions to reinforce knowledge; and Foundation and Higher examination questions to test students' understanding of the main topics covered in the preceding group of units.

Final exam practice To build upon this constant examination practice, there are now three separate papers for final exam practice at the end of the book. These cover different types of questions and the most common topics which students are likely to encounter in the real examination. They are at both Foundation and Higher level.

Revised text There are a number of completely new units, especially on e-commerce. The rest of the text has been extensively revised and rewritten to take account of all the rapidly changing developments in the business world, and to cover the approaches and topics laid down in the new specifications. The book covers all the specifications for the GCSE examinations starting in 2003 for both full, modular and short courses including virtually all options.

Key skills and citizenship To meet the new specifications, opportunities for providing evidence of key skills are highlighted throughout the book. These form an integral part of each unit and students should do these tasks whether they are to be used as evidence or not. (Many IT tasks can also be carried out manually if IT equipment is not available.) The book also provides good opportunities for contributing towards the teaching of citizenship. In this connection, the most useful units are: 6, 19, 21, 22, 44, 52, 53, 55, 60, 62, 68, 69, 73, 74, 75, 76. There is more information about key skills and citizenship opportunities in the Teachers' Resource Pack.

Online help This is the only GCSE Business Studies book to have its own teachers' support website which contains useful resource material on key examination questions, coursework, etc. There are further details in the Teachers' Resource Pack.

Finally, I should like to thank my many personal friends in the business world who have given me invaluable advice and information during the writing of the four editions of this book.

Renée Huggett.

Section 1

Elements of business

Business opportunities

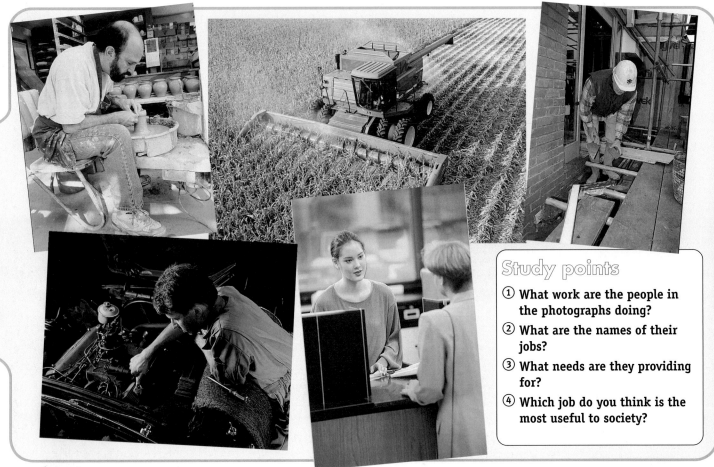

The business person is always looking out for chances to provide the **goods** and **services** that we all need. There are some things that we cannot do without. These five **basic needs** are:

- food
- water
- shelter
- clothes
- warmth.

No human being could survive for long if these basic needs were not met. They are just as important for people in the developed societies of the western world as they are for the few tribal societies in remote corners of the developing world. Look at Figure 1, which shows the total amount spent by British **consumers** (the people who buy goods and services) in a single year. Which of the goods and services in the chart are meeting our basic needs? What percentage do we spend on basic needs?

Figure 1: Consumer spending in a single year

	£ m
Cars and other vehicles	28,355
Other durable, long-lasting goods	24,247
Food	54,175
Alcohol and tobacco	41,866
Clothing and footwear	31,571
Energy products	28,215
Other goods	66,491
Rent, water and sewerage charges	70,755
Catering and eating out	46,009
Transport and communication	50,205
Financial services	24,164
Other services	61,518
Total	**527,571**

Source: adapted from *Monthly Digest of Statistics*, Office for National Statistics, February, 2000

Providing for our needs

One of the main differences between primitive societies and our own is that we let other people provide for most of our needs. It was once usual for human beings to collect wild plants, hunt animals and grow crops for their own use. Most people in the western world rely on others to provide their food. The farmer grows wheat on the land. The grain is sold to a merchant, who resells it to a miller who makes the flour. This is then sold to a baker who makes the loaves of bread. Without their labour, there would be no bread for us to buy. Each of them makes a **profit** on their part of the deal. Some of this money is invested in buying all the other goods, such as tractors, combine harvesters, milling wheels and dough-mixing machines, which are needed so that the process can be repeated again and again. These goods are called **capital**.

With all goods there is a chain of

production similar to the one for bread. With services, there is a general dependence on other firms. Plumbers, for instance, have to buy tools and equipment before they can do their work.

The whole of the business world is interdependent in this way. Money goes round and round from one person or firm to another to keep the economy working. People get a job – if they can – so that they will have enough money to pay for their needs. Business people – and public bodies such as State schools – provide the goods and services which other people need and make a profit to pay for their own needs.

Providing for our wants

Although there are some things which we cannot do without, there are others which we may not really need, but which are very pleasant to have. No one really needs a car. It is possible to live without one. However, travel is much easier if you do have one. Although most people like to have a microwave or a freezer, you could live without one. In modern societies there are hundreds, if not thousands, of **wants** of this kind.

Business provides for these wants, as well as for our basic needs. Modern societies could not exist as they do today unless people's wants were always increasing. At the end of the Second World War, only rich people could afford to fly. Now that air travel is something that nearly everyone can afford, lots of new industries have been created. Jobs have been provided for millions of people, both in the UK and abroad.

Electronics has brought many new inventions into our homes, from video recorders to compact disc players. As a result, many more skilled engineers have been needed to design and build these machines. In a similar way, computers have created a need for new skills, which has brought about great changes in education and training. The world is always changing. The business person is always looking for new ways to meet new needs.

Figure 2: Production of a loaf of bread

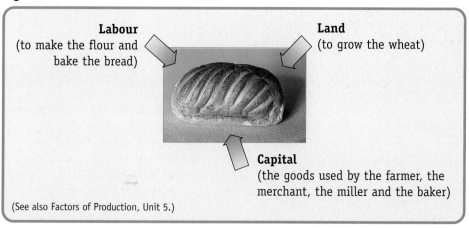

Labour
(to make the flour and bake the bread)

Land
(to grow the wheat)

Capital
(the goods used by the farmer, the merchant, the miller and the baker)

(See also Factors of Production, Unit 5.)

KEY TERMS

Basic needs Food, water, shelter, clothes and warmth, i.e. things that are essential for existence.
Capital Manufactured goods that are used to produce other goods and services.
Consumers People who buy goods or services for their own use.
Goods Physical objects that can be bought at a price, e.g. a packet of crisps at 25p or so.
Profit The difference between the selling price and the cost of production.
Services Non-physical products, ranging from education to medical care and from tourism to entertainment. They are also bought, or paid for, sometimes through taxes and rates, e.g. State education.
Wants Desires to obtain goods or services that one does not have.

CHECKPOINTS

❶ What are the five basic needs?

❷ What is the main difference between a basic need and a want?

❸ For each of our basic needs, list three craftspeople, kinds of firm and of organization which are involved in providing it.

❹ What other industries have been created or expanded as a result of air travel being made available to many more people?

❺ Explain how a want can become a need in modern western societies.

❻ What kind of business would you set up to meet new needs? Give reasons for your choice.

Key skills
Number and IT

A bar chart is a visual device which at a glance how things compare with each other. The vertical bar chart in Figure 3 shows how the annual sales of an imaginary company compare over a three-year period.

Figure 3: Company Sales

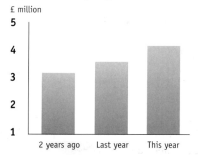

£ million

5		
4		
3		
2		
1		
	2 years ago	Last year	This year

Construct a bar chart showing the amounts spent in a year by consumers on food, alcohol and tobacco, and clothing and footwear, using the figures given in Figure 1. Use a spreadsheet or chart-making programme to construct the chart.

Markets

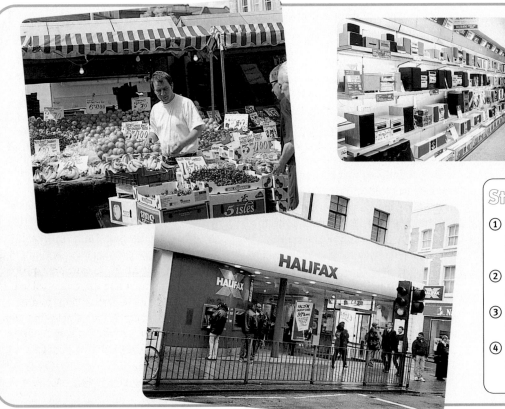

Buyers and sellers

The business person is constantly seeking **markets** for his or her **products**. In early societies, where even basic needs could not always be met, there was only one kind of market. Producers and traders would go from town to town or set up their stalls at a suitable crossroads to sell their goods or services.

That kind of market still exists in modern societies. Consumers come from miles around to buy food, clothes, shoes and other goods in street markets or at car boot sales. Most markets, however, do not exist in only one place. Buyers and sellers are scattered all over the country or even over the whole world. A market brings buyers and sellers together so that an exchange of goods or services can take place at a price. It can exist in a street market, in an auction room, or in a newspaper which advertises goods and services for sale, over the telephone, as with the Bank of Scotland's Banking Direct service, and on the internet. There are also

many other kinds of markets which cannot be seen. There is a market for cars, even though the buyers and sellers do not all come together in one place at one time. There is another for private education, television sets and so on.

The number of wants in modern societies is so great that there are thousands of different markets. Business people have to choose their market carefully if they are to succeed (see Unit 36). First of all, they must decide what type of market they are going to enter.

Different market types

There are four main types of market (see Figure 1).

- The non-durable (not lasting) consumer market exists to provide all the goods that people consume quickly.

- The consumer durable market deals in goods which last longer and which consumers will continue to use until they break or are replaced.

- The industrial or organizational market supplies goods to other manufacturers and organizations, who may sell their finished goods to consumers or to other manufacturers. (A small engineering firm, for example, may make parts of an oil rig, which is used by a multinational oil company to produce oil, which is then refined and sold by a garage to the consumer.)

- The services market deals with non-physical products of all kinds which are needed by both consumers and businesses. This market, which is now the biggest and the one which is expanding most rapidly, deals in such things as hairdressing, insurance, transport and so on.

A market exists whenever some people want to buy and others want to sell. If you made something – a dress, for example – or offered a service – such as cleaning windows – and no one wanted to buy,

Figure 1: Markets

Type of market	How long the product lasts	Examples of products
Non-durable consumer	Brief	Food, drinks, tobacco, newspapers, ice-cream
Consumer durable	Years	Electrical goods, cars, clothes, refrigerators
Industrial or organizational	Years	Ready-mixed concrete, industrial machinery, car components
Services	As long as need lasts	Education, loans, tourism, publicity

CHECKPOINTS

❶ What is a market?

❷ Why is the market so important for the business person?

❸ Use the Yellow Pages to find two examples of each of the four main types of market.

❹ How do markets help to fix prices?

❺ If you were setting up a business, state which of the four types of market you would go into.

there would be no market. In a similar way, if people wanted to buy something and there were no sellers, there would be no market either. (In that case, however, some keen business person would almost certainly start making the product if there were enough buyers for him or her to make a profit.)

Price

The price of goods and services is decided in the market. Basically, the price depends upon the **supply** (how many goods and services are available) and the **demand** (how many buyers there are), though there

Figure 2: Supply and demand

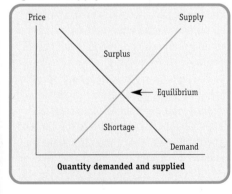

are also many other factors involved (see Unit 43).

If supply is bigger than demand, producers will cut back production and reduce prices.

If demand increases, producers will increase production and put up prices.

When the amount demanded equals the amount supplied, the equilibrium price will be reached.

These **market forces** can be seen at work most clearly whenever there is a face-to-face meeting between buyer and seller. A house owner may reduce the price of his or her house if there have not been many enquiries. In an auction sale, bidders drop out until only one is left, when demand is equal to supply.

Figure 3: Output

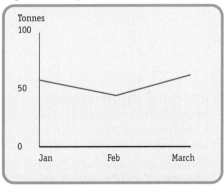

These market forces of supply and demand can be expressed in the form of a graph (see Figure 2). Graphs are equally useful when only one value is involved. In this case, a single-line graph would be used, as in Figure 3. This single-line graph shows the amount of ice-cream produced by a manufacturer in the first three months of a year.

Amounts (tonnes in this case) are usually shown on the vertical axis and time (months in this case) on the horizontal axis.

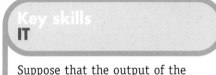

Key skills

IT

Suppose that the output of the ice-cream manufacturer in Figure 3 for the first six months of the year was:

January, 60 tonnes
February, 50 tonnes
March, 65 tonnes
April, 95 tonnes
May, 75 tonnes
June, 105 tonnes.

Key these values into a spreadsheet. Choose the type of graph required (i.e. single line graph) and create the graph. Label the vertical axis and give the graph a title. Print a hard copy.

KEY TERMS

Demand The number of goods or services that buyers are willing and able to buy over a period of time.

Market forces The forces of demand and supply which help to decide the price and control what should be produced.

Markets Putting buyers and sellers in touch so that an exchange of goods or services can take place.

Products Any goods or services.

Supply The number of goods or services offered for sale over a period of time.

Types of production

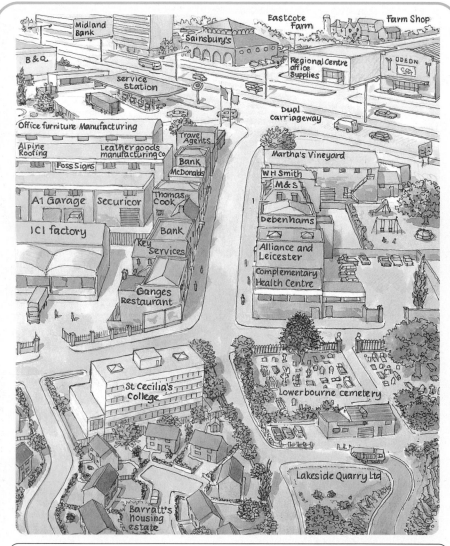

There are three main kinds of production.

- **Primary production**, which involves extracting natural resources from the earth, such as oil; and growing food and other crops.
- **Secondary production**, which includes the manufacturing of goods and semi-finished goods, such as metal sheets and rods; building; and supplying water, gas and electricity.
- **Tertiary production**, which provides services of all kinds to consumers and organizations.

Interdependence

It might seem that a tourist agency, which is in the tertiary sector, has very little connection with either primary or secondary production. Its main job is to book holidays and flights for customers. It doesn't grow anything or extract anything from the sea or land; and neither does it manufacture any goods.

However, it does depend greatly on other people or firms who do. Without its computers, it would do little business, but a firm in the secondary sector had to make the machines. Other firms in secondary production have made the paper, the desks, the tables and all the other goods that the agency uses.

Without a supply of electricity, the agency's computers would not work. For this, the agency depends on miners in the primary sector who produce coal or uranium from which electricity is generated.

The agency is also dependent on other firms in tertiary production – from the solicitor who gives legal advice and the bank manager who provides loans, to the window-cleaner who shines the plate-glass windows to attract customers.

Links in a chain

With services, there is a general **interdependence** with other types of industry, but with goods the links are far more direct (see Unit 1). There is a **chain of production** which links all three kinds of industry. The chains of production for a chair and for a hand-made woollen sweater are shown in Figure 1.

The more **specialization** there is, the more interdependence there will be, as each business will be making only a small part of the total product.

Study points

(Look at the Key Terms on the opposite page first.)

① Make three lists showing the primary, secondary and tertiary production shown in the illustration above.

② What kind of production would you normally expect to find in a high street?

③ Why is primary production usually found outside town centres?

④ Apart from secondary, what other kinds of production would you expect to find on an industrial estate? Explain why these other kinds are also located there.

⑤ Find a town, or part of a city, which once had big factories or industrial plants which have now closed. What kind of industry was it? Why did it decline? What changes, if any, have been made in the area since then? If there are no examples where you live, find one example in a library or on the internet.

Figure 1: Chains of production for a chair and a hand-made woollen sweater

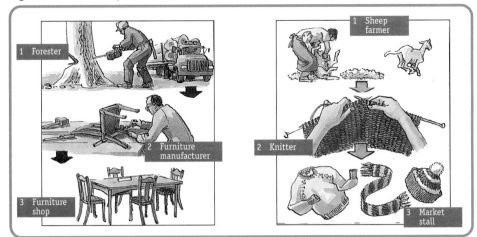

Figure 2: Gross domestic product by industry

	£ million	
	1990	*1998*
Agriculture, hunting, forestry and fishing	9,700	9.656
Mining and quarrying	13,404	12,748
Manufacturing	114,809	147,306
Electricity, gas and water supply	11,618	16,737
Construction	34,555	39,262
Wholesale and retail trade	70,948	113,070
Transport and communication	41,934	63,340
Financial services	97,457	176,977
Public administration and defence	33,021	40,495
Education, health and social work	53,428	89,041
Other services	18,867	38,912

Source: adapted from Office for National Statistics,
Annual Abstract of Statistics, 2000, Stationery Office, 2000

Profitable industry

Business people who can spot a gap in the market for goods or services will always be on to a winner. It is no good going into a declining industry and hoping to make a profit unless you have a really brilliant idea. So it reduces risk to enter an industry which is booming, where the chances of success are high. Look at Figure 2, which shows the amounts that various industries contributed to the **gross domestic product (GDP)** in 1990 and 1998. Which industry showed the biggest rise and which showed the biggest fall? Business people have to study information of this kind very carefully before they choose their product.

KEY TERMS

Chain of production The various stages, from raw material to finished product, through which goods pass before they are sold to consumers.
Gross domestic product (GDP) The total value of all goods and services produced by a country in a year.
Primary production Getting raw materials, such as oil, fish or coal, from the land or sea, or using the earth to grow things, such as crops or trees.
Secondary production Processing raw materials into finished goods.
Tertiary production Providing a service to any branch of industry or direct to consumers. This includes distributing and transporting goods.
Interdependence The dependence of businesses upon each other.
Specialization Businesses or people who concentrate on one particular activity.

CHECKPOINTS

1 What are the three main types of production? Give two examples of each.

2 What is a chain of production?

3 Draw charts showing the chain of production for a china cup; a plastic bag; a metal nail.

4 Why do you think all industries are dependent on one another?

5 Suggest reasons for the big increase (shown in Figure 2) in financial services between 1990 and 1998.

Key skills
Number and IT

PIE CHARTS

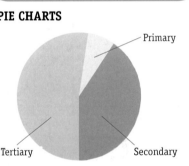

Contribution of primary, secondary and tertiary production to GDP

Pie charts show the relationship of parts to the whole in visual form. Use the figures in Figure 2 to work out the total amount contributed by primary, secondary and tertiary industries to the gross domestic product in 1998. Calculate the percentage share of each (rounding the figures to the nearest whole number).

Use a computer and suitable software package to construct a pie chart similar to the one above and print a hard copy of your chart. (If you do not have access to a computer, draw the pie chart by hand.)

The internet

Yell UK Web Awards

With the internet and e-commerce playing an increasingly important role in all aspects of our lives, the awards provide a unique opportunity to allow you to nominate your favourite site.

Entries will be judged by a panel of independent experts. The award categories include:
- best e-commerce site (business-to-business)
- best e-commerce site (business-to-consumer)
- best site for small and medium-sized enterprises (SMEs)

A number of criteria will be considered for all categories:
- overall site design
- ease of navigation around the site
- frequency with which the site is updated
- use of relevant technology and overuse of unnecessary technology
- the extent to which the site is engaging, captures the imagination and surprises.

Source: adapted from Yell UK Web Awards website.

Online shopping

Recent research shows that 25 per cent of internet users have already purchased goods via the internet. The most popular items bought online are computers and books.

Have you bought online?

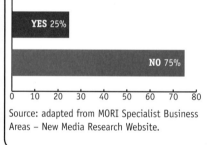

YES 25%

NO 75%

0   10   20   30   40   50   60   70   80

Source: adapted from MORI Specialist Business Areas – New Media Research Website.

David Bowie is a very enthusiastic supporter of the internet and was the first major artist to use it for chats with fans. He has his own website with a newsletter, chats with special guests and samples of his artwork. His last album was released on the internet.

The internet has many official sites for artists, fans and live concerts. A new technology, MP3, which compresses audio files, has made it easy to send and download music on the internet. This has provided new bands and acts with an opportunity to show off their talents, though very few have made it to the big time. It has also allowed individuals from all parts of the world to make thousands of pirated tracks of established acts available illegally on the internet.

The British record industry has a turnover, or total sales, of over £3 billion a year. Many record retailers now sell CDs over the internet as well as in their stores.

The **internet** provides a cheap and speedy way of communicating with other people all over the world by means of words, pictures and sounds. It is as revolutionary as the invention of printing in the fifteenth century – more than 500 years ago. The internet has two main aspects:
- the worldwide web (www.) consisting of millions of websites which provide information in both words and pictures about every imaginable topic and event
- e-mail (electronic mail) which provides an instant and cheap means of sending messages, documents and pictures to any other computer in the world.

Until recently, the internet was available only on computers, but it is fast becoming possible to go online using digital televisions, WAP (wireless application protocol) mobile phones, and games consoles (see Unit 65).

An estimated 18 million people in Britain have access to the internet, and about two-thirds are regular users. It is forecast that the number of internet users

Study points

1. What percentage of internet users have bought goods online?
2. Which are the two most popular kinds of goods for online buyers?
3. What is the annual turnover of the record industry in Britain?
4. Where do you prefer to buy CDs: in a store or online? State your reasons.
5. Look at some business-to-consumer websites which sell goods or services to consumers online. Which one would you put first? Give reasons for your choice.

Online links

www.yell.com
www. mori.com
www.davidbowie.com

Figure 1: Online banking advert

in Britain will more than double to 40 million by 2004. There is a similar growth in all developed countries throughout the world. As a result billions of people, of all ages, social classes and nationalities will soon be online.

Business-to-consumer

The growth of the internet has produced a revolution in businesses of all kinds. In retailing, **entrepreneurs** have created a new kind of business, the **dot com company**, which sells goods and services to customers online. These business-to-consumer companies (known as B2C), exist only in cyberspace but take the whole of the world as their market. There are now over 20 million dot.com companies.

For example, the pioneer online bookshop www.amazon.com, sells millions of books in America, Britain and other countries, even though it doesn't have a single bookshop. There are thousands of other B2C companies of a similar kind, selling a great variety of goods.

Very few, if any of these dot com companies have ever made a profit, yet many of their founders have become millionaires! Investors of all kinds have been so keen to buy a stake in these new

e-companies that they have been willing to pay inflated prices for their shares. As a result, the value of the founders' own shares has increased dramatically.

Cut in values

Recently, however, the value of some of these companies' shares has fallen as they face increasing competition, not only from other dot com companies, but also from existing retailers in the old economy which have gone online. For example, practically all the big booksellers, such as Waterstones, now have their own websites where books may be ordered. These companies, which have both shops and websites, are known as clicks and mortar companies.

There has been a similar growth in the services industries with both established banks such as Barclays, and new banks such as Egg, going online. In all, almost half of the big British companies and just over a quarter of small businesses now have their own websites.

Competition has become so intense that some of the wealthiest and best-known dot com companies have gone into liquidation, including living.com, the top online furniture store and boo.com, the online fashion retailer (see Unit 14).

More of these new companies will probably go the same way, until there are a much smaller number of successful companies, which might then start to make the huge profits that investors have been hoping for.

Although e-commerce (electronic commerce) is still a very small percentage of total British retail spending, it was forecast to increase to £10 billion in 2000, and to rise even further in future years. However, many consumers still have doubts about internet shopping. One of their main fears is that hackers might steal their credit card details if they shop

online. Consumers are also worried that firms they contact can collect masses of data about them which they can use later for their own purposes. They are also concerned that delivery of goods might be late or that they may not even arrive at all if they have had the bad luck to deal with a rogue firm.

Business-to-business

Recently, there has been a great increase in business-to-business (B2B) commerce which may have an even bigger long-term impact on business. In the past, big manufacturers such as Ford had to order thousands of different parts from hundreds of engineering firms. When different parts were needed for new models, the purchasing department had to tell suppliers what was wanted and ask them to make a **tender** to supply the parts. This was a long and costly process.

Now, car manufacturers have joined together to set up electronic exchanges. Manufacturers state the exact specification of the parts required on the electronic exchange. Suppliers from all parts of the world then put in their bids to do the job. This not only speeds up the process, but cuts manufacturers' costs as they no longer need large purchasing departments. Because of global competition, suppliers will be forced to cut their prices. It is estimated that manufacturers could save 10 per cent or more of their total costs.

Similar worldwide electronic exchanges are being set up in many other industries, including food, chemicals, clothes and oil. However, these new exchanges are currently being investigated by the European Union to see if they break competition rules.

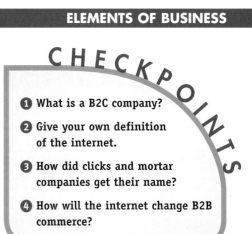

CHECKPOINTS

1. What is a B2C company?
2. Give your own definition of the internet.
3. How did clicks and mortar companies get their name?
4. How will the internet change B2B commerce?

KEY TERMS

Dot com company A business which does all of its trade on the internet. Its web address, or URL, ends in 'com'.

Entrepreneurs People who believe in enterprise and are willing to take risks to set up and develop a business, often backing their idea with their own money.

Internet A communication network which links millions of computers and other electronic devices all over the world through telephone, cable and wireless links.

Tender An offer to do a specified job at a stated price.

Government involvement

Forecast public spending and receipts for 2001

Public spending was expected to be about £370 billion in 2001, or around £6,000 for each person in the United Kingdom. If the government spends more money than it receives in taxes, it has to make up the difference by borrowing from financial institutions such as banks, or from the public. This money is known as the public sector borrowing requirement, or PSBR.

Expenditure (£ billion)

- NHS £54bn
- Transport £46bn
- Education £46bn
- Defence £23bn
- Debt interest £28bn
- Industry & agriculture £15bn
- Law & order £20bn
- Housing & Environment £14bn
- Other expenditure £59bn
- Social security £103bn

Receipts (£ billion)

- Council tax £14bn
- Other £55bn
- Business rates £16bn
- Income tax £96bn
- VAT £60bn
- National Insurance £59bn
- Excise duties £37bn
- Corporation tax £34bn

VAT

NHS

Income tax

Law and order

Raising revenue

Although private businesses earn almost all of the country's money, the government decides how almost half of it should be spent. During the last 20 years, it has spent up to 45 per cent of the gross domestic product (total value of all goods and services produced in the UK in that year).

The government raises money through **direct taxes** on individuals and businesses, **indirect taxes** on goods and services, and national insurance contributions, which are paid by both employers and employees. Then it decides – on behalf of the nation – how much should be spent on defence, health, public order and other items.

Government powers

The government's power does not stop there. It also controls and influences business in other ways.

- The government provides much of the physical and social **infrastructure** which contributes to business performance.
- It provides most of the educational services.
- It makes large purchases of goods and services.
- It is the largest employer.

Study points

① What does the government spend most money on?

② What is the biggest amount of money the government receives?

③ How much money does business pay in corporation tax and business rates?

④ Look at the amounts of money the government is expecting to spend. If you were the Chancellor of the Exchequer, what changes would you make, keeping the same total? State the reasons for your changes.

Online links
www.hm-treasury.gov.uk
www.open.gov.uk

Figure 1: Factors of production

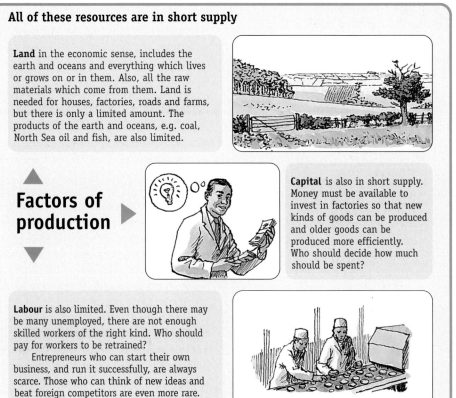

All of these resources are in short supply

Land in the economic sense, includes the earth and oceans and everything which lives or grows on or in them. Also, all the raw materials which come from them. Land is needed for houses, factories, roads and farms, but there is only a limited amount. The products of the earth and oceans, e.g. coal, North Sea oil and fish, are also limited.

Factors of production

Capital is also in short supply. Money must be available to invest in factories so that new kinds of goods can be produced and older goods can be produced more efficiently. Who should decide how much should be spent?

Labour is also limited. Even though there may be many unemployed, there are not enough skilled workers of the right kind. Who should pay for workers to be retrained?

Entrepreneurs who can start their own business, and run it successfully, are always scarce. Those who can think of new ideas and beat foreign competitors are even more rare.

In addition, the government has a great influence on business by controlling income tax and other financial aspects of the economy or business world (see Unit 71).

Factors of production

Although there may be no limit to wants, each country has only limited resources.

All goods or services produced need an input of land, labour and capital. These resources are known as the **factors of production**. All businesses and the people who work in them contribute **added value** to all the goods and services which are produced. As a result, a finished piece of furniture is worth much more than the wood which was cut from a tree to make it. It is now thought that entrepreneurs add most value because they are willing to take

chances. Without their special quality of **enterprise**, many businesses would not even exist. This is particularly important in this new information-based age, which has already produced great opportunities for many new kinds of business in communications, science, health and learning.

The factors of production are scarce, so we cannot have all we want. We have to make a choice – or let business or the government make one for us. If we choose to have one thing, we cannot have another. If you, as an individual, choose to spend all your money on clothes, you can't then afford to go to the cinema. If we, as a nation, choose to spend money on housing, there will be less money available for education, roads or social security. Economists call the value of this sacrifice – the thing which has to be given up – **the opportunity cost.**

The opportunity cost of a sweater might be a visit to the cinema. The opportunity cost of a new school might be two swimming baths. Look at your answer to Question 4 in the Study Points. Did you make the best choice?

KEY TERMS

Added value The amount, which can be expressed in money terms, that is added to a product as it is being made or distributed.

Direct taxes Taxes taken by the government on income and wealth. For example, individuals pay income tax and firms pay corporation tax. These taxes are collected by the Inland Revenue.

Enterprise A willingness to try out new ideas, working methods and kinds of business.

Factors of production Land, labour, capital and entrepreneurship.

Indirect taxes Taxes and duties taken by the government on spending, such as VAT and duties on drink and tobacco. These are collected by Customs and Excise.

Infrastructure The human-made environment such as roads, railways, housing, etc.

Opportunity cost The alternative which is given up when you choose one thing in business instead of another.

Planned, market and mixed economies

Nottingham tram gets final go-ahead

Nottingham's new trams are to be based on ADtranz designs

Minister for Transport Lord MacDonald has announced the final go-ahead for Nottingham's new £180 million tram system. Nottingham Express Transit (NET) will be receiving revenue support.

Lord MacDonald said: 'I am delighted that the government is backing Nottingham's new £180 million tram system. The new system will offer quicker, safer, cleaner and smarter transport for local people. It will make it easier for people to choose to use public transport and leave the car behind.'

The scheme will be built and operated by a private sector consortium, Arrow, comprising ADtranz

The ADtranz group
The international group ADtranz is one of the world's leading providers of railway systems, products and solutions. Internationally, ADtranz is the largest company in the rail industry, with marketing, development and production in 60 countries, representation in another 40 countries and 24,000 employees worldwide.

Source: ADtranz Group website

Total Rail Systems Ltd. based at Derby (where the trams will be built), Carillion (civil engineering contractors), Transdev SA (French public transport operators) and Nottingham City Transport (major local bus operator).

Source: adapted from Tenders on the Web News website.

Study points

① How much will Nottingham's new transport system cost?

② What is the total number of ADtranz employees?

③ How many public and private sector bodies are involved in the scheme? Why are there so many?

④ What are the main advantages of the scheme for:
(a) the people of Nottingham
(b) ADtranz
(c) Nottingham City Transport?

Online links
www.tenders.co.uk
www.adtranz.com

Managing the economy
There are three main ways in which a nation can manage its economy. It can have a:
● market economy
● planned economy
● mixed economy.

Market economies
In a **market economy**, everything would be controlled by supply and demand, i.e. market forces (see Unit 2). There would be no government interference of any kind. Everything would be left to private firms.

There are no real-life examples of market economies. The United States probably comes closest to this model; but even there, the government controls many services such as defence and the federal police force. It also has a big voice in how the economy is managed.

Planned economies
Another way of running the economy is a **planned economy**, in which business is totally controlled and financed by the State, or government. The State decides how many factories should be built; where they should be situated; what they should make; how much they should produce; who should be employed; and what they should be paid. In Communist countries, the whole of the economy was managed in this way. For example, there were no private shops, only State shops.

Russia was the first country to have a Communist government. It was followed by China, and, after the Second World War, by the countries of Eastern Europe. There were also Communist governments in the Far East. Even in Western Europe, there were very large Communist parties, though none of them ever gained total power.

In theory, there should have been great benefits from Communism. Everyone was supposed to be equal. Work was done not for private profit, but the public good.

In practice, Communist countries struggled to make their planned (or command) economies work. Their governments drew up five-year plans which set targets for the production of goods and services. Most of these plans never worked.

Gradually, the Communist countries became poorer and more and more backward. There were increasing shortages of basic goods, from soap to shoes. Now Russia and the whole of Eastern Europe have got rid of their Communist governments and are trying to set up mixed economies like those in Western Europe. China is still a Communist country, but it allows the **private sector** more and more freedom. Only Cuba still keeps an old-style Communist economy.

Mixed economies

In a **mixed economy**, most goods and services are provided by the businesses in the private sector, but others are provided by the **public sector**, such as the government and local authorities, or councils. For example, defence – the Royal Navy, the Royal Air Force and the Army – is paid for and controlled by the government. Parks and public libraries are run and paid for by local councils.

Until recently, the public sector provided many other goods and services, such as coal and electricity. These industries were owned by the government and run by public corporations. In the 1980s and 1990s, Conservative governments privatized most of these State-owned industries by selling them off to private shareholders. There are now only a few industries still in the public sector, including London Underground and the National Air Traffic Control services. The Labour government is planning to set up a **public private partnership** (PPP) in both these services (see Unit 13).

Partnerships

In the past, Conservative governments tried to create a closer partnership with the private sector by setting up **enterprise zones** in poor inner city areas. Private firms which set up businesses there gained a number of benefits. These included:

- exemption from, or a lower level of business rates
- 100 per cent tax allowances for new buildings
- easier planning permission.

There are still a few enterprise zones, but there are no plans to create new ones.

The Labour government has created even closer links with the private sector with its public private partnerships and private finance initiative (PFI) deals. In these schemes, private firms compete with each other to provide public sector buildings such as schools and colleges, or services, such as the new Nottingham tram scheme. Private firms provide the finance and their skills. They also bear the risk if anything goes wrong and can be fined if they are late in delivery. In return, the public authority pays them for providing the service or maintaining the building in good order for a fixed number of years. For example, Nottingham Express Transit, in the case study, has a 30-year contract to build and operate the tram system. Trams are due to be running on the 14-kilometre track by 2003.

London Underground

London Underground has already signed five PFI deals, worth £1 billion, which will provide improved ticketing systems, communications, and new rolling stock on the Northern Line. The government plans to use PPPs to raise a further £7 billion to modernise the system.

London Underground will still be in charge of running trains, signalling, stations and safety. The PPP partners will be responsible for upgrading and maintaining the infrastructure. The government claims that the Underground is not being privatized, as the assets will be returned to the public sector in an improved condition at the end of the contract. Critics claim that this is a partial privatisation and that the work could be done more cheaply through issuing public sector bonds.

KEY TERMS

Enterprise zones Inner city areas with business concessions on tax and business rates and easier planning permission.

Market economy A system in which the economy is governed by supply and demand without any interference by the State. No country in real life has a total market economy.

Mixed economy An economy in which some resources are controlled by the State and some by private firms and individuals, i.e. where a public and a private sector coexist.

Planned economy A system in which the State plans and controls the whole economy.

Public private partnership (PPP) A public sector project which is managed and financed by the private sector which also bears the risks. The public sector pays for the project over a number of years.

Private sector That part of the economy controlled by private firms and individuals.

Public sector That part of the economy which is controlled by the government, local authorities and public corporations.

PERCENTAGES

The following formula is used to calculate a percentage (%).

$$\frac{\text{quantity of one item}}{\text{total quantity}} \times 100$$

If one partner in a PFI consortium contributed £27 million to the total cost of £180 million, what would its percentage share of the whole be?

Revision and exam practice units 1–6

REVIEW POINTS

1 Explain why we cannot have all that we want.
2 What is a market? Why is it important for business?
3 Construct a table showing the main advantages and disadvantages of (a) mixed and (b) planned economies.
4 What is the main role of business in society?
5 What is opportunity cost? Give an example of opportunity cost in a small business.
6 Describe the three main types of goods.
7 Explain how the factors of production are involved in all business activity.
8 What is enterprise?

Extended questions

1 The price of goods and services is decided by supply and demand.
   (a) What is meant by 'supply' and 'demand'?
   (b) Use an example of one kind of goods and one kind of service to explain how their supply and demand might affect the price of each product.
2 (a) Explain what is meant by
      (i) a planned economy
      (ii) a market economy
      (iii) a mixed economy.
   (b) What type of economy do we have in Britain?
   (c) Give examples of how things might be different in Britain if we had another kind of economy. Give reasons for your answers.

Case study 1

Ducati bike sales at full throttle

Ducati, Bologna's manufacturer of high performance motorcycles, was on the ropes four years ago, unable to pay its employees and its suppliers. Its output had declined to a mere 20 motorcycles a day, and their reliability was questioned. The company was bought in 1996 by Texas Pacific Group. Since then, it has staged a fairytale recovery. It was successfully floated on both the Milan and New York stock exchanges last year, and sold 33,000 motorcycles in 1999. Now it has claimed Italy's single biggest online sale.

Federico Minoli, its president and chief executive, was surprised by the result of his novel idea to develop a super sports bike and to sell it only online. In 31 minutes, a year's production of the new €15,000 ($14,850) MH900, – named after the former world champion Mike Hailwood – was sold on 1 January.

'Our original plan was to produce 500 bikes this year,' explains Pierfrancesco Caliari, Ducati's spokesman. Following the remarkable response, the company has decided to increase production of the MH900 to 2,000 bikes this year. At the end of January, it had already sold 1,500 of the machines.

Ducati says its website receives an average of 150,000 hits a day. It has also launched a number of other sites, including Desmobid, where bike components and other gadgets are auctioned to fans after a championship race. It has also launched a business-to-business network to connect the company with its dealers throughout the world.

The bike was also aimed at the global market – more particularly, the 'global village of Ducati fans' – rather than at domestic buyers.

Source: adapted from FT.com – European e-business review website

1 How many machines was the company selling four years ago?

2 How many did it sell in 1999?

3 How long did it take to sell a year's production of 500 of the new MH900 motorcycles on 1 January, online?

4 Explain how the business-to-business network which Ducati has set up will affect its relationship with its dealers.

5 How does a company benefit financially by selling on the internet?

6 How has the internet expanded the company's global markets?

Online links
www.ft.com
www.ducati.com

Case study 2

CBI puts £200 billion price tag on plan to salvage UK transport system

Salvaging Britain's crisis-hit transport system will cost more than £200 billion over the next ten years, according to the Confederation of British Industry (CBI).

Digby Jones, CBI Director-General, said: 'After years of under-investment and delayed projects, the present transport system is failing business and society. That is damaging to wealth creation, social inclusion and employment. It goes to the heart of productivity for business.

'Now is the time for the government to turn words into action by making tough spending and funding choices. That is the only way to tackle the poor services, overcrowding, unacceptable congestion and concerns about safety.'

The total includes £25 billion on trunk roads and motorways, £79 billion on local transport, £62 billion on rail, £9 billion on aviation, £3 billion on ports and motorways and £2 billion on

research into technology.

Motorway congestion is set to rise 130 per cent between 1996 and 2010. Extra spending on all transport, coupled with smarter ways of managing traffic, would cut this to 37 per cent.

Digby Jones said: 'Twenty-five years ago the government spent almost as much on roads and local public transport

as it raised in road taxes. Now it spends half that amount in real terms – about £6 billion annually, yet it raises some £36 billion from road users.'

Source: adapted from CBI press release website

1   How much does the CBI think should be spent annually on the transport system over the next ten years?

2   How much is the government currently spending?

3   How do you think an integrated transport system helps in wealth creation?

4   In your view, how does a poor transport system affect (a) the environment (b) individuals (c) enterprise?

Case study 3

Markets revival gives a £65 million boost to farmers

A revival of farmers' markets in towns and cities has proved so popular that they are now generating an extra £65 million a year for the ailing agricultural industry.

Turnover is expected to rise to £100 million by next spring if the current rate of expansion continues. A report, compiled by the National Farmers Union of England and Wales, shows that there are now about 200 markets in Britain where producers sell their fresh meat, dairy products, fruit, vegetables and flowers directly to the public.

These markets, where farmers cut out the middle men and avoid price and supply controls set by supermarket chains, are expected to attract more than 5.2 million customers in the next 12 months.

The survey says that shoppers spend between £10 and £15 a visit on average.

It shows that 75 per cent of these markets are thriving and that the vast majority of stallholders are smaller, family-owned food producers whose place of production is usually within 40 miles of the market.

'British agriculture has, in recent times, been a bleak and often isolated industry. Many farmers have gained great comfort from socialising with fellow producers and shoppers at farmers' markets,' the report says.

Farmers reported that they gained valuable information about their customers' needs and many said they wanted their customers to visit their farms to see for themselves how their food is produced.

Sally Hales, a smallholder, who sells free range eggs for £1 a dozen at a farmers' market, said: 'We can sell people a fresh, high quality product without giving our profits away to the supermarkets who are killing the British farmers with the low prices they are giving us.'

Source: adapted from the *Daily Telegraph*, 25 May 2000

1   Which type of market is a farmers' market?

2   Which kind of production are farmers engaged in?

3   By selling direct to the customer, which kind of production are they using?

4   Why is it more beneficial to farmers to sell in these markets?

5   Describe the advantages to the consumer of shopping in a farmers' market.

6   If these markets expanded, explain what the effects could be on (a) health (b) small traders (c) supermarkets (d) town centres.

Case study 4

Sainsbury's – first UK food retailer to hold global online reverse auction

Sainsbury's today became the first UK food retailer to hold a global online reverse auction to purchase products which will be sold in its 432 stores. This was conducted on GlobalNetXchange, the major worldwide business-to-business online exchange for retailers.*

The first product to be bought was Sainsbury's economy mild cheddar. The companies taking part in the auction are suppliers who meet Sainsbury's quality and delivery standards. They were bidding to supply cheese to Sainsbury's for three months.

The standard bidding process can take up to six weeks. The auction lasted for four hours on the internet. The name of the successful bidder will not be known to the other bidders. The final decision was not just based on price.

Patrick McHugh, Sainsbury's Group Director for e-commerce and an executive board member of GlobalNetXchange said, 'GlobalNetXchange means retailers and suppliers no longer have to use paper catalogues and make costly computer system conversions in order to do business with each other.'

The GlobalNetXchange has the potential to manage some £200 billion of trade and become the industry leader.

The advantages of GlobalNetXchange to Sainsbury's businesses include:
- greater efficiencies and cost savings in buying on the web
- more efficient planning and forecasting in the supply chain
- increased range and choice of sourced goods, particularly in own label goods.

Source: adapted from Sainsbury's website – news release, 18 May 2000.

* In a normal auction, prices rise. In a reverse auction, sellers compete against each other to offer goods and services at the lowest possible price.

1 **How many stores does Sainsbury's have?**

2 **What savings will Sainsbury's make?**

3 **What might the benefits to the consumer be?**

Online links

www.j-sainsbury.co.uk

EXAM PRACTICE

Foundation

Valerie Dean runs a small stained-glass business from her home in a country town. She makes goods such as lampshades, windows and clocks.

1 What kind of production is Valerie engaged in? (1 mark)

2 Name the two other kinds of production. (2 marks)

3 Give one example of people engaged in each of the three kinds of production. (3 marks)

4 Name two primary kinds of production Valerie is dependent on. Give reasons for your answer. (4 marks)

Higher

Valerie Dean runs a small stained-glass business from her home in a country town. She makes furnishings such as lampshades, windows, clocks and other household ornaments. She has decided to move to the industrial estate where the council has built ten units for local craftspeople. Her boyfriend Garry, who makes hand-crafted golf clubs, will share the unit with her. They both sell their finished products to shops in the town.

1 What kind of production are Valerie and Garry engaged in? (1 mark)

2 Give one example of a business activity in each of the three kinds of production which you might find on an industrial estate. (3 marks)

3 What is meant by the interdependence of all areas of production? (4 marks)

4 Describe the links in the chain of production which have preceded the purchase of one of Garry's golf clubs. (6 marks)

Section 2

Structure and control of business

Sole proprietors

Personality check

The questions below will help you to assess whether you have the right personal qualities for running your own business. Make a list of the numbers and your answers – a, b or c – then check your scores at the end.

1 **If you find studying at home difficult, do you:**
   a) keep trying
   b) have a rest and then go on with it again
   c) give it up and do something else?

2 **Would you rather have:**
   a) a job you really liked even if you didn't make much money
   b) a steady job
   c) an easy job with lots of money?

3 **Do you like taking risks:**
   a) if you have to
   b) often
   c) never?

4 **Would you say you are enthusiastic about:**
   a) everything you do
   b) things you like doing
   c) very few things?

5 **Do other people come to you for help and advice:**
   a) almost never
   b) occasionally
   c) often?

6 **Do you think a business person is someone:**
   a) who makes use of the workers
   b) makes a reasonable profit
   c) provides a useful service for society?

7 **Do any members of your own family have their own business:**
   a) none
   b) one
   c) more than one?

8 **Do you enjoy working alone:**
   a) never
   b) always
   c) whenever you need to?

9 **If you were left a large amount of money, would you:**
   a) buy a house
   b) invest it in something you'd always wanted to do
   c) spend it wildly on all the things you've always wanted?

10 **Do your friends ask you to organize events:**
   a) sometimes
   b) frequently
   c) never?

11 **Do you write down what you intend to do during the next week:**
   a) always
   b) sometimes
   c) never?

12 **If you were doing a complicated task would you:**
   a) ask other people who knew more about it for advice
   b) try to do everything yourself
   c) not bother with the difficult parts?

Score chart
Questions 1-4   a)5 b)2 c)0
Questions 5-8   a)0 b)2 c)5
Questions 9-12   a)2 b)5 c)0
Add up your total number of points. The maximum is 60.

What your score means
40-60 You have excellent personal qualities for setting up your own business.
20-40 You could do well in your own business, but you might be happier working for a firm.
0-20 You need to think seriously about your personal characteristics if you want to get a job at all.

Look at the bottom of the page to work out your score.

I'VE GOT 60 POINTS!!!

Study points

When you have found out your score, get into groups to discuss the results and the following points.

① **From the way the marks are given in the quiz, which personal qualities are thought to be important in running your own business?**

② **Which, in your view, is the most important quality?**

③ **Are there any other personal qualities which you would have included?**

④ **How far are these qualities reflected in any person you know who runs a small business successfully, either in real life or in a television programme?**

⑤ **What else, apart from personal qualities, might be important for starting your own business?**

Businesses in the private sector range from those which are owned and run by one person to multinationals which employ thousands of people in many countries. They differ also in ownership and control, how they raise money and distribute profits.

Setting up on your own

The majority of businesses are owned by **sole proprietors**. The owner has complete control of the business and is totally responsible for its success or failure. Running your own business is extremely hard work. The risks are great, but so are the rewards in job satisfaction.

The main advantages of this form of business are:

- *Small start-up costs*. It is simple and inexpensive to set up as a sole proprietor. However, you must tell the income tax authorities and the Department of Social Security, as you will be taxed under **Schedule D** and will pay self-employed National Insurance contributions. You must also keep proper business accounts.
- *Profits are all kept*. The owner keeps all the profits, though he or she must save enough money to pay tax, interest charges on loans and VAT.
- *Offset of losses*. Losses made in the first year may be offset, or balanced, against tax paid earlier in the same financial year.
- *Flexibility*. The small business is very flexible. If one kind of activity is not profitable, the owner can quickly switch to something else.

Disadvantages

There are also certain disadvantages:
- *Unlimited liability*. This means that owners are personally responsible for all the debts of their business.
- *High risks*. The risks of failure are high as there is usually great competition.

- *Difficulties in raising money*. It is often difficult to raise capital, though government schemes have made this somewhat easier.
- *Slow growth*. The firm's growth is often slow as one person can do only a limited amount of work.
- *Lack of continuity*. The business stops with the owner's death.

For these, and other reasons, there is a high failure rate among one-person businesses.

What is required?

To set up your own business you must be dedicated, hard-working, adaptable and willing to take risks and to overcome problems.

You must have a good basic trading idea and investigate the market thoroughly. A profit and loss budget must be drawn up to make sure that the business will be profitable.

A cash-flow plan will increase your chances of getting a loan from a bank, which will be your main source of outside finance. (See Units 24 and 30.)

You will need to find a suitable site to work from. You could start at home, but without planning permission from your local council, you could run into trouble for making too much noise, or having too many visitors. Many businesses, e.g. mobile shops, street traders and scrap-metal dealers, usually have to be licensed by the local council.

You will need a business plan with both short- and long-term objectives. (See Unit 27.)

You will also need to cope with the administration or general organizing – financial records, correspondence and filing.

You will need to have a proper marketing plan, pricing policy and publicity campaign (see Units 36–45 and Unit 47).

Finally, you will need to have your own

letterhead – a printed sheet of paper containing details of the business, which is used for correspondence. The letterhead must state the business's (or your own) name, address, telephone number and, if appropriate, fax number and e-mail address (see Unit 64). It may also include the business's logo and a brief description of the firm.

Key skills
IT

Use a computer, and possibly a scanner, to design a letterhead for a business you would like to start. You should include at least one image in the letterhead. Print a hard copy.

KEY TERMS

Schedule D The part of the law or schedule under which self-employed people are taxed. They are allowed to take away from their turnover any expenses which arise for business purposes only and these are not taxed.

Sole proprietors People who run their own businesses. They have complete control, but bear all the risks and have unlimited liability.

Partnerships

John Lewis Partnership toasts golden jubilee

The 50,000 staff at one of Britain's biggest retail organizations will today raise a glass to celebrate the experiment in industrial democracy which was once described as an act of madness. The day marks the fiftieth anniversary of the handing over of all the assets of the John Lewis Partnership to a trust for the benefit of all permanent employees (known as partners).

The occasion will be observed in all the 25 department stores, 130 Waitrose food shops, five manufacturing units, distribution centres and warehouses.

In the 50 years since the signing of the trust settlement by the firm's founder, John Spedan Lewis, the business has expanded year by year. Turnover is nearly £4 billion.

All the profits are used for the benefit of the business and those who work in it. Last month, all 40,000 partners received a bonus equivalent to 15 per cent of their annual pay.

Source: adapted from John Lewis Partnership website, press release, 26 April, 2000

Partnership structure

'Every member of staff (partner) has a say in how the company is run and an annual share in the profits.'

Source: John Lewis Partnership website.

Study points

① How many department stores does the John Lewis Partnership own?

② What other kinds of store does it own?

③ When was the partnership started?

④ What percentage of the workforce are not partners?

⑤ What are the main benefits of being a partner?

Online links

www.john-lewis-partnership.co.uk

John Lewis is one of the biggest and most unusual partnerships in the world. As in all partnerships:

- the partners own the business
- all the partners share in the profits
- each partner has a voice in the way the firm is run.

Most partnerships, however, are very much smaller – just a handful of people. Partnerships are usually formed by professional people, such as doctors, solicitors, accountants and architects.

There are also some partnerships in the retail trade and in small manufacturing businesses and among craft workers, such as potters and weavers.

The main advantages of these smaller partnerships is that they can provide a much greater range of skills than a sole proprietor, as each of the partners can specialize. In a firm of solicitors, for example, one partner might specialize in wills and trusts, another in conveyancing and a third in criminal law.

There are other advantages. As more people (usually up to a maximum of 20) are involved, the partnership may have more profitable ideas than a sole proprietor. It may also be easier to raise capital as each partner contributes a share.

Disagreements

There are also many drawbacks. Although some partnerships have worked successfully for years, there are probably more chances of argument in partnerships than in any other form of business organization.

Steps to success in partnership

Before forming a partnership, the persons involved should consider:

1. Name and type of business and starting date.
2. Amount of capital provided by each partner.
3. Dividing up of profits and losses.
4. Voting rights: do the partners have equal or unequal control?
5. Arrangements for retirement, death or change of partners.
6. Choosing whether to have joint or separate bank accounts.
7. The preparation and auditing of annual accounts.
8. Arrangements to cover long absence through sickness or accident.
9. Insurance: both general and against death or illness of partners.

Adapted from: Small Firms Service

CHECKPOINTS

1. What is usually the maximum number of partners?
2. What is a sleeping partner?
3. Who owns a partnership and how is it controlled? What is its main source of finance?
4. Explain the main advantages of partnerships. In what types of business are they usually found?

Some of the most common disputes are caused by:
- the sharing of profits
- the control of the business
- the different responsibilities of each partner
- resentment that one partner is not doing his or her share of the work.

Many lifelong friendships have been ruined by people setting up in business together without drawing up a **deed of partnership** first.

This document should cover all the possible points of disagreement that could arise. How much capital should each partner provide? How should profits be shared – equally or in proportion to capital provided? Who should control the business? Should it be one partner, one vote, or should one partner be in control? What arrangements should be made for the partnership to be dissolved or for one partner to withdraw? How should the value

of the business in terms of its reputation and its clients' loyalty, i.e. the goodwill, be decided if one of the partners withdraws, retires or dies?

There is also one big drawback. Like sole proprietors, all partners have unlimited liability for the business's debts. This includes **sleeping partners** who invest money in the business and take a share of the profits, but who play no part in running the business.

However, this disadvantage may soon end. The government is creating a new kind of business structure: a limited liability partnership (LLP). Partners will retain all their present advantages of control, flexibility and tax status, but will no longer have unlimited liability.

If you enter into a partnership, make sure that a solicitor or an accountant draws up a proper deed of partnership before, or soon after, the business starts.

Most professional partnerships have quite a large turnover. Therefore, they have

to include **Value Added Tax (VAT)** in their prices. Only very small businesses with annual turnovers of, currently, £52,000 or less, are exempt.

VAT is paid at every stage of production, but businesses can offset, or balance, the VAT they pay on supplies against VAT received on their sales. For example, a furniture manufacturer pays VAT on the wood he or she buys from the supplier – the input tax. When the manufacturer sells a finished table to a consumer he or she charges VAT on the sales price – the output tax. The manufacturer pays the difference between the output and the input tax to the Customs and Excise. However, if the input tax is larger than the output tax, he or she can claim the difference back from the Customs and Excise. Only consumers cannot claim back VAT. Therefore, they are the ones who ultimately pay this tax on goods and services.

KEY TERMS

Deed of partnership A legal document which covers such matters as who provides the capital, control of the business, distribution of profits, settling disputes and so on.

Sleeping partners People who lend money, or their name, to a partnership for a share of the profits, but who have no part in its management.

Value Added Tax (VAT) A tax paid on practically all goods and services, though a few items, such as magazines and books, are zero-rated, or exempt. The current rate of VAT is 17.5 per cent.

Key skills
Number

VALUE ADDED TAX
A manufacturer's input tax in a year was £67,832, and his output tax was £139,231.

How much VAT did he or she pay to the Customs and Excise?

Co-operatives

Tower Colliery acquired the pre-packed coal outlet Welsh Dragon, which was threatened with closure, saving seven jobs.

UK co-operative movement: facts and figures

Co-operative Retail Societies

Turnover	£7.8 billion
Staff	68,000
Number of shops	4,663
	(79 superstores)
Number of members	8,281,000

The Co-operative Wholesale Society

Turnover	£3 billion
Number of CWS food shops	658

The Co-operative Bank Group

Assets	£3.9 billion
Customer accounts	1.5 million

The Co-operative Insurance Society

Total income	£2 billion
Families insured	3.5 million

Shoefayre	294 branches
Co-operative Opticians	80 practices
National Co-operative Chemists	236 branches
Worker Co-operatives	1,500

Source: adapted from CWS website

Tower Colliery Ltd

On 22 April 1994, the miners from Tower Colliery went home feeling defeated. After a two-week struggle with British Coal, the men had finally to accept the closure of the pit, the last deep mine in South Wales.

The National Union of Mineworkers committee decided to put the case to the workforce for an employee buy-out of the colliery. At a general meeting of the workforce, it was decided to accept this idea and a working party of six was appointed, known as the TEBO team.

Many fund-raising activities were organised. By the time the bid had to be submitted to buy the colliery, the team had raised £1.93million – each miner investing £8,000 – and secured a £1.5 million loan from Barclays Bank.

In October 1994, it was announced that the team were the preferred bidders. Eight months after the bitter taste of defeat, the workforce returned to the colliery on 3 January 1995, accompanied by their families and a brass band, and with the union banner in the lead. Of the 320 men employed at Tower before closure, 200 became shareholders in the new company.

During 1995, Tower Colliery produced 460,000 tonnes of anthracite which was sold in Britain, Ireland, France, Belgium, Spain and Germany.

By December 1995, the company had returned first year pre-tax profits exceeding £4 million.

Source: adapted from Tower Colliery website

Study points

1. How many worker co-operatives are there in Britain?
2. What is the total number of Co-op superstores?
3. Why were the Tower Colliery miners forced to buy the pit?
4. How much did each miner contribute?
5. Do you think it was a good idea for the miners to buy the colliery?

Online links

www.tower-coal.co.uk
www. co-op.co.uk

Worker co-operatives

A **worker co-operative** is different from any other type of business. It is owned and run by the whole workforce. Its members believe in co-operation – working together for a common purpose. It tries to ensure that everyone has a say in how the business is run. In a worker co-operative:

- membership is open to all workers
- each member has one vote
- any profit is distributed to members in a fair way
- members are in control, not outside shareholders, though some worker co-operatives employ a general manager
- the members sometimes form a limited company so that they do not have unlimited liability if the business goes into liquidation.

Supporters of the co-operative aim believe that it could create a happier and fairer society. They say that:

- the co-operative aim would reduce argument because the worker and the owner is the same person
- members would have a greater sense of responsibility and work harder to make the business succeed
- work would become more enjoyable and provide greater job satisfaction
- increased motivation among the workforce would provide better goods and services
- as local people are involved in the business, the co-operative would have closer links with the local community.

Problems to overcome

Like Tower Colliery in the case study, co-operatives are often formed by the workers in a plant which has been closed by a big company. If a big company with all its resources cannot make the plant succeed, the chances of the worker co-operative doing so are small. Yet, like all other private sector businesses, a worker co-operative must make a profit if it is to survive. There are also many other problems.

- Idealistic beliefs may clash with the harsh realities of the real world.
- Profit may be sacrificed to ideals.
- The co-operative may not be sufficiently competitive.
- Financial control is often weak unless an independent manager or accountant is employed.
- There may be difficulties in raising finance, as banks are sometimes unwilling to lend to co-operatives.
- It may not be easy to make decisions as everyone has a vote whether they have any knowledge or experience of the matter involved.

Some of the most popular sectors for worker co-operatives are catering, computers, dressmaking and cleaning.

Consumer co-operatives

Britain had the biggest co-operative movement in Europe in the nineteenth century. The first successful co-operative society, formed by a group of Rochdale weavers in 1844, was a **consumer co-operative**. It bought food at wholesale prices and sold it to members at the market price.

Today, co-operative societies have more than eight million members and a turnover of £7.8 billion a year. However, they still have many smaller shops that find it difficult to compete with big supermarkets. These local stores are kept partly for social reasons, as some of their older or less well-off customers find it impossible to visit out-of-town stores.

This idealism, or faith that the world could be a better place, is found in many co-operative businesses. The Co-operative Bank, for example, will not invest money in countries or in companies which it considers unethical or likely to do harm. So it does not invest in countries with oppressive rulers who persecute minorities, or in firms which produce arms or pollute the environment.

Marketing

Marketing has always been a big problem for small businesses. One answer is to form a **marketing co-operative** which markets and sells the products of a number of producers in the same kind of business. There are quite a number of marketing co-operatives in Europe and the United States, but there are very few in Britain. Even in the hard-pressed farming sector, there are only a few dairy co-operatives. Recently however, some farmers have set up farmers' markets to sell their goods direct to consumers (see case study 3 on page 15). The **Co-operative Union** links the various co-operative organizations in Britain and acts as their spokesperson.

CHECKPOINTS

1. State three kinds of co-operative. Give one example of each.
2. Who owns a worker co-operative and how is it controlled?
3. How do the beliefs of co-operative firms make them different from other kinds of businesses?
4. What are the main reasons why co-operatives do not always succeed?

KEY TERMS

Consumer co-operatives High street stores that share net profits among members.

Co-operative Union Founded in 1869 to form new co-operative societies. It now provides a link between the retail co-operative societies, the Co-operative Wholesale Society (CWS), the Co-operative Insurance Society, Co-operative Press and other co-operative bodies.

Marketing co-operative This provides joint services for producers.

Worker co-operatives Businesses that are owned and run by the whole workforce.

Key skills
Working with others

Form groups. You have decided to set up a co-operative, such as a restaurant, a sports centre or a newspaper. Decide what the business should be and how you would start and run it.

Franchises

Franchise fact file

Number of franchises
The number of business format franchises has increased by five per cent to 596.

Size of sector
Annual turnover of business format franchises is estimated at £7.4 billion. Taking into account other franchise related sectors, annual turnover is estimated at £57.9 billion. (Franchise related sectors include car, petrol and computer retailers who are selling another company's branded goods.)

Franchising now accounts for 29 per cent of all retail sales.

Numbers employed
Estimated at 303,000 people, including 14,900 employed by franchisees.

Franchise performance
Some 89 per cent of franchisees report profitability; 58 per cent claim their businesses are highly or quite profitable.

Finance
The total average outlay for setting up a franchise is £49,900. The average ongoing management service fee and advertising levy is 11.4 per cent of gross turnover. Fifty-nine per cent borrowed money to set up the franchise. The average amount borrowed was £25,500.

Source: adapted from Franinfo website – Franchising in the UK

Study points

① What is the total number of business format franchises?

② How many people are employed in this sector?

③ What is the estimated turnover?

④ What is meant by 'franchise related sectors'? Give one example.

⑤ Why do you think Tania succeeded better as a franchisee than as an independent retailer?

Online links
www.franinfo.co.uk
www.pronuptia.com

Young businesswoman reaps the rewards of franchising

It's been a little over one year since Tania Ashurst from Kent invested in the Pronuptia franchise and began trading, 'Yet,' she says, 'it has proved to be the most successful decision I have ever made.'

Tania originally worked as a secretary in Knightsbridge, London, but at the age of 19 she decided to return home to help her mother run her curtain shop in Ashford. The shop also stocked dress fabrics and the mother and daughter team decided to extend this by launching a bridal section in the store. Despite starting from scratch, Tania's Bridal Wear grew progressively and in 1992, they launched Men's Formal Wear to work hand in hand with it.

Tania felt there was more potential with a bigger name and decided to look at the possibility of trading with the Pronuptia name. In December 1998, Tania refitted her current

premises with a more modern feel and went ahead with Pronuptia.

After only one full year of trading with the new name and look, the shop's turnover had risen by 30 per cent.

Source: adapted from Franinfo – Franchise News, 29 February 2000

Joint ventures
Franchising is another form of co-operation – often between a big firm and a sole proprietor.

The big firm has a well-known product with its own brand name (see Unit 40) such as Wimpy, or a service such as Dyno-Rod, or a special kind of shop such as Holland and Barrett. In return for an initial fee and continuing **royalty payments**, the **franchiser** allows the **franchisee** to set up his or her own business and to use the firm's brand name.

Two well-known franchise operations

How does it work?

How does franchising – or **business format franchising** to use its full name – work? A big firm may decide that it wants to expand without investing large amounts of capital. So it decides to go into franchising instead. First of all, it carries out a pilot operation or trial run to see if the idea is practical. If this trial franchise, which is owned and run by the company, makes a fair profit in the first year, excluding investment costs and overheads, then the company decides to go ahead.

The company sets up a training scheme for franchisees, based on what has been learnt in the pilot operation. When all is ready, it advertises for franchisees. The advertisements bring many replies. The most promising applicants are interviewed, but most of them are unsuitable. The franchiser must be very careful in selecting franchisees. If they do not succeed, they could ruin the company's reputation.

A few people are finally chosen who have the necessary capital and the right qualities. After training, they are given exclusive trading rights in their own areas and set up successful businesses. A few more people are granted franchises in the second year. Later, say in the third year, the franchiser starts to make a profit which increases greatly in later years, as the number of franchises grows.

Advantages

There are great advantages for the franchisees, too. They have a much greater chance of success than most small businesses as the product has been tried and tested and has a secure place in the market. Franchisees also benefit from being able to use a brand name which is advertised nationally. The franchiser provides continuous support. If there are any snags or problems, the franchisee can get good advice quickly. There is a better chance of solving problems as they may already have been met and overcome in other franchises.

The franchisee will probably find it easier to raise money from the banks as they are taking less of a risk with a franchise operation than with an untried small business. Some banks will provide medium-term loans of five to ten years for up to two-thirds of the start-up costs and an overdraft for working capital or money to run the business with.

Disadvantages

On the other hand, there are some disadvantages. The franchisee:

- has less independence than other sole proprietors
- will not be able to sell the business without the franchiser's agreement
- does not always have the right to renew the franchise automatically
- has to make continuing royalty payments to the franchiser
- sometimes has to pay a mark-up, or percentage of the price, on supplies from the franchiser.

KEY TERMS

Business format franchising Trading under the brand name of another firm.

Franchisee A person who pays an initial fee and royalty payments for the privilege of trading under another firm's name.

Franchiser A firm which allows another person to use its tried-and-tested product, and to trade under its name, for a fee.

Royalty payments A percentage payment made for the use of another person or firm's invention or property.

Private limited companies

Why it paid to be an amber gambler

Bob Rontaler was working as a manager in a gold and silver jewellery business when a Polish friend tried to interest him in selling amber. 'I had never worked with amber. The impression I had was of old ladies with very heavy amber rings and necklaces', he said.

But Rontaler was eventually persuaded and ordered around £3,500 worth of amber from Poland. That was back in the mid-1980s. Since then the annual turnover of his company, Goldmajor Ltd, which imports and distributes amber jewellery, has passed £1 million.

Rontaler's parents were Polish. He met his Polish wife, Jaga, when she visited London 20 years ago. Both are directors of Goldmajor.

The bulk of the amber jewellery Rontaler buys is produced in Poland. Rontaler now also uses manufacturers in Thailand, because of the low labour costs, and in Israel.

Around half of Goldmajor's sales are to retail jewellers. Just under 20 per cent are to the Past Times chain of gift shops, 15 per cent are to other gift shops and six per cent are to department stores. Just under ten per cent of sales are for export.

The company employs ten full-time and two part-time staff, and has three agents who work on a percentage basis.

Source: adapted from the Financial Times, 25 November 1995

GOLDMAJOR
DESIGNERS & MANUFACTURERS OF QUALITY AMBER JEWELLERY

Established in 1985 and specialising in amber, the company is now a leader in the amber jewellery field in the UK.

Our designs are UK generated, many of which are copyrighted. Our designs are manufactured to the highest possible standard with a large UK manufacturing base. Part of our manufacturing is carried out at the source of the prime product, that of amber, where our artisans have the source of supply and the greatest experience.

Source: adapted from Goldmajor – company profile website

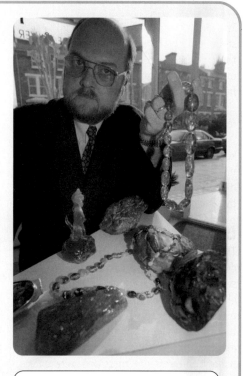

Study points

① **When did Bob form his company?**

② **Where does he make his jewellery?**

③ **Who are his main customers?**

④ **Which sector had the highest number of insolvencies (when companies cannot pay their debts) in a) 1989 and b) 1998?**

⑤ **Why do you think there was a steep rise in the number of insolvencies between 1989 and 1993, and a fall between 1993 and 1998?**

⑥ **How do you explain Goldmajor's success when so many other companies fail?**

	1989	1993	1998
Agriculture	78	157	65
Manufacturing	3,041	4,590	2,493
Construction and transport	2,227	4,271	1,829
Wholesaling	659	1,012	563
Retailing	1,039	2,005	1,153
Services	1,490	3,748	2,344
Other	1,922	4,925	4,756
Total	10,456	20,708	13,203

Source: adapted from Annual Abstract of Statistics, Office for National Statistics, 2000

Figure 1: Company insolvencies (England and Wales)

Online links
www.ft.com
www.gemnet.unet.com/goldmajor/profile1.htm

The next step up the business ladder is forming a **private limited company**. (This gives the company the right to add the abbreviation Ltd to its name.)

Shareholders

The **shareholders** own the company. The shareholders are usually family members of the people who set up the business. Some of the shares may also be owned by family friends, business associates and employees. Under European law, one person can now form a private limited company.

Part of the company's profits may be kept back, or retained, to pay for improvements to the business, and some is distributed to shareholders in the form of **dividends**.

Benefits

The founders of the business – or their descendants – are usually the main shareholders and **directors** of the firm. The chairperson of the board of directors takes a leading part in deciding the company's policy. He or she is often also the managing director who carries out the policy day by day. In practice, therefore, the people who started the business actually own the company and control it.

However, their financial liability is limited to the **nominal capital** they invested. Unlike the sole proprietor, who has unlimited liability for his or her debts, a company has only **limited liability**.

A company may become insolvent and go into **liquidation** owing thousands of pounds, but the people who own the company – the shareholders – would not have to pay those debts out of their own money. Their responsibility for the debts, or their liability, would be limited to the money they had invested in the company. If they had invested £1,000 in the company by buying shares for that amount, they might lose all of that, but not a penny more.

Limited liability *Advantages*

Limited liability is the main advantage of forming a company. There are other benefits, too.

A company is legally a separate entity, distinct from the persons who run it, which means that it has certain rights that are recognised by the courts. It can buy and sell assets, make contracts, sue other companies and individuals, and can itself be sued.

A company's shares can be bought and sold. Unlike a sole proprietor business, which ends with the death of the owner, a company can carry on after the person who started it has sold it or died. The shares can be sold to someone else and the company survives.

Small companies like Goldmajor Ltd are often far more enterprising and willing to try out new ideas than big established companies. For that reason, they have provided far more new jobs in recent years than have much bigger firms.

Disadvantages

There are some disadvantages in forming a limited company.

- It is more expensive to set up a company than to start a sole proprietor business. A company has to be registered with the Companies Registration Office. To do this it has to employ a solicitor, or a firm specializing in this work, which will cost anything from £100 to £180.

- A big company's accounts must be audited, which means that it has to employ an auditor as well as an accountant. (As a sole proprietor, there is no legal obligation to employ an accountant at all.)

- There are other legal formalities: for example, a company must hold an annual general meeting (AGM) and send details of the company's financial affairs to the Companies Registration Office every year.

- A company is less flexible in some ways than a sole proprietor business, as it is governed by two documents which state the nature of the business, the amount of capital and how the business should be run.

CHECKPOINTS

1. Who owns a private limited company?
2. What is the main advantage of forming a private limited company?
3. Who usually controls a private limited company in a) theory and b) practice?
4. How might a company's profits be distributed?
5. State the three main disadvantages of private limited companies.

KEY TERMS

Directors People who have been elected to the board of a company by the shareholders to make decisions about its management and policies.

Dividends Annual payments made to shareholders for each share they hold in a company.

Limited liability Limiting the financial liability of shareholders to the money they have invested.

Liquidation The closing or 'winding up' of a company, which may be either voluntary or compulsory, and which involves selling the assets of a firm to pay off its debts.

Nominal capital The amount of money which a company can raise from its shareholders. It is also known as authorized capital.

Private limited company A firm whose financial liabilities are limited to the amount of money put up by shareholders. To conform with European Union law, one person alone can now form a private limited company. Its shares cannot be sold to the public.

Shareholders People who have bought shares in a company which gives them a share in the ownership of the company and a share of any profits.

Public limited companies

A **public limited company (plc)** is different from a private limited company as its shares can be bought and sold by the public. To become a plc, a firm must have a minimum of £50,000 **share capital**, the money invested in its shares. Most plcs have a much bigger share capital totalling millions of pounds.

Share prices

The shares can be bought and sold through a bank or a firm which deals in shares. Their current price is quoted on the Stock Exchange. The nominal, or original, price of the share when it was issued by the company may be £1. However, the price of the shares will rise or fall according to how well or how badly the company is performing.

Regardless of the price of the shares, the shareholders are responsible only for the amount they invest in the company. Limited liability applies to plcs just as it does to private limited companies.

Control of plcs

The majority of shares in practically all companies are owned by **institutional investors.** Their huge blocks of shares give them great influence over companies' policies and the way in which they are run. The institutions' votes at company annual

Manchester United shares are down

While Manchester United has continued its dominance of the Premier League with its sixth title in eight years, its shares have lost ground over the past month.

Shares in the world's richest football club have slipped 18 per cent from a peak of 412.5p on March 23 to 337.5p on May 16. At that level, the company had a market value of £904.6 million.

Analysts said shares in the club had been hit by turbulence in technology and internet stocks.

The club's website receives eight million hits a month and from 2002 will be able to show highlights of the club's games. The club eventually hopes to offer its fans free global internet access.

Julian Easthorpe of Warburg Dillon Read [the investment bank] said the company's growth potential remained unrealized. 'There will be a number of internet winners and the ones with the best content will be the ones that win – and Manchester United has fantastic content.

'In Thailand recently ten million people sent in entries in a competition to win 20 tickets to visit Old Trafford. There is a huge untapped market in Asia.'

Source: adapted from Financial Times website, 26 April, 2000

Study points

① How many hits does the Manchester United website receive a month?

② What was the peak price of Manchester United shares?

③ Find out the current price of the shares.

④ State your view of the club's website.

⑤ Why do you think Manchester United became a public company?

Online links

www.ft.com
www.manutd.com

general meetings (AGMs) frequently decide who should be elected to the board of directors. If a company is performing badly, institutional investors can force a chairman or even a whole board of directors to resign. Companies can never ignore their immense power.

In contrast, the private investor, such as a Manchester United fan with a few shares, has very little influence.

Figure 1: Control in a plc

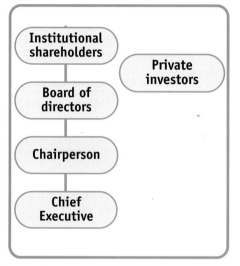

Top jobs

In a plc, the two most important people are the **chairperson** and the **chief executive**. In general terms, the chairperson represents the company in the outside world and takes a leading part in making policy. The chief executive is responsible for carrying out company policy and the day-to-day management of the firm.

Occasionally, the chairperson may also be the chief executive. A managing director is then appointed to carry out the routine tasks of running the business day by day.

Leadership

In recent years, there have been changes in the ways some companies are managed or run (see Unit 21). They have become more open and democratic with a bigger emphasis on teamwork. However, all organizations need **leaders** who can keep employees working together towards agreed aims or objectives.

There are three main kinds of leader.

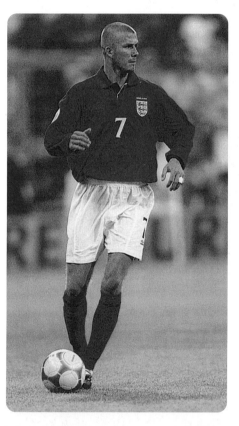

- *Autocratic leaders* like to tell other people what to do, to make as many decisions as possible and to keep a firm control over employees. There are still many autocratic leaders running big companies.
- *Democratic leaders* like all employees to have a say, encourage people to work on their own or in a team, and are willing to delegate, or give up, some of their own power to others. This kind of leader is found in only a minority of companies.
- *Charismatic leaders* have big personalities which appeal to their employees and inspire them to succeed. They delegate much of their work, are easy to approach and like to be called by their first name. There are few leaders of this type.

KEY TERMS

Chairperson A person elected by the board of directors to represent the firm and to help form and carry out its policy.

Chief executive A person appointed by the board who is in charge of the day-to-day running of the firm.

Institutional investors Financial institutions, such as banks, insurance companies and pension funds, which have billions of pounds to invest.

Leader A person who can keep the needs of individual workers and the aims or objectives of the company in harmony.

Public limited company (plc) A limited company whose shares can be bought and sold by the public and other firms. The company has the right to use the abbreviation plc after its name.

Share capital The money a business obtains by selling shares to investors.

The role of the public and voluntary sectors

About 20 years ago, much of Britain's industry was owned by the State. The government owned more than 100 businesses, including steel making, coal mining, oil production, car manufacturing, railways, airlines, road transport services, ports, telecommunications and the **public utilities**, such as gas, electricity and water.

Many of these huge industries were run by **public corporations**. For example, the coal industry, which then employed hundreds of thousands of miners, was run by the National Coal Board. Like some of the other State industries, it had a **monopoly**, as it was the only business which was allowed to run underground coal mines.

These nationalized industries did not have to make a profit. They were expected

Heathrow jets miss by 200 feet

Aircraft movements handled by Area Control Centres ('000s)			
	1998	**1999**	**% growth**
Total UK	1,703	1,828	7
London Centre	1,658	1,778	7
Source: NATS website: Facts and Figures			

Two British jets, together carrying 470 passengers, came within 200 feet of colliding at Heathrow Airport, it emerged yesterday.

The scare came when a British Airways 747 was cleared to land on a runway just as a British Midlands Airbus was cleared for take-off from the same runway. The incoming aircraft was directed to abort its landing and carved a path over the stationery Airbus.

The incident sparked concern that air traffic controllers are coming under pressure to fit in too many landings and take-offs at Heathrow's two runways, especially during the busy summer period. The airport already deals with more takes-offs and landings than any of its European counterparts, some of which have four or more runways.

Source: adapted from *The Times* website: Britain

Air traffic sale wins approval

Labour rebels denounced the government's plan for Britain's air traffic control system as they voted against the public-private partnership scheme and claimed it would compromise safety.

Forty-five Labour MPs backed a series of rebel amendments, seeking to keep National Air Traffic Control Services (NATS) in the public sector. The clauses were defeated comfortably, 307 votes to 99, by the government.

John Prescott, the Deputy Prime Minister and Transport Secretary, insisted that safety would not be undermined by the plan to sell off 51 per cent of the service under plans for a public-private partnership.

But Mrs Gwyneth Dunwoody MP said the best way to ensure standards was to keep NATS as a non-profit making company or publicly-owned corporation.

Source: adapted from *The Times* website: Politics

Study points

1. How many runways are there at Heathrow?
2. By what percentage did landings and take-offs increase there in 1998–9?
3. What does the government plan to do with the air traffic control system?
4. Explain the main alternatives to this proposal.
5. In your view, would it be a good idea to sell off part of the air traffic control system? Give your reasons.

Online links

www.the-times.co.uk
www.nats.co.uk

to break even so that their spending was the same as their income. However, if they spent more than they received, the government would usually give them a **subsidy** to make up the difference.

Public sector revolution

From 1979 onwards, there has been a revolution in the **public sector**. In that year, the government sold off its shares in British Petroleum. Other State-owned industries, such as the British Airports Authority, were changed into plcs and sold to private investors. In all, more than 100 public sector businesses were **privatized**.

Very few industries now remain in the public sector. The main ones are British Nuclear Fuels, the Post Office, London Underground and the air traffic control system (NATS). As the case study has shown, the government plans to partially privatize NATS through a public private partnership (see Unit 6). There are also plans to modernize London Underground with a PPP.

Partial privatizations

There has also been partial privatization in other State-owned organizations. Many new National Health Service hospitals are being built under private finance initiative (PFI) deals, for example. The private sector provides the capital and expertise to build and maintain the hospitals and is paid a fee by the public sector for the duration of the contract.

Colleges and schools are also being built through PFI deals. The NHS is sending some of its patients to private hospitals in order to free beds for more urgent cases. The BBC remains a public corporation, but

it sells some of its products in private sector markets and is obliged to buy a certain proportion of its programmes from the private sector. In addition, the private sector provides many services which were once controlled by the State, for example, running prisons and cleaning hospitals.

Local authorities

The powers of local councils have also been greatly reduced. Just over ten years ago, local councils had a monopoly of street cleaning, refuse collection, managing sports centres and many other kinds of services. In 1988, the Conservative government decided that private firms should be allowed to tender, or bid, for all these services. The council's own departments had to put in a bid to do the work. The lowest bid got the contract.

This system of compulsory competitive tendering has now been replaced by a new system. Under Labour's new Best Value system, councils are not forced to put the services out to tender. However, they are obliged to make sure that they offer best value by setting themselves targets which they have to reach. The private sector may be brought in if they fail. Many other services, such as residential care for poor, elderly people, continue to be provided by private nursing homes whose fees are paid by local councils.

Councils have also lost responsibility for many other services. Council homes have been sold off to tenants. The remaining houses are often managed by housing associations, which now provide most of the new rented homes. Schools have their own budgets. Most local bus services are provided by private firms. Some roads are built and maintained by private companies under PFI contracts.

KEY TERMS

Monopoly A market in which one firm controls the total output of the product.
Privatize Transferring businesses from the public to the private sector and also allowing the private sector to provide public services.
Public corporation A government-owned organization which is controlled by a board of governors chosen by the government.
Public sector Organizations and businesses which are owned and controlled by the government and other public authorities.
Public utilities Publicly-owned businesses which supply essential services such as water.
Subsidy A grant from the public authority which allows a product to be sold below the market price.

The private sector has triumphed. However, critics complain that some of the privatized companies providing goods and services for the public sector are making massive profits even though the level of service provided has declined.

A wide range of information is offered by public and voluntary organizations

Voluntary sector

With some encouragement from the government, non-profit organizations (NPOs) in the voluntary sector have provided more services in the last 20 years. Many charities provide a targeted service for particular sections of the community. Age Concern, for example, provides services and support for pensioners.

There are about 135,000 charities in the UK, although 90 per cent are very small. The top 10 per cent get most of the income and do most of the work. The sector's annual income is £13.1 billion. It has nearly half-a-million paid employees, a quarter of whom are graduates, and more than three million volunteers.

Revision and exam practice units 7–13

1 What are the differences between a worker and a consumer co-operative?

2 What are the main advantages of limited liability?

3 Draw a chart showing the differences in objectives, ownership and control of the kinds of business described in Units 7–12.

4 State what you think the most suitable business organization would be for:

- a group of people who wanted to open a Caribbean restaurant in a city

- a young person, whose hobby is restoring old cars, who has always wanted to set up his own business and has just been left £25,000

- a person who has invented a new kind of home-lift for handicapped people

- three transport and distribution executives who have been given golden handshakes and want to set up their own business in the same field.

Give full reasons for your choice in each case.

5 Co-operatives and franchises both depend on co-operation. Draw a chart showing the main differences between them.

6 Give one example of when it would be appropriate for a sole proprietor to make his or her business into a) a partnership and b) a private limited company. Give reasons for your choice, supported by financial calculations. Describe how he or she would go about setting up the company.

Case study 1

Husband and wife team celebrate 25th anniversary and a year of success with card franchise

Franchisees Mike and Sue Humphry recently celebrated 25 years of marriage. Mike spent 27 years with British Telecom. Sue previously worked in the catering industry. Mike has always liked the idea of working for himself. He contacted the British Franchise Association and examined the information on the many franchises available within the UK market.

'We had discussed opening some kind of retail outlet,' explained Mike. 'We then turned our attention to franchising because it offers a proven business format and eliminates a certain amount of risk. We focused on the greeting card sector. Card Line Greetings was the first company I contacted and I was immediately impressed by the fact that the company had a five-year track record in the franchising industry and more than 30 years in the greetings card industry. I could make as many visits to the HQ in the Midlands as I felt we needed.'

The Card Line proposition is simple. Each franchisee is allocated a precisely calculated geographical area and supplies a wide range of high-quality greeting cards to retailers on a sale or return basis. Retailers receive regular visits by the franchisee to merchandise the display, keeping stocks high and ensuring good product rotation.

This allows the customers greater choice and cuts down the work for the retailer. Card Line invests in new designs and ranges which ensures the displays are always fresh and interesting.

Source: adapted from Franinfo – Franchise News website, 29 February 2000

1 To whom do Mike and Sue sell their cards?

2 What services do they give to their customers?

3 Explain in your own words the advantages of franchising to Sue and Mike.

Online links

www.franinfo.co.uk

Case study 2

£39m rail profit fury

One of Britain's worst-performing rail companies has announced record profits despite a slump in its standard of service.

Commuters reacted angrily to the figures from South West Trains, which showed that operating profits have jumped from £33.8 million to £39 million.

It means SWT, which runs local and long-distance trains from the south-west into Waterloo, now tops the earnings league for all Britain's 25 privatized train operators. Only last week the firm, owned by transport giant Stagecoach, appeared on the Strategic Rail Authority's list of the 13 worst rail operators in Britain.

SWT managed to run only 79 per cent of its trains on time during the six months to the end of March. The firm was also fined £4 million last year for its dismal performance on punctuality and for running trains with too few carriages, making them overcrowded.

Chief executive Keith Cochrane pledged that SWT would 'continue to strive' for punctuality improvements.

Some commuters in London yesterday were not impressed with SWT's profits. City banker John Bancroft said: 'This is nothing short of a scandal. The trains are late and dirty, and nothing has improved since privatization. They should give passengers a refund.'

Many of the 25 train operating companies blame Railtrack, which owns the track and the signalling, for some of the delays.

Source: adapted from the *Daily Mail*, 15 June 2000

1 **How many privatized train operators are there?**

2 **What are the main criticisms levelled against SWT?**

3 **Do you think public services such as British Rail should have been privatized? Give reasons for your answers.**

Case study 3

Any small company which wants to succeed needs to advertise its activities, particularly in the Yellow Pages. Which of these advertisements is the most effective? Give your reasons. Design a Yellow Pages advertisement of a similar size for a private limited company you would like to set up.

Extended questions

1 Choose examples of a small, a medium-sized and a large business, each showing different types of business organization.
   a) Describe what each business does, how big it is and how it is organized.
   b) For each business, examine how its size, its growth and the risks it takes all depend on each other.
   Discuss the relationships between these factors.

2 'Small is beautiful.' Discuss the advantages and disadvantages of being small for:
   a) a sole proprietor,
   b) a small partnership and
   c) a small co-operative.

BUSINESS VITAE: JOSH

COMPANY STATEMENT: JOSH is a state of the art salon for Afro and European hairdressing, which up till now has only been available in the West End, can now be found

With about 14 years experience in the industry, JOSH is driven by love and enthusiasm for hairdressing and the need to offer immediate and friendly customer service – always making sure that the customer is happy with their hair.

JOSH has some of London's highly qualified and experienced stylists and beauticians who listen to, and deliver on, customers' needs.

YEAR FORMED: 1999

EMPLOYEES: 4

CORE SKILLS: Taking care of clients every need – the hair, the pampering, the courtesy and the consultation that is usually missing at other salons. Essentially, it means giving the client the 'finish' as it were. JOSH also has a bridal section offering special bridal packages to would-be bides – JOSH has done 14 weddings so far this year.

KEY CLIENTS: Rio (Gladiators); Paula Taja; Local residents – mainly professionals including doctors, lawyers and company directors and ordinary residents.

1 How many years' experience has Josh had?

2 How many people does he employ?

3 Who are his key clients?

4 What personal qualities do you think Josh has which will help him to succeed as a sole proprietor?

5 Do you think this is a satisfactory way of presenting information about a business? How would you change it or what other information you would provide?

Online links
www.blackbritain.co.uk

EXAM PRACTICE

Foundation

Seaview is a ten-room bed and breakfast boarding house at a seaside resort on the north-east coast. At present, it is open for eight months of the year, from 1 April to 1 December, but many of the rooms remain unlet. The owners have three plans to attract more customers.

Plan 1 – to offer evening meals.

Plan 2 – to reduce prices, although these are competitive with similar establishments in the town.

Plan 3 – to open for the whole year.

1 (a) Explain the possible effects on the business of each plan. (6 marks)
(b) Which plan do you think is likely to be most effective? Give reasons for your views. (4 marks)

2 How would the boarding house be affected by the falling prices of Continental holidays? (2 marks)

Higher

Seaview is a small, select, ten-roomed hotel at a seaside resort on the east coast. The three partners who run the hotel as a partnership are thinking of changing it to a private company.

1 How would the source of finance for a company be different from a partnership's and what benefits would it offer? (4 marks)

2 How might the business be affected by a general increase in wages and salaries? (2 marks)

Section 3

Business aims and organization

Business objectives

1: Tracey's failed pottery venture

Ever since Tracey left school, she had wanted to have her own pottery. Instead, she had been forced to take a job as a receptionist. After she got married, she started going to pottery classes in the evening, while her husband watched TV.

Her pots were admired by everyone. One evening, when she got back from her class, she told her husband Bill that she would like to give up her job and start a pottery in the garage. He thought it was a good idea.

They worked out that if Tracey gave up her job she would save £750 a year on fares to work; £3,000 on child minder's fees; and another £900 on lunches and clothes for work that she would no longer have to buy. In addition, her tax bill would certainly be lower, perhaps by £1,000 a year. If she could make a profit of £4,000 a year, which didn't seem very much, they would be almost as well off.

They decided to spend their savings of £5,000 on pottery equipment. Tracey worked hard and soon had a stock of pots. One weekend, they took some samples round to local shops, but failed to get a single order. A craft fair was being held the following weekend. Tracey hired a stall for £15, but she sold only £20 worth of pottery. Meanwhile, the household bills were mounting up. Tracey's wages had helped to pay these bills before she gave up her job. Tracey went on with her business for six more months. Finally, she was forced to sell the pottery equipment at a loss and to take a job as a receptionist again.

Tracey and her husband lost most of their savings, but things could have been far more serious. They did not get planning permission for the pottery. If neighbours had complained to the council's environmental health officer about the noise or the increased fire risk, the council might have closed the business before it had even got started.

As well as this, Tracey failed to tell her insurance company that she was using a kiln in her garage. If it had caught fire and the blaze had spread to the house, she might have lost their home as well. The insurance company would almost certainly have refused to pay because it had not been told that the use of the garage had changed and there was now a greater risk of fire.

Study points

① What enquiries should Tracey have made before she started her business?

② After she had started the pottery, what could she have done to make the business more likely to succeed?

③ If Tracey had opened the pottery in your area, what kind of pottery would you have advised her to produce? Explain your reasons.

2: What happened to Boo.com?

Boo.com was launched six months ago in a blaze of publicity as the first global online retailer selling fashion sportswear in 18 markets worldwide. With £91 million in backing from investors, it was one of the best funded internet start-ups.

But the company experienced difficulties almost from the outset. Two months after the launch, Boo.com was forced to lay off 90 staff and discount some product ranges by 40 per cent.

In recent weeks, Boo.com frantically searched for more funding to stay afloat. With only £500,000 of the original funds remaining, a further £20 million was needed for a dramatic restructuring programme to help cut costs. The appeal for more money fell on deaf ears and on Thursday morning Boo.com appointed a liquidator.

The key to the failure of Boo.com was the rate at which the company was spending money. Boo.com was the first UK internet start-up to go under. However, it is unlikely to be the last.

Source: adapted from *The Times* online special: Boo.com

Study points

① What could have been done to prevent Boo.com from going under?

Online links
www.the-times.co.uk

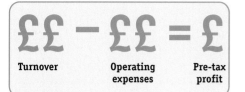

Turnover — Operating expenses = Pre-tax profit

Making a profit

The main aim of every business is to survive. The only way it can do this is to make a profit. Its **turnover** – the goods or services it sells – must be bigger than its operating expenses, or the day-to-day cost of running the business.

If a limited company fails to make a profit, it will not have enough money to:
- pay the wages; so it will lose workers
- pay its suppliers; so it cannot buy raw materials and services
- pay interest charges; so it cannot borrow money
- pay a **dividend** (a part of the profits) to its shareholders (people who own a share of the company); so the price of its shares will fall
- invest money to allow it to grow and expand; so it will not do very well against rival businesses. If this continues for long, the firm will go out of business or be taken over by a more efficient company.

This basic law of survival applies to all firms in the private sector, both sole proprietors and much larger companies.

Other objectives

In addition to making a profit, a business can have other aims or **objectives**. These might include:
- size and growth – in money invested in the business, turnover, stock market value and the number of employees

- an increase in a company's or a product's, **market share** – for example, if the total value of new houses built in Britain during a year was £6,000 million, a house-builder with a turnover of £300 million would have a five per cent market share
- product development – which will increase turnover and market share
- keeping customers happy – which some companies now see as the prime aim or objective.

(See Unit 17 for a further discussion of these aims and how success in achieving them may be judged.)

Small businesses

These aims apply to small businesses too. Before Tracey made a single pot, she should have made a thorough investigation of the market to find out what kinds of pottery were wanted (see Unit 36). Was it kitchenware, garden pottery, gifts or individual art items? This would have helped her decide what her core business would be. Then she should have set herself clear objectives. These objectives should be specific, measurable, easy to explain and practical.
- *Specific*. Tracey should have decided what her competitive priorities (the things which are most important in competing against other businesses) were going to be. Was she going to concentrate, for example, on: reliable products and deliveries, good quality, lower prices, large numbers of cheaper pots with lower profits, or expensive pots with higher profits?
- *Measurable* in terms of money and number of pots being made.
- *Easy to explain* to the bank manager for a loan, to employees and so on.

CHECKPOINTS

1. What is the main aim of every business in the private sector?

2. What would happen to a business which failed to make a profit?

3. Say in your own words why it is important for any business to have clear objectives.

4. Why do you think both long-term and short-term objectives are needed?

- *Practical*. What was the best way for Tracey to sell her goods: retail (selling in small numbers to individuals), wholesale (selling in large numbers to shops who then retail them), car boot sales, fairs and exhibitions or local businesses such as cafés, restaurants and public houses?

Public sector

Before 1979, the public sector was not expected to make a profit, but to provide the best possible service for the whole community (see Unit 13).

In recent years, however, public sector organizations have been expected to make a profit if possible. In some cases, a free service is provided, as with the fire or ambulance service. These organizations are expected to meet strict financial targets.

Key skills
IT

Use a computer and any clip art available to design a **logo** for Tracey's business or one you would like to start yourself. Print a hard copy.

KEY TERMS

Dividend A small part of the profits of a company which is paid each year to all the shareholders.

Logo A logo is a symbol – a letter or a small drawing – representing a business or a brand.

Market share The proportion of the total sales of a market that a product – or a business – holds.

Objectives The aims which a business sets for itself so that it can measure how successful it has been in reaching its targets.

Turnover The total sales of a business during a set period, usually a year.

Growth and expansion

About 3i

3i is Europe's leading **venture capital company.** We make share and loan investments in growing businesses. Our main activity is investing in start-up companies, growing businesses, management buy-outs, management buy-ins and share purchases.

3i invests in a wide range of businesses and industry sectors. We look at each business individually and in-depth. The ability and integrity of the management and the growth potential of the business are the key factors 3i considers when deciding whether or not to invest.

3i has over 50 years' experience and has invested almost £11 billion in more than 13,200 businesses.

Source: adapted from About 3i website

"We work with management teams to develop imaginative responses to business opportunities and share the risks and rewards in achieving them"

EAT

One of 3i's core objectives is to help young companies reach their full potential.

A good example is the EAT (Excellence and Taste) chain of sandwich, coffee and soup outlets in central London. We were initially approached in autumn 1997 by Niall MacArthur, an ex-investment banker who had swapped his pinstripe suit for an apron to open a sandwich bar in Villiers Street, near Charing Cross, with two partners.

MacArthur had ambitious plans to expand the business, believing that an opportunity existed for another player to succeed at the premium end of the market alongside the successful Pret à Manger chain.

MacArthur had researched the market very thoroughly. He had clearly identified a market niche, namely for high quality, innovative, home-cooked lunch products sold from strongly-branded and well-located premises. The

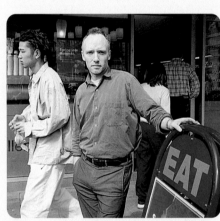

range of items offered was wider than the competition, with new recipes trialled and rolled out every month. He had huge amounts of energy and enthusiasm. In November 1997, we injected an initial £350,000 of capital into the business.

By the time we sat down again with the team in the late summer of 1998 to review progress, they had opened two further shops, just turned in their first break-even monthly performance and won the coveted Sandwich Bar of the Year award. All fresh produce was manufactured and supplied by their central kitchen in Camberwell, which was now running 24 hours a day. MacArthur had identified further

Study points

① What does EAT stand for?

② How much did 3i invest in EAT at first?

③ What kind of production is EAT involved in?

④ What is a venture capital company?

⑤ Why did 3i decide to finance this company at first?

⑥ What persuaded them to give EAT more finance?

Online links
www.3i.com

high-profile sites for expansion.

We have recently committed a further £2.6 million of funding to support the three-year plan of expanding the chain to 30 sites. By March 1999, seven EAT outlets will be established and the business is now well placed to continue its rapid growth into the coming year.

Source: adapted from About 3i website

Figure 1: Mergers and takeovers

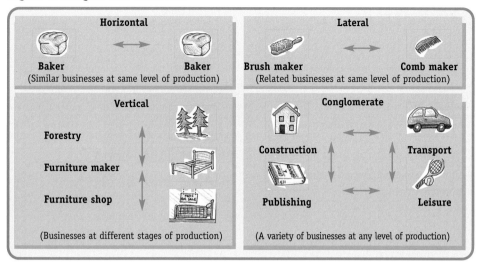

Horizontal

Baker — Baker
(Similar businesses at same level of production)

Lateral

Brush maker — Comb maker
(Related businesses at same level of production)

Vertical

Forestry
Furniture maker
Furniture shop
(Businesses at different stages of production)

Conglomerate

Construction — Transport
Publishing — Leisure
(A variety of businesses at any level of production)

CHECKPOINTS

❶ What are the two main company attitudes towards mergers?

❷ Name the two chief advantages of horizontal mergers. Give two examples of this kind of merger.

❸ State three advantages of lateral mergers and give one example .

❹ Give one actual example of a vertical merger. What would be the main advantages for the purchasing firm?

No business can afford to stand still for long, particularly in today's cut-throat environment, when fashion changes consumers' wants so quickly and rapid advances in technology create new business opportunities almost every day. Those businesses which do not keep up with the changing times will soon find that other firms have started to steal their market share.

Entrepreneurs like Niall MacArthur in the case study welcome this competitive environment. MacArthur was not put off by the fact that there are many start-up failures in the sandwich bar market and a strong, firmly-established market leader, Pret à Manger. He was determined to make his business succeed. The steps he took could be a model for other entrepreneurs.
● He carried out thorough market research.
● He found a **niche market** for high-quality, home-cooked products.
● He introduced competitive products.

It was this thoroughness and attention to detail which was responsible for his success and made it possible to open new branches of EAT with the financial assistance of the venture capital firm, 3i.

Ways of expanding

There are other ways of expanding as well as growing a business. Company A can agree to merge with Company B to form a new company, Company C. Or Company A can make a **takeover bid** for Company B by offering to buy its shares. If the bid is accepted, the two businesses merge to form a new business, Company C. There are three main kinds of **merger**.

Horizontal merger

Horizontal integration can provide:
● economies of scale which reduce unit costs (see Unit 17)
● reduced competition when rival firms are taken over.

This kind of merger has been common among high-street retailers recently.

Lateral merger

Lateral integration helps to:
● give the firm a greater share of the market

● extend the product mix
● provide new opportunities when a core product is reaching the end of its life cycle (see Unit 43)
● gain technological skills by taking over a smaller, more advanced company.
● use the firm's own skills in another sphere.

For example, a chain of retailers with its own transport fleet might take over a contract-hire car and van firm; or a computer firm might take over a software manufacturer.

Vertical merger

Vertical integration may be either backwards or forwards. In the first case, for example, a big retailer might take over a small manufacturer to ensure continuity of supplies. In the second, a brewery might take over a chain of pubs to give it a secure outlet for the sale of its beers.

There are many other reasons for takeovers. The assets of the company which is taken over may have been undervalued, so the purchasing company can make a quick profit by selling some of them off. The company may have a tax loss which the purchaser can offset against its own profits. The purchasing company may believe that its more highly skilled management will make the other company profitable. Or, it may feel there is a need to diversify from declining industries.

KEY TERMS

Merger The joining of two firms to form one new company, which is jointly owned by shareholders of the former companies.

Niche market A segment, or small section, of a market.

Takeover bid An offer by one company for the shares of another so that it can gain a controlling interest.

Venture capital company A firm which invests money in other companies which it thinks might succeed.

Multinationals

A new century of success

In last year's report to shareholders I said no company had had a greater impact on the lives of people around the world in the 20th century than Ford. I want Ford to have an even greater impact on people's lives in the 21st century.

In 1999 we made a fast start. We launched innovative products around the world. We strengthened our existing global brands and added valuable new ones.

Our immediate and ongoing focus is on satisfying customers. That hasn't changed since the company was founded nearly 100 years ago. We want to make customers' lives easier, safer, healthier, more entertaining, more fun. We want to give people choices and solutions. We also want to make it easy to do business with us.

The internet is a powerful tool in this effort. I believe that the internet will be the moving assembly line of the 21st century. It is going to improve productivity, lower costs and delight customers that much.

William Clay Ford, Jr. Chairman of the board.

Source: adapted from Ford Motor Company website – 1999 Annual Report

William Clay Ford Jr, chairman of the board

Automotive operations

- Established 1903
- World's largest manufacturer of trucks and second largest manufacturer of cars and trucks combined
- Operations in 40 countries
- 114 plants
- 247,500 employees
- Over 20,000 dealers serving over 200 markets
- 1999 revenue mix: North America, 73%; Europe, 22%; South America, 2%; Other, 3%.

Source: adapted from Ford Motor Company website – 1999 Annual Report

Aston Martin cars

Founded in 1914 by Lionel Martin and Robert Bamford in a small West London workshop, Aston Martin has grown over more than 80 years to become a world renowned manufacturer of the finest, exclusive, luxury sports cars.

The sense of family is strong at Aston Martin, with a number of father/son teams employed in our workshops. Owners' sons have grown up alongside their fathers' Aston Martins and later became owners themselves. In fact, owning an Aston Martin is like being part of one of the most exclusive clubs in the world. In more than 80 years, a little over 14,000 cars have been made and it says much of our company and our customers that some three-quarters of them are still in use.

The V8 series of Aston Martin cars are as unmistakable today as they were when first launched in 1970. The use of the very finest materials – Connolly leather, burr walnut veneers, Wilton carpets – unashamed luxury combined with exhilarating yet refined performance, all point to the cars' unique ancestry. And most important, each and every engine bears the signature of the craftsman who hand-built it.

Source: adapted from Aston Martin Lagonda Limited website

Study points

1. When was the Ford Motor Company founded?
2. How many countries does it operate in?
3. What is its main geographical market?
4. What kind of market does Aston Martin cater for?
5. How does Ford benefit by producing different brands of cars?
6. What did the chairman of the board mean by saying that the internet will be 'the moving assembly line of the 21st century'? Do you agree?

Major brands

Ford: genuine, progressive, smart
Mercury: innovative, expressive, individualistic
Aston Martin: the most exclusive club
Jaguar: elegant, sensuous, original, refined power
Lincoln: American luxury
Volvo: safety for life.

Online links
www.ford.com
www.astonmartin.com

Multinationals like the Ford Motor Company are the kings of the business world. Their turnover is often greater than the national income of small countries.

In 1999, for example, Ford sold a record number of 7,200,000 vehicles. As the case study shows, Ford directly employs 247,500 people and has more than 20,000 dealers serving over 200 markets worldwide. In addition, it provides employment for many more firms which supply it with parts and other services.

Record earnings

Although Ford had record earnings in North America, its main market, it did not do so well in Europe and the rest of the world. For example, in Britain, it made a pre-tax loss of £119 million against a profit of £61 million in the previous year.

The company put the blame for its loss partly on the Consumers' Association campaign against the high price of cars in Britain compared with the price for the same models on the Continent. As a result, all car manufacturers in Britain, including Ford, were forced to cut their prices to keep their customers happy.

But there were also deeper reasons. Sales of Ford vehicles fell from 490,024 in the previous year to 464,341. The car industry has become very much more competitive, not only in Britain but throughout the whole of Europe.

For these reasons, Ford is restructuring its operations in Europe. One consequence is that car production at Dagenham will end in 2002 with the loss of 1,400 jobs. However, Ford will invest about £330 million in the plant to make it the main diesel engine production centre.

Changing environments

Multinationals have to take into account factors such as these, and many more, in managing their global operations, as the business environment varies so greatly

from one country to another and is subject to endless change. In deciding where it should increase or decrease its activity and investments it has to take dozens of factors into account. Some of the main ones are:

- the economic, political and social stability of the country which is essential to protect the multinational's investment
- the value, and potential, of the market for its goods or services in that country
- the infrastructure of roads, railways and airports and public utility supplies
- the education and skills of the country's population
- the laws relating to worker protection and redundancy
- government and local authority aid and support for business
- trade union power
- interest and exchange rates.

Main objectives

The main objectives of multinationals are to expand their operations in the most profitable areas, to gain as large a share as possible of the world market and to use their skills and expertise for the benefit of all the companies in the group.

To do this, multinationals need stable exchange rates between currencies, so that they can make firm plans for the future. In addition, they need a free flow of international trade which is not restricted by **protectionism**, or policies of high duties on imported goods.

Foreign subsidiaries

The parent company keeps control over its global operations through its foreign **subsidiaries**. These are firms which have either been set up by the parent company to produce or market its products, or they are foreign companies which have been taken over. The parent company may own them entirely, or may hold a controlling

CHECKPOINTS

❶ What are the main ways in which a multinational is different from other firms?

❷ What are the main international problems for multinationals?

❸ Explain how changes in foreign countries can influence a multinational's decisions.

❹ Describe how a multinational controls its operations in foreign countries.

interest by having 51 per cent or more of the voting shares.

In addition, the parent company is often a large shareholder in other companies. Even if it does not have a controlling interest of 51 per cent or more, it can still influence boardroom decisions if it owns a large number of shares.

Advantages

Some of multinationals' advantages are:
- economies of scale (see Unit 17)
- greater global access to capital
- avoiding tariffs, e.g. Japanese car manufacturers in Britain escaping European Union tariffs and duties
- government grants and subsidies for new factories
- reduced tax bills by declaring profits in a low-tax country.

Disadvantages

There are also some disadvantages including:
- difficulties in control and communication
- host country restrictions on redundancies, repatriating profits etc
- changes in exchange rates.

KEY TERMS

Multinationals Large conglomerates which operate in many countries.
Protectionism Putting tariffs or other restrictions on imports to protect a country's own industries.
Subsidiaries Smaller companies which are controlled by bigger companies.

Ways of measuring success

'BP's goal is to play a leading role in meeting the world's energy needs without damaging the environment'

Adapted from Exploring Alaska on BP website

bp

Top 10 UK companies by market capitalisation*

	Company	Business sector	Value (£m)
1	BP Amoco	Oil and gas	87,734
2	Glaxo/Wellcome	Pharmaceuticals	74,852
3	BT	Telecommunications	58,501
4	SmithKline Beecham	Pharmaceuticals	46,863
5	Lloyds TSB	Retail banking	46,461
6	HSBC	Retail banking	41,995
7	Shell	Oil and gas	36,707
8	Vodafone	Telecommunications	30,195
9	Zeneca	Pharmaceuticals	24,855
10	Diageo	Alcoholic drinks	24,492

Source: adapted from *Britain 2000*, Office of National Statistics, 1999

* Market capitalisation is the amount of money that a company is worth on the stock exchange. It is calculated by multiplying the number of shares the company has issued by their current price on the stock exchange. As most shares go up and down in price almost every day, their market capitalisation, or stock market values, constantly change.

Study points

① What was the stock market value of the top company?

② What kinds of business are the top ten companies involved in?

③ How would BP Amoco measure its own success?

④ Do you think this is the only way in which the company would judge its success?

⑤ In your view, is market value a realistic way of calculating a company's true value?

Profit

As you have seen in Unit 14, profit is necessary for any business to survive. For shareholders in particular, it is a strong measure of success, as big profits usually mean big dividends. Making the biggest possible profit – or **profit maximization** – is not always the most useful objective. For example, small proprietors may not want to work much harder to make a bigger profit if they are satisfied with their present income and lifestyle. A big company may decide to make a lower profit for a time so that it can sell a product more cheaply to break into a new market (see Unit 43).

Profit is very important, but a better way of measuring the real success of a business is the return on capital employed (see Unit 33).

Company size

Another way of measuring success is by company size. Small companies are defined as those which have at least two of the following features:

● an annual turnover of less than £2.8 million
● assets of £1.4 million or less
● 50 or fewer employees.

Although these small companies can obtain certain benefits, such as a lower rate of corporation (or business) tax and some government grants, most entrepreneurs prefer to see their company grow and expand.

Stock market value

As the case study shows, companies can also be ranked according to their stock market value. However, this does not always reflect the true value or success of a business, but only investors' views of it. In 1999, investors hoping to make a quick fortune bought huge quantities of shares in new technology companies, which sent their share price soaring. But what goes up, can always come down again. Psion, Baltimore Technologies, Kingston Communications and Thus joined the FTSE 100 in March 2000, but were ejected only three months later.

Turnover, or sales, is another way of measuring success. But, by itself, it is not enough. A company may have a very high turnover, but make little profit. The number of employees is another measure of size and success. However, this is not a

Figure 1: Business objectives

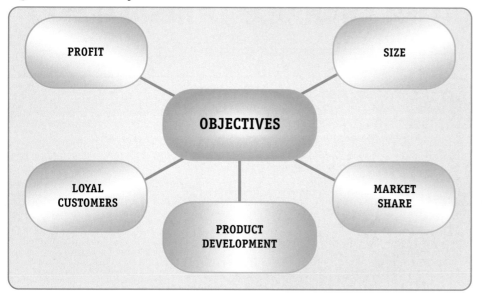

1. How is profit calculated?
2. Why are some businesses opposed to making as much profit as possible?
3. Make a list of the main internal economies of scale.
4. Describe when a demerger might occur
5. Why is market share important for businesses?

true value again, as the company may be inefficient and employing more people than it needs.

Economies of scale

Big companies, however, do have many advantages. These benefits are known as **economies of scale.** These are some of the main economies, or savings in cost.

- *Technical*. The reduction in unit costs as more goods are produced owing to the use of more efficient, labour-saving machinery and the **division of labour** which makes production more efficient.
- *Buying*. Big firms can obtain a discount, or a reduction in price, because they buy raw materials and parts in bulk or large quantities.
- *Financial*. Large companies often pay less interest on the money they borrow than small firms or sole proprietors do, as their size gives them the power to bargain with the lender.

- *Marketing*. The costs of advertising and promotion are spread over a large number of units and are, therefore, proportionally cheaper.
- *Managerial*. The costs of management are also proportionally lower as they are spread over a larger volume of production.
- *Distribution*. Bulk delivery of goods is proportionally cheaper.

Diseconomies of scale

A company, however, can become too big. It then becomes difficult for the managers to run the business efficiently. The company may become rigid and inflexible in its views. Smaller competitors may start to win market share. This inefficiency produces **diseconomies of scale** which cause costs to rise.

The only answer to these problems may be a **demerger** which breaks up a business into two separate companies.

Market share

As you have seen in Unit 14, market share is the percentage that a product, or a company, holds of a total market. Market share is measured by either value or volume. (See the case study in Unit 41.)

Market share is a much better measure of success than size, as it shows that a business is performing more efficiently than its competitors.

Product development

The main strength of a business is its products. If a business is to succeed in an increasingly competitive world, it must continuously update its products and develop new ones (see Unit 41). Satisfying customers is also important. In the long term, customer loyalty and repeat purchases and orders are the final test.

SMALL COMPANIES
State which of the following are small companies.

	Company		
	A	**B**	**C**
Turnover	£1.5m	£1m	£2.9m
Assets	£1m	£0.75m	£1.2m
Employees	64	28	51

KEY TERMS

Demerger Breaking up a large company into two separate businesses.

Diseconomies of scale An increase in costs which occurs when a firm becomes too big to be managed effectively.

Division of labour Dividing production into separate tasks which can be done by individual workers. These specialist workers need little training and can work faster.

Economies of scale The reduction in costs which arises through a firm growing in size.

Profit maximization Making the biggest profit possible.

Revision and exam practice units 14–17

Case study 1

REVIEW POINTS

1 Give one example of horizontal, lateral and vertical integration. Explain the main reasons for each type.

2 Why does a business need to have clear objectives? Give an example of a short-term and a long-term objective. Why do you think it is important to have both?

3 What are the main ways of measuring the success of a business?

Extended questions

1 'All businesses must be dedicated to growth.'
   a) What must all businesses do in order to survive?
   b) Give the two main objectives for most businesses.
   c) Do you agree with the above statement? Give reasons for your answer.

2 Large companies and multinationals can focus on a small number of core businesses or spread their interests over a wide range of products.
   a) What are the main advantages of having i) a focused and ii) a diversified strategy?
   b) Explain the main dangers there might be in each of these strategies.

10,000 new jobs as furniture giant triples UK stores

The Swedish furniture giant IKEA is to triple the number of stores it has in Britain, promising 10,000 new jobs and price cuts of at least 20 per cent. Forecasts suggest the company will attract 20 million shoppers this year.

The ten-year expansion will increase the number of stores to 30 and triple the current work-force of 5,000. It will be concentrated in parts of the UK which have suffered worst from the demise of traditional manufacturing industries. The new stores will retain the company's traditional format of large out-of-town warehouses.

IKEA's total sales in the UK reached £585 million last year. This year sales are expected to top £750 million.

The expansion will cost the company an estimated £700 million, while the new jobs will be a mix of full and part-time. The first stage will involve a £300 million investment on eight new stores and two distribution centres, creating a total of 4,500 new jobs.

Defending the decision not to look at town centres, UK managing director Goran Nilsson said: 'Selling bulky goods means the concept does not fit easily in town. We are looking at ten-acre plus sites, often bringing real economic benefits in areas of regeneration.'

A spokesman said: 'IKEA's business idea is to provide a wide range of good quality furnishing items at a price that the majority of people can afford.

'Twenty new stores will enable IKEA to double sales and reduce prices by at least 20 per cent.'

The UK is IKEA's second biggest market after Germany, accounting for 11 per cent of the company's total £5 billion turnover. It employs 50,000 around the world.

Source: adapted from *Daily Mail*, 20 June 2000

1 What kind of business organisation is IKEA?

2 How much were IKEA's sales in the UK last year?

3 What is the company's total turnover?

4 How much does it intend to spend on expansion?

5 Why is it concentrating on out-of-town sites?

6 What factors influence a company such as IKEA to expand into foreign markets?

7 What do you think IKEA's main business objectives are?

Case study 2

Shops go up for grabs in the battle of the high street

A record 1,200 shops have flooded onto the property market this year as high street retailers give up the battle to survive in the face of unprecedented competition.

'Fierce competition in every sector is leading to the distinct feeling that there are just too many shops,' property consultancy Colliers Conrad Ritblat Erdman (CCRE) warns in a report.

Arcadia has put 400 shops up for sale, while Barclays attempts to unload 200 branches and Centrica 240.

The consultants say that demand is now concentrated on the big shopping malls, and on out-of-town shopping centres. There is also growing demand from DIY operators, which fuels rent rises as B & Q and Homebase compete head to head for sites.

But CCRE says bloodshed in the high street does not spell the end of the nation's traditional way of shopping.

A new breed of retailer is emerging. Smaller outlets are badly needed by coffee shop operators, opticians and mobile phone firms.

Larger stores – like those being vacated by C & A – are attractive to retailers such as Gap and discounters like Peacocks and Primark. For investors, though, the chances of significant rent rises appear some way off.

Source: adapted from *Daily Mail*, 20 June 2000 (see also case study in Unit 46)

1 **How many high street shops had closed during the year?**

2 **According to the report, what are the main causes?**

3 **Why are small businesses sometimes more successful in the high street than some larger companies?**

EXAM PRACTICE 1

A medium-sized firm, making fashion jewellery, has won three large contracts in the Netherlands. As a result, it has decided to set up a company in Rotterdam.

The subsidiary company will produce and market the jewellery, with the parent company in England maintaining a controlling interest.

Another Dutch company has suggested a merger with the British company.

Foundation

1 What is a subsidiary company?
(1 mark)

2 What is meant by 'a controlling interest'?
(2 marks)

3 What factors will the company have taken into account before expanding into a foreign country?
(4 marks)

Higher

1 What factors would the company need to consider before expanding into a foreign country?
(6 marks)

2 What were the company's objectives in relation to its new venture?
(2 marks)

3 What effect would a merger be likely to have on the company's market share? What (a) advantages and (b) problems would a merger create for the parent company?
(6 marks)

4 What problems might it create for the firm in relation to (a) decision-making (b) communication? Suggest how these might be solved.
(6 marks)

EXAM PRACTICE 2

Andrew Pearson worked in a garden centre in the suburbs of a large city. As he had been there for seven years, he thought he had sufficient experience to offer his services as a jobbing gardener. He estimated that he would need a minimum of £70 a week for his personal expenses, £30 a week to pay for the instalments on his second-hand van, and £50 a week for the rent of a flat which he shares with a friend. Petrol, heating and electricity, and incidental business expenses he estimated at a further £40 a week. With help from his grandparents, he had saved £4,000 and his father offered to lend him £1,000 to buy the necessary tools and a shed in which to keep them. He thought that while he was building up his business, he could work a 40-hour week for 46 weeks of the year.

Foundation

1 What is the total annual amount that Andrew estimated he would need?
(2 marks)

2 How much would Andrew need to make a week to cover his estimated expenses?
(3 marks)

3 If he worked a 40-hour week, what would Andrew need to charge per hour to break even and cover his own expenses?
(3 marks)

4 What do you think should be Andrew's business objectives for the future?
(4 marks)

Higher

1 Do you think Andrew's estimates are realistic or are there any vital expenditures he has missed? Explain your reasons for your answer.
(4 marks)

2 Which of Andrew's conclusions are based on fact and which on opinion?
(4 marks)

Organization of small and large businesses

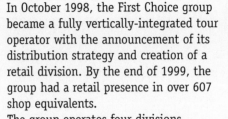

Overview

First Choice Holidays is one of the UK's leading tour operators. The business was formed in 1973.

In 1994 the company was restructured and rebranded as First Choice Holidays plc.

In October 1998, the First Choice group became a fully vertically-integrated tour operator with the announcement of its distribution strategy and creation of a retail division. By the end of 1999, the group had a retail presence in over 607 shop equivalents.

The group operates four divisions.

- UK and Ireland tour operators, both mainstream, such as First Choice Holidays and Unijet Travel and specialist businesses including Flexiski and Lakes and Mountains.
- International tour operations, including the Canadian tour operations, Signature Vacations, and the leading yacht charter and watersports company, Sunsail.
- Airline and aviation, comprising charter airline Air 2000 and seat broker Viking Aviation.
- UK distribution, including the retail travel agency chain Bakers Dolphin, the direct retailer Travel Choice Direct and Holiday Hypermarkets.

Small businesses

If you were self-employed – as a painter or a gardener – you would have to do everything yourself. Before you started your business you would have investigated the market and set objectives for yourself (see Unit 14). It would be your responsibility to see that these objectives were carried out. You would have to look after the production – painting rooms or mowing lawns. In addition, you would have to do all your own buying – tins of paint or garden plants.

It would be your job, too, to market your services by advertising in the local newspaper or by putting leaflets through letter boxes. If you needed finance – to buy a new van, a set of ladders or a lawn mower – you would have to arrange a loan from a bank. There are many other things

Study points

1. Who is the most important person in the company?
2. Who is the next most important person?
3. Which people are of equal importance?
4. Describe in your own words the work of the company's four divisions.
5. What is a fully vertically integrated firm?
6. In your view, how does First Choice Holidays benefit from this integration?

Online links

www.firstchoiceholidaysplc.com

Organisation Chart

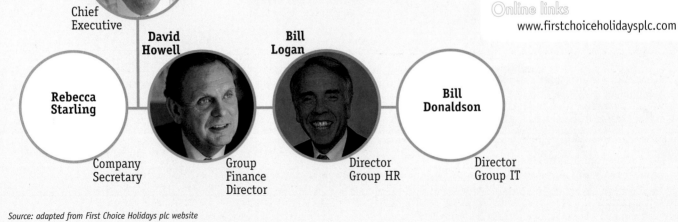

Ian Clubb   Chairman

Peter Long

Chief Executive

Rebecca Starling

David Howell

Bill Logan

Bill Donaldson

Company Secretary

Group Finance Director

Director Group HR

Director Group IT

Source: adapted from First Choice Holidays plc website

you would also have to do, such as sending out bills, writing letters, keeping business accounts. You could get help with some of these matters from an accountant or a typist – for a fee. Or you could do everything yourself.

If your business expanded later, so that you had to employ other people, you would have even more responsibility. You would have to give orders and see that they were carried out. You would have to take income tax and national insurance contributions from your employees' wages. You would also need to know far more about the law and employees' rights (see Unit 63).

Larger businesses

The more people you employed, the more complicated it would be to run the firm. Big firms cope with these problems by **organization**. In all businesses above the self-employed level, there must be people in **authority** who give the orders and see that they are carried out. There is a **chain of command** which runs right the way down an organization from the top, the chairperson, through the chief executive and the heads of departments to the bottom – the shop floor and office workers who carry out the final orders.

Organization charts

The way in which a plc is organized can be shown in the form of a chart. The firm in the case study, First Choice Holidays plc, is organized by **function** – the jobs that people do. This is the most common form of organization.

The vertical lines of authority represent the chain of command, with orders going down from one level to the one below. The

horizontal lines show that people are of equal rank, or importance.

At the top is Ian Clubb, the chairman of the board of directors. The board is responsible to the shareholders who have invested money in the firm. As chairman, Ian Clubb is the most important person in the company, as he decides what the policy and the objectives of the firm should be (see Unit 14).

At the next level is the chief executive, Peter Long, who is in day-to-day control of the firm and who is also a member of the board of directors. He has to decide and plan how the firm will achieve its objectives and also has the responsibility, or duty, of reporting back to the board. Very occasionally, the chairperson of the board is also the chief executive.

Main divisions

The four people at the next level of the chart are the heads of the four main divisions in the group. With the chief executive they make up the top management team. Their titles describe their function. Rebecca Starling is responsible for general administration and legal matters. David Howell is in charge of the group's financial affairs. Bill Logan, the head of the human resources division, is responsible for everything connected with the company's employees. Bill Donaldson is in charge of information technology, which plays an increasingly important role in the firm's operations.

Although many firms have an organization similar to this, it is not a rigid structure. The organization of a firm develops to suit its own needs. For example, in manufacturing firms there would be a production division or department and sometimes a purchasing division, too.

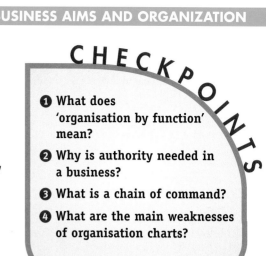

CHECKPOINTS

1. What does 'organisation by function' mean?
2. Why is authority needed in a business?
3. What is a chain of command?
4. What are the main weaknesses of organisation charts?

Organization charts can only show what it is hoped will happen in a firm – not what actually does. Some powerful chairpersons often bypass the formal structure and make deals of their own without the top management's knowledge or go-ahead. On the other hand, there are some chief executives who are so powerful that the chairperson is no real match for them and has relatively little power.

Informal groups

In all organizations, there are also **informal groups**, cutting right across the formal structure, which can have a great effect on the way in which a firm is run. These groups do not appear on the organization chart.

However, they can have a great impact on the firm's performance. Satisfied groups can increase a firm's productivity by helping each other and people who work for them, and by working hard so that the business succeeds.

Groups of discontented employees can have a harmful effect by always complaining, being awkward, destroying team spirit, or even wrecking projects.

KEY TERMS

Authority The right to give orders to people at a lower level in the organization.

Chain of command The levels through which an order has to pass before it can be carried out.

Function The jobs that people do which form the basis of an organization's structure.

Informal groups Loose associations of people sharing common attitudes, interests, or views, which exist outside an organization's formal structure.

Organization The way in which a business is structured, or arranged, so that it can achieve its objectives.

Key skills
Communication and IT

Construct suitable organization charts for:
a) a firm manufacturing women's clothing and
b) a car rental firm.
Print hard copies.

Company structures

CASE STUDY

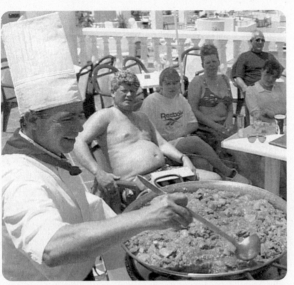

Poolside food at the Tenerife Ocean Beach Aparthotel from the First Choice It's Summer brochure

Dividing up the work

Every person in an organization has his or her own job to do; but each of them is also a member of a **formal group** – such as a division or a department. The chairperson and the chief executive officer are members of the board of directors (see Unit 18). Below that level of the **hierarchy**, everyone is a member of a division or a department, each of which is controlled by a working director or a manager.

As the case study shows, the organization of a firm can be split horizontally into divisions – e.g. UK distribution and Airline and aviation – and vertically into increasingly smaller departments and sections.

Why formal groups?

Why should firms be split up into formal groups? There are advantages for both employees and the firm itself. For employees, the main benefits are as follows.

- It gives them a greater sense of unity and purpose as they can see themselves as members of a team.
- It is easier to get help, as they can ask experienced colleagues or take the more difficult problems to their boss.

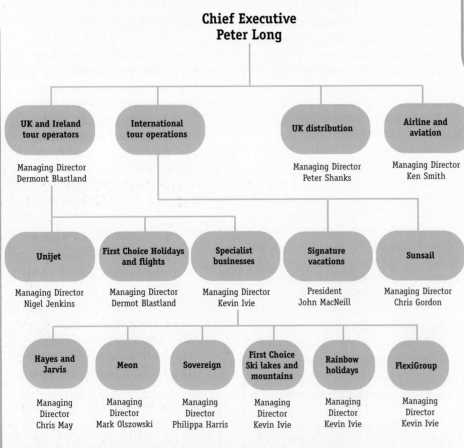

Figure 1: Part of First Choice Holidays organization chart

Source: adapted from First Choice Holidays PLC website

Study points

① What does Ken Smith do?

② What are the names of the other three divisions?

③ Who is in charge of UK and Ireland tour operators?

④ What other parts of the business is he or she responsible for?

⑤ Who is in charge of the specialist businesses?

⑥ How many managing directors of specialist businesses report directly to him or her?

⑦ Describe in your own words the advantages of these arrangements.

Online links
www.firstchoiceholidaysplc.com

- It makes it easier to carry out joint projects as everyone involved is working together.

There are even bigger benefits for the company.

- There are economies of scale as specialist staff can do work more efficiently.
- Communications from top to bottom are better, as there are definite channels through which orders can flow.
- Each person has only one immediate superior so that there is unity of command. An employee gets orders only from his or her own boss.
- It is much easier to check that work has been carried out as there are managers or supervisors at all levels.
- Co-ordination between departments is easier since each manager can speak for all the employees he or she controls.

Span of control

If the organization is to work effectively, there must be a suitable **span of control**. This is the number of subordinates, or people lower in the hierarchy, that a manager can directly control. He or she is called their **line manager**. The number of employees line managers control depends on certain factors.

- How good at their jobs the managers and his or her subordinates are.
- The type of work – simple work needs less supervision, or watching over.
- The ease of communication. People who are not in the same building are more difficult to control.
- The kinds of decision that have to be made. If they are difficult, the span of control will be narrower, because more time will have to be spent in making them.

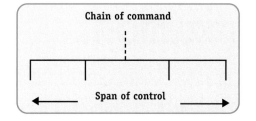

Chain of command

Span of control

Delegation

Another important factor affecting the span of control is **delegation**. This means giving people lower in the hierarchy the authority to carry out tasks and make decision themselves.

If a manager is willing to delegate a lot of work, he or she can have a wider span of control, as his or her subordinates are doing much of the work instead. If, on the other hand, the manager does not give his or her subordinates much authority, they may be working less effectively than they could, and the manager will be snowed under with too much work.

The amount of delegation depends on the structure of the organization and the type of leader. In a bureaucratic organization, that is one that is run by a central management, everything has to be approved and checked by all levels according to fixed rules and procedures. There will, therefore, be little delegation.

In a commercial organization the amount of delegation will depend on what the leader or manager is like. An autocratic leader, i.e. one who likes to have total control, will want to make all the decisions him or herself. There will be little delegation. A democratic leader, i.e. one who likes everyone to have a say, will be far more likely to delegate. He or she will listen to other people's views. The charismatic leader is one who depends on the appeal of his or her personality; this type of leader will delegate according to their mood at the time (see Unit 12).

CHECKPOINTS

1. What is a formal group?
2. What is the meaning of a hierarchy in business?
3. What are the main advantages for employees and firms of working in groups?
4. In what kinds of organization would you expect to find a) the most delegation and b) the least? Explain the reasons for your answers.

Managers' attitudes to employees still vary widely. The two main views were summarised by Douglas McGregor in The Human Side of Enterprise, published in 1960.

Autocratic leaders believe in Theory X which assumes that workers:

- are lazy
- lack ambition and responsibility
- must be forced to work
- want security.

Liberal leaders believe in Theory Y which specifies that workers:

- like work
- want responsibility
- can exercise self-control
- are not motivated only by security.

'Excuse me, Sir, please may I empty my waste-paper bin?'

KEY TERMS

Delegation Giving a subordinate authority to do a job without being supervised or watched over, or authority to make decisions in a particular area of work.

Formal group A group in an organization which is set up to carry out clearly defined tasks.

Hierarchy The different levels of authority in an organization, each one above another.

Line manager A manager who is directly in charge of a group of employees.

Span of control The number of subordinates controlled by a manager.

Types of organization

CASE STUDIES

Figure 1: Organization chart of First Choice Holidays plc

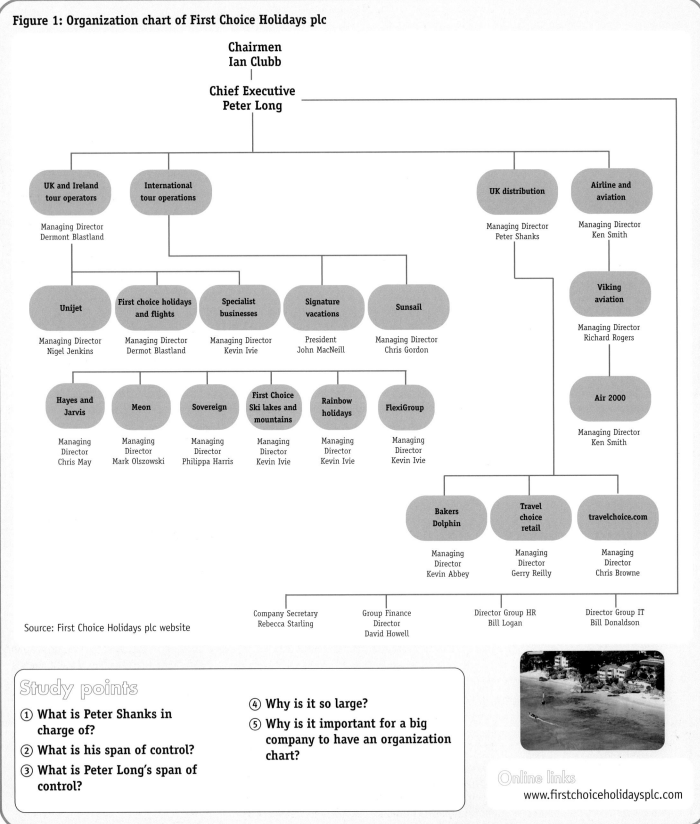

Chairmen
Ian Clubb

Chief Executive
Peter Long

UK and Ireland tour operators
Managing Director
Dermont Blastland

International tour operations

Unijet
Managing Director
Nigel Jenkins

First choice holidays and flights
Managing Director
Dermot Blastland

Specialist businesses
Managing Director
Kevin Ivie

Signature vacations
President
John MacNeill

Sunsail
Managing Director
Chris Gordon

Hayes and Jarvis
Managing Director
Chris May

Meon
Managing Director
Mark Olszowski

Sovereign
Managing Director
Philippa Harris

First Choice Ski lakes and mountains
Managing Director
Kevin Ivie

Rainbow holidays
Managing Director
Kevin Ivie

FlexiGroup
Managing Director
Kevin Ivie

UK distribution
Managing Director
Peter Shanks

Airline and aviation
Managing Director
Ken Smith

Viking aviation
Managing Director
Richard Rogers

Air 2000
Managing Director
Ken Smith

Bakers Dolphin
Managing Director
Kevin Abbey

Travel choice retail
Managing Director
Gerry Reilly

travelchoice.com
Managing Director
Chris Browne

Company Secretary
Rebecca Starling

Group Finance Director
David Howell

Director Group HR
Bill Logan

Director Group IT
Bill Donaldson

Source: First Choice Holidays plc website

Study points

① What is Peter Shanks in charge of?

② What is his span of control?

③ What is Peter Long's span of control?

④ Why is it so large?

⑤ Why is it important for a big company to have an organization chart?

Online links
www.firstchoiceholidaysplc.com

2: Unilever brands and business groups

Our portfolio of leading brands includes Magnum ice cream and Lipton tea. Many brands have international appeal, others are leaders in local markets.

The core building block in Unilever is the local operating company. These companies are organised into twelve business groups. This grouping is based on geographical markets.

In the consumer businesses, we operate in eight regions. In most, all Unilever companies form one business group. However, some operations are too large to be managed as a single group. In Europe and North America we have organized companies in two or three business groups, so that they can each focus on specific product areas.

Our professional cleaning group, DiverseyLever, on the other hand, is organized globally, with its operations managed on a worldwide basis.

Source: adapted from Unilever website

Study Points

① What kind of market is Unilever's organization based on?

② Why has Unilever chosen this organizational structure?

CHECKPOINTS

❶ What is a geographical organization? Which kinds of firm would use it?

❷ Why would a firm normally change from a functional to a geographical organization?

❸ State two other kinds of organization and give examples of firms that would use them.

❹ What kind of market is First Choice Holidays' organization based on?

❺ What are the main organizational problems for multinationals? How do they attempt to solve them?

It is often difficult for even a small firm to find the right kind of organization to achieve its objectives. These problems are obviously much greater with bigger firms, especially multinationals, operating in a number of continents. Deciding how power should be divided between the parent company and the operating companies in foreign countries, or how communications should be organized, is not easy.

Functional

Whatever kind of organization is chosen, it will usually be based, at least in part, on function, because the advantages are so great (see Unit 18). There are economies of scale, division of responsibility is easy and the chain of command is clear. On the other hand, it may produce a narrow outlook. Departments may become more concerned with their own affairs than with the objectives of the whole company. They could become too remote from the market.

Geographical

As a firm expands and its activities spread, it has to give local managers more responsibility. They are more in touch with local markets – for their products, labour and supplies. Production can be organized regionally so that the distribution costs are reduced.

A large firm might divide Britain into seven regions. Each would be allowed to run most of its own affairs, with senior managers in charge of production, planning, finance, personnel, etc. Although these managers would have a large amount of power, central management would still have to check their work.

It would be useful, for instance, for firms making farm equipment to be organized geographically, as farmers' needs vary around the country.

Market-based

With a market-based organization, the business is divided up according to the various groups of consumers or clients – the market segments (see Unit 36). Some examples are:
- insurance companies with separate departments for car and life policies
- publishing firms with separate divisions for educational and general books
- record companies with divisions for classical and pop, cassette and CD
- BBC radio with its separate stations for five different kinds of listener.

Product-based

Very large firms which make a wide range of products usually have separate groups or divisions for each product, such as one for paint, another for fertilizers, etc. One advantage is great economies of scale by each department concentrating on just one product. Another is that each product group can have its own profit targets so that it is easy for the parent company to judge if that group is doing well.

In practice, most multinationals use a mixture of organizations and try to combine them into a whole. One problem is always how much **centralization** or **decentralization** there should be in a firm. Both have benefits and drawbacks.
- Centralization produces economies of scale – in the use of skills, in buying supplies, etc. However, long lines of communication can result in slow decision-making.
- Decentralization helps firms to respond quickly to market changes and speeds decision-making. But, it can also cause doubling up of effort and may weaken the power of the parent company.

In practice, most multinationals give a large amount of autonomy to their operating companies. However, general policy, finance, appointment of top managers and relations with other businesses are usually centrally controlled.

KEY TERMS

Centralization When a firm is organized in such a way that policies and decisions for all branches or offices are made by a central body.
Decentralization When the policies and decisions are made regionally. Each office or branch of a firm makes its own decisions about how it will be run.

New organizational structures

Winner of a UK Business Excellence Award: NatWest Insurance Services

NatWest Insurance Services is one of 13 key businesses within the NatWest Group. It faced a major challenge when, in 1993, the creation of NatWest Life removed half the income and two-thirds of the profit from the business. The management team decided to rebuild and reposition the company, concentrating on its core businesses.

NatWest Insurance Services's subsequent success has been based on just three key principles: putting the customer at the heart of the company, offering outstanding value for money, and delivering exemplary service.

The assessors of the award were impressed by the way in which self-assessment has been integrated throughout the business and is now a way of life. People management processes were felt to be particularly powerful, linked to continuous improvement in most areas.

All of this activity made **empowerment** a reality in the company, rather than just a buzzword.

Source: adapted from the British Quality Foundation website

The Hawk, the Harrier vertical take-off jet and the Eurofighter. The manufacturer, the Military Aircraft and Aerostructures department of British Aerospace, also won a UK Business Excellence Award in 1999.

Study points

① How many major business units are there in the NatWest group?

② What is the name of another business unit within the group?

③ Explain in your own words the three key principles NatWest Insurance Services used to achieve excellence.

④ How do you think
a) employees and
b) the business benefit when empowerment is introduced into a firm?

Departmental functions

Figure 1 shows part of the organization chart of an engineering firm which is run in a formal, hierarchical way, with four main departments, each controlled by a director or manager. The work of each department is then divided, with each smaller section controlled by a manager. For example, the production department has four separate sections, each controlled by a manager, who reports to the production director.

Each of the major departments has its own specialized functions.

- *The production department* (under the production director) controls production; keeps quality standards up and costs down; uses research and development (R & D) to develop new products; and keeps up with the latest technological and electronic methods of production (see Units 48–52).
- *The marketing department* (under the marketing director) deals with market research; finding the right market; brands and packaging; and the 'four Ps' – product, price, promotion and place (see Units 37–45).
- *The finance department* (under the finance director) is responsible for raising money; budgets, cash flow and breakeven; and the production and analysis of accounts (see Units 23 and 25–30 and 34–35).
- *The personnel department* (under the personnel manager) is in charge of human resources including wages, salaries and fringe benefits; recruitment and selection; training; and industrial relations (see Units 53–63).

These departments do not work in isolation. They are constantly talking to each about any matters that affect the firm. For example, no company would think of making a new product without consulting all the key departments. However, the talks always start at the top – between members of the board of directors or the senior managers. Other discussions are then held at lower levels of

Figure 1: Hierarchical organization in an engineering firm – vertical authority

the hierarchy until, finally, the people at the bottom, who actually produce the goods or services, are told what to do. There are several advantages for both the business and its employees in this system (see Unit 19); but there are also many disadvantages.

Drawbacks

Some of the chief disadvantages are as follows.

- Hierarchies usually have tall organizational structures with perhaps seven or eight levels of authority. This means that there is a long chain of command.
- Each employee is concerned mainly with his or her own function, or specialized work, and often has only a limited amount of contact with employees in other departments.
- There is a natural tendency for managers to protect the interests of their own department. This may make them more concerned with office politics than with the interests of the whole firm.

- The hierarchical system emphasizes rank. This may create divisions, reflected in separate car-parking spaces for managers, longer holidays for **white collar workers** and separate canteens for **blue collar workers**.

From the 1980s, progressive British companies started to introduce **quality management systems**, which had started in Japan. Their main features are:

- flat organizational structures instead of tall structures
- emphasis on teamwork rather than on function
- outward looking instead of inward looking
- emphasis on performance rather than on rank.

Flat structures

Many businesses have reduced the number of management levels from seven or eight to just four or five. This means that there is a shorter chain of command. Decisions can be made more quickly because fewer managers are involved.

The increasing use of **information technology (IT)** and the internet has

CHECKPOINTS

❶ What are the main responsibilities of the key departments in a firm with a functional system?

❷ State the main disadvantages of hierarchical management systems.

❸ What are the main features of quality management systems?

❹ How has information technology affected management structures?

❺ Describe how a quality circle works and what it does.

speeded up this process even more. Many routine tasks, such as sending out orders, invoices and statements were once done by clerks under the control of a supervisor or middle manager. All of this work can now be done by a few computer operators.

IT has made it much easier for senior managers to obtain all kinds of information about the business on their own computer screens, which has also reduced the need for middle managers.

Teamwork

Teamwork helps to give each employee greater responsibility and a bigger outlet for his or her skills. Employees also become more deeply involved in their work and gain a greater sense of achievement.

In car factories, shop-floor workers often work together as members of small teams. Supervisors are no longer used to inspect and check the products for quality. Instead, the assembly-line workers carry out continual checks of their own products and make adjustments to their machines if necessary (see Unit 52).

Some manufacturing companies have encouraged employees to take more responsibility for their own work by setting up **quality circles**. These voluntary groups of a dozen or so employees meet regularly to discuss in an open and democratic way how the quality of their own production could be improved. They make suggestions to managers that are then put into effect. The groups consist of shop-floor workers, supervisors and, sometimes, managers.

KEY TERMS

Blue collar workers Employees who work mainly with their hands.

Empowerment Giving employees more responsibility and the right to make some decisions.

Information technology (IT) The storing, classifying and using of information by electronic means, particularly computers.

Quality circles Small groups of employees who discuss how the quality of production could be improved.

Quality management systems Systems which emphasize quality, or the highest possible standards, in all aspects of the business.

White collar workers Employees, such as clerks and managers, who do very little physical work.

Conflicts of interest

CASE STUDY

Johnson & Johnson

General Robert Wood Johnson, who guided Johnson & Johnson from a small, family-owned business to a worldwide enterprise, had a very perceptive view of a corporation's responsibilities beyond the manufacturing and marketing of products.

In 1943, Johnson wrote and published the Johnson & Johnson Credo, a one-page document outlining these responsibilities. The Credo received wide public attention and acclaim. Putting customers first, and stockholders [shareholders] last, was a refreshing approach to the management of a business. But Johnson was a practical, minded businessman. He believed that by putting the customer first the business would be well served, and it was.

Today the Credo lives on in Johnson & Johnson stronger than ever. Over the years, some of the language of the Credo has been updated and new areas recognising the environment and the balance between work and family have been added. But the spirit of the document remains the same today as when it was first written.

Johnson & Johnson, with approximately 98,000 employees, is the world's most comprehensive and broadly-based manufacturer of health care products. It has more than 190 companies selling its products in more than 175 countries.

Source: adapted from Johnson & Johnson Credo website

Our Credo

'We believe our first responsibility is to the doctors, nurses and patients, to mothers and fathers and all others who use our products and services. In meeting their needs everything we do must be of high quality. We must constantly strive to reduce our costs in order to maintain reasonable prices. Our suppliers and distributors must have an opportunity to make a fair profit.

'We are responsible to our employees, the men and women who work with us throughout the world. Everyone must be considered as an individual. We must respect their dignity and recognize their merit. They must have a sense of security in their jobs. Compensation must be fair and adequate, and working conditions clean, orderly and safe. We must be mindful of ways to help our employees fulfil their family responsibilities. We must provide competent management and their actions must be just and ethical.

'We are responsible to the communities in which we live and work and to the world community as well. We must be good citizens – support good works and charities, and bear our fair share of taxes. We must encourage civic improvements and better health and education. We must maintain in good order the property we are privileged to use, protecting the environment and natural resources.

'Our final responsibility is to our stockholders. Business must make a sound profit. We must experiment with new ideas. Research must be carried on. New equipment must be purchased, new facilities provided and new products launched. Reserves must be created to provide for adverse times. When we operate according to these principles, the stockholders should realize a fair return.'

Source: adapted from Johnson & Johnson Credo – United Kingdom – website

Study points

① How many people does Johnson & Johnson employ?

② What kind of goods does the company produce?

③ When was the Credo first published?

④ For which groups of people does the business have a responsibility?

⑤ Why was the Credo revolutionary?

⑥ How do you think the firm has benefited from the Credo?

Online links
www.jnj.com

Figure 1: Distribution of profits in a plc

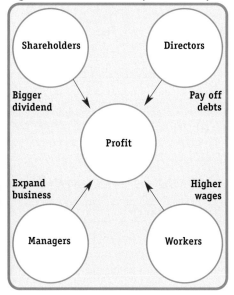

Conflicts of interest may occur in all kinds of business because the people and groups involved want different things. For example, a sole proprietor, who makes machine parts for a larger firm, may want a higher price for his products because he needs to buy some new machines. The larger firm, however, may want to keep the price at its present level because it has just had to give its own work force a large pay rise. One partner in a small legal firm may want to open an office in the city centre because she is ambitious to succeed. Her partner, however, may not wish to do so because he does not want to take the risk. As you can see, the conflicts may be external, as with a supplier and a larger firm; or internal, as with two partners.

Distribution of profits
The bigger the business the greater the chance of conflict because there are more people and more groups involved. One of the most likely sources of conflict in a plc is the sharing of profits.

As Figure 1 shows, there is inevitably a conflict of interest over how the profit should be used because different groups have different wants. The shareholders want a bigger dividend as a reward for taking the risk of investing their money. The directors want to pay off some of the firm's debt so that it does not have to pay its bank such large amounts of interest every year. The managers think it would be better to buy another company which would greatly increase profits in the long run. The workers want higher wages because the cost of living has increased and they have had only a small pay rise for the last two years.

The directors decide how the profits should be used, but the other groups can all exert pressure. If the shareholders do not receive a reasonable dividend they may sell their shares. If the managers do not get their way, they may resign. If the workers do not get a fair pay rise, they may work less efficiently. It is the directors' task to balance out all these demands so that all the groups are satisfied in some way.

Government
There can also be external conflicts. Government policies can sometimes create conflict with business. Big food retailers have not been pleased by the planning restrictions on out-of-town shopping. They developed superstores to provide good (and free) car parking, low prices, and a wider range of goods and services. The government, however, has to take a wider view of the whole nation's interest. The government believes that superstores:
- do not benefit poorer shoppers without cars
- increase car use
- destroy city centres.

For those reasons, the government has decided to restrict out-of-town developments in the hope that town centres will benefit.

Other external conflicts
Business can have conflicts of interest with many other external authorities and groups. These could include conflicts with:

CHECKPOINTS
❶ Why are there conflicts of interest in a business?

❷ Explain why there could be conflicts over the sharing of profits in a plc.

❸ Who might be involved in external conflicts with a business?

❹ Describe the policies a progressive company might adopt towards its stakeholders.

- local communities over factory noise or other forms of pollution
- suppliers over delays in payment
- customers over prices
- pressure groups over any issue which affects them, particularly environmental ones (see Units 74 and 75).

Stakeholders
Companies with quality management systems try to take into account as many of these opposing views as possible when they are making policy decisions. Instead of thinking of their shareholders first, they try to consider all the **stakeholders**, who have a stake, or an interest, in the business. They try to find policies which will give the greatest satisfaction to the greatest number of stakeholders.

General Robert Wood Johnson who wrote the Credo in the case study was years ahead of his time. He was the first businessman to realize that many different groups of people had a stake in his business – and that the company's aim should be to satisfy as many of them as it could.

It has taken half a century for most other big corporations to catch up. Now many of them publish a mission statement. This sets out in broad terms the basic beliefs of the company, the main reasons for its existence and the different groups of people it hopes to satisfy.

One company has carried the process a stage further by introducing an independent assessment of how far it has achieved some of its aims (see Unit 76).

KEY TERMS
Stakeholders Internal or external groups which are affected by the activities of a business.

Revision and exam practice units 18–22

Case study 1

1 List the main advantages and disadvantages of
   a) centralization and
   b) decentralization.

2 What is meant by a functional organization? Why is this type of organization usually included in the structure of all businesses?

3 What kind of company would be likely to have a product-based organization?

4 What is meant by span of control? Which factors decide how wide it should be?

5 In a bureaucratic organization, how likely are the managers to delegate authority? Explain why this is the case.

6 Explain the purpose of a chain of command.

7 List the benefits of formal groups to an organization.

8 Draw an organization chart for a market-based company. Explain why you have chosen this form of organization.

9 If you were the managing director of a firm producing dairy-farm equipment, what kind of organization would you have? Explain your reasons.

10 List the main tasks of the key departments in a manufacturing firm.

11 List the main differences between hierarchical and quality management systems.

12 What are the main external and internal conflicts of interest in a plc?

Top bosses grab 30 per cent pay rises

Bosses of Britain's biggest companies saw their pay soar by 30 per cent last year – six times the growth in average earnings and more than 13 times the rate of inflation.

On average, the chiefs of the 100 largest companies on the stock market are picking up £1.2 million a year in pay and bonuses – nearly £5,000 every working day and 50 times what a junior hospital doctor expects to earn.

The figures underline the yawning gap between Britain's super-rich and the majority of the population, flying in the face of the government's agenda to reduce social exclusion.

The often huge windfalls from directors' share options are not included in the earnings figures.

Bosses' soaraway earnings have been an embarrassment for successive administrations trying to keep a lid on wider pay demands.

Shipping group P&O, for example, has run into trouble after trying to peg a wage rise for seafarers at below two per cent when its directors netted a collective 20 per cent increase last year.

TUC general secretary John Monks said it was now clear who were the 'guilty culprits' awarding themselves excessive pay rises as the Bank of England warned of the threat to inflation and interest rates.

Nearly half of all the companies in our survey have cut staff in the past year.

The boards at oil colossus BP Amoco, British American Tobacco and financial services group Legal And General received the largest proportional increases, with rises of 113 per cent, 98 per cent and 74 per cent respectively.

Source: adapted from *Financial Mail on Sunday*, 28 May 2000

1 How much do the chiefs of the 100 largest companies earn on average?

2 Why does the government want to curb excessive payments to directors?

3 Why are they a threat to (a) inflation (b) interest rates?

4 How could this money be distributed in a different way?

Online links
www.thisismoney.co.uk

Case study 2

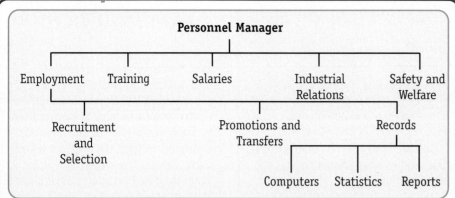

The organization chart shows the structure of the personnel department in a large company. Say which person or section in the department, and/or in other departments, would make decisions about the following matters.

1 Whether a member of staff should be sent on a training course.

2 Whether a member of staff should be promoted.

3 Whether a service engineer should be called in to repair a computer.

4 Whether an applicant, or person applying for a job, should be chosen for that job.

5 Whether a pay rise should be give to employees.

6 Whether employees who are on strike should be given what they want so that they go back to work.

7 Whether someone should be transferred from the computer section to the reports section.

8 A complaint from an employee that the temperature in one part of the factory is below the legal level.

9 A request from another department for the names of all the people in the company over the age of 58.

Extended questions

1 'Skills in dealing with people are more important for a manager than organizing ability.'

  a) What sorts of skill are needed when dealing with people? How might a manager use these skills to do his or her job better?

  b) What is meant by 'organizing ability'? Explain why this is important in managing a department or division of a company.

  c) Do you think the opening statement above is true? Give reasons for your answer.

Case study 3

Narendra Nanji's small business

Narendra Nanji, a qualified electrician, didn't get on well with his employer, so he decided to leave his job and set up on his own. At first he had to work twice as hard for half the wages. His wife helped him with the correspondence and accounts every weekend.

It went on like that for two years. Then he had a lucky break. He got a big contract to rewire a large house which was being converted into a health centre. He couldn't cope with all the work himself, so he decided to take on a cousin, Harish, as a full-time employee, hoping that he could get enough work to make his decision to expand worthwhile.

Narendra never looked back after that. Within four years, he was employing nine electricians. He was working 65 hours a week – getting contracts, ordering supplies, organizing all the work and even helping out with jobs which weren't going fast enough. He still did all the paperwork, with the help of a full-time secretary.

The stress of his job, however, took its toll and he had a heart attack. When he recovered, he decided that he would have to reorganize his business so that he delegated more authority.

1 Show how organization could reduce Narendra's problems and draw a chart to illustrate your answer.

Case study 4

£250 million loss a threat to village post offices

The Post Office will announce today that it has plunged £250 million into the red, its first annual loss for 23 years.

The reverse will bring new fears for the future of 8,000 village sub-post offices which are already fighting to survive.

They are subsidised by the Post Office at a cost of £30 million a year. In fact, the huge loss is mostly due to a doomed attempt to save them. It involved a £1 billion scheme to equip 19,000 sub-post offices with computers.

The small post offices currently pay out State benefits, including pensions, mostly using payment books and paper forms. The introduction of computers and plastic swipe cards was meant to help them keep that business, which post office chiefs feared might be lost to banks.

But last year, ministers decided that the benefits would be paid through the banks from 2003, cutting out sub-post offices completely.

That system will cost the Department of Social Security less to operate – but could sound the death knell for nearly half the business-starved sub-post offices, according to rural campaigners.

The switch has also left the Post Office with a bill for £571 million which will be shown as a write-off in its annual accounts.

Without that write-off, the Post Office would have made a profit of about £300 million.

The financial picture casts doubt on whether the Post Office can continue to subsidise the more remote sub-post offices.

Last year, 383 sub-post offices closed on top of 233 in 1998. The Post Office is required to operate as a commercial concern, though in State ownership, and pay the Treasury a large chunk of its revenue. This year that will amount to £175 million, despite the loss.

Source: adapted from *Daily Mail,* 19 June 2000

1　How much did the post office lose in 1999?

2　What is the main cause of the loss?

3　Why did the government change the method of paying benefits?

4　In what way is the Post Office both State-controlled and a private concern?

5　What are the conflicts of interest between the three main stakeholders?

6　What other groups of people are involved (a) financially and (b) personally, if the sub-post offices are forced to close?

7　What other solutions do you think the government might introduce which would be of benefit to all the parties?

EXAM PRACTICE

ABC Typewriters was a large international billion pounds organisation which was founded nearly a century ago. They produced typewriters in the UK and America, and later, computers, and marketed them all over the world. For many years they had been a market leader. They were organised in a centralized hierarchical structure, with a weak chief executive in charge of the heads of departments, most of whom had been with the company for many years. The heads of these four departments – production, marketing, personnel and finance – were all specialists and failed to work together as a team. The chairman and the board of directors were responsible for company policy.

Because of greater competition from other manufacturers selling computers direct to customers on the internet, lack of control over foreign subsidiaries and weak management, the company was forced to issue a profit warning. The final loss for the half-year was £300 million.

Foundation

1　How many departments were there?
(2 marks)

2　What are the advantages of a hierarchical structure for
(a) the company
(b) the employees
(c) the customer?　(6 marks)

3　What steps do you think could be taken to restore the company's fortunes?　(4 marks)

Higher

1　Explain how a centralized hierarchical structure operates.　(4 marks)

2　Why do you think the company was slow to react to competition?
(4 marks)

Section 4

Sources and uses of finance

Management accounting

Crops tainted by GM seeds to be ploughed up

The government is advising farmers to plough up oilseed rape crops tainted by genetically modified seeds after securing European Commission funding for affected farms.

Advanta, the company which supplied the seeds, demanded urgent talks with ministers. David Buckridge, Advanta's European business director, said destroying the crops was an 'over-reaction'.

A spokesman for the Ministry of Agriculture said that its legal experts had now determined that any harvest from the affected fields would be illegal within the European Union because the crop did not have commercial consents.

'Farmers who have the affected crops will be able to replace them with other appropriate crops up to June 15 and still qualify for payments,' he said.

However, he admitted that farmers were still likely to be out of pocket because of the labour and other costs linked with destroying the plants and re-planting new ones.

The Marquess of Lansdowne, who has already destroyed around 250 acres of the tainted oilseed rape, said it had cost him an estimated £5,000 in labour and chemicals.

Source: adapted from *The Times*, 29 May 2000

Firms move to avoid risk of contamination

Some of the world's biggest seed companies are moving their operations to countries free of genetically modified production to reduce the risk of contamination.

Advanta said it had abandoned producing seed in Western Canada because the risk of cross pollination from GM crops was now too high.

David Buckridge said the company had moved some of its production to New Zealand, where no GM production takes place, and the rest to New Brunswick in Eastern Canada and Montana in the United States.

Source: adapted from *The Times*, 29 May 2000

Farmers to get payout for rogue GM crops

Compensation payments are to be made to up to 600 farmers who unwittingly planted rogue genetically modified crops.

The pledge to farmers who destroyed their contaminated spring oilseed rape crop was given by the company at the centre of the controversy, Advanta Seeds UK. Final sums are to be decided by an advisory panel of experts.

The company said: 'Advanta is making this gesture, not because of any liability, but because it has always, and continues to put the interests of its merchants and their farmer customers first.'

Source: adapted from *The Times*, 3 June 2000

Exercising financial control

No business of any size can succeed unless it keeps a close watch on its financial affairs to see that the firm's resources are being used in the most profitable way. This is the main task of **management accounting**. It uses a wide range of financial information to control a firm's activities and to provide a sound financial basis on which management decisions can be made. Some of its main functions are:

- to make sure that there is enough capital
- to analyse costs and keep them as low as possible
- to plan for the future by making forecasts and exercising budgetary controls
- to analyse a firm's financial performance
- to make comparisons with similar firms.

Study points

1. Who supplied the oilseed rape seeds?
2. What action has the company taken to prevent similar incidents occurring again?
3. What is GM food?
4. Evaluate how the businesses involved have been affected.
5. Assume you are the public relations officer for Advanta. Write a letter to the farmers affected, explaining your firm's actions. Use a computer if possible. Include one appropriate chart or graph, and print a hard copy.

In addition, management accounting also has to cope with day-to-day changes and risks, or uncertainties about success or failure, by using techniques such as **risk analysis**. As the Study points have shown, business is greatly affected by external events over which it has no control and which are often very difficult or impossible to forecast. The speed of change is now so rapid and the interdependence of countries so great that no business, even the smallest, can avoid these risks.

Effects of chance events

For example:

- An airline's business could be damaged by a series of fatal air crashes in other countries and an unexpected rise in the price of fuel. Both these situations could be totally outside the airline's control, but there could be a double loss. The crashes could result in a fall in passenger bookings, while the higher fuel prices would increase costs.

- A shoe manufacturer's sales might be cut by a sudden increase in VAT and a big increase in competition from low-price shoes imported from India and Cyprus. Again, the shoe manufacturer has no control over either event.

- A butcher's sales could be greatly reduced by a long hot summer, when people tend to eat less fresh meat, and a sudden increase in BSE cases among cattle. Once again, these changes cannot be forecast. There are some changes which are more predictable. For example, every butcher knows that more and more people are changing to a vegetarian diet. Butchers can try to do something about that – by making their meat cheaper or more appealing or easier to cook.

- Farmers could have unknowingly planted genetically modified crops, as in the case study. This event was outside the control of the farmers and the firm which supplied the seeds.

- A British firm ordered $1 million of parts from an American firm when the exchange rate was £1 = $1.48. But when it was time to pay, the exchange rate had changed to £1 = $1.42. This change in the exchange rate could make a great difference to the amount the British firm had to pay.

Management of change

Businesses have to learn to live with such risks. This has made contingency planning (planning for chance events) or **management of change** even more important for firms. In making decisions, allowance is made for external events over which a firm has no control. Mathematical models are used to determine the probability of certain events and the best and the worst effects that they could have on a business. These help a firm to make decisions which appear to produce the highest profit and the least risk.

Financial accounting

Businesses also employ financial accountants. Their task is to keep an up-to-date record of all financial transactions, including purchases, sales, payments, debts, etc., so that a business's financial situation can be immediately known at any time. These records were once written by hand in special books called ledgers, but they are now usually entered and stored on computers. There are many software programs specially designed for keeping accounts.

Financial accountants also produce the annual accounts that public limited liability companies are obliged by law to publish every year (see Unit 34).

KEY TERMS

Management accounting Using financial information to control a firm's operations and to make management decisions.

Management of change Making allowances for external events, such as strikes or a rise in prices, by calculating the best and worst effects they could have on a business.

Risk analysis A way of including variations when estimating sales, costs, etc., so that possible effects on profits, and therefore the risk attached to each situation, can be looked at.

CHECKPOINTS

❶ Explain in your own words the main functions of management accounting.

❷ What is risk? Name three external risks which might affect a firm.

❸ A decrease in car accidents, a rise in the birth rate and a severe winter are all chance events. Which kinds of business might be affected by each event and what might the main effects be?

❹ Rule a line down the centre of a page. Head the columns a) Development and b) Effects. Copy into column a) the developments given below. Then write down in column b) all the ways in which they might affect a business, including the risks involved and the opportunities arising.

Development	Effects
Equal opportunities	*Higher pay for women, possible prosecutions, male resistance, etc.*
Immigrants	
New technology	
Lower fuel prices	
Arms reductions	
A fall in cigarette smoking	

Key skills

IT

Using a spreadsheet, set up a conversion table for the values of the pound and the dollar given in the text above. What would be the effect of the change on the British firm which owed $1 million?

Print a hard copy of the results.

Sources of finance for the self-employed

The Prince's Trust to create 30,000 new businesses by 2005

The Prince's Trust aims to help 30,000 more young people into business by 2005. The expansion will cost a total of £100 million. The government has pledged to fund half that cost if The Trust can secure a matching £50 million of funding.

HRH Prince of Wales was joined at the Battersea Park launch by young, Prince's Trust supported entrepreneurs. All were unemployed or failing to fulfil their potential before The Trust gave them the advice

and capital necessary to start their own businesses.

One was 22-year-old Michelle Fry, proprietor of a café in Sussex. Michelle, who is a wheelchair user, had been unemployed for several years before receiving assistance from The Trust. She now runs a thriving business which employs three people.

Source: adapted from press release, 17 June 1999, The Prince's Trust website.

Be your own boss

Want to work for yourself, but can't get the money you need to start your own business? If you're 18 to 30 and unemployed or in a part-time or temporary job that's not fulfilling your potential, The Prince's Trust's business start-up could help you. The Prince's Trust can offer:

- a low interest loan of up to £5,000
- test marketing grants of up to £250
- advice from a volunteer from the local business community during your first three years of trading
- other support including discounted exhibition space and advice.

Source: The Prince's Trust website.

Study points

1. How many start-up businesses does The Prince's Trust plan to create by 2005?
2. What will be the total cost of this project?
3. How much of the total amount will The Prince's Trust have to find?
4. What kind of entrepreneurs does The Trust help?
5. What is the maximum low-interest loan that can be granted?
6. Where else could a young entrepreneur go for business advice and financial help?

Online links

www.princes-trust.org.uk

Obtaining assets

If you wanted to buy a games console, you could either pay for it out of your savings or you could try to borrow the money from someone, for example an uncle. If you were a sole proprietor, you would have a similar kind of choice if you wanted to buy an asset such as a new machine. You could buy it from **internal sources**, such as your profits; or from **external sources**, such as a bank. This unit and Unit 25 show how businesses obtain money for capital expenditure on assets such as machinery, vehicles, buildings and land (see Unit 28).

Internal sources

The main internal sources of finance for sole proprietors are as follows.

- *Owner's funds*. Sole proprietors will usually use some, or all, of their own money to start their business. Young entrepreneurs might be able to get start-up money from their family or a family friend.
- *Selling personal assets*. Very often sole proprietors have to sell a valuable asset, such as a second car or an inherited collection of coins, to provide funds to start their business.
- *Profits*. This is the main internal source for successful businesses. However, tax, national insurance contributions and the sole proprietor's drawings – or money to live on – also have to come out of the profits.
- *Depreciation*. This is another useful source of finance for sole proprietors (and all other businesses). If a business buys a new computer, its value falls immediately it is bought and continues to fall (usually very rapidly) every year after that. The business is allowed to deduct the cost of this fall in value from its profits. This reduces the profits of the business, so that it has to pay less corporation, or business, tax. The business also benefits in another way. It has allowed for an expense that it doesn't have to pay immediately. Therefore, it has more cash available to spend on other items. Of course, the business will have to replace the asset in the end, when it will probably take out a loan to do so. (For the ways in which **depreciation** is calculated, see Unit 32.)

Figure 1: Main internal sources of finance for sole proprietors

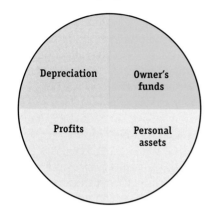

External sources

The main external sources of finance for sole proprietors are as follows.

- *Bank loans*. These are the main external source for small proprietors. Banks provide business loans for many different purposes, including loans to start a business. A bank's decision to lend money or not depends to a large extent on whether it likes the sole proprietor's business plan (see Unit 27). Banks usually want security, such as the borrower's house, which is pledged, or given as a guarantee, for the loan.

- *Mortgage loans*. Businesses can obtain mortgage loans to buy property in the same way as an individual obtains a mortgage to buy a home. The money has to be paid back over an agreed period. Banks and insurance companies give mortgage loans to businesses.

- *Grants and loans*. There are still a few European Union, government and local authority grants and loans for small businesses available in some areas. The government also guarantees some bank loans made to small businesses. As the case study shows, The Prince's Trust provides loans for 18–30 year-olds who are unemployed or under-employed.

- *Hiring and leasing*. These allow sole proprietors (and other businesses) to acquire assets, such as vehicles or machinery, by paying for them at regular intervals without spending large amounts of cash.

Figure 2: Main external sources of finance for sole proprietors

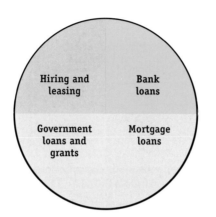

Hiring and leasing

There are three main kinds of hiring and leasing: hire purchase, finance lease and contract hire. Each of them has advantages and disadvantages.

- *Hire-purchase*. A finance house buys an asset, such as a vehicle or a machine, and the business pays the finance house back in monthly instalments (comprising a fixed sum, plus interest). Usually, a deposit has to be paid. The asset does not actually belong to the business until the last instalment has been paid.

- *Finance lease*. Assets can also be leased. Equal payments are made at regular intervals for a fixed period, as with hire-purchase. Usually, no deposit has to be paid. The sole proprietor never owns the asset, but at the end of the fixed term, he or she receives a proportion of the amount for which it is sold.

- *Contract hire*. A sole proprietor hires, or rents, a vehicle for a fixed period of time, but never owns it. Contract hire can be obtained with or without maintenance. Contract hire with maintenance is useful for sole proprietors, as they do not have to worry about their car or van, but can concentrate on their core business.

Other small businesses

Partnerships have more or less the same kind of sources of finance as sole proprietors. They can also raise money from 'sleeping partners' who invest in the business but, legally, take no part in running it.

Franchisees are in a different situation from most other businesses. The franchisers usually decide how much capital is needed to start the business and how it should be spent. Although a few small franchising companies quote a start-up fee of a few thousand pounds, the average start-up costs of setting up a franchise are quite high, nearly £50,000 (see Unit 10).

Because franchisees have a higher rate of success than sole proprietors, the government is more likely to guarantee a bank loan to cover part of the franchisee's start up costs. In 1998–1999, the government provided nearly £200 million under its Small Firms Loan Guarantee scheme.

KEY TERMS

Depreciation The reduction in the value of an asset over a period of time.
External sources Capital obtained from financial institutions, such as banks, and from individuals willing to provide finance.
Internal sources Finance which comes mainly from own funds, profits and depreciation.

Sources of finance for companies

Pet food firm acquires well-known brand name

An expanding own brand pet food manufacturer has taken a bigger bite of the UK market by taking over one of the industry's famous names.

In a deal put together in Leeds, Primetime Pet Foods has acquired Pascoe's – a well-known pet food name and manufacturer with a strong supermarket presence – creating a business with a combined turnover of almost £11 million.

The deal – the total value of which is undisclosed – was funded with the help of £2 million from Lloyds TSB Commercial Finance, and a further £1.575 million from NatWest.

Peter Scaife of Lloyds TSB Commercial Finance said: 'This is an extremely good deal for Primetime. It gives them access to Pascoe's well-established and comprehensive distribution network, and opens the door to whole new area of potential sales.'

Mr John Walgate, Primetime's finance director and newly appointed managing director of Pascoe's said: 'This acquisition opens up some massive sales opportunities, because Pascoe's sells to supermarkets that Primetime currently doesn't deal with.'

Source: adapted from press release 11/99 on Lloyds TSB Commercial Finance website

Pascoe's sponsor the Rockwood dog display team

Dog display team

The Rockwood dog deliver display team deliver a fun-packed show full of daring stunts and clever routines.

Rockwood dogs are trained for films and commercials. TV and film credits include appearances on Wogan and That's Life, plus 'lead' roles alongside the likes of James Coburn, Edward Woodward and Anthony Hopkins. Recent film credits include 101 Dalmatians and Twintown.

All the dogs are fed on Pascoe's Lifeplan.

Source: adapted from Pascoes Dog Food website

Organic dog food

Pascoe's have launched the first Organic complete dog food onto the UK market. The entire range of Pascoe's dog foods are now made with non-GM ingredients.

Source: adapted from Pascoe's Dog Food website

Companies use many of the same sources of finance for capital expenditure as the self-employed (see Unit 24). They are:

- profits
- depreciation
- bank loans
- mortgage loans
- loans and grants
- hiring and leasing.

Bank loans

As the case study shows, bank loans are still one of the main ways in which companies can finance their expansion. It is usually much easier for medium-sized companies to obtain a bank loan than it is for a sole proprietor or a small company. One of the reasons is that it usually has much bigger fixed assets, such as freehold property and plant and machinery, which it can offer as security for a bank loan.

Lloyds TSB offers **asset-based finance** as one of its main methods of borrowing for middle market businesses with annual turnovers of £3 million or more. The deal also includes a percentage of the amount of money owed to the company which helps to maximize the size of the loan.

Because of their structure and their size, companies also have other sources which are not available to the self-

Study points

1. What will be the turnover of the new business?
2. Who provided the money for Primetime Pet Foods to buy Pascoe's?
3. What is the distinctive feature of Pascoe's dog foods?
4. Why did Primetime want to buy Pascoe's?
5. What other financial sources could Primetime have used to buy Pascoe's?

Online links

www.ltsbcf.co.uk
www.pascoes.co.uk

employed. Let's look at the main additional sources of finance for companies.

Selling assets

Selling an asset, or a thing that a business owns, is a quick way of raising money. However, it is short-sighted to sell assets if they are still making a big contribution to profits. For example, let's say that a Third Division football club sells for £100,000 a player it bought for £20,000. The club makes a profit of £80,000. It uses most of the money to pay for urgently needed repairs to its stands. However, now that the club has lost its only star player, it starts to lose games. Fewer people come to watch the team and the gate receipts drop from £300,000 to £200,000 – a fall of £100,000. The club has lost more than it gained by selling its star player.

This is the kind of financial problem that faces many smaller Third Division clubs with an annual budget of £1 million or so. Generally, assets should only be sold if they do not fit in with the business's plan or if they are not contributing to profit. The sale of assets always needs careful consideration.

Venture capital

Small companies with new ideas may find it difficult to obtain finance from the normal sources, such as the high-street banks. They can sometimes obtain venture, or risk, capital from other financial organizations or from groups of rich people who invest in companies which have good ideas. In return for the risk they are taking, the venture capitalists often demand a seat on the board of directors. (See Unit 15.)

Going public

Medium-sized companies often find it difficult to raise enough money to expand

their business. One solution is to go public, or become a public limited company (plc), which provides many other ways of raising money. These include the following.

- *Debentures.* The public lends money to a plc for a fixed period of time at a fixed rate of interest. The terms of the loan are set out in a document called a debenture. The interest on the debenture has to be paid even if the firm does not make a profit.
- *Foreign loans.* Plcs with high credit ratings can borrow money from foreign banks. Multinationals also use the banks in the countries where they operate.
- *Sale and leaseback.* Instead of selling a building outright, plcs often sell the asset and then lease it back from the new owner. In this way, they obtain the cash they want, but still keep the use of the asset.
- *Selling subsidiaries.* Big plcs often sell their smaller subsidiary companies if they no longer fit in with their plans for future growth.

However, the main way plcs raise money is through issuing shares.

Share capital

Share capital is the money a business obtains by selling shares to institutional investors and the public. The shares may be of two main kinds: **ordinary shares** with a varying dividend and **preference shares** with a fixed dividend. A company can issue shares up to the limit of its nominal, or authorized, capital (see Unit 11).

This method of raising money has one big advantage compared with borrowing money. If a business borrows money from a bank, it will have to pay back all the money in the end. With share capital, the

CHECKPOINTS

❶ What are the three main additional sources of finance for private limited companies?

❷ State the two advantages of sale and leaseback.

❸ Explain in your own words the benefits of shares for a) investors and b) companies.

money never has to be repaid, though some big companies with surplus cash now buy back some shares from their shareholders.

Shares also have another advantage. When money is borrowed from a bank, interest has to be paid at fixed intervals (see Unit 26). With shares, a dividend, or interest, is paid to shareholders every year or half-year, but there is no legal obligation on the company to pay a dividend. In fact, if the company has financial problems, it could save money by reducing dividends or not paying one at all.

A company, however, could not miss paying a dividend year after year without some harmful effects. If it did, shareholders would start to sell their shares.

There are also great advantages for investors in owning shares compared with having other forms of savings. Not only do they get interest payments, but the value of the shares may also rise.

Key skills
Number

HIRE OR LEASE?
Choose the vehicle you would need for any business that you would like to set up. Find out from a local garage what it would cost to acquire
a) on hire-purchase and
b) on a fixed-term lease.

Calculate which would be better for your business, using a chart to illustrate your answer.

KEY TERMS

Asset-based finance Giving the assets of the business as security for a loan.
Ordinary shares Shares, also known as equities, which pay a varying dividend. These shares give the shareholder one vote for each share held at annual (and extraordinary) general meetings.
Preference shares Shares which pay a fixed dividend every year. Holders of preference shares have priority over ordinary shareholders in the payment of dividends. Most big companies no longer issue preference shares.

Short-term and long-term finance

Victor and Jo Forman, who are both in their thirties, have been in the hotel business ever since they left school. Victor worked his way up to become manager of a Manchester hotel with 125 rooms and Jo, who is a qualified cook, has also been a hotel receptionist. Seven years ago, they gave up their jobs and bought a small guest house in Southampton at a bargain price which they have just sold for a good profit.

The Formans have now bought a bigger, 10-bedroom hotel just outside Southampton which has been unoccupied for a number of months. It is in need of some urgent repairs and also needs to be redecorated and refurbished. Later, they plan to build a small health and fitness centre.

They are hoping to borrow most of the money they need from their bank. They can offer as security the business itself and a house they own in Manchester.

Study points

(Look at Figure 1 on the facing page before you answer the questions.)

① Study the sketch above. What seem to be the two most urgent jobs the Formans have to do?

② What are the other main tasks that they will have to do before the hotel can reopen?

③ Draw a plan or make a sketch of the hotel's new fitness centre.

④ Which of the loans shown in Figure 1 might the Formans use for the repairs and refurbishment (excluding the building of a fitness centre)?

All businesses need to borrow money for varying lengths of time. Some is needed for medium- or long-term capital expenditure on permanent assets such as expensive machinery or land (see Units 24 and 25). Some money is also required for shorter periods of a year or so (see Unit 28) for paying the running expenses of the business, such as rent and wages, starting a small business and buying a vehicle or office equipment.

Short-term finance

Short-term finance can be obtained in various ways.

- *Bank overdrafts*. These allow a business to spend more than it has in its current bank account, up to a limit agreed with the bank manager. The business pays **interest** only on the amount overdrawn each day, so this is a relatively cheap way of borrowing. Businesses with an uneven cash flow have a special need of overdrafts (see Unit 30). Farmers, for example, have to spend large sums on fertilizing their land and sowing seed, but they get no financial return for months. An overdraft covers their expenses until they start to sell their crops.

- *Factoring*. This is another way of obtaining short-term finance for an existing firm which is owed a large amount of money. The firm can 'sell' its debts (money owed to it by customers) to a **factor**. The factor pays the firm immediately for about three-quarters of the debts. The factor then collects all the amounts due and pays the firm the remaining amount, less the charges for the factoring service. Although the charges can be high, the firm gets an immediate payment of cash and saves money by not having to employ its own staff for collecting debts.

- *Trade credit*. Firms do not normally have to pay their suppliers immediately, but usually have 30 days of credit in which they do not have to pay their bills. By using the full credit period, a firm can use the money saved for other purposes or to pay other bills. Small firms can now claim interest from larger firms or the public sector if they exceed the normal or agreed period of payment.

Figure 1: Business loans

Type of loan	Amount	Loan period
Business overdraft	As agreed	1–12 months
Starter loan	£1,000+	2 years
Small business loan	£1,000–£15,000	1–7 years
Business loan	£15,001+	1–20 years
Business mortgage	£15,001+	1–20 years

Source: adapted from Business Loans, Lloyds Bank

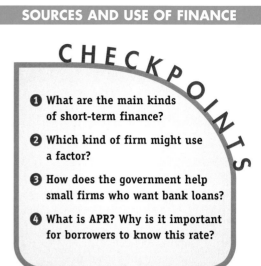

CHECKPOINTS

❶ What are the main kinds of short-term finance?

❷ Which kind of firm might use a factor?

❸ How does the government help small firms who want bank loans?

❹ What is APR? Why is it important for borrowers to know this rate?

● *Short-term bank loans*. These include starter loans which provide short-term finance for a new business (see Figure 1).

Longer-term finance

Medium-term loans, like the small business loan in Figure 1, last for up to seven years. There are also some medium-term loans for small firms which are guaranteed by the government. The Small Firms Loan Guarantee Scheme helps firms which do not have enough **security** to obtain a normal bank loan. It guarantees loans of up to £250,000 for established businesses. The average size of the loan is just over £40,000.

There are also a number of other European Union and government grants to which small businesses may be entitled. Most of them are given to firms in areas of high unemployment, lack of opportunities, and general neglect. Other grants are given to develop promising-looking enterprises

and for introducing technology and training.

Long-term finance is commonly needed for a variety of purposes, including buying property, equipment and other businesses. Bank loans and mortgages are available for periods of up to 20 years (see Figure 1). Other long-term sources of finance for plcs include debentures and share issues (see Unit 25).

Interest rates

Interest has to be paid on all bank loans. The rate of interest is calculated from the **base rate**. The bank adds a certain percentage to the base rate according to the degree of risk involved in giving the loan. Let's say the base rate is seven per cent. A big company with a good credit rating might pay only two per cent over base rate, making a total rate of nine per cent. A small firm with a lower credit rating might pay five per cent over base rate, making 12 per cent in all.

In addition to the amount of risk involved and the credit rating of the

borrower, the size of the loan and its duration also affect the interest rate charged. With some loans, the rate of interest can be fixed so that it remains the same throughout the whole time of the loan. With others, the rate of interest can vary so that it changes as general interest rates rise and fall.

If you borrowed £100 at a **nominal interest rate** of eight per cent for a year, the total amount you would have to repay would be £108. This would be divided into 12 equal monthly repayments of £9.

However, the nominal interest rate does not give a true picture of the interest rate you are paying. Each time a monthly repayment is made, some of the original loan is paid off. Since the repayments are the same each month while the amount of loan still left to be paid off is decreasing, the true interest being paid each month is increasing. This rate, expressed as the average percentage interest paid over the whole period of the loan, is the **annual percentage rate (APR)**. It is usually about twice as much as the nominal rate.

KEY TERMS

Annual percentage rate (APR) The true annual rate of interest paid when money is borrowed or goods are obtained on credit. The APR is higher than the nominal interest rate.

Base rate The rate of interest, based on the rate that banks charge each other. It is used to calculate interest rates on bank loans and overdrafts.

Factor A specialist firm or bank which takes over the collecting of the debts of another firm for a fee.

Interest The payment a borrower makes to a lender for the use of money.

Nominal interest rate The rate of interest stated by a lender, applied to the whole loan at the start of the loan period.

Security An asset which a borrower offers as a guarantee so that it could be used to repay a loan if that became necessary. The security could be a house or an insurance policy.

Key skills
Number

NOMINAL INTEREST RATE
If you borrowed £2,500 for two years at a nominal interest rate of 20 per cent:
a) how much would you have to pay back in total?
b) how much would your monthly instalments be?

Revision and exam practice units 23–26

REVIEW POINTS

1. What is meant by management of change?

2. What are the two most important tasks of management accounting?

3. Explain the differences between internal and external sources of finance and give two examples of each.

4. For how many years does a) short-term, b) medium-term and c) long-term finance usually last?

5. Explain how profit can be a source of finance for investment. Why is it such an important source?

6. What is APR?

Extended questions

1. Explain why businesses try to keep risk as small as possible. Give examples of how management accounting can help to achieve this.

2. Omar is starting a mobile TV repair service in an enterprise area. You have been asked to advise him.
   a) State where he might obtain finance for his capital expenditure.
   b) What kind of government aid might be available?
   c) How should he advertise his business?

Case study 1

Venture forward

Gaynor Connell is a member of the firm Jacksons Accountants. She says: 'I was recently privileged enough to be asked to get involved in a venture capitalist meeting. The meeting was extremely long because the guy trying to get funding was looking for between £10 million and £15 million capital to get his business up and running. Despite three hours sitting around a table the venture capitalist did ask, much to my delight, 'Is £15 million all you need?'

'I have to say that what sold the idea was the amount of time, effort and precision that was put into the presentation.

'The development of a business plan is an essential tool in raising finance – but it isn't the whole package.

'At the venture capitalist meeting I discovered that a great deal of importance was placed on market research, what your competitors were doing and how successful they were. I found the whole experience of the meeting was a fantastic insight into the amount of money available for business start-ups.

'So what are the benefits? Not only does the business owner have the benefit of not having to concern themselves with a bank's expensive borrowings but there are also massive tax concessions for the lender.

'In a nutshell: use your accountant, put forward the idea of going for venture capital and make the most of the opportunities out there.'

Source: adapted from *All about making money*, July 2000

1. What is meant by venture capital?

2. What kind of people are venture capitalists?

3. What is the benefit to them?

4. What is the most important feature in trying to raise such capital?

5. If you were a venture capitalist, state three questions you would ask a potential borrower.

Case study 2

Gordon's bookshop

During the 1990s Mark and Sophie Gordon opened a bookshop in the West Country. Although it was very small, they hoped they could enlarge the premises in the future.

In five years, they made enough profit for them to be able to repay a large part of their original borrowing. They had also been able to save enough money to help finance the bookshop's expansion. But they realised they would also need to borrow a large amount from their bank.

In addition to extending the shop so that the shelf space was more than doubled, the entire premises were extensively refurbished.

But Mark and Sophie had greatly underestimated the increased costs. Even though their profits rose, they found it difficult to cope with the high interest payments.

Then disaster struck. A chain bookstore moved into the town. Their sales fell immediately. Then interest rates rose by two per cent. People cut down on buying books and their sales really dropped.

The combination of these factors left the Gordons struggling to survive.

1   **What were the Gordons' original business objectives?**

2   **What did they do to achieve those aims?**

3   **What factors did they fail to consider when they expanded their business?**

4   **What course of action could they take to retrieve the situation?**

EXAM PRACTICE

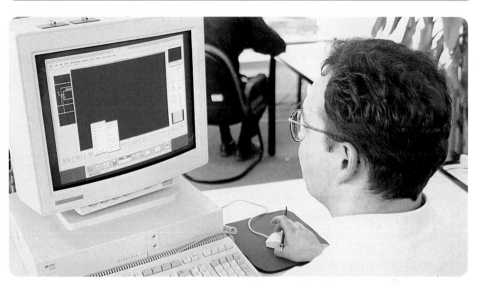

Robert left school when he was 16 with five GCSEs and enrolled on a carpentry course at his local FE college, gaining a special diploma as the most successful student on the two-year course.

He obtained a job in the design department of a local factory producing furniture kits for self-assembly and in eight years he had become the chief designer, with a good salary, a company car and an annual bonus.

But Robert was ambitious and wanted to use his designing skills to create original and individual pieces of furniture. He had saved sufficient capital for a mortgage deposit and had his own car.

He sent some of his designs to a high-class furniture manufacturer who asked for a finished sample, with the assurance that, if satisfactory, a firm order would be placed. Robert decided to resign from his job and start his own business.

Foundation

1   What internal sources of finance does Robert have?   (2 marks)

2   What external sources are available to him?   (3 marks)

3   How could he acquire machinery and equipment?   (4 marks

Higher

1   What will be Robert's chief internal source of finance?   (2 marks)

2   What advantages does Robert have which would encourage a bank to offer him a loan?   (4 marks)

3   Do you think Robert would qualify for any types of medium- or long-term finance? Give your reasons for your answer.   (4 marks)

4   What factors does Robert need to take into account when borrowing larger sums of money?   (4 marks)

   a) What is Robert likely to lose now by leaving his full-time job?   (4 marks)

   b) What does he hope to gain in the future?   (4 marks)

The business plan

Your business plan

You have to draw up a business plan to help you to understand what your financial needs are likely to be and to show to anyone from whom you may be borrowing or receiving money.

A business plan is a concise report which explains your business – what it is and how it will make money – and gives a financial forecast. This all has to be explained clearly and fully and, preferably, briefly. No one wants to wade through a 20-page report on a small business you are running from your back bedroom; two pages should suffice.

Source: adapted from Start Up – Your Business Plan on Virginbiz website

The Hypatia Trust

Our objective is to establish a residential centre for the arts and literature in Penzance, Cornwall. It will be called Hypatia House.
Our primary focus will be on:
- research, documentation and communication activities through the study of literary, scientific, and artistic records
- the exhibition of women's arts and crafts
- the publication of related texts.

The purposes of our proposed multi-resource residential centre are to:
- house the library, currently running to 20,000 volumes
- pioneer local educational opportunities

- offer new employment opportunities to the local community
- provide cultural and educational tourism on a year-round basis
- restore a linked group of heritage buildings including a Georgian theatre.

The Union Hotel in Chapel Street is a listed set of buildings, some parts dating to Tudor times. The site includes Grade II assembly rooms and a rare derelict Georgian theatre.

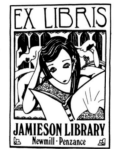

Business plan for Hypatia House

Residential arts centre (including catering); bookshop/gift shop.
First phase: purchase and restoration of the Union Hotel: £1.5 million.
Second phase: restoration of the Georgian theatre: £1.2 million.

Set-up costs

Education and research facilities: £150,000
Specialist library and arts collections: £150,000
Information technology (IT): £65,000
Publishing and printing: £90,000
Healthy living, including small gym: £70,000
Business enterprise management and advisory services: £50,000 (including staffing costs).

Source: adapted from Business Plan for Hypatia House on Hypatia Trust website.

All businesses, particularly start-ups, need to have a good **business plan**. As the case study shows, the plan needs to explain what the business is and to state what finance is needed. The plan sets out aims and objectives and shows how they will be achieved. It should be based on firm facts and realistic assessments. If the business is in the private sector, it usually includes a forecast of when the business will break even (if it is a start-up) or what its profits will be.

Forecasting

Forecasting is one of a business person's most difficult activities. All forecasts attempt to estimate what is likely to happen in the future based on what has happened in the past. They range from what the weather will be on Christmas Day to whether a new pop group will reach the top of the charts.

Business people cannot afford to make hopeful guesses. They use various methods to make forecasts which are as accurate as possible. They use these forecasts to make a business plan. As circumstances change they make adjustments to their plans.

Short-term planning is easier than **long-term planning** because fewer changes are likely. It is possible to forecast with some accuracy how much a new machine will cost next year, what new products will be required or where the markets for those products might be. It is much more difficult to make a similar forecast for ten years' time.

Short-term planning

It is vital for any business to know what its turnover is likely to be in the following year. Otherwise, it would not know whether it was likely to make a profit or not, whether it was wise to make capital expenditure or even how to plan its production schedules.

Short-term forecasts are based on both internal and external sources. Firms use their own records of what has happened in the past to make predictions about the future.

Figure 1 shows sales figures for the past three years for Brand X, a non-biological detergent. These figures show that sales have gone up over the last three years, but not at a steady rate. There was an increase of 10 per cent in 2000, but only 4.5 per cent in 2001. Was this a temporary drop or does it mark the beginning of a downward trend? External sources can be used to check what is happening in the whole market (see Unit 37). Are people buying less non-biological detergent? Has competition increased? These questions – and many more – must be answered before a reasonable forecast can be made about the following year's sales of Brand X.

Budgets

In a big firm, forecasts are made about the firm's capital expenditure, demand for manpower, materials, etc. These forecasts are used to make the firm's **budget** for the following year.

Forecasts are only a prediction about what is likely to happen in the future. Budgets are a detailed statement of the objectives – or targets – month by month, or quarter by quarter, for the coming year. Each department has to prepare its own budget.

These are then put together to make a master budget for the whole firm. Departmental budgets provide a valuable check on performance, as the forecasts in the budgets can be compared with actual results. If there is a large gap between them, reasons can be found and action taken. This is known as **budgetary control**.

Long-term planning

Long-term planning needs great skill. Many projects may take years to develop or to show any return on the investment – which can be millions of pounds – so it is vital to

Figure 1: Brand X sales (£ million)

1999	2000	2001
10	11	11.5

CHECKPOINTS

❶ What is the importance of a budget?

❷ How does budgetary control make it easier to manage a firm?

❸ Which of the following forecasts could the directors of a company reasonably make for a ten-year period based on present situations?

  a) The price of oil will increase.

  b) There will be increasing opportunities to trade with countries in Eastern Europe.

  c) Further privatization of public industries will give possible opportunities for expansion.

make some plans for the future. However, there is no way of knowing how high interest rates may be in 10 years' time or what the unemployment rate might be. Long-term planning, therefore, is more about applying principles than about definite amounts of money. It shows intentions rather than decisions.

Figure 2: Making a budget

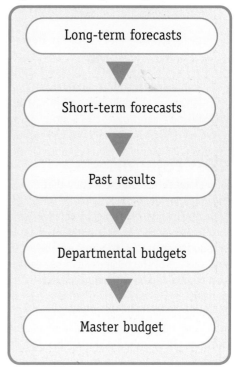

Long-term forecasts
↓
Short-term forecasts
↓
Past results
↓
Departmental budgets
↓
Master budget

Costs

1: Sonia's flower stall

Sonia got a part-time Saturday job in a florist's shop while she was still at school. The owner thought she had promise and trained her to make displays of various kinds, wreaths and bouquets.

When Sonia left school, she decided that she could make a living by having a flower stall of her own. She knew that flowers bought wholesale for, say, £1.25 a bunch were sold in the shop at £2.50. Wreaths sold for £25 or more and simple displays were anything from £15, while more elaborate ones sold for £35 upwards.

Sonia hired a stall in the local covered market for £30 a day. That was her main cost. She also needed moss, wrapping paper, tools, tape, a cover for the stall, accounts books and many other items.

Figure 1: Time and costs for items sold

	Time taken	Selling price	Cost of materials
Simple bouquet	15 minutes	£16	£7
Horizontal basket	30 minutes	£25	£10
Wired bouquet	1 hour	£35	£12

Cost categories

In general terms, all the money that a business spends on producing its goods or services is its costs. In accounting, these costs have to be put into separate categories or groups and analysed before a true picture of the business can be seen. **Capital expenditure** is money spent on permanent acquisitions – such as buildings, land, vehicles or equipment – which are necessary for the running of a business. In accounting terms, this normally includes anything that lasts for more than a year. Capital expenditure appears as assets in a firm's balance sheet (see Unit 33).

Revenue expenditure is all the money that is paid out to run a business. This will include the cost of buying stock, expenses like rent and heating bills, and any losses (such as discounts or unsaleable stock). Revenue expenditure appears in the profit and loss account, which sums up exactly how much profit or loss a business has made during the year (see Unit 32).

It is important to distinguish between capital and revenue expenditure, because only revenue expenditure affects profit. Sometimes the line between what is capital expenditure and what is revenue expenditure may vary a little, depending on the kind of business being carried on. For example, a furniture shop buys furniture as part of its stock for re-sale. Is this capital or revenue expenditure? A builder buys furniture to furnish his new office extension. Is this capital or revenue expenditure?

2: Capital and revenue expenditure

Each of the items below, labelled A to D, might be a capital expense for one kind of business, but a revenue expense for another.

Study points

① State which of the items might be bought by the following businesses and say in each case whether it would be capital or revenue expenditure
   a) electronic equipment retailer
   b) farmer
   c) taxi driver
   d) museum
   e) secretarial agency
   f) children's zoo
   g) new car dealer.

CHECKPOINTS

❶ A building firm pays out money on the following items: ladders, cement, scaffolding, lorries, repainting the premises (the cost will be spread over three years), stationery and printed invoices, small hammers, wages for permanent staff, an extension to the offices. Which of them are items of capital expenditure?

❷ List some of the items of capital expenditure a hairdresser might have.

❸ What would be the revenue expenditure of a high-street shop selling electrical goods?

❹ A firm decides to expand and move to larger premises. It also decides to give the executive staff smarter offices and to employ more office staff. Which of the firm's fixed costs will change?

❺ Say which of the following costs are fixed and which are variable: electricity, transport goods, rent, materials, rates, maintenance of equipment, interest on loans, salaries, insurance.

Further cost breakdown

To get a more detailed financial picture of a business, its revenue expenditure is broken down again into two more categories.

Some of the costs under revenue expenditure have to be paid for whether a firm is making a profit or not and they are not affected by the amount of sales or production. These are called **fixed costs**. Examples of fixed costs are rent or mortgage repayments, rates and salaries. There will be changes in these from time to time due to outside factors: for example, rates may rise or salaries increase.

Other costs relate to how many goods are produced or how much is being sold. For example, to produce more goods, more materials will be needed, more electricity may be used and more overtime may have to be worked. These costs are higher at some periods than at others and are not known for certain in advance. They are called **variable costs**. Other examples are petrol and repairs.

KEY TERMS

Capital expenditure Money spent on acquiring assets for a business which will normally last for more than a year.

Fixed costs Expenditure which is not affected by the amount of trade done by a firm or by the number of goods produced. A business cost which must be paid whether a firm is making money or not.

Revenue expenditure Money paid out for the running of a business.

Variable costs Any costs which change according to the amount of business done or the number of goods produced.

Breakeven and decision-making

Nottingham City Hospital NHS Trust

Overall position: The income and expenditure of the Trust for the period to 30 June 1999 shows a deficit against the plan to date of £137,200. This is an increase on the previous month's position which showed a deficit against the plan of £72,600 and gives rise for concern. Assuming this trend were to continue, the Trust would be reporting a deficit against the plan of around £550,000 at the year end.

Expenditure position: The table below sets out the financial position of those directorates showing a significant adverse variance to date, together with the cause.

Year end position: The hospital is still planning to meet its financial targets and plans a small surplus of £38,000 for 1999–2000.

Capital payments: The 1999–2000 capital programme allows for cash spend totalling £4.999 million.

Management costs: Management costs for 1999–2000 are forecast to be within the target set by the NHS Executive of £5.648 million.

Source: adapted from Nottingham City Hospital Trust website

Directorate /Department	Variance	Cause
Breast services	£45,816	Replacement of X-Ray tube and pay costs
Integrated medicine	£39,938	Non-pay and drug costs
Mobility centre	£37,509	Over performance of contract activity
Radiology	£36,167	Radiographers staffing changes
Renal	£35,757	High drug costs
Paediatrics	£23,578	Nursing costs

Study points

(You should read the unit first before you attempt the study points.)

① **How much was the deficit against the plan on 30 June?**

② **By how much had the deficit increased during the month?**

③ **Which department showed the biggest variation from its planned expenditure?**

④ **What were the causes?**

⑤ **In your view, how could the Trust achieve breakeven?**

Online links

www.ncht.org.uk

Breakeven is the point reached in a business after which its activities begin to become profitable. It is, of course, essential for any business in the private sector to pass this point because it could not continue for very long if it just managed to cover its costs.

Finding breakeven

By adding together fixed and variable costs and comparing these with sales revenue we can see at which point average costs equal average revenue – the **breakeven point**.

This can be shown graphically by a **breakeven chart**. Look at Figure 1 which shows the breakeven point for a small shop in a country town which sells all its goods for £1. Its fixed costs are £21,000; the average cost of buying each item of stock (or variable costs) is 40p, and each item is sold for £1.

- The fixed costs are £21,000 a year. These have to be paid whether the shop sells a single item or not, so they are shown as a straight line across the graph at £21,000 on the vertical axis.

- The cost price of each item sold (or variable costs) have to be added to the fixed costs to find the total costs. The variable costs, therefore, start at £21,000 on the vertical axis on the left. As the average cost of each item is 40p, the cost of 10,000 items would be £4,000 (40p x 10,000 = 400,000p ÷ 100 = £4,000). The total cost would be £25,000 (£21,000 fixed costs + £4,000 variable costs). The total costs are calculated in the same way for, say, 40,000 items and 90,000 items. These points are then joined to create the total costs line in Figure 1.

- All items are sold for £1. The revenue for 10,000 items would therefore be £10,000 and so on. The revenue line is plotted on the graph, starting at 0, with the first point being made opposite £10,000 on the vertical axis as in Figure 1. The next point is made for 20,000 goods and so on. The points are then joined to form the revenue line as in Figure 1.

Breakeven point

The breakeven point is where the revenue line and the total costs line intersect, or cross each other. Below that point, there is a loss. Above that point, there is a profit.

Figure 1: Breakeven chart for the pound shop

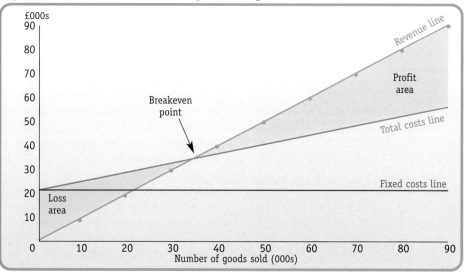

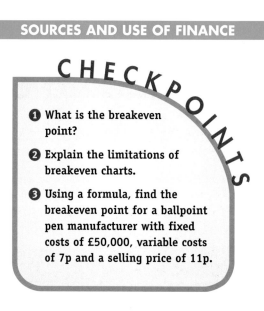

1. What is the breakeven point?

2. Explain the limitations of breakeven charts.

3. Using a formula, find the breakeven point for a ballpoint pen manufacturer with fixed costs of £50,000, variable costs of 7p and a selling price of 11p.

As you can see in Figure 1, the breakeven point is 35,000 items a year. This would be 673 items a week, or 112 items a day for a six-day week. To break even, therefore, the pound shop would have to sell 112 items every day. The number of items above the breakeven point is known as the **margin of safety**. That is where the pound shop would need to be if it was going to make a profit.

The breakeven point can also be calculated without using a graph. The formula is:

$$\frac{\text{fixed costs}}{\text{selling price} - \text{variable costs}}$$

With the pound shop, the fixed costs were £21,000. The selling price less the variable costs was 60p (£1 – 40p = 60p). Therefore the breakeven point was 35,000 items (21,000 ÷ 0.6 = 35,000). A breakeven chart shows immediately what profit a firm is likely to make at varying levels of sales, or production in the case of a manufacturing firm. The chart makes it easier to decide whether a firm is likely to be profitable or not.

Limitations

Breakeven charts have limitations. They do not give an entirely accurate picture of the whole situation. There are a number of reasons for this.

- The chart is only a forecast based on the current situation.
- Variable costs cannot be accurately estimated. For example, the pound shop might find that fewer manufacturers had surplus stock to dispose of, so it could no longer buy in its goods for an average cost of 40p. Or a manufacturing company might have to work a lot of overtime to fulfil an order on time, which would put up its wages costs.
- It does not allow for unexpected rises in fixed costs, such as buying a new machine.
- A breakeven chart is less useful in businesses providing services as their charges for each job can vary greatly according to customers' financial circumstances and need.

- Selling prices might have to be cut because of increased competition.
- The chart assumes that all stock will be sold, though this is not always the case.
- It gives no indication of suitable prices to charge, or the mark-up.

Margins and mark-ups

There is a big difference between the profit (or margin) and mark-up. The mark-up is the amount that must be added to the cost price to obtain a desired profit. Both the margin and the mark-up are expressed as percentages.

The margin is calculated by expressing the gross profit as a percentage of the selling price. With the pound shop, the margin is 60 per cent (60 ÷ 100 x 100 = 60%).

The mark-up is calculated by expressing the gross profit as a percentage of the cost price. With the pound shop, the mark-up is 150 per cent (60 ÷ 40 x 100 = 150%).

The mark-up is always higher than the margin. For example:

Margin	Mark-up
25%	33.3%
50%	100%
60%	150%

As this table shows, the higher the gross margin, the higher, proportionately, is the mark-up.

KEY TERMS

Breakeven The relation of income and costs to the amount produced.

Breakeven chart A graph showing the point at which sales and costs are equal.

Breakeven point The point at which costs and expenses are exactly equal to sales, so that no profit or loss has been made.

Margin of safety The amount produced after the breakeven point has been reached.

Managing cash flow

Doomed Dome was bankrupt by second month

There was a shadow hanging over the Millennium Dome from the outset because of 'inherently risky' visitor number targets and a system of 'weak' financial management, the National Audit Office concluded yesterday.

In July 1997, the Millennium Commission approved a lottery grant of up to £449 million – with £50 million to be repaid – to the New Millennium Experience Company to build and operate the Dome.

Since the Dome opened on January 1, 2000, the commission has awarded four additional grants to the company. This brings the total grant funding of the project to £628 million.

The target of 12 million paying visitors was a broad brush estimate. In May 1995, the commission had planned for 15 to 30 million visitors. In July 1997, this target had been scaled down to 12 million with a breakeven figure of 11 million.

However, at this stage the final decision had not been taken on the content of the Dome ticket prices, and whether there would be access by car for the purpose of dropping off and picking up visitors.

The company recognized that it would have to be a 'must-see' attraction with the necessary 'wow' factor. But by the end of September 2000, the Dome had attracted just 3.8 million paying visitors.

In May 1997, the company expected £195 million in private sponsorship. By the end of September 2000, this figure had been reduced to £115 million.

Media coverage that undermined confidence, word of mouth not spreading, failure to explain the content to visitors and the perception that travel costs were too high created negative perceptions.

The systems in place within the company and the information available had hindered the company's ability to produce reliable financial forecasts.

Source: adapted from *The Times* website, 10 November 2000

Study points

1. **In 1995, how many people did the Millennium Commission expect would visit the Dome?**
2. **What was the new visitor target set two years later?**
3. **How many paying visitors had actually visited the Dome by the end of September 2000?**
4. **What was the breakeven figure?**
5. **Why is the breakeven point important?**
6. **If you had been in charge of the Dome what actions would you have taken to ensure that it passed the breakeven point?**

Online links

www.the-times.co.uk

Cash flow refers to money coming into and being paid out of a business over a period of time. Unit 27 shows that businesses make forecasts of what their profits will be in the future. Detailed budgets may show that sales can be maintained and increased; that there is a definite market; that the business is being run efficiently; and that at the end of the year a healthy profit will be made. This is very encouraging – but is it enough?

What about the day-to-day financial situation? Will the firm be able to meet its commitments as they become due? Will it have the cash to pay the staff every week or month? Many promising companies have been forced to close simply because they did not have that ready cash when it was needed. In other words they had a **liquidity problem**: they did not have enough working capital that they could lay their hands on immediately to pay their bills (see Unit 34).

E-commerce problems

Recently, this has happened to a number of big e-commerce companies. It could have happened to the New Millennium Experience Company in the case study if it had not been bailed out by public money. The Dome, which was meant to be the centrepiece of the Millennium celebrations, had a cash flow problem because it never attracted enough visitors to pay its way. It was expected to attract 12 million paying visitors in the 12 months of its existence; but it had much less than half of that number. As a result, its receipts were much lower than planned.

It is very important for any business to know exactly what cash will be available month by month or even week by week – and to make forecasts for the immediate future.

Cash-flow forecasts

Look at Figure 1, which shows the three-month **cash-flow forecast** for a sole proprietor. You can see that in January, it is forecast that the receipts will be more than the payments so that the business will have a surplus of £250. This will be added to the £250 in the bank to make a total balance of £500. In February, the receipts are again expected to be higher than the payments by £200. So the balance would increase to £700. In March, however, receipts are predicted to drop, and bills are expected to increase. This would swallow up all the money in the bank (£700) and still leave a deficit of £600. The deficit is shown in brackets (£600) in Figure 1, which indicates in accounting that it is money which is owed.

Figure 1: Cash-flow forecast for a sole proprietor

	Jan £	Feb £	March £
Receipts	1,250	1,000	700
Payments	1,000	800	2,000
Opening bank balance	250	500	700
Closing bank balance	500	700	(600)

Any business can have a sudden demand for money or a fall in receipts which could not be predicted. But, more often, as in this case, it should have been possible to forecast the situation. The sole proprietor should have known the bills were coming; and the fall in sales might have always happened at this time of the year, as many businesses are seasonal. The owner should have planned in advance what action to take and discussed the matter with a bank before it happened. Banks will often give an overdraft to a business in these circumstances, particularly if only a few hundred pounds is involved for a short period of time. Or payment of bills might have been delayed, or debtors could have been asked to pay their bills more promptly.

Bigger firms keep a far more detailed cash-flow forecast, as in Figure 2. However, they also sometimes have cash-flow problems. They can apply the same kinds of remedies as a sole proprietor. In addition, they usually have more assets to sell off, or they might ask a factor to advance the money owed to them which gives them more immediate cash (see Unit 26).

CHECKPOINTS

❶ What are cash-flow forecasts?

❷ Why are they important for all types of business?

❸ Study Figure 3 which shows a hotel's forecasts and actual receipts and expenditure up to July and its forecasts for August. Then answer the following questions.

   a) If the hotel had an opening bank balance of £4,000 at the beginning of June, what would be the balance at the end of July?

   b) If there is a cash-flow problem, would the forecast figures for August solve it?

Figure 3: Cash-flow forecast

	June	July	August
Receipts (£)			
Forecast	70,000	60,000	55,000
Actual	68,000	45,000	
Expenditure (£)			
Forecast	65,000	55,000	50,000
Actual	62,000	59,000	

Figure 2: Cash-flow forecast form

For: (name of firm)		
Enter period (e.g. monthly or quarterly)		
	BUDGET	ACTUAL
RECEIPTS		
REVENUE ITEMS		
Collections from debtors		
Cash sales		
Other income		
Commissions		
Rent		
Investment income		
Repayment of VAT		
Repayment of Corporation tax		
Other – specify 1		
2		
CAPITAL ITEMS		
Net proceeds on disposal of assets		
Loans received		
Capital grants		
Capital introduced		
TOTAL RECEIPTS A		
PAYMENTS		
REVENUE ITEMS		
Trading expenses		
Payments to trade creditors		
Cash purchases		
Gross wages (including NHI)		
Administration expenses		
Gross salaries (including NHI)		
Directors' remuneration		
Rent		
Rates		
Insurance		
Repairs and renewals		
Heat, light and power		
Hire and leasing charges		
Printing and stationery		
Legal and professional		
Postage and telephone		
Vehicle running costs		
Entertaining and travelling		
Selling and distribution costs		
Advertising		
Carriage and packing		
Finance costs		
Overdraft/loan interest		
Bank charges		
CAPITAL ITEMS		
Capital purchases		
HP instalments (plus interest)		
Loan payments		
OTHER PAYMENTS		
VAT		
Corporation Tax		
Dividends		
Sundry – specify 1		
2		
TOTAL PAYMENTS B		
If A greater than B: surplus		
If B greater than A: deficit shown thus ( )		
OPENING BANK BALANCE C		
CLOSING BANK BALANCE		

Source: Barclays Bank

KEY TERMS

Cash flow The relationship between money coming into a business (receipts) and money going out of a business (payments).

Cash-flow forecast A statement of estimates of cash receipts and payments over a future period.

Liquidity problem A lack of cash at the time it is needed because a firm's receipts cannot keep pace with its payments.

Revision and exam practice units 27–30

REVIEW POINTS

1 Why is a satisfactory cash flow important for a business?

2 When might a cash-flow forecast be prepared? What use might be made of it?

3 What are the main differences between short-term and long-term planning?

4 Why are both short-term and long-term planning necessary for the good management of a business?

5 What is the difference between fixed and variable costs?

6 List the costs a minicab driver might have and group them into fixed and variable.

7 Explain the concept of breakeven and draw a chart to illustrate it.

Extended questions

1 You are running a club which has a liquidity problem. You have decided to take urgent action on three fronts. Explain how you would:
   a) prepare a cash-flow forecast for a bank
   b) make immediate cuts in costs
   c) plan to increase revenue.

1 Study the questionnaire from the Business Plan section of Lloyds Bank's information pack called Working for Yourself.

2 Think of a business you would like to start or buy. Answer the questions.

Case study 1

Working for yourself

Setting out a business plan is not as daunting as it may sound. Writing down the answers to the questions it poses is simply an effective way of testing your ideas.

A THE BUSINESS IDEA

Is the type of business:

        Start-up   Franchise   Existing business?

        ☐   ☐   ☐

Product/Service supplied/Principal activity:

How will you be trading?

        Sole trader   Partnership   Limited company

        ☐   ☐   ☐

Reasons for starting your own business:

B THE MARKET

Who will your customers be? ....

Who are your major competitors? ....

What do they charge for a similar product or service?.............

What are their strengths/weaknesses...........................

What makes your business idea better/different?...................

C PEOPLE

Who are the principals and what will you each bring to the business?

Name: ....   Age: ....

Experience: ....Skills: ....

Role in the business: ....

D MARKETING AND ADVERTISING

How do your competitors promote their products/service?

How are you going to promote your idea?

E SALES AND PRICING

What will you be charging your customers?

How do these charges differ from those of your competitors?

F PREMISES

Can you work from home?   Yes   ☐   No   ☐

If no, what kind of premises do you need? ....

How little space can you start off with?....................................

Are you: buying ☐   renting ☐   leasing ☐   the premises?

G EQUIPMENT

What kind of equipment do you need? (e.g. plant, transportation, office, etc.)

Type: ....   Supplier: ....   Cost: £ ....

Will you lease or buy this equipment?   Lease ☐   Buy ☐

H SETTING-UP COSTS

What have you estimated the total cost of setting up to be?

How will you cover these costs?

Own contribution: £..............   Other contribution (grant, family): £..............

Bank finance £..............

Source adapted from *Working for Yourself*, Lloyds Bank

Case study 2

Technical side good, but cash still a struggle

John Lambkin is the manager of Easton Lodge, a farm near Stanford in Lincolnshire.

The fixed costs for the year ended Nov 30, 1999 were:

Fixed costs	1999	1998
Labour	49,765	51,154
Power and machinery		
Machinery and vehicle repairs	19,409	16,330
Fuel and oil	7,114	7,883
Electricity	3,155	3,064
Vehicle tax and insurance	40	80
Contract and hire	10,328	12,041
Plant and machinery depreciation	22,676	23,601
Loss (profit) sale of fixed assets	2,288	(5,747)
Total		
Property charges		
Water rates	1,263	1,081
Property repairs	2,342	5,556
Depreciation	2,972	2,484
Total		
Other overheads		
Professional	1,393	3,339
Telephone	2,458	2,579
Office	5,290	7,628
Subscriptions	1,552	1,482
Sundry expenses	1,212	993
Total		
Rent	28,000	29,288

As far as cash flow is involved, the business generated £49,000 during 1999, £12,700 more than the previous year. Funds from other sources, including a large reduction in the amount of cash owed to the business, added another £23,400.

But replacing the old materials handler could no longer be put off, and just under £30,000 had to be found to buy a replacement machine. That, coupled with £27,000 in drawings and a similar amount tied up in unsold grain meant a net outflow of over £14,000 from the business during the year.

Source: adapted from *Farmers Weekly*, June 30, 2000

1 **Add up the totals for each section of the account.**

2 **Are there any fixed costs on which the farmer might be able to economize?**

3 **What was his cash flow situation for the year?**

4 **What other methods could he have used to acquire the replacement machine?**

5 **Discuss the factors outside the farmer's control which will affect (a) his productivity (b) his profits.**

EXAM PRACTICE

Gary has been running a repair garage in north London for three years, with his two brothers, Marcus and Steve. They have made a simple chart of their revenue and expenses for the three years.

	Revenue(£)	Expenses(£)
Year 1	95,000	35,000
Year 2	140,000	42,000
Year 3	190,000	65,000

They share all the profits equally between them. They plan to install a drive-in car-wash for £200,000, and to accept credit cards from customers.

Foundation

1 Draw a bar chart illustrating the brothers' profits for the three years. (2 marks)

2 How could they finance their plan to buy a car-wash? (4 marks)

3 Draw up a business plan which the brothers might present to their bank in order to obtain a loan. (4 marks)

4 How would the introduction of a credit card facility affect their cash flow? (2 marks)

Higher

1 Why is it important for the brothers to make a business plan before buying the car-wash? (2 marks)

2 How will the decision to buy affect their cash flow? (2 marks)

3 What benefits are the brothers likely to get from the credit card facility? (2 marks)

4 Suggest and explain what you think would be the best method to finance the car-wash purchase. (3 marks)

5 What problems might arise if there is an unexpected recession? (4 marks)

6 Evaluate the brothers' financial position and assess if this was a good business decision. (4 marks)

Trading accounts

Eidos sees shares fall after loss

Shares in Eidos, the computer games publisher behind the cyber-heroine Lara Croft, slumped eight per cent yesterday as the company plunged into the red and gave warning that trading conditions would stay tough for at least six months.

Eidos, which has issued two profit warnings since January, said that there would be no improvement in adverse trading conditions in its sector until a new generation of games consoles, due later this year, was 'properly established in the market'.

This was not expected until well into 2001.

Eidos blamed the market conditions for an underlying loss of £26.8 million for the year to March 31 – worse than analysts' revised expectations and down from a pre-tax profit of £39.2 million previously. There is again no dividend.

Mike McGarvey, chief operating officer, said: 'Make no mistake, nobody is immune to this market downturn.'

Source: adapted from *The Times*, 14 June 2000

Eidos acts to cut operating costs

Eidos, the troubled video games company in takeover talks with France's Infogrames, yesterday reported flat second-quarter results and said it expected operating costs to be up to £10 million lower by the end of the year.

The company said its quick expansion had led to a sharp rise in

operating costs. Eidos has tackled this by reducing the size of its workforce. Eidos said it was expecting healthy Christmas trading.

Second-quarter sales were unchanged at £16.8 million, while pre-tax losses increased 6.7 per cent to £22.3 million.

Source: adapted from *The Times*, 1 September, 2000

Every year, all businesses have to prepare annual accounts which provide a financial record of their trading activities. They are the **trading account**; the profit and loss account (see Unit 32); the balance sheet (see Unit 33); and the cash flow statement which shows the flow of cash in and out of the business (see Unit 30).

A retailer's trading account shows how much was spent on buying **stock**, how much was made when the stock was sold, and the **gross profit** made during the year. A manufacturer's account also shows the cost of producing the goods.

With big companies, such as Eidos in the case study, the trading account is usually included in a consolidated, or combined, profit and loss account.

Sarah's gift shop

Sarah has a gift shop in a cathedral city. Look at Figure 1 which shows her trading account for the last financial year.

- The first item in the debit column (left-hand side of table) shows the value of Sarah's stock at the beginning of the financial year.
- The second item – **purchases** – is the value of goods for re-sale which Sarah bought during the year. The figure of £160,000 is reduced to £158,000 as some faulty goods were returned to the manufacturer. This reduces the total stock figure to £198,000.

Study points

1. What does Eidos produce?
2. How much did the firm lose in the second quarter of the year?
3. What has caused Eidos's losses?
4. What action is the firm taking to reduce its losses?
5. In your view, what other actions could it have taken?

Online links
www.eidosinteractive.com

Fig 1: Sarah's gift shop

Trading account	£	£		£
Opening stock		40,000	Sales	150,000
Purchases	160,000			
less returns	2,000	158,000		
Total stock available for sale		198,000		
less closing stock		90,000		
Cost of sales		108,000		
Gross profit		42,000		
		150,000		150,000

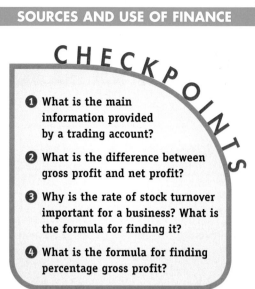

CHECKPOINTS

❶ What is the main information provided by a trading account?

❷ What is the difference between gross profit and net profit?

❸ Why is the rate of stock turnover important for a business? What is the formula for finding it?

❹ What is the formula for finding percentage gross profit?

- The cost of the goods sold during the year is found by subtracting the amount of stock held at the end of the year (still unsold) from the total value of stock. This produces a figure of £108,000.
- Now look at the credit column (right-hand side of table). **Sales (turnover)** during the year totalled £150,000. If the cost of sales figure is taken away from the sales figure (£150,000 – £108,000), it shows that Sarah's gross profit was £42,000.

This doesn't mean that Sarah actually made £42,000 during the year. All the expenses of running the business and the overhead costs now have to be subtracted to find the **net profit** (see Unit 32). Even then, the figures have to be compared with past results and forecasts or with those of similar firms before you can see if the business is doing well.

Comparing figures

Various **ratios** are used to make comparisons easier. Two important comparisons we need to make when looking at trading accounts are: a) gross profit, expressed as a percentage of sales, and b) rate of stock turnover.

The gross profit (or gross profit margin) shows what percentage of sales is actual gross profit. The formula for calculating this is:

$$\frac{\text{gross profit}}{\text{sales}} \times 100 = \text{percentage gross profit}$$

In the case of Sarah's gift shop, the answer would be:

$$\frac{£42,000}{£150,000} \times 100 = 28\%$$

Sarah's gross profit ratio of 28 per cent is not a particularly high margin – many similar businesses would have a margin of 50 per cent or more.

Stock turnover

Another good indication of how well a business is doing is the rate of stock turnover which shows how quickly or slowly a business is selling its stock of goods. To work this out we first have to find the average stock held.

This is given by the formula:

$$\frac{\text{stock at start} + \text{stock at end}}{2} = \text{average stock held}$$

In Sarah's case, the figures would be:

$$\frac{£40,000 + £90,000}{2} = £65,000$$

The rate of stock turnover is worked out by another simple formula:

$$\frac{\text{cost of sales}}{\text{average stock held}} = \text{rate of stock turnover}$$

The gift shop's rate of stock turnover for the year was:

$$\frac{£108,000}{£65,000} = 1.7 \text{ times}$$

This calculation shows that Sarah has sold her average stock 1.7 times in the year. This is very poor for this type of business and it means that either trade is slow or she is holding too much stock at a time.

To find out what percentage of the sales value went on buying goods, use the following formula:

$$\frac{\text{cost of sales}}{\text{sales}} \times 100 = \text{cost of goods to sales ratio}$$

In the case of Sarah's gift shop, this would be:

$$\frac{£108,000}{£150,000} \times 100 = 72\%$$

The rest (28%) is gross profit.

Profit and loss accounts

Love leather at DFS

Leather is quite simply the most stylish, sophisticated and sexy of all natural materials – the ultimate in luxury, and yet amazingly affordable at DFS. We've got dozens of designs for you to choose from, from traditional to trendy, and all exclusive too. So why not call in and take a good look – you're sure to fall in love with leather at DFS!

Source: DFS website

DFS Furniture

DFS Furniture is to open new stores in Swansea, Romford, Liverpool, Glasgow and Edinburgh this year, and also has planning permission for a store in Belfast.

Source: UK Business Park website

Upholstered furniture maker good value

The home furnishings sector remains highly competitive, but DFS has shown itself more adept than most at handling the pressure. A combination of trendy design, good marketing, a clever pricing policy, and investment into in-house manufacturing capabilities, helped the company achieve record first-half profits.

And the second half is looking just as good, with sales and orders showing substantial double digit growth. With trading so buoyant and the order book standing at £90 million, Charterhouse Securities has upgraded its full-year profits forecast. It now expects £43m pre-tax.

Having adapted well to the fast-changing fashion in home furnishing, DFS is now seeking new ways to increase its market share, which is currently 14 per cent. Over the coming year, five new stores will be added to the 53 existing stores. And the recently launched website, which has so far served only as a product guide, will be enabled for e-commerce within a year.

Half year 29 January	Turnover £m	Pre-tax profit £m	Stated earnings per share (p)
1999	138	12.0	7.8
2000	169	22.1	14.2

Investors' Chronicle view: Admittedly, along with the rest of the sector, DFS remains vulnerable to rising interest rates and a cooling in the housing market. But prospects still remain good given the trend for shorter fashion cycles in home design. Good value.

Source: adapted from the
Investors Chronicle, 5 May 2000

Credits

A **profit and loss account** shows the net profit after all the permanent (or fixed) costs have been deducted from the gross profit. This is the real amount that the business has made.

gross profit – fixed costs = net profit

Big firms, like DFS Furniture in the case study, usually publish their financial results every six months. These are eagerly awaited by the shareholders as they are sometimes also paid a dividend then if the firm has made a good profit.

A business's profits are greatly affected not only by its own efforts, but also by the state of the market in which it operates. DFS Furniture benefited from the state of the furniture market; Eidos, the computer games company which was studied in Unit 31, was badly affected by the downturn in its market. You will read much more about markets – and their importance – in the next section, Marketing Strategies.

With big companies, the way in which the net profit is calculated is usually

Study points

① How many stores does DFS Furniture have?

② Where were the new stores which were due to be opened in 2000 located?

③ What was the company's pre-tax profit for the first half of the financial year?

④ By what percentage did DFS's profit increase compared with the previous first half?

⑤ How did the business achieve such record profits?

⑥ If the general economy became less buoyant, what effects would this be likely to have on DFS Furniture's prices?

Online links

www.dfs-online.co.uk
www.ukbusinesspark.co.uk

Figure 1: Sarah's gift shop

Profit and loss account		
	£	£
Wages	15,000	Gross profit 42,000
Rent, rates and insurance	16,000	
Heat and lighting	1,000	
Bad debts	500	
Depreciation – Equipment and fittings	400	
Net profit	9,100	
	42,000	42,000

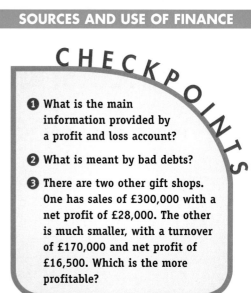

CHECKPOINTS

❶ What is the main information provided by a profit and loss account?

❷ What is meant by bad debts?

❸ There are two other gift shops. One has sales of £300,000 with a net profit of £28,000. The other is much smaller, with a turnover of £170,000 and net profit of £16,500. Which is the more profitable?

shown in notes attached to the accounts. With a sole proprietor, the calculations are shown in the accounts.

Sarah's gift shop

Let us look again at the accounts for Sarah's gift shop. Figure 1 shows her profit and loss account. Her gross profit was £42,000 (see Unit 31). This is entered on the credit (right-hand) side of the account. Any additional income received, such as discounts, commissions, rent or interest, would also be entered on that side.

All expenses, losses and costs are entered on the debit (left-hand) side of the account. In Sarah's case, these are wages; rent, rates and insurance; heating and lighting. The fourth item is a **provision** for **bad debts**. Any business is likely to have some bills which will never be paid and these are included as an expense (written off). The final item is another provision, for **depreciation**.

Depreciation

Fixed assets, such as equipment, machinery and vehicles, lose value over time through wear and tear and becoming out-of-date. Businesses are allowed to deduct a certain amount for this depreciation from their profit so that they pay less tax.

There are two ways of calculating depreciation. In the reducing balance method, a percentage, say 25 per cent, of the asset's value is written off each year. With a car which cost £10,000, 25 per cent (or £2,500) would be allowed in the first year. The car's value would be reduced to £7,500. Therefore, in the second year, the depreciation would be £1,875 (25 per cent of £7,500). In the third year it would be £1,406 (25 per cent of £5,625) and so on.

Straight line method

The other way of calculating depreciation is the straight line method, in which the same allowance is made each year. This method is often used with large machines. It is estimated how long the machine will last and what its scrap, or residual, value would then be. The following formula is used to work out the depreciation:

$$\frac{\text{original cost} - \text{scrap value}}{\text{useful life in years}} = \frac{\text{annual}}{\text{depreciation}}$$

For example, a machine costs £40,000 and has a useful life of six years when it will be worth £4,000. Therefore the straight line depreciation would be £6,000 a year (£40,000 – £4,000 = £36,000 ÷ 6 = £6,000).

Comparing profits

When Sarah has taken away all her expenses, including depreciation, from her gross profit, she has a net profit of only £9,100, as Figure 1 shows. This is certainly a very low figure, but it doesn't tell us much by itself. How do we compare it with the profits of similar shops which have lower or higher total sales? As before, it is easier to compare figures when they are expressed as a percentage.

Another ratio – the percentage net profit to sales – provides the answer. This ratio shows how much of the income from sales is net profit. The formula is:

$$\frac{\text{net profit}}{\text{sales}} \times 100 = \begin{array}{c}\text{percentage} \\ \text{net profit to} \\ \text{sales ratio}\end{array}$$

In Sarah's case the net profit, or margin, would be:

$$\frac{£9,100}{£150,00} \times 100 = \quad 6\%$$

In comparison with other gift shops, six per cent is a low percentage. Sarah might be better off putting her money into a savings account which earns a nominal rate of interest of 6 per cent.

KEY TERMS

Bad debts Bills which will never be paid and which are written off (and therefore treated as an expense of a business).

Depreciation Reduction in the value of an asset over a period of time.

Profit and loss account A summary of the expenses, losses and overheads of a firm which is used to calculate the net profit over a period.

Provisions Allowances for general or specific losses which may occur. A provision does not involve any actual expenditure.

Key skills
Number

The depreciation on the car mentioned in the text was £1,406 in the third year. What was the depreciation in the fourth and fifth years?

Balance sheets for small businesses

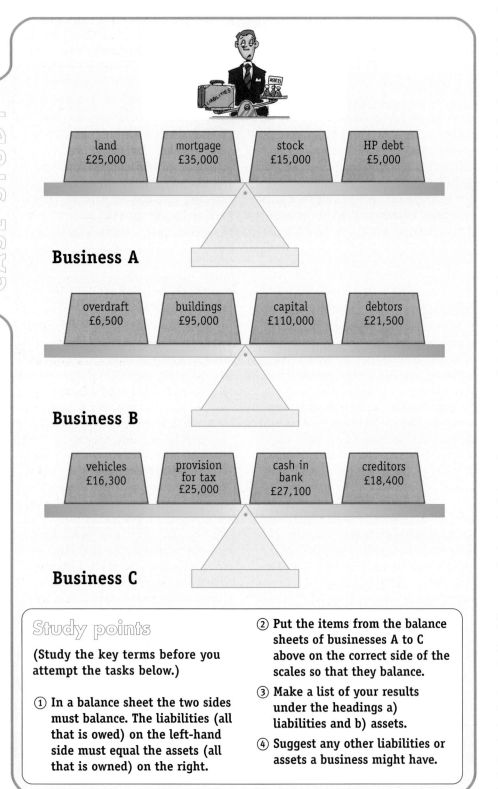

Business A

| land £25,000 | mortgage £35,000 | stock £15,000 | HP debt £5,000 |

Business B

| overdraft £6,500 | buildings £95,000 | capital £110,000 | debtors £21,500 |

Business C

| vehicles £16,300 | provision for tax £25,000 | cash in bank £27,100 | creditors £18,400 |

Study points

(Study the key terms before you attempt the tasks below.)

① In a balance sheet the two sides must balance. The liabilities (all that is owed) on the left-hand side must equal the assets (all that is owned) on the right.

② Put the items from the balance sheets of businesses A to C above on the correct side of the scales so that they balance.

③ Make a list of your results under the headings a) liabilities and b) assets.

④ Suggest any other liabilities or assets a business might have.

What is a **balance sheet**? It is a statement of the financial position of a business at one moment in time, showing all that it owes (its liabilities) and owns (its assets).

Liabilities

Let's go back to Sarah's gift shop again and look at her balance sheet for the previous year (see Figure 1). The first item – **capital** – shows the amount that was invested in the business at the beginning of the year.

You may be wondering why the capital is a liability; but just think a minute! We are not considering Sarah's own financial affairs, but those of her shop. The capital is the amount of money that the shop owes to Sarah, the amount she has put into the business.

The capital of £100,000 has increased by £9,100 during the year, thanks to the net profit which was calculated in the profit and loss account (see Unit 32). During the year, Sarah drew £8,000 out of the business to live on, which reduces the total to £101,000.

The final item on the liabilities side is the **creditors** – the firms or people to whom the shop owes money. These are **current liabilities**. The shop has no **long-term liabilities** – debts, such as mortgages or loans, which do not have to be paid within a year. Normally, these are listed before the current liabilities.

Assets

Now let's look at the other side of the account – the assets. The equipment and fittings, which are **fixed assets**, were worth £4,000 at the beginning of the year; but depreciation of £400 has reduced the figure to £3,600 (see Unit 32). Stock at the end of the year was valued at £90,000.

Debtors owed the shop £3,500; but a provision has been made for bad debts of £500, which reduces the figure to £3,000. There was £9,100 in the bank and another £400 in cash. These are **current (or circulating) assets**. If you study the balance sheet, you will see that most of the assets consist of stock. As we saw in the trading account (see Unit 31), the value of stock had risen by £50,000 during the year. This is always a bad sign as it shows that the business is not attracting enough customers or is choosing stock that people do not want to buy.

Figure 1: Balance sheet for Sarah's gift shop

Balance sheet

Liabilities	£	Assets	£	£
Capital	100,000	Equipment & fittings	4,000	
Net profit	9,100	Depreciation	400	3,600
	109,100			
less Drawings	8,000	Stock		90,000
	101,100	Debtors	3,500	
Creditors	5,000	*less* Bad debts	500	3,000
		Bank		9,100
		Cash		400
	106,100			106,100

Return on capital

Another way of judging the success (or failure) of a business is by using a ratio – **return on capital employed (ROCE)**. This shows how well the business is using the capital invested in it to make a profit. The ROCE, which is expressed as a percentage, is calculated by using the following formula:

$$\frac{\text{net profit}}{\text{capital employed}} \times 100$$

Sarah's gift shop has a net profit of £9,100 (see Unit 32). The capital employed is £106,100 as shown in Figure 1. Therefore the ROCE is:

$$\frac{9,100}{106,100} \times 100 = 8.6\%$$

This percentage can then be compared with the ROCE of the business in previous years and with the ROCEs of other businesses operating in the same market.

The average ROCE varies greatly from one industry to another. But by almost any standard, the ROCE of Sarah's gift shop is extremely low. Some retailers have a ROCE of 25 per cent.

CHECKPOINTS

❶ Give one example of a fixed asset.

❷ Give two examples of a current asset.

❸ These are the current assets of a business – £141,000 of stock, £21,258 at bank and £765 in cash. What are the total current assets?

❹ What are the main business meanings of 'capital'?

❺ A small business has the following liabilities and assets:

Cash at bank: £15,000
Cash in hand: 500
Premises: 145,000
Bank loan: 50,000
Creditors: 55,000
Stock: 79,000

a) Which are the assets and which are the liabilities?
b) What is the value of the assets and the liabilities?

Sarah's net profit is only £9,100 a year, which is very little more than the interest she would receive each year if she invested the capital in an internet savings account. She would then be free to find a job which would provide a real income!

It would probably be sensible for Sarah to sell the business – if she could find a buyer. Very often, when a business is sold, an extra charge is made for **goodwill** representing the loyal contacts the business has built up with its customers over the years. Unfortunately for Sarah, the goodwill of her business would be worth virtually nothing.

KEY TERMS

Balance sheet A statement of the financial situation of a business at a specified moment in time.

Capital Money invested in a business representing a claim on the assets.

Creditor A business or person to whom money is owed.

Current (or circulating) assets Asset items which constantly change and are easily converted into cash, such as stock, debts owed to the business (debtors) and cash in the bank or in hand.

Current liabilities Debts demanding short-term payment, such as tax, money owed to creditors and overdrafts.

Debtor A person or business who owes money.

Fixed assets Permanent possessions which enable a business to function, such as buildings, machinery, vehicles and land.

Goodwill The financial value of customer contacts built up by a business.

Long-term liabilities Debts not due for payment within one year, such as mortgages and bank loans.

Return on capital employed (ROCE) An important ratio which shows how efficiently a business is using its capital to make a profit.

Key skills
Number

A big company had a pre-tax profit of £304.9 million. The capital employed was £1,215.4 million. What was the ROCE?

Company balance sheets

McCarthy & Stone plc

One of the best-known builders of retirement flats, McCarthy & Stone has won many top building awards. It has been the House Builder of the Year (medium-sized builder) in four of the last six years and won the Daily Express House Builder of the Year award in both 1999 and 2000.

Group balance sheet as at 29 February, 2000 (half year results)

	£m
Fixed assets	
Tangible assets: investment properties	9.8
Tangible assets: other	9.4
Investments	0.2
	19.4
Current assets	
Stocks	136.1
Debtors: amounts due after one year	15.7
Debtors: within one year	2.4
Cash at bank and in hand	52.9
	207.1
Creditors falling due within one year	
Borrowings	–
Other amounts	52.4
Net current assets	154.7
Total assets less current liabilities	174.1
Creditors falling due after more than one year	
Convertible unsecured loan stock	13.0
Lease and hire purchase contracts	13.8
Net assets	147.3
Capital and reserves	
Equity interests	20.3
Non-equity interests	22.2
Called-up share capital	42.5
Share premium account	38.8
Capital redemption reserve	1.4
Revaluation reserve	0.2
Profit and loss account	64.4
Shareholders' funds	147.3

Source: adapted from McCarthy & Stone website – Investor information

THE NATURAL CHOICE
FOR A HAPPY RETIREMENT

A sole proprietor does not have to show his or her accounts to anyone, except the Inland Revenue, and the Customs and Excise if he or she is liable to pay VAT. A plc, however, is bound by law to publish an annual report and final accounts each year because millions of people may have money invested in the company. These companies also usually issue interim accounts giving financial information for the previous six months only. Their accounts must also be audited. This means that they have been checked by an independent **auditor**.

The balance sheet

Look at the balance sheet in the case study. You will notice that the accounts are set out in a different way from those of a small proprietor (see Figure 1 in Unit 33). Most sole proprietors, and some small companies, still use the traditional form of accounts, where assets and liabilities are set out in two columns side by side. Practically all big companies use a vertical format instead which uses only one column.

Study points

(Read the unit before you attempt the study points.)

① **What is the difference between tangible and intangible assets?**

② **Do you think that McCarthy & Stone's working capital was adequate?**

③ **What was the company's current ratio?**

④ **Would McCarthy & Stone pass the acid test?**

⑤ **Do you think McCarthy & Stone would be a good company to invest in?**

Online links

www.mccarthyandstone.co.uk

Let's look at some of the most important items in the balance sheet. The fixed assets include both tangible (physical) assets, such as property, vehicles and machinery, and intangible (non-physical) assets such as investments, goodwill and patents. (Note that McCarthy & Stone has no intangible assets.) These fixed assets are likely to stay in the business for more than a year.

The current assets, on the other hand, can vary daily as goods are sold and then replaced. The current assets include stock, cash in hand, which is immediately available, cash in the bank, and money that is owed to the business within one year and later.

The next section shows all the debts which have to be paid within a year. When these are deducted from the current assets, it gives the net current assets, or **working capital** (£207.1m – £52.4m = £154.7m). If you then add on the fixed assets to the net current assets, you obtain the total assets (£154.7m + £19.4m = £174.1m).

Finally, if you deduct the other debts which have to be paid after more than a year, you will find the net assets (£174.1m – 26.8m = £147.3m).

Capital and reserves

The second part of the balance sheet shows the capital, or the amount of money that the owners have put into the business, and the reserves, or the extra money that has been built up over the life of the business. These include the share premium account, when shares were issued at a higher price than their nominal value; the revaluation reserve when assets were revalued because of inflation; and the profit and loss account which shows the

profit which has been retained in the business.

You do not need to know very much about the capital and reserves section for the examination. However, you should note that the capital and reserves, or the money owed to shareholders, is the same amount as the net assets. This is because accounts are all based on the principle of **double entry**.

Solvency

One of the most important figures in the balance sheet is the net current assets, or working capital:

$$\text{current assets} - \text{current liabilities} = \text{working capital}$$

This shows whether the company is solvent – that is, able to pay its debts. It is vital for a business to have enough to pay its debts as they arise, or it could have a cash-flow or liquidity problem (see Unit 30).

Ratios

Several important ratios can be calculated from the balance sheet. One is the **current ratio**. The formula is:

$$\frac{\text{current assets}}{\text{current liabilities}} = \text{current ratio}$$

This shows how many times a company could afford to pay its current liabilities out of its current assets. For example, if a company had current assets of £60 million and current liabilities of £50 million, it would have a current ratio of 1.2:1. In the past, companies would not have been happy with such a low ratio, but a number of companies now operate with that kind of figure, or even less. However, the higher the ratio, the safer investments will be.

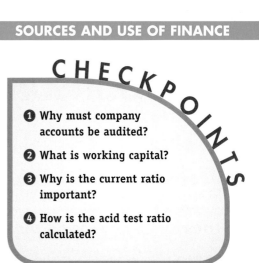

CHECKPOINTS

❶ Why must company accounts be audited?

❷ What is working capital?

❸ Why is the current ratio important?

❹ How is the acid test ratio calculated?

The acid test ratio is an even stricter test of a company's liquidity. Stocks, which cannot necessarily be sold immediately, are first deducted from current assets. The formula is:

$$\frac{\text{current assets} - \text{stocks}}{\text{current liabilities}}$$

At one time, all companies were expected to have a positive ratio, i.e. higher than 1:1 so that if all the company's short-term creditors wanted to be paid immediately, the company could do so by using cash and liquid assets and chasing its own debtors – the firms and individuals who owed the company money. Now, many companies work with a lower ratio, believing that stock turnover and cash flow are more important indicators of economic health. Again, a company with a high ratio would be very safe; but investors would need to make sure that it was using its assets to the greatest advantage.

Limitations of ratios

Ratios are very useful for comparing a company's current performance with budget forecasts, previous years' performance, and with competitors in the same sector. However, they do have a number of limitations.

Ratios deal with the past. Therefore, they do not give a picture of the present or the future.

Comparisons with other firms may be inaccurate, because they may have different objectives, markets or accounting procedures.

Ratios do not take into account the state of the market or of the general economy.

KEY TERMS

Auditor A qualified, independent person who examines a company's accounts to make sure that they have been properly kept and that they give a true and fair picture of the company's financial situation.

Current ratio The relationship between current assets and current liabilities.

Double entry The accounting principle that records each financial transaction twice: as a credit, (money owed by you), and a debit (money owed to you).

Working capital The amount of capital available to pay immediate debts, or the net current assets.

Comparisons of final accounts

Barton Babyfoods plc

Figure 1: Profit and loss account

		This year		Last year
	£m	£m	£m	£m
Sales		34		18
Cost of sales		(17)		(9)
Gross profit		17		9
Administration	(6)		(4)	
Distribution	(2)		(1)	
Operating profit		9		4
Tax		(3.5)		(1.5)
Profit after tax		5.5		2.5
Dividends paid		(2.5)		(2)
Retained profit		3		0.5

Figure 2: Balance sheet

	£m	£m	£m	£m
Fixed assets		1		1
Current assets				
Stocks	8		4	
Debtors	6		4	
Cash	1		0.5	
TOTAL	**15**		**8.5**	
Current liabilities				
Creditors	(12)		(6.5)	
Net current assets		3		2
TOTAL assets less current liabilities		**4**		**3**

Note: Numbers in brackets – such as (17) – show minus values

Who reads accounts?

Company reports and accounts are eagerly awaited and read by a wide range of people. These include:

- stockbrokers and day traders, who deal in shares
- shareholders who want to see what dividends they will get and how their company is doing
- unions looking for information to support their case for better wages and conditions for their members
- other firms which might want to make a takeover bid
- stock exchange speculators, like **bears** who want to sell shares and **bulls** who want to buy them in the hope of making a profit
- creditors who want to make sure the company can pay its bills
- financial journalists and City analysts, so that they can keep up to date with business trends.

Interpreting accounts

Skilled analysts sift carefully through accounts looking for clues to a company's performance. But how can that be judged?

Study points

(Study the simplified profit and loss account and balance sheet of the imaginary firm, Bartons Babyfoods plc, in Figures 1 and 2 and then answer the following questions.)

① What has been the percentage rise in Bartons' sales over the year?

② How do you find the gross profit?

③ What makes up current assets? By how much have they increased compared with last year?

④ For what reasons might the level of stocks have increased?

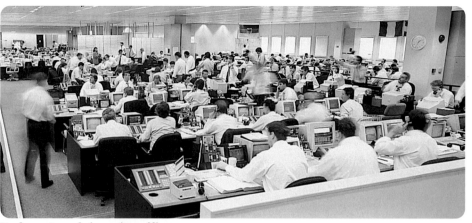

Dealers at work in a city office

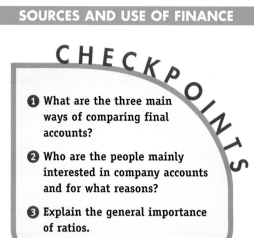

CHECKPOINTS

❶ What are the three main ways of comparing final accounts?

❷ Who are the people mainly interested in company accounts and for what reasons?

❸ Explain the general importance of ratios.

One way is to compare the current year's result with those of previous years, using ratios where possible (see Units 32 and 34).

Another way is to compare a company's performance with those of similar companies.

A third way is to compare the performance with a budget (see Unit 27). Only managers who work in the firm can do this, however, as a company's budgets are not published.

First, let us compare one year against another, using some of the ratios used in previous units.

Profitable?

The case study shows that Bartons Babyfoods plc had an 88.8 per cent rise in sales during the year, which looks good. However, we need to know how much it cost the company to sell its products. The following formula gives the net profit on each pound of sales (see Unit 32):

$$\frac{\text{net profit}}{\text{sales}} \times 100 = \begin{array}{l}\text{net profit}\\\text{per pound}\\\text{of sales}\end{array}$$

Net profit, or pre-tax profit, is the amount of operating profit that remains after a company has paid any interest on loans and overdrafts and received any interest on its investments. As these items are omitted from Bartons' simplified accounts, the operating profit is used.

Using the formula above, the net profit ratios for the two years show a respectable rise of 4.3 per cent:

This year $\frac{9}{34} \times 100 = 26.5\%$

Last year $\frac{4}{18} \times 100 = 22.2\%$

Solvent?

Now let's look at the balance sheet. This year the current assets increased by £6.5 million, which looks good. During that period, however, Bartons' liabilities increased from £6.5 million to £12 million. What do these figures really mean?

To find out, we have to calculate the current ratio, which was discussed in Unit 34. The formula is:

$$\frac{\text{current assets}}{\text{current liabilities}} = \text{current ratio}$$

The ratios for the two years show that there has been a decline:

This year $\frac{15}{12} = 1.25$ Last year $\frac{8.5}{6.5} = 1.3$

The ratio, however, is satisfactory as the current assets will still cover current liabilities, but a downward trend needs to be watched.

The stock turnover rate is calculated by the formula:

$$\frac{\text{cost of sales}}{\text{average stock}}$$

The average stock was $(8 + 4) \div 2 = 6$. The cost of sales was £17 million. Therefore the stock turnover rate was:

$$\frac{17}{6} = 2.83$$

This rate is not satisfactory and management should take immediate action to increase it.

Efficiently run?

Finally, let's see how often the current assets were turned over in each year. The formula is:

$$\frac{\text{sales}}{\text{current sales}}$$

The figures for the two years are:

This year $\frac{34}{15} = 2.3$ Last year $\frac{18}{8.5} = 2.1$

In this respect, Bartons Babyfoods plc is operating more efficiently, as more sales are resulting from the same value of current assets.

KEY TERMS

Bears Speculators on the Stock Exchange who sell shares in anticipation of a fall in their price, when they will buy them back.

Bulls Speculators who buy shares in the hope that they will rise in price, when they will sell them for gain.

Revision and exam practice units 31–35

Case study 1

REVIEW POINTS

1 What is a trading account?

2 What are ratios and why are they important in interpreting accounts?

3 In comparison with a trading account, what additional information is provided by a profit and loss account?

4 What information does a balance sheet provide?

5 What are the three main purposes of a balance sheet?

6 Name three kinds of assets and say which ones are fixed and which are current.

7 What is depreciation?

8 What is the main difference between current and long-term liabilities?

9 What information is not provided in a balance sheet?

10 Explain the difference between a bull market and a bear market.

Extended questions

1 What is the importance of balance sheets for:
   a) investors
   b) takeover bidders
   c) the labour force?

2 A friend has asked you to help her get a bank loan to start her own business. What advice would you give her in relation to:
   a) filling in a loan application form
   b) other documents she might send
   c) the interest she might have to pay on the loan?

Boots Company

The Boots Company comprises eight separate businesses. Each business operates independently for most purposes with an executive board and management team totally focused on the opportunities to create value within its chosen markets.

Our aim as a group is to ensure that they maximize their opportunities and generate strong cash flows by meeting their customers' needs. To achieve that we maintain a high level of investment in growing and extending our businesses and in increasing their efficiency and competitiveness.

About our business

Our goal is to become the global leader in health and beauty by drawing on our knowledge and experience to offer excellent products and services through a wide variety of channels to consumers around the world.

Underpinning all of this is our objective to maximize the value of the company for the benefit of its shareholders. While vigorously pursuing our commercial interests at all times we seek to enhance our reputation as a well managed, ethical and socially responsible company.

Online links
www.boots-plc.co.uk

1 How many businesses are there in the group?

2 How does meeting customers' needs generate strong cash flows for the company?

3 How can the board try to maximize the value of a company for the benefit of the shareholders?

4 What are the totals for fixed assets, current assets, net current assets and net assets for the two years? (See balance sheet opposite.)

5 What is the current ratio for the two years?

6 (a) What were the acid test ratios for 1999 and 2000?

   (b) Do you think the company should be concerned about these ratios?

7 What does the working capital in 2000 tell you about the company in relation to its debts?

Case study 1 continued

Financial performance

Group balance sheet 31st March 2000

	2000 £m	1999 £m
Fixed assets		
Intangible assets	62.3	64.4
Tangible assets	1,799.0	1,788.6
Investment in joint venture	8.0	6.2
Other investments	133.2	106.2
Current assets		
Stocks	689.5	722.0
Debtors falling due within one year	404.5	388.1
Debtors falling due after more than one year	4.0	14.1
Current asset investments and deposits	379.2	105.8
Cash at bank and in hand	43.0	32.2
Creditors:		
Amounts falling due within one year	(1,153.2)	(1,191.0)
Net current assets		
Total assets less current liabilities	2,369.5	2,036.6
Creditors: Amounts falling due after more than one year	(489.2)	(230.7)
Provisions for liabilities and charges	(26.8)	(25.3)
Net assets		
Capital and reserves		
Called up share capital	224.8	228.8
Share premium account	252.5	252.0
Revaluation reserve	266.9	276.2
Capital redemption reserve	40.8	36.8
Profit and loss account	1,066.6	986.4
Equity shareholders' funds	1,851.6	1,780.2

Source: adapted from The Boots Company website – About Boots

Case study 2

Cash boost operation

Avon Health Authority has agreed to sell Horfield Health Centre so it can pay for improvements at other surgeries.

The centre, which was built in 1969 and serves more than 18,000 patients, is valued at £375,000. It is expected to be bought by a consortium of GPs currently renting the premises.

The sale is the latest in a series of sell-offs prompted by a lack of capital funding for refurbishment.

Avon Health Authority spokeswoman Vicky O'Loughlin said, 'The health authority has a lot of health centres but it doesn't have very much capital funding to improve them.

'If the consortium of GPs buys Horfield Health Centre they will be able to raise money to carry out improvements that will benefit patients.

'This is a way of firstly letting them develop their health services and secondly giving us money to put into health centres.'

Now GPs involved in the consortium are looking at ways of raising loan funds to buy the health centre.

Source: adapted from *Bristol Evening Post*, 1 July 2000

1 Why is the Avon Health Authority selling the health centre?

2 If the GPs buy the centre, will this be capital or revenue expenditure?

3 Are the funds raised by the Avon Health Authority from the sale to go to capital or revenue expenditure?

4 If the doctors bought the centre, where would it be shown in their balance sheet?

5 How would the doctors benefit by buying the centre?

Case study 3

Tesco staff set for multi-million savings payout

Over 55,000 Tesco employees will share an estimated £83 million payout this month as two of the company's Save As You Earn schemes mature.

The staff, who have invested between £5 and £250 every four-week period in the three and the five years savings plans, will receive news of the value of their investment over the next few days.

Based on the current Tesco share price, those putting aside the average saving of £26 per period into the five-year scheme will receive payouts of over £4,500. Those fortunate enough to have invested their full entitlement of £250 per period will have seen the value of their savings rise to just less than £44,000.

The Save As You Earn scheme works by giving savers options to buy company shares at a discounted rate. Staff who invest for the duration of the savings scheme also receive a bonus equivalent to the value of nine period payments if they saved in the five-year scheme and three period payments for the three-year scheme.

Tesco chief executive Terry Leahy said, 'The Tesco Save As You Earn

scheme has enabled over 55,000 of our staff to share in the success of our company with a record estimated £83 million payout.'

The final payout figures are based on a Tesco share price of £1.57.

Source: adapted from Tesco Newscentre website, 8 February 2000

1 **What was the average amount saved?**

2 **How much would the person have had to save over the five-year period?**

3 **How much profit would they have made?**

4 **What are the costs and benefits to Tesco of the scheme?**

Online links
www.tesco.co.uk

EXAM PRACTICE

Rosemary Carter runs a secretarial agency in a small town in East Anglia with three women doing secretarial and computer work, and a receptionist. She is calculating her final accounts for the year and is studying her previous year's profit and loss account.

	£
Wages	43,000
Rent, rates and insurance	21,000
Heat and lighting	5,000
Advertising	2,500
Telephone	1,300
Car expenses	2,100
Provision for bad debts	2,000
Depreciation – Computers	2,000
Furniture	2,500

Foundation

1 Calculate Rosemary's total expenses for the year.   (2 marks)

2 Describe in your own words the two methods of calculating depreciation.   (4 marks)

3 Which items in the account do not involve actual expenditure?   (4 marks)

Higher

1 Calculate Rosemary's total expenses for the year.   (2 marks)

2 Which two items will also appear in another account?   (4 marks)

3 In what way are depreciation and provisions only book-keeping items rather than actual expenditure?   (4 marks)

Section 5

Marketing strategies

Finding the market

In Britain there are great differences in income and spending patterns between regions. Firms have to take these differences into account in finding a market for their goods or services.

Figure 1: Household spending on goods and services

	Housing	Fuel, light and power	Food	Alcohol and tobacco	Clothing and footwear	Household goods and services	Motoring and fares	Leisure goods and services	Miscellaneous and personal goods and services	Average household expenditure
£ per week										
United Kingdom	49.70	12.90	55.80	19.30	18.90	42.20	50.20	51.60	13.20	313.70
North East	40.60	12.70	48.30	20.30	17.30	33.50	38.70	44.40	10.40	266.20
North West	45.50	13.10	54.70	23.10	20.40	38.90	49.60	50.30	12.50	308.20
Yorkshire & Humberside	42.90	12.70	52.00	20.70	18.00	40.60	43.00	48.50	13.50	292.00
East Midlands	46.70	12.70	55.10	19.80	19.10	42.10	52.50	50.70	13.10	311.90
West Midlands	45.00	13.00	54.00	19.80	17.30	39.80	48.10	49.90	11.20	298.20
East	51.90	12.50	56.50	16.20	19.80	44.90	51.60	54.70	14.10	322.20
London	64.10	12.10	61.60	18.90	21.40	48.30	52.50	59.10	16.30	354.20
South East	60.70	12.40	57.20	17.50	18.70	47.10	59.80	59.60	14.90	347.80
South West	50.30	12.50	54.00	16.90	17.50	41.50	48.20	47.50	12.50	301.00
England	51.50	12.60	55.60	19.20	19.00	42.80	50.80	52.80	13.50	317.90
Wales	43.00	14.20	53.30	18.80	16.50	41.60	45.10	47.30	11.80	291.60
Scotland	42.20	13.80	56.80	20.90	18.30	37.00	47.80	45.20	11.00	293.00
Northern Ireland	29.40	15.80	61.10	19.30	23.00	40.70	48.60	41.50	13.60	293.10

Source: adapted from *Regional Trends*, Central Statistical Office, 1995

Figure 2: Average income per household per week

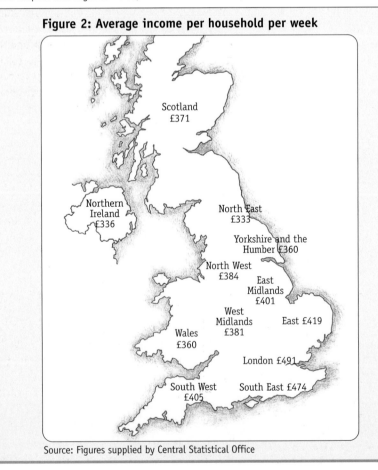

Scotland £371
Northern Ireland £336
North East £333
Yorkshire and the Humber £360
North West £384
East Midlands £401
West Midlands £381
East £419
Wales £360
London £491
South West £405
South East £474

Source: Figures supplied by Central Statistical Office

Study points

① Which region or country has a) the highest and b) the lowest household income?

② Which region or country spends most on a) alcohol and tobacco b) housing and c) food?

③ What percentage of house-holds' total spending goes on motoring and fares in a) the North East and b) London?

④ Which region has a) the lowest and b) the highest average expenditure per household per week. Suggest reasons for this.

⑤ You work for a big leisure company, with interests in cinemas, theatres and clubs, which is planning to expand its activities in England. Which seems to be the best region for expansion?

In today's highly competitive markets, very few firms can afford to be entirely **product-orientated**. A century ago, markets were more local and more limited; most people had only enough money to buy the basic necessities of life. A retailer's or manufacturer's main concern was the quality and the price of a product.

Today, markets are international. The range of goods and services on the market is enormous and most, though not all, British consumers have enough money to satisfy their needs and still spend on their wants or desires (see Unit 1).

Marketing

As a result, most firms are now **market-orientated**. They have to identify the wants and desires of the consumer, both now and in the future, and provide the right goods or services to satisfy the customer and make a profit for the firm. That, in brief, is what marketing is all about. Marketing is based on the theory that people who are like each other buy similar products. For example, most pop records are bought by young people. As the case study shows, people's income and where they live also have an effect on what people buy. Other influences include sex, or gender, life styles and socioeconomic grouping (see Unit 37).

Market segments

A big group of people who are similar in a number of ways form a **market segment**. For example, in the car market, there is a market segment for large family cars. A small group of people who are like each other in one or two ways form a market niche. In the car market, there is a niche for sports cars (see Unit 15). Marketing people try to find market segments or niches so that products can be developed to meet their needs.

Age is one of the most important factors in market segmentation. As the proportion of old people in the population increases, there will be a rise in demand for medicine, old people's homes and hospital services (both State and private).

However, there is also a desire among many old people to look younger and keep fit. There are also a growing number of old people with large company pensions and more leisure time for spending money. How might a marketing person make use of these business opportunities?

Similar investigations are made into what young people spend their money on, what they are likely to spend more on in the future and what goods are likely to become less popular.

Gender is also important. Women still spend more on clothes, cosmetics and jewellery than men. However, there have been changes in the market; sex roles have weakened. Look at jeans or unisex hairdressers!

Income is another important factor. Marketing people put everybody into social grades, or socioeconomic groups, according to the income of the head of the household (see Unit 37). Different responsibilities and life styles also need to be taken into account. A single woman on the same income as a married man with three children will spend her money very differently.

Education also has a great influence, but less, perhaps, than it once did, mainly because more students now receive the same kind of education. The influence of marketing has also helped to create a more general taste for foreign travel, luxury homes or expensive cars.

A marketing person puts all this information together and tries to find the market segment in which the largest number of people share a want for a product or service. If the segment has not been catered for by other firms, so much the better.

However, people's tastes are always changing, so that the size and shape of segments are in a constant state of flux. Take the market for young people's clothes. Most girls want cheap, stylish clothes, while most boys want casual clothes. Stores which do provide these goods have had to change or go out of business. But in five years' time, or less, fashion could change again.

There is an element of impulse in all buying, so that many goods are bought on the spur of the moment, without any plan. One example is buying bars of chocolate at supermarket check-outs. There are many more ways of tempting consumers to buy. As people's incomes increase, so do the numbers of **impulse buyers**.

CHECKPOINTS

1. What does product-orientated mean?

2. Why do businesses need to be market-orientated?

3. Give one example each of market segments for a) watches b) cars and c) furniture.

4. How do different levels of education affect spending patterns? Why has the influence of education weakened?

5. What might be a profitable market segment for a) a museum b) a florist and c) a computer-dating agency?

KEY TERMS

Impulse buyers People who can be easily tempted to buy goods.

Market-orientated Where market research is carried out to find out what consumers want before starting production. A product is then made to suit the market.

Market segments Groups of consumers within a market who have similar wants or desires.

Product-orientated Where a product and its price are the most important concerns. A manufacturer decides on a product, makes it, prices it and tries to sell it without first investigating to see if a market exists for the product.

Key skills
Communication

Give a short talk on three items that you have bought on impulse. Explain how the marketing of these products – advertising, price, packaging, design, place – may have influenced your decision.

Market research

How Britain shops for music and video

Woolworths

HMV store

Music and video retailers face a gigantic upheaval in the market because of free downloading from the internet. Verdict's consumer research points to the chains that are in the best shape to face the music. HMV and Woolworths lead two distinct parts of the market – HMV for connoisseurs and Woolworths for older, more middle-market consumers.

Comparing the two leaders, the latest report reveals that of HMV's loyal customers, 71.7 per cent gave range of offer as the most important reason for their loyalty. This compares with 50.7 per cent of Woolworths' loyalists. Price and convenience are relatively more important for Woolworths loyalists.

Some 40 per cent of music and video shoppers visit HMV and 21.2 per cent use it as their main store; 37.2 per cent of shoppers visit Woolworths and 18.4 per cent use it as their main store.

HMV has a very strong following among the 15–24 age group. Its main user profile is also biased to males and the more upmarket music consumer. Woolworths performs well among females, 35–44s and C2DE social grades.

Virgin is placed third, gaining 10.9 per cent of main users. Its main user profile is similar to HMV.

Our Price is changing its format to concentrate on mobile phones, DVD players and MP3 players for music downloaded from the internet. Its music and video offer will be much more limited in future.

WH Smith appeals to upmarket groups with a high penetration of ABs and C1s, also attracting female and middle-aged shoppers. The company has chosen to return to its roots and focus on books, magazines and stationery.

Source: adapted from Verdict on how Britain shops for music and videos 2000 website

Study points

(Study Figure 1 before you attempt the study points.)

① Which is the most popular music and video shop?

② What percentage of music and video consumers use it as their main shop?

③ What is their main reason for choosing it?

④ What is the main type of customer you would expect to find in an HMV, Woolworths and WH Smith shop?

⑤ If you were opening a music shop, explain how the information in the Verdict research report would be of use to you.

There are two main methods of **market research.**

- Desk research obtains **secondary data**, or information which already exists in printed form or in computer files.
- Field research obtains **primary data**, or data which did not previously exist, from people and organizations.

Kinds of data

There are two main types of secondary data: external and internal. Some comes from official external sources such as the European Union and government departments; some comes from unofficial sources such as trade associations, business directories and company reports. Internal data comes from the business's own accounts and reports.

Primary data is collected direct from a variety of people and organizations. Most businesses use specialist firms, like Verdict Research Ltd in the case study, to collect and analyse data for them.

Primary data is much more valuable than secondary data because it is more up to date and specific, but it is much more expensive and time-consuming to obtain.

Questionnaires

Questionnaires, long lists of carefully selected questions, are used in many forms of field research to collect primary data. The most important methods of field research are as follows.

- *Face-to-face interviews.* Data is collected by interviewers in the street, on the doorstep or at the workplace. This is an expensive, but much used method.
- *The internet.* E-mails are used. This method is becoming increasingly popular.
- *Telephone interviews.* Refusal rates are high, but this is a quick and cheap method.
- *Printed questionnaires.* These are placed in magazines and newspapers and through the mail. This method is more common than telephone interviews and even cheaper.
- *Focus groups.* Data is gathered through groups of people who express their deepest feelings. This is a popular method which obtains more detailed views and feelings.

Figure 1: Socioeconomic groups

Group	Job description	Examples
A	Higher managerial, administrative, professional	Chief executive, senior civil servant, surgeon
B	Intermediate managerial, administrative, professional	Bank manager, teacher
C1	Supervisory, clerical, junior managerial	Shop-floor supervisor, bank clerk, salesperson
C2	Skilled manual workers	Electrician, carpenter
D	Semi-skilled and unskilled manual workers	Assembly-line worker, refuse collector, messenger
E	Casual labourers, pensioners, unemployed	Pensioners without private pensions, anyone living on basic benefits

CHECKPOINTS

1. What kinds of data are used in market research?
2. What are the three main sources of secondary data?
3. State three kinds of information which might be obtained from secondary data.
4. What are the three main aims of surveys?
5. Write one question of each of three main types for a questionnaire on a breakfast cereal.

- *Hall tests*. With this method a group of people are brought in from the street to test a product and say what they think of it.
- *Observation*. Trained observers watch people to assess their reactions to a street advertisement or an in-store display. Observation is also used to check competitors' prices.

Collecting data

Primary data is collected in two main ways. Sometimes a random sample of the whole population is used. A computer chooses the people to be interviewed at random, in the same way as the computer, Ernie, picks Premium Bond winners.

More often a quota sample survey of a few thousand people is used. The people to be interviewed are chosen according to their socioeconomic group (see Figure 1) and their sex and age in proportion to the total number in the population. For example, in a general survey, you would include 51 per cent women and 49 per cent men, because at the last count of the total population in the United Kingdom there were roughly 29.1 million men and 30.1 million women.

Different groupings

Although this method still produces good results, some researchers have become increasingly dissatisfied with it. The structure of the population has changed greatly since the socioeconomic groups in Figure 1 were first drawn up 75 years ago. The six groups were based on the job of the head of the household who was always the man. However, many women now earn more than their partners. And some of the classes have merged so that most researchers talk of AB groups and C2D groups.

The Office for National Statistics is using a new social class structure of eight groups for the 2001 census, with seven classes for those in work and one for the long-term unemployed and sick. It also includes more middle class categories. Other market researchers use entirely different categories based on life styles or the television channels people watch.

Writing questionnaires

It is not easy to make up a good questionnaire. Before you start, you must have a clear idea of exactly what it is you want to find out (your objectives). The questions must be clear, precise and easily understood.

Questions in surveys may require:

- a direct '*Yes*' or '*No*' (or '*Don't know*') answer, for example: 'Have you ever bought Brand X?'
- a scale of answers, for example: 'How would you rate the cleaning power of Brand X?'
  Very good, Fairly good, Good, Poor, Bad, Very bad
- a range of answers, for example: 'Which of the following have you used in the last seven days?'
  Brand X, Brand Y, Brand Z

Care must be taken not to ask more than one question at a time. Always test the questions on someone else before you start and rewrite any that are unclear.

Personal interviews can also be used to test people's reactions to a brand name, packaging, an advertisement or the product itself (see Unit 40).

KEY TERMS

Market research Getting information about consumers by studying statistics and reports and gathering new data by surveys of individuals or groups.

Primary data First-hand information from market-research surveys of consumers. It is collected by field research, for example street interviews.

Secondary data Information which already exists due to other people's research. It is collected by desk research, for example reading documents.

Key skills
Communication

Form groups. You have been asked to undertake a market research survey into pet ownership among young people between the ages of 11 and 16. Draw up a suitable questionnaire.

Revision and exam practice units 36–37

Extended questions

1 a) Why does a firm need to market its products?

   b) What changes in the business environment have led to marketing becoming more important in the modern world?

2 You are setting up a market-research firm. State

   a) what kinds of people you would employ as interviewers

   b) why you think the personal qualities looked for are important

   c) what sort of training you would provide for your new employees.

Case study 1

Carving a name for themselves

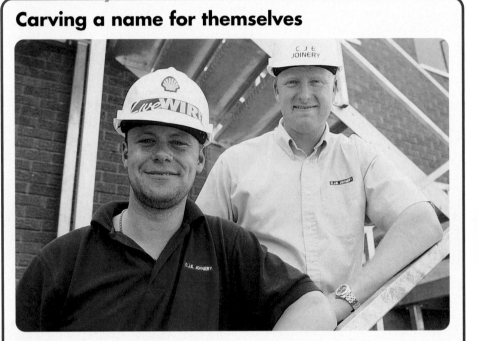

Joining together to start their own business seemed the natural thing to do for Colin and Wayne, who have been friends for over 14 years. They left college as qualified joiners and began working for other people, but realised that they could do a better job themselves. Having identified a gap in the market for them to set up their own business, the pair established CJE Joinery in November 1998.

The business specialises in joinery, concrete shuttering and Velvac window installation services for blue chip construction companies nationwide. After just 17 months in business, Colin and Wayne have certainly carved a name for themselves in the joinery industry, establishing a reputation for delivering a highly professional service and providing customers with quality workmanship and reliability. The business employs up to 40 staff and has already achieved a first year turnover of £750k. [Colin and Wayne were finalists in the Shell Livewire Start-up Business Awards, 2000].

Source: adapted from Shell Live Wire website

1 Why did Colin and Wayne decide to start their own business?

2 How do you think they discovered a gap in the market?

3 What market segment are Colin and Wayne catering for?

4 As well as being market orientated, in what way are they also product orientated?

5 What problems might Colin and Wayne's rapid expansion have caused for them?

Online links
www.shell-livewire.org

GROUP WORK

A supermarket chain has decided to open a new store in your area. You have been asked to carry out a market research survey about people's views of other supermarkets in the area. You have also been asked to conduct some in-depth interviews about their attitudes to shopping – their dislikes, their hopes, their needs, their reasons for shopping. The six groups of people you have chosen to interview are:

- men aged 18–25, social grades A, B, and C1

- women aged 18–25, social grades C2 and D

- men aged 26–45, social grades C2 and D

- women aged 26–45, social grades A, B, and C1

- men aged 46–65, social grades A, B and C1

- women aged 46–65, social grades C2 and D.

1 Make up a questionnaire as a group. Decide which of you will interview which category, or type, of people.
2 Interview, by yourself, one or more people in the category you have chosen. Bring the results back to your group.
3 Discuss the results as a group. Write a report by yourself, giving the results of your group's survey. In the report say what sort of store the supermarket chain should open if it wants to meet the needs and wants of the people you interviewed.

Case study 2

1 In your view, what personal qualities should the interviewer have?

2 What job skills would she need?

EXAM PRACTICE

Caroline and David Palmer lived in a semi-detached house in Essex. Caroline was a secretary in a firm of accountants. David was a self-employed decorator. When they went on a holiday to Wales, they were attracted by the comparatively cheap housing and the beautiful scenery.

They found an empty shop with three-bedroom accommodation and a lovely garden. Caroline had always wanted to run a souvenir shop and when she found there were none in the nearby towns, she pointed out to David that there would be no competition. Three months later, they had sold their house and moved to Wales.

They looked in Yellow Pages to find suppliers and decided to employ a firm of shopfitters and decorators, as it would take too long for David to do it alone. This, plus buying the stock, took most of their savings. Caroline bought the kinds of things she was interested in – miniature glass and porcelain bowls, bric-a-brac, artificial flowers, Chinese ornaments and hanging baskets.

Although it was a good summer, they found that the town attracted relatively few tourists. The locals didn't buy souvenirs. In six months, most of the profit from the sale of their Essex house had gone and they had to go to the bank for a loan. David decided to go back to decorating but realised it would take some time to re-establish himself in an unknown area.

Foundation

1 Before buying the shop, should Caroline and David have first (a) made out a business plan (b) consulted their bank manager (c) carried out market research (d) rented premises instead? (2 marks)
2 What secondary market research could they have carried out? (2 marks)
3 State and explain two other methods of market research Caroline and David could have conducted. (4 marks)
4 What experience did they each have which they could have made use of? (4 marks)
5 Make a list of the steps they should have taken before coming to the decision to move to Wales. (4 marks)

Higher

1 If Caroline and David had collected primary data during their two-week holiday, what would it have told them? (4 marks)
2 What secondary market research should they have carried out? (4 marks)
3 What demographic factors should the couple have considered? (4 marks)
4 Which existing market segments could they have targeted? (4 marks)
5 Suggest a suitable marketing strategy Caroline and David could adopt to retrieve the situation. (4 marks)

The marketing mix

Marks & Spencer unveils brand new look

BEFORE

AFTER

As part of an extensive programme of work undertaken over the last 12 months designed to reinforce the strengths of the Marks & Spencer brand, the company today unveiled its updated brand identity to 70,000 employees worldwide.

The new look complements a host of initiatives, including more staff on the sales floor to serve customers better, the modernization of stores across the country and the introduction of exciting new ranges.

The name Marks & Spencer will appear on all labels, packaging and literature in an updated 'stacked' logo written in the stylish Optima font. The Marks & Spencer carrier bag also receives special treatment: a range of co-ordinated shades of green will be added to the traditional colour. The new look will start to be introduced into 297 stores in the UK from the summer.

Source: adapted from Marks & Spencer website press releases 2000

Marks & Spencer plc preliminary results for year ended 31 March, 2000
Group sales £8.2 billion *(last year £8.2 billion)*
Profit before tax and exceptional items £557.2 million *(last year £628.4 million)*
Full year dividend of 9p proposed *(last year 14.4p)*

Exceptional items

The exceptional charge for UK restructuring is £63.3 million. Of this, £16 million of redundancy costs were reported at the half year following the rationalization of the UK store management structures and the closure of a distribution centre (Tyneside). The additional £47.3 million now provided for includes:

- head office costs of £18.5 million resulting mainly from restructuring of UK retail into customer business units.
- £28.8 million that relates mainly to the costs of restructuring store roles to refocus staff activities towards the customer.

Whenever a company is going through a bad patch, so that its sales or profits start to fall, it has to study carefully all aspects of the business. When it discovers what is wrong, it can then change the way in which the business works. The case study shows some of the actions a leading high-street retailer took when it was confronted with just such a problem.

Reviewing the brand

Marks & Spencer focused first on its **brand** (see Unit 40). For many years, the words 'Marks & Spencer' had meant a distinctive kind of high quality goods and refined shopping experience. However, in our new more stylish and competitive world, that image had begun to lose some of its appeal. This was reflected in the flat sales figures and the drop in profits.

As the case study shows, Marks & Spencer introduced a completely new look which involved fresh packaging of its products, carriers and brand name, and a whole new range of exciting new products.

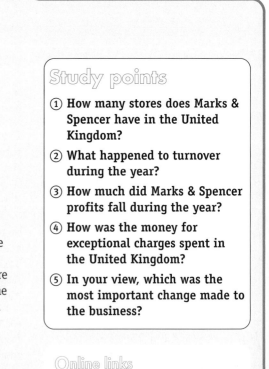

Study points

1. How many stores does Marks & Spencer have in the United Kingdom?
2. What happened to turnover during the year?
3. How much did Marks & Spencer profits fall during the year?
4. How was the money for exceptional charges spent in the United Kingdom?
5. In your view, which was the most important change made to the business?

Online links
www2.marksandspencer.com

Figure 1: The marketing mix

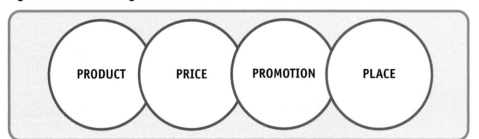

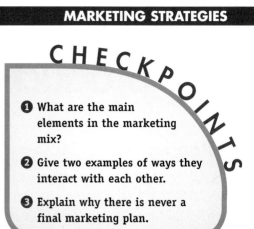

It also:

● established a customer insight unit to understand the shopping habits and age and sex structure of its customers
● changed store layouts and products to meet local needs
● introduced clearly differentiated ranges to broaden traditional markets
● created new product areas such as nursery and maternity wear, and mobile phones
● put 4,000 customer-facing advisors on the sales floors to deliver better customer service
● completed a transitional modernisation of 178 stores
● opened the first three of its new stores in Sutton, Fosse Park and Kensington.

Marks & Spencer also started to cut its costs, by changing its suppliers and other means, so that during the second half of 2000, it hoped to achieve cost savings of over £80 million. This was designed to make Marks & Spencer more competitive on price.

The aim of all these actions was to make the business more responsive to its customers' needs by making changes to its products, its prices, the way in which it sold its products and where it sold them.

The four Ps
All of these factors have to be taken into account whenever a company decides to refocus its business. For convenience, they

are grouped into four main categories – the **four Ps**. They are:

● *product*, which must be differentiated from its rivals' products
● *price*, which must be low enough to be competitive
● *promotion*, which is how customers will hear about the product
● *place*, which is where the customer will find the products and how they will be distributed to them.

In addition, packaging is now such an essential part of a company's or a product's image that these are always included in any refocusing exercise, as the case study has shown. Some business experts now call it the fifth P.

The right mix
Marketing strategy is such a big – and vital – topic that it is divided into the four or five Ps to make it easier to study. Each of them will be considered in much greater detail in the rest of this section. However, in the real world, they are never dealt with separately, as they all have to be blended together in the right amounts so that they create the best **marketing mix**. It is no good getting just one factor right. That rule applies whether we are considering a whole firm or a single product. What good would it be to stamp down prices really low (price), unless shoppers had heard about it through an advertising campaign (promotion)? What good would it be to produce and launch the best product in the world (product), if

it was so expensive that only a few people could afford to buy it (price)? What good would it be to spend millions of pounds advertising a product (promotion), if the company's distribution system was so bad that supplies ran out in the shops (place)?

These few examples, and the case study, show that each of the four Ps (and the fifth) is essential to success. They are all inter-related. As Figure 1 shows, they must be firmly linked together so that the whole package appeals to the target customers.

This mixing and remixing process does not occur only when a product is launched or when a company is having a tough time. It continues throughout the whole life of a product or a business. It is an on-going process which never ends.

KEY TERMS

Brand The features which distinguish a business, or one of its products, from all its rivals.
Four Ps The four main factors in the marketing mix – product, price, promotion and place.
Marketing mix Mixing the four Ps in the right amounts so that the product appeals to consumers in the chosen market segment.

The product

CASE STUDY

Panasonic ES8003S – it's so linear

What does it have?
Most shavers have rotating blades or foils. This shaver has a unique linear driver which sends the blades from side to side. This means that no matter what beard density the shaver encounters, the blade speed is the same.

Eh?
This means that the shaver gives you a closer and faster shave. In fact, the blades are moving back and forth 13,000 times a minute.

Waterproof
We don't know if any of you have a thing about shaving underwater, but you really can do it with this shaver if you want to. More likely perhaps, you can shave in the shower, if so inclined.

Twin gate slit blade
In some ways this feature is what really sets this shaver apart. The twin gate blade captures hair at the beginning and end of each stroke, so curly or long hairs cannot be missed.

Source: adapted from Shavers from BestStuff website

£115

Quick features list:
- *one-hour charge*
- *universal voltage*
- *charge status lamp*
- *three-dimensional shaving system*
- *twin gate slit blade*
- *five-stage battery monitor*
- *13,000 rpm linear motor drive*
- *waterproof*

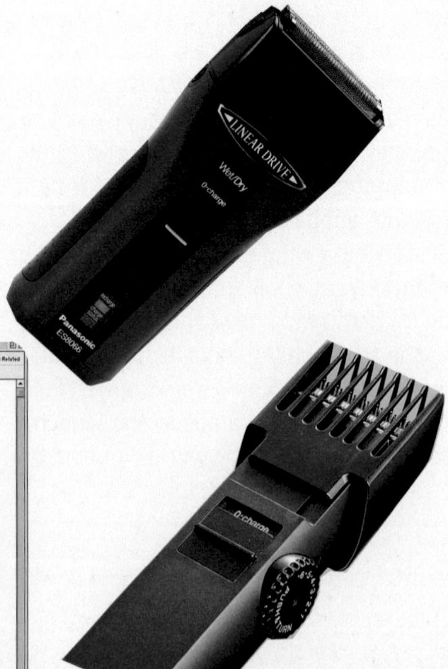

In some ways, the product is the most important of the four Ps. The product is the basis of the whole marketing process. Without a product, there could be no price, no promotion and no place! In fact, many businesses now believe that a high-quality product which provides good value for money is the main key to marketing success.

As you saw in Unit 2, products can be divided into two classes: non-durable consumer goods, such as food and drink, and durable consumer goods, like radios and shavers. However, there are many more differences in products than that.

Shaver market
As the case study shows, shavers have many contrasting characteristics, or features. Each shaver has a number of special features designed to appeal to different kinds of customer. Some manufacturers make up to 15 different models.

Let's see how this works out in practice. There are two main markets for shavers of all kinds: male and female. Within the male market, there are two main segments: men who wet-shave with foam, gel or oil using a razor and men who dry-shave with an electric shaver. Many Panasonic shavers are waterproof, dual-purpose shavers which can be used for either a wet or a dry shave, so that they cover both of the main segments. Beard

Study points
1. How much does the Panasonic shaver cost?
2. At what speed do the blades move?
3. What are the shaver's main features?
4. How could these features be used in marketing?

Online links
www.beststuff.co.uk
www.teenhq.co.uk

trimmers are also made to cover the smaller niche market of men with beards.

There are also the same two main segments for wet-shave razors and dry, electric shavers in the female market. In addition, there is a niche market for electric epilators, which pluck the hair instead of cutting it.

At first glance, many male shavers may look more or less the same – apart from the Philips shaver with its unique rotary, or revolving, head. In fact, they differ from each other in many ways. Some of the contrasting features include:

- chargeable or non-chargeable
- pop-up or extendable hair trimmer
- quick or long charge
- dual voltage or auto voltage.

It is now much easier for consumers to compare the different features of products by using internet sites such as the one in the case study. These 'e-tailers' also usually offer lower prices than bricks and mortar retailers.

Three kinds of features

All shavers – and every other product – have three main kinds of characteristics or features. They are as follows.

- *Objective*, or actual, features which exist in the product itself. One of the most important is the quality of the materials and workmanship. Another is the design, which includes colour, shape and size.
- *Subjective features* which exist in the customer's mind. One of the most important is the image that a particular product creates in the owner's – and other people's – mind. What would you feel like if you owned a Rolex watch – and what might your friends think?
- *Additional features* which are not part of the product but which are obtained when the product is purchased. These include after-sales service and extended guarantees.

Differentiation

Manufacturers make use of these features to produce goods which are different from each other and from those of rival firms. One shaver may have a de luxe pouch with zipper; another may have a silvery case instead of a black one. One shaver may have a year's guarantee; another may have a two-year guarantee. And so on. This marketing process is known as **differentiation**. These features make a product different from rival products and make it appeal to subgroups in the market segment through price, quality and use. In the past, some goods, such as milk, were not differentiated. Now, there is skimmed, semi-skimmed and full-fat, extended-life and long-life, and other kinds of milk to appeal to various groups in the market segment.

Creating a new product

It is a very lengthy process to create a new product. The main stages are shown in Figure 1. The first stage is to find an idea for a new product. This may come from a variety of sources, such as:

- a market research survey
- adapting a foreign product for the home market
- the research and development department (see Unit 49)
- a brainstorming session, in which a group produces as many ideas as possible, usually within a stated time
- an individual manager or technician.

In the second stage, the major departments of the firm – production, marketing, finance – examine and discuss the proposed product. Many proposals fail at this stage.

If the firm decides to go ahead with the product, the third stage will be for the research and development department to examine its feasibility. In the fourth stage, the production department will probably make a prototype before the firm goes into full production. Finally, there may be a trial

launch of the product in a **test market** in one region of the country to discover consumer reactions before the product is launched nationwide.

Services

At one time, there was little marketing of services. That is rapidly changing. Banks and building societies offer differentiated products with separate accounts for business, teenage and personal customers. Credit card companies offer differentiated products with up-market gold cards and varying credit limits. A swimming bath might offer a whole range of products with annual, monthly and weekly season tickets and other tickets which also provide fitness training.

CHECKPOINTS

1. What are the three main features of goods?

2. Why do most manufacturers make a range of products?

3. What are the main advantages of differentiation?

4. Explain how services are marketed.

5. Think of one idea for a new product. State how it might be developed and at what point it might fail.

KEY TERMS

Differentiation The ways in which a business makes its product differ from similar products. Branding and packaging are important methods (see Unit 40).

Test market A trial launch of a product in one area of the country.

Figure 1: Creating a product

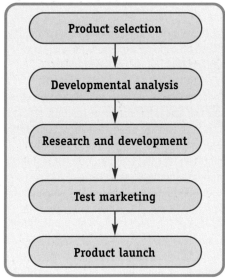

Product selection

↓

Developmental analysis

↓

Research and development

↓

Test marketing

↓

Product launch

Branding and packaging

1: Gap announces national distribution centre

Gap Inc. has announced plans to build a national distribution facility in Rugby to serve its Gap brand stores in the United Kingdom.

The 650,000-square-foot distribution centre, scheduled for completion in late 2001, will create about 500 jobs when operational.

Gap, which opened its first store in the UK more than a decade ago, currently operates more than 130 Gap and GapKids stores across the country. In 2000, the company planned to open more than 30 new stores in the UK.

Source: adapted from news release, 19 April 2000, on Gap Inc website

Study points

① Where and when was Gap founded?

② How many stores does the company have in Britain?

③ What percentage are the British stores of the worldwide total?

④ Gap wants to expand its operations in Britain again. You have been brought in as a consultant to suggest how the brand identity might be altered. Describe the changes you would suggest.

About us

A simple formula drives our brands: We strive to deliver style, service and value to everyone.

From jeans and T-shirts to khakis and jackets, Gap offers a balance of modern and seasonal styles in a clean organized, easy-to-shop environment. Merchandise ranges from clothing and accessories to personal-care products for adults, kids and baby.

Gap provides total access to the brand in Gap, GapKids, babyGap, Gap Outlet stores and US customers can shop online.

Gap was founded in 1969 in San Francisco, California, with a single store and a handful of employees. Currently, we employ over 110,000 people worldwide and operate more than 2,900 stores in the United States, Canada, France, Germany, Japan and the United Kingdom.

Source: adapted from Gap Inc website

Online links
www.gapinc.com

Branding, and its associated packaging, is now one of the most important matters for most consumer businesses. As you have seen in Unit 38, branding is of vital importance for retailers like Marks & Spencer which sell a wide range of goods and the Gap case study in this unit shows that it is equally important for a speciality retailer such as Gap. It is also just as important for the manufacturer of a single product, such as Daz or Persil.

The brand name can be the name of the firm, like Marks & Spencer, Gap, Ford, or Black and Decker, or it can be an invented name, like Kit Kat, Weetabix, Daz, or Virgin. When a new brand name has to be invented, a thesaurus, a special kind of

dictionary, is sometimes used, because it gives useful lists of words with similar meanings.

The Virgin brand now covers a wide range of businesses from music to trains and an airline. This process is known as **brand stretching**.

Benefits of branding

Businesses benefit greatly from branding. The main advantages are that:
- it clearly differentiates their products from rival products
- constant advertising creates brand loyalty and goodwill among customers
- brand loyalty makes it possible to charge a premium, or higher, price

- the brand name makes it easier for the product to be sold globally.

Challenges to branding

Recently, the branding of manufactured goods has come under attack from various quarters. Most branded goods are expensive. Therefore, cheaper, no-brand rival goods have been marketed which appeal to many shoppers. Smaller firms have also been quick to produce clones, or exact copies, of some branded goods, such as computers. There has also been a big, illegal global trade in pirated copies of some branded goods, such as CDs.

One of the most serious challenges has come from the supermarkets which now

2: Packaging problem

Three sixth-formers in East Anglia are setting up a business to sell their own brand of honey to up-market residents and wealthy weekenders with second homes. They are thinking of using the brand name of Honeyrich, Honeyhealth or Honeypure. They are also considering which shape of jar and what slogan would have the greatest appeal to their target market.

CHECKPOINTS

1. Give six examples of brand names.
2. Why are brand names used?
3. What are the main purposes of packaging?
4. Why do you think some supermarkets introduced their own brand goods?
5. What would be the main effects on businesses and the economy if brand names were abolished?

Study points

1. Choose the best brand name or suggest a better alternative. State your reasons for your choice.
2. Explain which jar you would choose, or draw a different shape you prefer.
3. Write an appropriate slogan.

the fifth P. As the case study above shows, part of the packaging – the label – is used to promote the brand name and the slogan. Labels and paper packaging are also used to advertise other promotions such as price cuts and special offers. They also contain information required by law, such as the ingredients of tinned food and the bar code used in the EPOS system for sales analysis (see Unit 46).

Packaging can also be used to help extend a product's life cycle (see Unit 41). To give the product a new look, changes can be made to:

- the container, such as changing its size or shape
- the packaging material, such as using plastic instead of paper
- the design on the packaging, for example altering the lettering or the colour of the words or label.

The packaging also plays an essential physical role in many consumer products. For example, liquids could not be sold without leak-proof containers of some kind.

Finally, packaging plays a vital role in the distribution of goods (see Unit 45). It

needs to be strong, secure, and easy to handle and transport. This reduces the cost of replacing broken or damaged goods and helps to prevent losses through tampering or theft. It must also be of a suitable shape and size, so that it can be displayed easily and attractively in shops and stores.

Criticisms of packaging

Critics complain that packaging is often so expensive that it puts up the price of goods unnecessarily. Yet, without attractive packaging, there might be much lower sales and, therefore, higher prices, because there would be fewer economies of scale.

Consumers frequently complain that packaging is difficult to open. This is often caused by the need to stop terrorists or criminals from tampering with the contents.

Environmental pressure groups complain that fancy packaging wastes scarce raw materials. However, much packaging is now recycled and used again.

sell many **own-brand products** in addition to the branded goods. These products are made by manufacturers but sold under the supermarket's own name or brand name. For example, Novon is Sainsbury's own brand of washing powder and liquid. These own-brand products now account for a large percentage of supermarket sales.

Packaging – the fifth P

Packaging is so closely associated with brand, and has so many links with the four Ps, that some business experts now call it

KEY TERMS

Own-brand product A product which is sold under the name of supermarket or other big retailer instead of the name of a manufacturer.
Brand stretching Using one brand name to cover a variety of different businesses.
Packaging The physical container or wrapping of a product, which is also used for promotion and selling appeal.

Key skills
Communication

Use a thesaurus to find a suitable name connected with light for
a) a lipstick
b) a pop group and
c) a furniture polish.

Product life cycles

CASE STUDY

Egg makers have market cracked

After the shiny packaging is discarded and the hollow eggs are demolished today, parents might reflect on how many chocolate bars they could have bought for the same money.

And well they might ask. Penny per gram, the most popular chocolate eggs cost about three times as much as bars of similar chocolate from the same manufacturers.

Special occasions give confectionery makers a perfect opportunity to inflate prices, as research shows that consumers are more concerned about their children liking their Easter eggs than whether the eggs offer value for money.

The extra packaging also pushes up the price, and manufacturers were criticized recently by trading standards officers for putting excessive wrapping on Easter eggs.

Chocolate-lovers tend to be conservative. Only eight per cent are interested in new products, which could be bad news for Cadbury's 'square egg', the Squegg, launched this year.

Source: adapted from *Financial Mail on Sunday*, 23 April 2000

Chocolate sales 1998

	Sales by value	Sales by volume
Year-round sales	£3,708m	561,000 tonnes
Seasonal sales*	£437m	40,000 tonnes

*Products designed for Christmas, Easter, Mother's Day, Father's Day, Valentine's Day

Online links
www.cadbury.co.uk
www.thortons.co.uk
www.vdbfoods.co.uk

Thornton's over-egged Easter bunny appetite

Thornton's appears to have over-estimated demand from the Easter bunny this year, admitting yesterday that it had 200,000 eggs left on its counters after the festival.

The sweetie shop, which boasts that it has been making 'chocolate heaven since 1911', said sales were six per cent better than last year.

But like many a sweet-toothed toddler, it seems Thornton's eyes were bigger than its, or the nation's, belly. Martin Allen, finance director, said, 'I am afraid we over-egged it a bit.'

Expensive adult eggs – costing upwards of £15 – proved hard to move. And the market for novelty eggs, such as one which contained a CD, was sickly. However, Mr Allen said the eggs raced off the shelves once the prices were cut in half to clear stock.

Thornton's 200,000 eggs were worth £1.4 million, but will lead to a £5 million loss after marketing expenditure is considered.

Source: adapted from *The Times*, 3 June 2000

Some manufactured goods have a short life, like some instant meals which disappear from the shelves almost as soon as they are launched, vividly-coloured, cotton or silk shell suits which lasted only three or four years, and some car models which disappear after only eight years or so. Yet some other products, like Oxo cubes, which were first produced in 1910, have existed for almost a century.

Chocolate Easter eggs, in the case study, have also been around for about the same length of time. However, the tradition of giving eggs for Easter goes back for many centuries, as Christians were once forbidden to eat eggs during Lent, the 40 days before Easter. Some primary products, such as sea salt, have also been used for many centuries, since it was first discovered that sea salt could be used to preserve meat during the grim winter months when food was scarce. People then acquired a taste for salt and started to use it to flavour all their food.

Sales patterns

Why do some products have such a long life and others last only a brief period of time? And how do business people try to extend the shelf life of their products?

The **product life cycle** has five main phases (see Figure 1).

Study points

1. How many chocolate eggs did Thornton's fail to sell at Easter?
2. What is the total amount spent on speciality chocolate sales.
3. Name one other occasion, apart from Easter, for speciality chocolate sales.
4. What percentage are seasonal sales of all chocolate sales by a) value and b) volume?
5. How could this information be used to help in deciding the selling price?
6. What evidence is there that most people have conservative tastes in Easter eggs? How could this factor be used in marketing?

Figure 1: Product life cycle

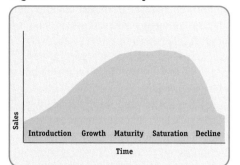

- *Introduction*. Sales are often brisk because the product is new. But marketing and development costs are high, so there is usually no profit.
- *Growth*. Sales start to rise, and costs fall because there are economies of scale in long production runs. The product begins to make a profit.
- *Maturity*. Sales are still increasing, but at a slower rate. Profits are high. However, there is greater competition from new rival products.
- *Saturation*. The market is now saturated with many similar products. Sales and profits start to fall.
- *Decline*. Demand shrinks and sales fall even more. The product starts to lose money and is withdrawn.

In economics, the product life cycle is shown with a rounded curve like that in Figure 1. However, in the real business world, there are very few examples of this kind. What actually happens is shown in the other three graphs.

Figure 3 Brand life cycle

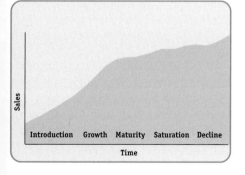

KEY TERMS

Product life cycle The phases a product goes through from its introduction to its final decline.

Figure 2: Extended life cycle

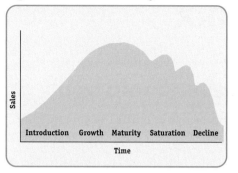

The life cycle for most products is shown in Figure 2. The product follows the economic pattern of increasing sales until maturity is reached. When sales begin to fall at saturation point, the marketing department starts to fight back by using a number of life extension techniques.

Extension techniques
There are many different ways of trying to extend the life of a product. These techniques can help to maintain sales.
- *New models*. New versions of products, with improved features or better design can be produced. This is constantly done with mobile phones, where models sometimes last for only a few months.
- *New uses*. New uses can be found for products. Trainers, first used for sport, achieved massive sales when they became used as everyday footwear.
- *More frequent use*. A mayonnaise manufacturer might be able to persuade consumers to use mayonnaise not only on salads, but in sandwiches, too.

Figure 4: Aborted life cycle

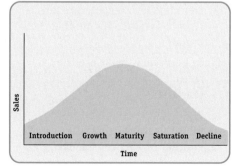

CHECKPOINTS

1. What are the five phases in a traditional product life cycle?
2. Why is the sales pattern shown in Figure 1 rarely found in the real business world?
3. Why do you think Figure 3 shows a continuous upwards trend?
4. Find two examples of products which might have had a life cycle like that in Figure 4. How could the pattern have been reversed?

- *Price reductions*. These can help to maintain sales of a declining product.
- *New outlets*. Paperbacks are no longer sold only in bookshops, but also in supermarkets and airport lounges.
- *Free gifts*. Magazines come with free CDs, garden seeds or cosmetics.

Branded goods
Some branded goods, like Oxo or Mars, seem to defy all life cycle laws and go on for many years after maturity, saturation and decline would normally have been reached. Their life cycle is illustrated in Figure 3.

Although the brand name remains the same, the product itself may be changing continuously to take advantage of all the latest developments in technology and to respond to changes in the market.

Aborted life cycle
Sometimes, the product life cycle looks like the one in Figure 4. There is a quick rise to maturity and an equally quick fall to decline – all within just a few months. There could be a number of reasons for its brief life.
- The product might not be popular.
- Poor marketing might have put people off.
- A competitor might have used industrial espionage, or spying, to discover how it was made and put its own product on the market before the original was launched.
- The product could have been ahead of its time.

The product mix

Bespoke service wherever it suits you

Individually hand-cut and finished suits measured and fitted in your office or home from £395 (New York from $775)

No longer do you need to struggle to your tailor for fittings or waste precious time trawling through the shops for an 'off the rack' suit.

Now the tailor comes to you. We cover most of the United Kingdom and now operate in New York. At Norton & Townsend we have years of experience in offering the finest in traditional tailoring, an impeccably efficient service and superb value for money.

Why not have one of our trained measurers take the strain out of buying a new suit?

- *Extensive range of top quality wool/worsteds from the world's leading merchants.*
- *Tropical 8oz travel suits to toasty, thick flannels and cashmeres.*
- *Orders completed in between six and eight weeks.*
- *Classic Savile Row cuts and Italian/American contemporary styles available.*
- *The usual range of bespoke options and specifications including coloured linings, pocket styles, working cuff buttons and many more.*

Source: adapted from Norton and Taylor Bespoke Tailoring website

Matthew Norton, a former marketing director for a wine company, who set up the visiting tailoring business in 1991. Since then, it has gone online and become a limited company.

Study points

(Look at the key terms before you do the study points.)

① When was the firm started?
② How much does it charge for a suit?
③ What is the firm's product range?
④ Would it be advisable for the firm to increase its product range?
⑤ In your view, what are the strengths and weaknesses of the firm?
⑥ What other small businesses might profitably provide a visiting service for clients?

Online links
www.city2000.com

Sole-product businesses

Very few businesses have just one product. There are a number of successful sole-product businesses in primary production, e.g. small vineyards which produce only one kind of wine and farms which breed pedigree cattle. These businesses can succeed because they are producing high-quality products that customers cannot easily obtain elsewhere. Even so, these businesses run the risk of total disaster if their vines or their cattle get some disease, such as BSE, as they have no other products to sell. Subcontractors who work for only one manufacturing company run a similar risk. If a company decides it does not want a subcontractor's work or goes into liquidation, the small business loses all its work. Having only one product to sell increases business risk.

Product range

Most businesses, therefore, have more than one product. For example, the firm in the case study has a **product range** of suits. They are made in different styles and sizes and with different cloths. This provides the customer with greater choice by making suits for different kinds of activity. It also reduces the firm's risk as it no longer depends on just one product.

Some firms diversify even more by producing goods or services of many different kinds. Even smaller businesses sometimes have a wide product mix, such as making fireplaces, luxury kitchens, trouser-presses, cosmetic accessories, furniture and distributing DIY products. Businesses such as these have spread their risks over a number of products in different markets. If the sales of one product start to fall, the sales of other products may still be rising.

As you have seen in Unit 41, practically all products have a limited life cycle. Some disappear almost as soon as they are launched. Others have their life extended by marketing promotions. A few go on for many years, but most products eventually fade away. All businesses are faced with the constant need to cut their losses on failing products and to support new products which might succeed. How do businesses decide?

Figure 1: The Boston Matrix

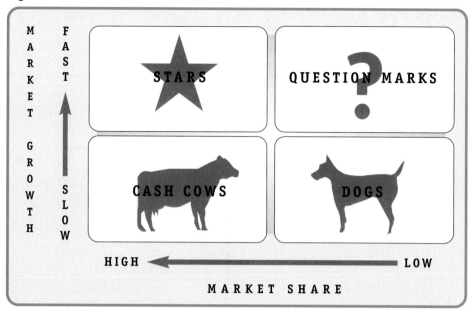

CHECKPOINTS

❶ What is the difference between a product mix and a product range? Give one example of each.

❷ Describe the four kinds of product in the Boston matrix.

❸ What is the main a) advantage and b) disadvantage of a wide product mix?

❹ If the following events were to happen, state whether they would be a) an opportunity b) a threat or c) have no effect at all on Norton & Townsend. Give your reasons.

(i) Marks & Spencer cuts the price of its business suits by 10 per cent.

(ii) There are dramatic crashes on the New York and London stock exchanges.

(iii) The number of women in top executive jobs rises by 7 per cent.

(iv) The structure of many big companies becomes far less hierarchical.

The Boston matrix

The Boston matrix, or framework, is a great help in making decisions. The matrix was developed by the Boston Consulting Group. It divides products into four main classes and describes the investment and the returns which might be expected from each (see Figure 1).

- Stars have a high market share in a market which is growing fast. Although the business has to support the product by advertising and promoting it, the cash returns will be worthwhile in the end if it succeeds.
- Cash cows are in a stable market which is no longer growing at its earlier rate. Cash cows are profitable as they are well-established products with a large share of a stable market. They can be 'milked' to finance other products.
- Question marks, or problem children, have a low share in a fast-growing market, so they need considerable investment to succeed. It is always difficult to decide how much time and cash should be invested in a question mark. If the product seems better than

its rivals, it is probably right to support it, as it could turn into a star and, finally, a cash cow.

- Dogs have a low market share in a slow-growing market and may not even be breaking even. These products are likely to be killed off. Businesses must make sure that they always have new products coming on stream to replace the dogs which have gone into final decline.

Although there are still some big businesses with a wide **product mix**, the number has declined. Competition is so fierce that many businesses have become highly focused on a couple of markets.

SWOT analysis

In this new era of global competition, big firms have to be constantly aware of what is happening in their own business and in the rest of the world. To measure their performance, they use another simple technique – a SWOT analysis.

In the first part of the exercise – the SW part – they look inwards at their own

Strengths and Weaknesses. For example, they might compare the time they take to answer a complaint from a customer with the time a major rival takes. They reply much quicker than their rival. So that is a strength. Then they look at the price of their goods. Their rival's prices are lower. So that is a weakness.

They then carry out the second part of the exercise – the OT part. For this, they look in the outside world at any Opportunities they might be missing or any Threats on the horizon. For example, the economy is booming, so that presents an opportunity to increase their sales. However, the government is talking of putting VAT on the goods they produce, so that is a threat.

Big companies use a SWOT analysis of this kind to improve their own performance and to plan their route ahead.

KEY TERMS

Product mix Different kinds of product made by a business, such as suits, raincoats and sports bags.

Product range Similar products made by a business, such as various kinds of suit.

Revision and exam practice units 38–42

Case study 1

REVIEW POINTS

1 What is differentiation? Why is it important?

2 What are the five main stages in a product life cycle? Give two examples of how marketing might be able to halt decline.

3 Describe the threats that manufacturers of branded goods have faced in recent years.

4 Why is packaging so important in marketing goods?

5 Describe the main features of products and explain how they can be used in marketing.

Extended questions

Branding is one of the most important aspects of product marketing. Explain its advantages and disadvantages for:
a) the producer
b) the retailer and
c) the customer.

National Packaging Group plc

National Packaging Group plc is the UK's largest packing distributor with a network of local branches throughout the UK offering customers a complete 'one-stop shop' for packaging products on a just-in-time basis.

Established six years ago by its parent company Charles Baynes plc, National Packaging has a current turnover of £52 million and employs over 250 people nationwide.

National Packaging Advantage is the service dedicated to the large corporate customer, ordering a variety of stock and custom-made products.

For your company, packaging materials represent a substantial investment in people space, stock and transport.

Your packaging is the visible face of your business; therefore it is vital that your packaging is well designed, safe, secure and environmentally friendly.

When you order from your local National Packaging branch you will be supplied with quality products from the best international manufacturers on a just-in-time basis and at consistently competitive prices.

Furthermore, every customer benefits from National Packaging's commitment to source and provide products that save time, money and the environment.

Source: adapted from National Packaging Group plc website

1 What is the business of the National Packaging Group?

2 Who are its customers?

3 In what way are packaging materials a substantial investment in people space, stock and transport?

4 What does National Packaging mean when it says it sources products?

5 Explain the various ways in which packaging is important to the company's customers.

Online links

www.national-packaging.co.uk

Case study 2

Easier shopping

Our performance in a tough market place, reflected in our sales, is being driven by the growing strength of the Safeway brand. Ever since we started repositioning our brand five years ago, we've been targeting young families as the customer group who offer us the best opportunity for profitable growth. We measure our success by the total spend we are attracting from family shoppers – up by 22 per cent since 1996. We're listening to them and giving them what they want in terms of product range and quality, availability, value for money and service.

Over the past few years we've been working hard to meet their expectations which, like much else in our industry, are always rising. Today's bright idea is tomorrow's 'must have.' And over the past 18 months we've invested extra resources in our brand.

Our priority is to upgrade the quality of our product ranges, particularly those that are critical to family shoppers. We've increased the number of lines we carry in an average superstore by over 1,200.

Source: adapted from Safeway website

1 **Why does Safeway think its brand name is so important?**

2 **How does Safeway measure its success?**

3 **Why is it targeting young families?**

4 **Explain how the company has increased its appeal to its customers.**

5 **How does Safeway deal with its products' life cycle?**

6 **Describe four decisions Safeway made to make its brand distinctive.**

Online links

www.safeway.co.uk

Case study 3

Liberty's strategy

Liberty is a unique brand in world retailing. This year a new management team led by chairman Philip Bowman and managing director, Michele Jobling have been developing a new strategy to take Liberty successfully into the next century. The key elements are:

● to refurbish the store in London
● to strengthen the branded merchandise business by focusing and developing three capsule ranges: ladies apparel (clothing), gifts and homewares
● to develop distribution channels to ensure that the branded merchandise range is made available internationally.

Liberty is in touch and maintains its leadership in design, creativity and style with new fabrics, modern furniture and glass, avant garde jewellery and extreme fashion.

We look for quirky individuality, confident colours and respect for traditional materials used with modern flair.

Source: Liberty plc website

1 **What is Liberty's new strategy?**

2 **How will the branded merchandise business be strengthened?**

3 **Explain how this might help to reduce business risk.**

4 **In what way does Liberty use differentiation to sell its products?**

5 **Describe what you think would be a typical Liberty customer for ladies apparel (clothing) and gifts in relation to age, education and income.**

Online links

www.liberty.co.uk

EXAM PRACTICE

Foundation

1 What do you think will happen to these products by 2010?
   (a) Levi's (2 marks)
   (b) single-use cameras (2 marks)
   (c) skateboards (2 marks)
   (d) long-playing records. (2 marks)

2 Which socioeconomic and age groups do you think are mainly interested in the products in Q1? (8 marks)

3 How might market research help to extend the life cycle of a product? (4 marks)

4 What are the main problems for a manufacturer with a product facing an aborted life cycle? (4 marks)

Higher

1 What do you think will happen to these products by 2010?
   (a) Levi's (2 marks)
   (b) single-use cameras (2 marks)
   (c) skateboards (2 marks)
   (d) long-playing records? (2 marks)

2 How might market research help with an extended life cycle? (4 marks)

3 In the next ten years, what do you think will happen to demand for:
   (a) foreign holidays (3 marks)
   (b) internet shopping (3 marks)

4 In each of the following cases, a manufacturer is faced with falling sales because of rival products.
   (i) a top of the range lipstick
   (ii) a baby buggy sold mainly in superstores and large retail outlets
   (iii) a middle of the range divan sold in a large variety of retail outlets.
   Discuss how differentiation may be used to revitalise each product in relation to (a) quality, (b) image and (c) after sales. (6 marks)

5 Apart from any loss of profit, what other problems does a manufacturer have with a product which is reaching the end of its life cycle? (4 marks)

Price

Cabel and Wireless Connect
Save money on the internet by joining Connect

Unlike other companies, who either supply your internet connection or provide phone calls, we have been able to combine both our internet and national telephone services into one package to bring you big savings.

Connect is made up of three tailored packages designed to suit your individual needs. With Connect12 you pay just £5.99 per month and it includes 12 hours online for no extra cost*. After you've used up your free hours, calls cost just 2.4p per minute daytime and 0.8p per minute at all other times.

Moving up to Connect35, all you pay is £14.99 per month and this includes 35 hours online*. Even after you've used the free hours, calls cost just 2.1p per minute daytime and 0.7p per minute at all other times.

If you're a very regular user of the internet, Connect75 costs you just £29.99 per month and includes 75 hours online*. Calls cost just 1.8p per minute daytime and 0.6p per minute at all other times.

Calls to our technical support team are charged at the same low rates as calls to the internet and are included within your free hours.

The telephone service that comes with Connect gives you all the features you're used to – and a lot more besides.

National calls on Saturday for no more than 50p, where you chat for as long as you like, for a maximum of 50p per call.

A promise to save you money on your phone bill compared to BT, or double the difference back.

* Free hours are based on evening and weekend usage.

Source: adapted from Cable and Wireless website

C&W Internet Lite

Internet Lite has been the best performing free access ISP in *Internet* magazine's six-month lab tests. There are no registration or monthly fees. You just pay as you go for the calls you make, at rates similar to a local telephone call.

Calls to technical support are charged at 50p per minute, or at local call rates if you are a Cable & Wireless telephone customer.

Source: adapted from Cable & Wireless Internet website

Supply and demand

Price has always been an important factor in the marketing mix, but it is even more vital in today's competitive environment when firms have to compete ruthlessly with their rivals.

The economic laws of supply and demand (see Unit 2) still have a certain influence on prices, particularly in primary production. During the summer months, for example, when there are plenty of home-grown vegetables, prices tend to fall. In the late spring, when the prices of home-grown vegetables are high, prices tend to rise. If there are large supplies of oil, the price should fall to oil companies like Shell. If, on the other hand, OPEC (the Organization of Petroleum Exporting Countries) decides to restrict production, the cost of oil will rise. (The final price of petrol at the pumps is governed by many other factors, including the high rate of government tax in Britain.)

Although this economic law affects all businesses, it has much less force in the secondary and tertiary areas of production, such as manufacturing and retailing. Other factors, such as what competing firms

Study points

1. What does it cost to join Internet Lite?
2. How much do you pay per month if you want 35 free hours per month online on the Connect service?
3. At what times could you use the free calls?
4. Why are free calls given at those times?
5. In your view, how successful has Cable & Wireless been in using price to attract customers?

Online links
www.cwcom.net

charge for similar products, have an equally big influence.

Price-fixing methods

How do firms decide the price of their products? The simplest method is the **cost-plus** approach, that is:

unit cost + overheads + mark-up
= selling price

Some firms still set their prices in this way. In theory, they can never go bankrupt, but what happens if the labour force goes on strike for higher wages? Or if sales decline? Or if their price is undercut by cheap foreign imports?

Some of these problems can be avoided by using a **market-orientated price** instead. With this method, a firm finds out (by market research) what customers are prepared to pay before the price is set.

There is a **price plateau**, which represents the level of price that a market segment expects to pay for a particular product. If a firm's price is too much below the plateau, consumers will think the product is inferior, so they won't buy. If it is too far above the plateau, they won't buy either.

Pricing techniques

Prices are not always easy to understand. Some prices have so many variations and attached conditions, as in the case study, that consumers sometimes find it difficult to know exactly what they are getting or even what they are paying! Businesses use many professional techniques to set their prices. Some of the most important are as follows.

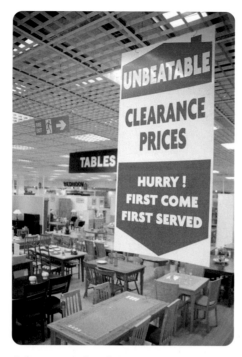

Sales promotion in a superstore

- *Critical point price*. Goods are rarely priced at £10 exactly, but at £9.99 instead, because it seems a much lower price, even though the difference is only one penny.
- *Complementary pricing*. One product may be sold at a relatively low price, but the product which goes with it, may have a relatively high price. For example, a ball-point pen might be relatively cheap and the refill dear.
- *Differential price*. Some stores charge higher prices in small towns than they do in cities where there is more competition. Some supermarkets are now considering charging lower prices at times of the day when there are fewer customers.

- *Discount price*. A reduction in price, or a discount, often given for large orders or cash payments, or to loyal customers. Two for the price of one is another example of discount pricing.
- *Sales*. Mark-downs – or sales – were once mainly seasonal, but they now take place at any time of the year.
- *Price cut*. Prices are often cut dramatically to sell slow-moving stock or at the end of a product's life.
- *Loss leaders*. Cheap goods are stacked in wire baskets at store entrances to attract shoppers into the store.

Effects of life cycle

The product life cycle (see Unit 41) can also have an influence on the price. In the introduction period, a low **penetration price** may be used to gain entry to a crowded market by undercutting rival prices; or a high **skimming price** may be used if the product is completely new and has no rivals.

In the growth period, a price plateau is established which is usually set by the market leader. Differential prices may become more common during the maturity phase. There may also be bigger discounts to retain market share.

In the saturation period, discounts may be given to prevent sales falling, and in decline, there may be big end-of-life price cuts to clear stocks.

KEY TERMS

Cost-plus pricing Fixing a price by adding a percentage to the cost of production.

Market-orientated price A price which is decided by the whole range of factors in the marketing mix instead of by the cost-plus price of a product.

Penetration price A price which is set low enough to allow a firm to enter a new market.

Price plateau The level of price that consumers expect to pay for a particular product.

Skimming price Charging a high price for a new product while it remains unique.

Promotion

Where to place advertisements

Direct mail
- pin-point targeting possible
- easy to measure effectiveness

but
- opposition to 'junk' mail
- mail shots often poorly targeted

Television
- emotional impact
- huge audience
- life-like

but
- ads can't be kept
- expensive
- targeting can be difficult

Radio
- relatively easy targeting
- low cost

but
- small audience

Internet
- global coverage

but
- often delays in downloading

Posters
- big impact
- seen by many people

but
- limited information
- difficult targeting

Press
- easy targeting of market segments
- ads can be kept
- colour available

but
- not as dramatic as television
- ads often unread

Study points

1. How much was spent in the year on advertising?
2. Which branch of the media had
   a) the biggest and
   b) the smallest share of advertising?
3. What are the main
   a) advantages and
   b) disadvantages of Press advertisements?
4. Put the different branches of the advertising media in order of effectiveness for targeting market segments.
5. Look at Figure 2. You are putting a display advertisement in a Manchester newspaper for a new upmarket women's magazine targeting affluent readers in the 35–44 age group. Assuming that advertising rates per reader were virtually the same in all the publications, which would you choose? State your reasons.

Figure 1: Main advertising expenditure by type

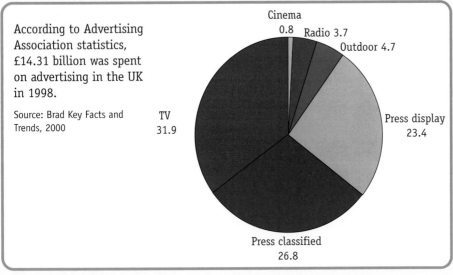

According to Advertising Association statistics, £14.31 billion was spent on advertising in the UK in 1998.

Source: Brad Key Facts and Trends, 2000

Cinema 0.8
Radio 3.7
Outdoor 4.7
Press display 23.4
TV 31.9
Press classified 26.8

Figure 2: Readership of Manchester newspapers (source: www.adweb.co.uk)

	Adults	Men	Women	ABC1	C2DE	15–24	25–34	35–44	45–54	55–64	65+
Manchester Evening News	121929	65303	56635	47102	74831	26397	24967	20175	15329	13363	21704
Manchester Metro News	166323	76152	90169	67291	99033	38027	31049	31328	21606	16438	27879
South Manchester Express	58157	28496	29663	34894	23263	12508	9374	11588	7416	6362	10912

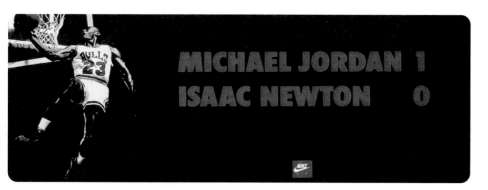

Purposes of advertising

> 'Advertisements are messages, paid for by those who send them, intended to inform or influence people who receive them.'
>
> Source: The Advertising Association

The main element in the third P – promotion – is advertising, though sales promotions also play a big part (see Unit 46). Advertising is big business. Over £14 billion is spent on advertisements in Britain every year. Advertisements are used in a number of ways, but the main purposes in order of importance are:

- to persuade people to buy some goods or service, from a £10 book to a £10 million house in central London
- to change people's attitudes or views, as with drink-driving campaigns
- to make people think better of a business or an organization, such as advertisements during general elections
- to provide simple information, such as legal notice to declare that a business has closed or gone into liquidation.

With a few exceptions, anyone can advertise what they have to sell. If you wanted to sell your bike, you could put a card in a shop window for a few pence or a **classified advertisement** in the local newspaper free or for a few pounds. A campaign to advertise a newly opened shop, using **display advertisements** in regional newspapers and a few short 'spot' advertisements on regional television, need cost no more than a few thousand pounds.

Choosing media

As the case study shows, it is important to choose the right branch of the media, or channels of communication, for advertisements. There is an astonishing variety of newspapers and magazines. *Willings Press Guide* lists 14 national dailies, 11 national Sunday newspapers, 300 regional dailies and Sundays, 1,135 local weeklies, 933 free local weeklies, 3,533 consumer magazines for the general reader and 6,319 trade, business and professional magazines! The choice depends on a number of factors, including:

- the message the advertiser wants to put across
- the market segment a business wants to reach
- whether the likely customers are local, regional, national or international
- the special qualities that the branch of the media has to offer.
- how much the advertiser can spend.

Advertising agencies

Advertising is highly skilled and involves the work of so many different specialists that it would be uneconomic for even the biggest firm to have its own staff. So a firm decides how much it can spend – its advertising budget – and then chooses an independent **advertising agency** to run the advertising campaign. The chosen agency appoints an account executive to be in charge of the campaign.

- The media department buys television and radio time, and space in newspapers and magazines.
- The creative department takes care of the advertisements themselves. A copywriter writes the text. The artwork is done by a visualizer (who does the general presentation), an artist (who does the drawing) and a layout person (who does the detailed design).
- The art buying department gets a photographer and a film production company to make the television commercials.

Public relations

The main difference between advertising and **public relations (PR)** is cost. Advertising has to be paid for, but PR gets free publicity. Most firms and organizations – unless they are tiny – have their own PR department or employ a firm. One of the main tasks is sending out press releases to the media – information about a new product, an appeal for funds or just a story about something a famous person is doing – in the hope that it will be printed or broadcast free of charge.

KEY TERMS

Advertising agency A firm which produces advertisements for other firms or organizations.

Classified advertisement An advertisement in small type, which is charged according to the number of lines.

Display advertisement A larger advertisement, which is ruled off from others and charged according to the number of single column centimetres or by the proportion of a page it takes up.

Public relations (PR) Distributing information about a firm or an organization with the aim of improving its public image.

Place

Business Post

Business Post Group plc is one of the fastest growing overnight express parcel and mail companies in the UK, with a customer base in excess of 18,000 ranging from large multinationals to smaller users.

Business Post's nationwide collection and delivery network consists of over 60 strategically positioned locations (a combination of regional hubs and franchised local depots). The key operating centre is the national hub in Birmingham.

Domestic Services A nationwide service providing speed, flexibility in delivery times and value for money.

- Premier Delivery. Next day delivery, with priority options.
- Premier Packs. Small items or mail, 5kg and 10kg weight limits.
- Maildoc. 1kg weight limit. Now also available to key international commercial centres.

HomeServe.net, the principal UK carrier for Tiny Computers Ltd, is a next day nationwide home delivery service enabling businesses to add extra value to their products by giving customers a choice of three standard delivery windows, 8–12, 12–5 pm, and 5–8 pm. At the point of collection, details are also taken of a secondary delivery address or secure location.

Web Despatch This facility enables customers to use the internet to book collections and enter consignment information online, so that a label can be printed out.

Franchising BP franchising started in 1988 and now has 37 successful locations, including 14 franchisees who have been with the firm for nine years. They operate out of warehoused units of approximately 600 square metres.

Source: adapted from Business Post website

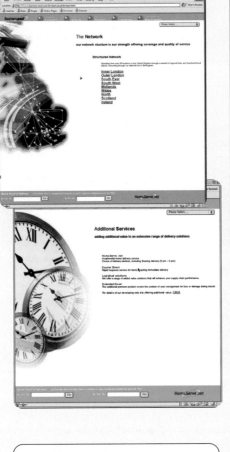

Study points

1. Where is the operating centre of Business Post's distribution network?
2. How many customers does it have?
3. What is its main business?
4. Which kind of production is it involved in?
5. Do you think it is a good idea for Business Post to have franchisees?
6. What effects might the internet have on the firm?

Online links

www.business-post.com

The last of the four Ps – place – deals with how a business distributes its products. Although it is the last, it is just as important as the others.

As the case study shows, distribution is a complicated business demanding speed and many hours of work. Most goods – over 80 per cent – are distributed in Britain by road against less than five per cent by rail. There are more than 420,000 heavy goods vehicles on Britain's roads, plus many foreign lorries delivering goods from the Continent.

Channels of distribution

Figure 1 shows the three main **channels of distribution**. The traditional way of distributing goods is shown as channel A. A **wholesaler** buys goods in bulk, or large quantities, from producers and then sells and delivers them in smaller quantities to retailers. Sometimes, the goods are already packaged. All the wholesaler has to do is to split them up into smaller quantities. Other goods, like screws, are bought unsorted. A specialist firm then sorts the screws and puts them into small, convenient packages, which are delivered to the retailer.

The process of dividing large quantities into smaller lots is known as **break bulk**.

There are over 110,000 wholesalers and dealers, employing more than 1,100,000 people. The food and drink sector has the largest number of wholesalers, including many 'cash and carry' wholesalers, such as Makro and Booker.

Many independent, convenience stores and village shops obtain their goods through groups, such as Cost Cutter, Spar and Londis, which buy goods in bulk and deliver them at discount prices to their members. Most supermarkets and other big chains of retailers have set up their own central buying and distribution systems.

Distribution centres

Each supermarket has its own **regional distribution centres (RDCs)** throughout the country. Manufacturers and suppliers deliver their goods to the RDCs. The goods are then delivered as required to all the branches in the region. This channel, which cuts out the wholesaler, is shown as type B in Figure 1.

Figure 1: Main channels of distribution

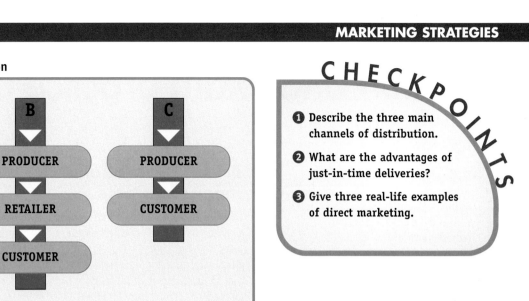

CHECKPOINTS

❶ Describe the three main channels of distribution.

❷ What are the advantages of just-in-time deliveries?

❸ Give three real-life examples of direct marketing.

Stock is ordered automatically by electronic means (see Unit 46). Lorries deliver the new stock of all the items required to the store once or twice a day, or with larger superstores, even more frequently. Big manufacturers have their own highly automated national distribution centres to speed up the supply of goods to RDCs and wholesalers. Delivering stock, or **inventory**, just-in-time, or just before it runs out, reduces costs.

Specialist firms

Distribution has become such a skilled task that multiple retailers contract part, or the whole, of the work to outside firms. These specialist firms provide a whole range of services, including vehicles with the retailers' own distinctive colours or liveries. They provide vans and lorries of many different sizes, including refrigerated lorries for frozen food. The majority of goods are transported in Britain by road, though rail is still used for bulk freight such as coal and metal.

Direct marketing

The third channel of distribution (type C in Figure 1) cuts out both the wholesaler and retailer. **Direct marketing** tries to build a personal long-term link with targeted customers through:

- websites (popular sites get millions of 'hits' a month)
- e-mails (sent regularly to registered customers)
- direct mail (personalized letters to chosen customers)
- mail-order catalogues
- press advertisements or magazine inserts with reply coupons
- telephone calls.

These direct channels are often used for services, such as insurance, and for complex machines, such as computers, where any problems can often be solved only by the manufacturer.

Agents

In all three channels of distribution, there are also agents who provide a link between sellers and buyers. For example, with some mail order catalogue firms, customers act as agents. Like most agents, they do not own the goods or services they provide, and do not receive a salary. Instead, they take a **commission** on every sale they make.

Agents are often used for selling houses, holidays, and tickets for sports and entertainment events. Exporters also sometimes use agents to sell their goods in foreign countries. It is cheaper for firms to use agents than to set up their own selling organization. The agents' inside knowledge of their own country is valuable in marketing the firm's products.

KEY TERMS

Break bulk The repacking of goods which have been bought in large quantities into smaller packages for resale to retailers.

Channels of distribution The methods by which goods and services are distributed from producers to consumers.

Commission A payment based on a percentage of the value of the goods sold. For example, an estate agent who sold a £100,000 house for a two per cent commission would make £2,000.

Direct marketing Selling direct to customers through the post or some other means.

Inventory The stock of finished goods, semi-finished goods or raw materials stored by a firm.

Regional distribution centre (RDC) A large warehouse, usually of 250,000 square feet or more, with the latest computer systems and automated handling equipment, which distributes goods to all the branches of a multiple retailer in one region.

Wholesaler The link between a producer and a retailer.

Revision and exam practice units 43–45

1 What is the difference between a classified and a display advertisement?

2 How does public relations differ from advertising?

3 What is the meaning of a price plateau? Who would be likely to use a penetration price?

4 Describe the main channels of distribution and explain why they are used.

Extended questions

Jill is opening a boutique in a small country town. She has asked you to give her some advice – for a fee – about a) publicity in local newspapers b) promotional events on the opening day c) advertising on local radio and TV stations. Write a report giving your advice.

Business lounge at Bristol International Airport

Case study 1

Bristol International means business

Success in attracting an increasing number of business passengers has been the key to the rising fortunes of Bristol International. Over the last five years, the number of business passengers flying from the South West's premier airport has almost doubled to 620,000 per year. How is Bristol International achieving this?

The growth of business passengers and business routes has been central to the airport's strategy. June 1999 saw the launch of Navigator, the UK's first frequent flyer programme exclusively for business customers of an airport rather than individual airlines. Navigator cardholders benefit from parking close to the terminal, with preferential discounted rates and one free use of the executive business lounge, complete with complimentary refreshments and business facilities.

Compass points

The Navigator card is swiped at the airport each time the business traveller visits, accruing valuable 'compass points' which can be exchanged for a range of savings and special offers from the airport, and its business partners in the region.

Development of new routes at Bristol International is paramount if it is to permanently lure away commuters from the London airports and the Birmingham Eurohub. In a recent survey by top South West law firm Burges Salmon, 67 per cent of the region's business travellers flying to the United States would utilise a daily service to New York from Bristol International. Securing such a service remains one of the airport's primary aims.

Improving access to the airport for business passengers has also been a priority for the management team. A dedicated luxury coach service connects the public transport hubs of Bristol Temple Meads railway station and the city's bus station.

However, the most fundamental improvement to the business facilities at Bristol International has been the opening of its £27 million passenger terminal at the beginning of March. The new building boasts two sumptuous business lounges, with superb views of the airfield and the latest in business facilities. Business passengers can also use the airport's express check-in.

Bristol International has identified that growing the facilities, routes and services it can offer its business passengers is a cornerstone to its continued success.

Source: adapted from Somerset Business, June 2000

1 How many business passengers does Bristol International currently have a year?

2 What has been the airport's main business objective?

3 Name three services Bristol International has offered to promote the airport.

4 Explain how two of the services would attract business people.

5 Assess the effect of the airport's expansion on
a) the local community
b) the business passenger
c) local businesses

6 What effect does the expansion have on
a) the economy
b) manufacturing industry?

Case study 2

BRITAIN	
Chicken	£4.09
Apples	£2.00
Onions	£1.09
Potatoes	£1.00
Carrots	£1.60
Oranges	£1.59

GERMANY	
Apples	£1.50
Onions	91p
Potatoes	76p
Carrots	98p

DENMARK	
Chicken	£3.75
Apples	£1.77
Onions	68p
Potatoes	52p
Carrots	£1.04

FRANCE	
Chicken	£3.50
Apples	£1.69
Onions	70p
Potatoes	£1.70
Carrots	£1.40

BELGIUM	
Chicken	£4.20
Apples	£1.75
Onions	70p
Potatoes	70p
Carrots	82p
Oranges	£1.10

ITALY	
Apples	£1.40
Onions	£1.50
Potatoes	£1.20
Carrots	£1.20
Oranges	£1.30

Prices (per kg) are typical
High Street prices

Organic food rip-off

British shoppers are paying some of the highest prices in Europe for organic food. One of the main reasons produce is so expensive is that 70 per cent has to be imported because UK farmers have not been given sufficient incentives to switch from conventional growing methods. Currently there are around 3,000 organic farms here. Organic food sales have been growing at 40 per cent a year since 1995. The market is expected to reach £500 million this year and top £1 billion by 2002. But it has not brought lower prices.

'Organic food is far too expensive,' said Liberal Democrat MP Paul Tyler. 'For many years, the government treated organic farming as a peripheral issue and didn't help farmers develop their land while European governments encouraged it.'

Only three per cent of British farmland produces organic food, forcing supermarkets to buy abroad. But this does not go the whole way to justify the mark-ups by most stores.

The Agriculture Ministry admitted there is no shortage of farmers keen to go organic – but said there is not enough money to cover the costs of converting. Once farmers decide to abandon conventional methods, they face a two-year wait before supermarkets accept their produce as genuinely organic. Without a subsidy they are unwilling to take the financial risk.

Source: adapted from *Daily Mail*, 13 May 2000

1 In which country are organic apples
   a) most expensive
   b) cheapest?

2 How many organic farms are there in the United Kingdom?

3 What are the main reasons why organic food is expensive?

4 What problems do you think conversion to organic farming creates for farmers?

EXAM PRACTICE

Malcolm is a qualified plumber who lives in a large industrial town in Yorkshire. He has worked for the same firm since he left school at 16 and attended a two-year day release course at his local college. He has now decided, in his thirties, to start his own firm. His bank adviser has approved his detailed business plan. Some of the main items were: employing three qualified plumbers; plumbing and heating equipment repairs; installation; emergency services 365 days of the year for all domestic, commercial and industrial requirements.

Malcolm hopes to attract customers from a wide area. He now has to decide how he will advertise his new business.

Foundation

1 What would be Malcolm's first step?
   (2 marks)

2 Suggest two places where he might advertise for staff. (2 marks)

3 Design a classified advertisement for a local paper which you think would attract employees. (4 marks)

3 Suggest two methods of advertising Malcolm's services for a) domestic customers b) industrial businesses.
   (4 marks)

Higher

1 Suggest three ways Malcolm could obtain suitably qualified staff.
   (6 marks)

2 Design a general display advertisement advertising his services. (4 marks)

3 Discuss the suitability or otherwise of using the following methods of promotion a) local radio b) regional TV c) direct mail d) random phone calls e) internet. (10 marks)

4 Apart from the services he intends to offer, suggest two other services Malcolm could provide to compete with rivals. (4 marks)

Retailing

Verdict on High Street 2000

High streets – new and old

High streets have huge public support. Only 16 per cent of shoppers would like to see more out-of-town development. For the second year running, Verdict has produced a ranking of the top 100 UK high streets and shopping malls. Oxford Street remains in top place.

The high street is staging something of a revival after suffering a falling share of sales and selling space over the last 10 years, due mainly to rapid out-of-town expansion. Reinvestment back in the high street is now taking place with major schemes such as Brighton's Churchill Square (1998) and Reading's Oracle (1999).

Retailers on the high street have faced many threats and challenges in the last year, from the internet, intensified price competition and weak consumer demand. Increases in rates and rents have put even greater strain on the margins of retailers.

The threat to the high street from online retailing is very real. Verdict estimates that consumer spending for consumer goods online will grow by more than 1,000 per cent in the next five years. While sales will only account for 3.1 per cent of the UK total, the vast majority will be cannibalised from traditional home shopping or existing stores, including the high street.

Nevertheless, Verdict believes that the high street's position has stabilised, with the slowing down of out-of-town development and reinvestment in traditional high streets and covered malls leading off them.

The report estimates that total retail sales in 1999 were £197.2 billion. High street sales were £93.8 billion, or just under 48 per cent of total sales. The phenomenal out-of-town sales growth over the last ten years has seen the share of sales accounted for by the high street fall from 52 per cent in 1990.

Source: adapted from Verdict on High Street 2000 website (see also case studies 1 and 2 in Revision and exam practice 14–17)

Retailing is very big business. As the case study shows, retail turnover is nearly £200 billion a year, and rising. Retailing employs about 2.4 million people. There are over 200,000 shops and stores.

Nearly 80 per cent of shops are owned by sole proprietors and partnerships. Although they are in a majority, their total market share is falling, and many of them, particularly in the grocery trade, could not survive without the aid of buying groups such as Londis and Cost Cutter.

Recently, they have had to face a new threat from convenience stores on garage forecourts, some of which are open 24 hours a day. However, small businesses which are run efficiently and with entrepreneurial style can still survive (see Unit 47).

Multiples rule

Retailing is increasingly dominated by **multiple retailers**, or chains of shops owned by a single company, including supermarkets, like Tesco, which now sell an increasing variety of goods, and specialists, like Curry's. These big chains still rule the high streets, though some have moved to new out-of-town developments.

Study points

1. **What percentage of shoppers would like to see more out-of-town developments?**
2. **Why has high street shopping decreased?**
3. **How are high streets likely to be affected by the internet?**
4. **What are the main advantages of out-of-town shopping?**
5. **In your view, what more could high streets do to regain a bigger market share?**

Online links
www.verdict.co.uk

Out-of-town centres

There are eight huge regional out-of-town centres like Cribbs Causeway just outside Bristol. The latest, Bluewater, near Dartford in Kent, is the biggest in Europe with 320 shops and parking for 13,000 cars. There are many other smaller retail parks with cheap, warehouse-type sheds for supermarkets and retailers of DIY, electricals, computers, furniture and so on. Factory shop centres are a newer development selling end-of-line and overstocked goods at discount prices.

Although the government is now less keen on out-of-town developments, there are still a number in the pipeline for which planning permission has already been obtained.

Electronic orders

All of the big multiples use electronic means to record sales and order new replacement stock. The system is completely automatic. As each item is sold, the check-out assistant moves its bar code over the scanning window of an **electronic point of sale (EPOS)** terminal. The bar code is a combination of narrow and broad stripes containing the item's unique number. It is registered by the laser beam of the EPOS terminal and recorded by a computer.

When the stock of any item starts to run out, new supplies are automatically ordered just-in-time from the company's regional distribution centre by **electronic data interchange (EDI)** between computers. The new stock is then delivered to the branch.

Use of data

This recorded data is used in many other ways. It allows head office managers to find out precisely how many goods are being sold every minute of the day in all of its branches throughout the country. The data is also transmitted direct to market research firms who are then able to produce national sales statistics for each item purchased.

Retail sales have been boosted by credit cards, which give instant credit up to an agreed amount, and debit cards which automatically deduct the amount due from the shopper's bank account. The latter also provide a useful cash-back facility for shoppers.

Sales promotions

In the long term, sales can be increased only by efficient marketing, management and sales planning. In the short term, however, sales can often be boosted by **sales promotions**. Some of the most common are:

- *Loyalty cards*. Given for purchases in some supermarkets and multiples. Points provide discounts on goods, free airmiles, cinema tickets etc.
- *Free gifts*. Favourites of garages and chemists. For example, customers collect enough tokens and get a gardening tool, a wine glass, etc; or buy two bars of soap and get another one free.
- *Competitions*. Often used by newspapers, which offer cash or other prizes. Scratch cards have become increasingly popular.
- *Special offers*. Used by many manufacturers. They range from 3p off a bar of chocolate to £50 trade-in on your old cooker.

CHECKPOINTS

❶ What is the main
  a) advantage and
  b) disadvantage of sales promotions?

❷ Give two examples from your own observation of point-of-sale material.

❸ Describe three examples of any sales promotions you have seen yourself.

- *Better-value offers*. Widely used. For example, manufacturers produce bigger bars of chocolate for the same price or improved quality detergent.
- *Special-purchase offers*. Widely used. For example, a customer buys six packets of an item and can send for a cookery book at a reduced price.
- *PR promotions*. Occasionally used. For each product a customer buys the firm will donate money to a charity.

Sales promotions sometimes produce enormous increases in sales, but these are often temporary. Once the promotion ends, consumers switch to other brands.

Point-of-sale material

Point-of-sale material may also help to increase sales. Examples of this include:
- posters.
- show cards.
- display stands and cases.
- dump bins (wire or plastic containers filled with one brand of goods).
- wire racks (like those at checkouts full of chocolate for impulse buyers).
- illuminated displays.
- pavement models (such as a fisherman outside a fish shop).

There are many examples. Businesses use anything, in other words, which will attract consumers' attention to the goods or the firm.

KEY TERMS

Electronic data interchange (EDI) A means of transmitting orders and invoices and other information between computers.

Electronic point of sale system (EPOS) A system of recording sales automatically by scanning the bar code on goods.

Multiple retailers A chain of shops or stores owned by one firm.

Point-of-sale material Physical objects designed to draw consumers' attention to a product or a firm.

Sales promotions Schemes which offer customers a special bargain in the hope of increasing sales.

Marketing in small businesses

Fruit aficionados put the squeeze on coffee

This could be the start of genuinely healthy competition to international chains of coffee bars. A rival group of juice bars is hoping to threaten the supremacy of the custom-made latte or triple espresso.

Leading the juice revolution are Crussh Juice Bars, the owners of which announced this week that they had bought their nearest competitor, Fresh N Smooth, based in Canary Wharf, East London. Crussh plans to open 30 branches across Britain by the end of next year.

Crussh began in October 1998 as a café in the City that sold fresh juice and food. The founders, James Learmond, a former property developer, and Christoph Brooke, a former restaurant manager, have three other Crussh bars, all based in Central London, with another due to open shortly.

Mr Learmond, 33, said: 'People who think that this will be a fad are wrong. Sooner or later they are going to have to

try it. Anyway, how long ago was it that coffee was just something you made in your office? No one dreamt that coffee bars would be so popular.'

The most popular of 15 cocktails is Love Juice, a gentle potion of peach, strawberry, orange and banana. All juices are pressed in front of the customers at the counter.

Source: adapted from *The Times, 19* February 2000

Shell *LiveWIRE* Young Entrepreneur of the Year 2000 and winner of £10,000

Jenine Parkynn, 26, set up her company, Fender Sturrock, in Peebles in November 1998. The promotions and marketing company provides blue chip clients with skilled staff for publicity campaigns at clubs, pubs and trade shows across the UK. It also provides marketing ideas for product launches and promotions and has nationwide sales teams to carry out field marketing activities for major banking institutes.

Fender Sturrock now employs 225 full time staff across Britain. The projected turnover this year is just over £10 million.

Source: adapted from Shell LiveWire Finalists website

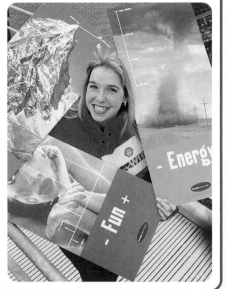

More closures and fewer start-ups

In the first quarter of 2000, 108,000 businesses closed in England and Wales, an increase of nine per cent on the first quarter of 1999. There were 111,200 start-ups during the same period.

Alastair Camp, managing director, Barclays Small Business Banking, said: 'Business closures are part of the natural ebb and flow of commercial life. Mergers, takeovers, retirement and re-entry into paid employment result in a fairly constant level of closure activity.'

Source: adapted from Barclays New Release website, 20 June 2000

Study points

1. How many businesses closed in England and Wales in the first three months of 2000?
2. State two reasons why businesses close.
3. In your view, why did James Learmond and Jenine Parkynn succeed in business?
4. Where might James and Christoph obtain money to finance their expansion?
5. What should they state in their business plan when they try to borrow the money?

Online links

www.the-times.co.uk
www.newsroom.barclays.co.uk
www.shell-livewire.org

The four Ps and principles of marketing are just as important for small firms and the self-employed as they are for big corporations. As the case study shows, over 100,000 businesses closed in three months, sometimes for justifiable reasons, but often through the failure to make out a proper business and marketing plan.

All sole proprietors need to do a SWOT analysis before the business is launched (see Unit 42) and at regular intervals after that. The analysis may help the owners to find a market niche which they can exploit.

Although small firms cannot compete with big firms in many ways, they do have certain natural advantages. They:
- are far more flexible
- have far closer contact with customers
- have lower overheads
- can afford to be more adventurous as they have less to lose.

The internet has also helped to create a more level playing field for small businesses, as it provides an opportunity to contact new customers all over the world at little cost.

Market research

Small firms can never hope to spend a fraction of the vast amounts that big firms spend on, say, elaborate market research reports, but much research can be carried out quite cheaply in other ways. Trade fairs can provide a large amount of information about market trends and new developments. Trade magazines are full of up-to-date information. Chambers of Commerce can provide information about local markets and business trends. Mintel, and other organizations, publish excellent market reports on all types of business.

Some field research can also be carried out. Friends and possible customers can be questioned about the idea. A short, simple questionnaire could be used. For example, a person who is thinking of making toddlers' clothes or toys could ask playgroup parents to fill in a questionnaire.

Product

As you have seen in Unit 39, the product is all-important. The self-employed have some advantages. For example, it is much easier for a small manufacturer to make a product to a customer's design. A small insurance broker can take the time to find an insurance policy to match a customer's exact needs. Small grocery shops can sell specialized goods that supermarkets do not stock. The self-employed can also compete on quality. For example, a local tailor could use better cloth for suits than multiple stores.

Small businesses can also compete on customer care. Corner grocery shops can provide ethnic, high-quality or organic foods that supermarkets do not stock. They should also be able to give their customers better advice on what goods to buy. A small business can also provide better after-sales service. For example, a local specialist will often repair a computer more quickly, and more cheaply, than a large firm.

Price and promotion

Many small businesses, particularly manufacturers, fail through charging prices which are either much too high or much too low. A very high price is uncompetitive, so the product will not sell. A very low price may not cover costs, so the business will fail. Small businesses must find the right price for a product's position in its life cycle (see Unit 43).

Small businesses usually do better in promotion than in pricing. The best form of promotion in a local or an industrial market is word-of-mouth recommendation, especially as it's free! Leaflets, commercial directories and the Yellow Pages in particular are all important in promoting a business. Small firms in industrial markets can use the trade press to advertise their business; other small firms can use local newspapers. Firms sometimes neglect the chance of getting free publicity by sending news items about themselves to the newspapers and magazines in which they advertise. Another useful form of public relations is sponsoring local sporting or artistic events, or helping community projects.

Place

Small businesses have great advantages in distributing their products as they can offer a more personal service. Big firms usually contract delivery of their goods to specialist firms who can often give only a general idea of when the delivery will be made. Small firms, which distribute their own goods, can deliver at a time to suit the customer. Some small traders, such as newsagents, milkmen and greengrocers, provide a doorstep service.

Many self-employed people save the expense of renting a shop or office by providing a mail-order service from home or by teleworking for bigger organizations. Manufacturers can sell their goods direct to customers at fairs and exhibitions. If they produce small amounts of goods, they can sell direct to retailers (for example craft workers, such as potters, often sell their products to selected shops and department stores).

Excellent advice

The self-employed no longer lack advice on how to start and run their businesses successfully. All the high street banks produce free material, giving excellent detailed advice to people who want to start their own business. As the case study shows, there can be big rewards, but the risks are equally great!

CHECKPOINTS

1. What are the three main advantages of being small in business?
2. Describe the market research a small business should carry out.
3. State four kinds of promotion small firms can use.
4. What advantages do small businesses have in distribution?
5. What are the main dangers in pricing and how can they be overcome?

Key skills
IT and communication

You have decided to go ahead and start your own business. Key in a report on a computer showing how you would apply the four Ps to make it a success. Include an image in your report, such as a logo.

1 Describe the main
   a) advantages and
   b) disadvantages for customers of three different kinds of retail outlet.

2 How do niche markets benefit small firms?

3 What is the difference between sales promotions and point-of-sale material? Give two examples of each.

4 Describe how a small firm of your own choice could carry out its market research.

Extended questions

1 Explain the advantages that a small firm can have over a large firm in
   a) distribution and
   b) product.

   What effects would these benefits have on the firm's marketing strategy?

Case study 1

Online retailers fail to deliver on service

British retailers that are online such as Virgin, Harrods and lastminute.com have been criticised for falling below customer service standards, while a new report suggests the gap is growing wider between companies' online expectations and reality.

Eighty per cent of online retailers did not have clear policies on returns, terms and conditions or even physical addresses and phone numbers where they could be contacted by consumers, according to a study by Trust-On-Line, which offers an accreditation service for internet shops.

A list of sites run by such companies as Sainsbury's, Tesco, Iceland and Interflora all failed on various criteria that would be required of a normal shop. Said Dermont Hill, the managing director of Trust-on-Line, 'Customers need to know where to return items if there is a problem.'

At the same time, the services group CMG has found that France now leads the UK in the proportion of business done online. It reports that the number of companies doing more than one per cent of their sales over the internet has fallen by 30 per cent since last June.

However, other analysts said that the findings needed careful interpretation and that while the proportion of companies doing a certain amount of business had fallen, the number involved is growing rapidly.

'The big retailers are only doing an average of 0.3 per cent of their sales online,' said Mike Godliman at Verdict Research. 'What we've found is that while CDs, books and computer software have taken off, we aren't seeing any appreciable sales online of things like electrical goods, furniture or DIY goods.

'We're predicting that by 2005, three per cent of all retail sales will happen online, which is a tenfold increase on today. But, of course, that's only three per cent.

'People get excited because it's the internet – but other areas are growing too.'

Source: adapted from *The Independent*, 23 May 2000

1 What percentage of online retailers do not have clear policies on returns, terms and conditions, and physical addresses and phone numbers?

2 Explain, in your own words, what is meant by the three phrases a) returns b) terms and conditions c) physical addresses and phone numbers.

3 Why do you think the number of companies doing more than one per cent of their sales on the internet has fallen by 30 per cent?

4 In your view, why do CDs, books and computer software sell better than other products?

5 Apart from the internet, which other retail areas do you think are growing?

Case study 2

Abbey's coffee bar an instant hit

1 What is Abbey National's core product?

2 Explain which of the 4 Ps is involved in its new initiative.

3 Why do you think Abbey National decided to introduce the coffee bar?

4 Why do you think the idea has proved so popular?

5 Suggest two other businesses where such a facility could expand a firm's business.

Carol Haste, manager of Abbey National in High Barnet, thought she had seen everything in her 22 years of service, but when the bank suggested renovating the branch and installing a Costas coffee bar, she laughed.

Today, ten days after its grand opening, Miss Haste is thrilled with Abbey's 'bold innovative move'. The branch in north London has already registered 100 new customers for its internet bank and is luring customers from other banks along the high street with its bright new image.

The High Barnet branch is light and airy, with signs in user-friendly and lower-case lettering, and 'meeters and greeters' to direct people.

A Costas coffee bar is on the right-hand side, surrounded by comfy sofas and a collection of books. Customers enjoying a quiet latte will not be disturbed by staff unless they ask to be.

The left-hand wall is filled with cash machines, and internet and digital TV screens, which children on holiday were showing their grannies how to use yesterday. Dorothy Lancaster, a customer for 40 years, said, 'I like anything different. I can't believe what they have done: I thought they would just install some coffee machines.'

Of course, not everybody is happy. There may be more branch staff but some customers are convinced there are fewer service points, while others miss the rope barrier to indicate where to queue.

Source: adapted from *Daily Telegraph*, 2 August 2000

Case study 3

Tesco and Asda top of the shops

House of Fraser, Littlewoods and Allied Carpets have emerged as the least loved retailers in Britain while food chains Tesco and Asda are firm favourites among investors and shoppers alike, according to a new survey.

Retail Intelligence, the retail analyst, found that City investors admire Tesco and Asda for their financial performance, strategic vision and quality of senior management.

The report, published today, adds that the stores groups are also shoppers' favourites because of their low-pricing policies, store layouts and geographic spread.

Allied Carpets is ranked last of the 27 retailers involved for its poor performance on all fronts. The company has been taken over by French rival Tapis Saint Maclou.

Storehouse, joint twenty-fifth with House of Fraser, has ceased to exist since its sale of the Bhs chain and a change of name to Mothercare. Marks & Spencer, which has suffered a worse press than most, is ranked twentieth.

Source: adapted from *The Times*, 26 June 2000

Online links
www.cbi.org

1 How many retailers were included in the survey?

2 What features do consumers appreciate in Tesco and Asda?

3 Why do you think they are popular with investors?

4 How would you define 'strategic vision'?

5 From your own experience, describe the three most important elements in a store's popularity.

6 Discuss three facilities large superstores can offer which are impossible for their smaller competitors to provide.

7 In what ways do you think that supermarkets enhance or detract from the quality of life? Give reasons.

EXAM PRACTICE

Foundation

A new out-of-town shopping centre has opened on the outskirts of a city in the North West. The proprietor of a small high street boutique, who opened her business five years ago specialising in teenage fashions, employs one full-time member of staff and two part-time. Faced with competition from the new shopping centre, she considers whether to a) run the business alone b) change her clientele and sell only more expensive, designer clothes c) specialise in only a few types of clothing such as lingerie or swimwear.

1 How long has the boutique been open? (1 mark)

2 Why is it difficult for the owner to compete with the stores in the shopping centre? (4 marks)

3 Which of her solutions would you choose? Give your reasons. (8 marks)

Higher

A new out-of-town shopping centre has opened on the outskirts of a city in the North West. The proprietor of a small high street boutique, who opened her business five years ago specialising in late-teenage and twenties fashions, employs one full-time member of staff and two part-time.

Her main business objectives have been to acquire a loyal clientele and to sell the kinds of products which interest her, while making a reasonable profit. But faced with competition from the new shopping centre, she realises she will need to take definite steps to survive.

She considers whether to a) expand the business by forming a partnership with two other people with business experience b) change her clientele and sell only more expensive, designer clothes c) specialise in only a few types of clothing such as lingerie or swimwear d) take out a bank loan to revamp the shop e) concentrate only on increasing sales by reducing prices and going down-market.

1 What has been the owner's measure of success in the past? (3 marks)

2 Which of her possible solutions involves product development? Explain your answer. (4 marks)

3 Discuss the benefits and problems which may arise from each course of action. (10 marks)

4 What do you think accounts for the popularity of out-of-town shopping malls and shopping centres? (4 marks)

Section 6

Production strategies

Producing goods

1: Ainsworth Finishing Company

Founded in the early 1800s, Ainsworth Mill has seen many changes. Through accurate market analysis and investment in both plant and staff, it maintains its position as Europe's largest commission bleaching and dyeing factory. It is situated between Bolton and Bury, providing easy access to the motorway network.

Recent capital investment involved the addition of a beam dyeing department enabling Ainsworth to offer a full range of dyed shades, literally from black to white. Lighter shades may be continuously processed.

As part of the company commitment to quality, inspection ensures goods leaving Ainsworth conform to our customers' and our own very high standards. Before breakdown into smaller customer specified roll lengths, the quality may be certified by our modern chemical and physical testing laboratory. Goods may be tested to virtually any BSI (British Standards Institution) standard.

Sampling is performed at every stage of production to ensure traceability and prompt identification of any faults that may appear.

Source: Ainsworth Finishing Company website

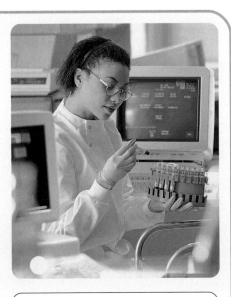

Study points

① When was Ainsworth Mill founded?

② Why is it useful to be near the motorway network?

③ How are the goods tested for quality during production?

④ What would be the likely effects if the firm's quality control system continually failed?

Online links

www.ainfinco.co.uk

How do manufacturers decide what goods to produce? There are a number of reasons:
- the research and development department may have come up with a new idea (see Unit 49)
- as the Express Dairies case study shows, a way may have been found of adding value (see Unit 5)
- an existing product may need redesigning
- a rival firm's product may have been copied, or cloned.

Essential features

The first stage in designing a product is to write a design brief stating the essential features of the new product. A more detailed specification will then be written, covering all of the following features.
- *Function*. Describes exactly what the product does.
- *Composition*. A detailed description of the materials to be used.
- *Design*. A product must be pleasing to look at and touch. It should also be easy to pack, transport and store.
- *Ease of use*. This is important for consumers and equally important in industrial markets, as employees would need less training to use the product.
- *Reliability*. Unreliable products increase costs, because of the constant need for replacement, and also harm the firm's reputation.
- *Easy maintenance*. Parts should be easy to replace.
- *Safety*. Products must match all current British and European Union laws, and must not harm the environment.
- *Cost*. The price must compete with rival products.

Once the specification has been agreed, a prototype, or first model, can be made and tested.

The production manager

The production manager decides how goods should be produced. The main tasks are to:
- see that production flows smoothly through efficient planning and control
- maintain, or improve, the quality of the products
- ensure that goods are produced on time by working out a production schedule
- keep costs within the **production budget.**

2: Express Dairies

During the summer of 1999, Express Dairies nationally launched a children's fresh milkshake, Shakey Jake, a whole milk drink of special appeal to children under eight. The product is being made at our creamery in Frome, Somerset, following its successful test market in the Granada television region. Additional processing capacity has been installed to meet demand.

Source: Express Dairies, Annual Report

Online links

www.express-dairies.co.uk

Study points

① What is Shakey Jake's target market?

② Why was a television region chosen for the test market?

CHECKPOINTS

❶ Name three firms which, in your opinion, produce high-quality goods. Give reasons for your choice.

❷ How can research and development help a production manager?

❸ What are the main functions of a production manager?

❹ Which in your view is more important a) the market or b) production? Explain the reasons for your answer.

To ensure that production flows smoothly, the production manager has to make the best use of physical and material resources. Production must be planned so that materials and components have to be moved for the shortest possible distances; this means finding the best layout of machinery. In this way, work will be speeded up and costs reduced. **Work study** may help the production manager to use the labour more efficiently. Workers are observed to find out how they do a job and how long each action takes. The detailed results are then studied closely to find out if there is a more efficient and quicker way of doing the task.

Quality control

Efficient **quality control** is important in all forms of production as it has become one of the main ways of satisfying customers.

In the past, quality control consisted mainly of carrying out inspections of individual products or samples from the assembly line. The Japanese were the first to use statistical process control. In this system, the machine operator checks that his or her machine is working correctly two or three times every shift.

Now, under new quality management systems, samples of the products, and the machines making them, are both checked at regular intervals throughout the working day. As Ainsworth Finishing Company case study shows, laboratories are also used to check that products are up to standard.

Quality circles are also used to improve production methods (see Unit 21). These small groups of workers, who discuss their way of working and how it might be improved, exist not only on the shopfloor, but usually in all other departments, too. In a big company, there may be as many as 100 separate quality circles.

Getting the timing right

However high the quality of the goods may be, they will never succeed if they are not produced at the right time to meet the demands that the sales department expect. The production schedule must be worked out to ensure that raw materials, components and labour are all available when needed and that equipment is all working at the right time (see Unit 52). Efficient progress control, making sure work flows smoothly through all stages, helps avoid delays in production.

Keeping costs down

A production manager must keep costs down so that the production budget is not exceeded. To help do this, he or she might use several methods: work study, improved machinery layout, new working methods, simplification of parts, reduction in power costs or buying in components from other manufacturers instead of making them. Other departments in the firm may also help the production manager to keep costs down. The research and development section (see Unit 49) may suggest improvements in production methods, while the **purchasing manager** can help by buying cheaper raw materials.

KEY TERMS

Production budget The total costs of production, including raw materials, labour and overheads.

Purchasing manager The manager who is responsible for buying all the raw materials and finished goods that a firm needs.

Quality control Inspecting samples of goods to see that they are up to a firm's usual standard.

Work study A method of measuring how long a job should take and how it should be performed.

Research and development

1: Robot cleaner hopes to sweep the market

Pushing a vacuum cleaner around will soon be as old-fashioned as washing clothes by hand, according to James Dyson, the domestic appliance entrepreneur. Today he launches his robot cleaner, which navigates its way around rooms. He is aiming at worldwide sales of £2 billion a year by 2005.

The cleaner goes on sale early next year retailing at about £2,500. Mr Dyson, chairman and owner of Dyson Domestic Appliances, hopes the device will repeat the success of the company's bagless vacuum cleaner launched in 1993, which now has half the UK market. The robot system has been developed by Dyson's team of 400 designers and engineers in a £5 million top-secret project.

'My hope is that every household will want one before too long,' said Mr Dyson. 'It could mean that the conventional vacuum cleaner goes the same way as the washing tub and mangle.'

The 9kg device contains three computers and 50 sensors that work out its position in relation to furniture,

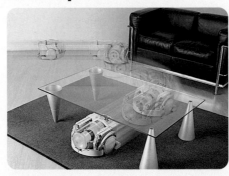

fittings, children and pets. Its electronic 'intelligence' enables it to steer around a room in the most logical way, using a similar suction device to Dyson's conventional bagless cleaners. The system uses rechargeable batteries, similar to those used in camcorders, and has enough energy for about half an hour under normal circumstances. New electronic techniques pioneered by Dyson's engineers mean the system can be recharged in about 40 minutes.

Mr Dyson believes that in the first year the company should sell 100,000 of the systems round the world, building up to one million a year after about five years. Although he hopes the price of

the machine will eventually come down, it is unlikely to be sold for less than £2,000. However, this should not put people off once they work out the opportunities for saving on drudgery, he reckons.

Source: adapted from Dyson.com – News website

Study points

① How much does the new cleaner weigh?

② What was the cost of the project?

③ How many engineers and designers were involved in the research and development?

④ Which consumers would you advise Dyson to target for his new cleaner?

Online links

www.dyson.co.uk
www.ft.com

Research and development (R & D) is a lengthy, expensive and risky process. It involves finding a suitable idea, investigating it, testing it to see if it is practical and, finally, developing the finished product. A large team of scientists, technicians and engineers may have to work on the project over many years.

As the Dyson case study above shows, 400 people were involved in researching and then developing the Dyson robot cleaner. The Dyson R & D team included new ideas developers, design engineers, laser scientists, specialists in fluid mechanics, acoustic engineers, thermo- and aero-dynamicists, polymer engineers, mechanical research engineers and people with vision.

Expensive

R & D is very expensive. Britain spends 1.8 per cent of its gross domestic product on all forms of R & D – some £14.7 billion. Most of this, or £12.5 billion, was spent on civilian R & D, with £2.2 billion on military projects. Many rival countries spend considerably more. About £9.6 billion was spent on industrial research. Business contributed over 70 per cent; the rest came from the government, charities and foreign companies. The biggest spenders were in the pharmaceuticals, aerospace, electronics, chemicals and car industries.

Risky

R & D remains a risky business. Years of research may lead nowhere and the costs of development are high as well. It is

estimated that about 30 per cent of new products fail in the laboratory and another 60 per cent during development. Some may even fail later as consumers may not like them or the market may have changed.

If R & D is so chancy, why do firms bother to do it at all? Some of them don't. In industries such as footwear or furniture, where the products do not change much from year to year, most firms rely on their trade associations or outside bodies for R & D. However, in high-tech industries, such as computers, the pace of change is more rapid. Samples of new products are quickly taken apart and copied by rivals, who produce their own, even better product. High-tech industries are forced to spend more on R & D to keep up with the competition.

2: Rolls-Royce: advanced engines for civil aircraft

Rolls-Royce is a world-leading producer of aero engines. With a range that extends from helicopter engines to the massive 104,000lb thrust of the Trent turbofan, Rolls-Royce is well placed to provide the power for the civil aircraft market.

Rolls-Royce market outlook, 1998–2017: aircraft demand

- 16,900 aircraft will be delivered between 1998 and 2017.
- Value of these aircraft deliveries will be $1,300 billion.
- 43,500 new engines (installed and spare) will be required for these aircraft.
- Value of these engine deliveries will be $280 billion.
- Passenger travel will grow on average 5.1% each year over next 20 years.
- Air cargo traffic will grow at an average of 6.5% each year.

Source: adapted from Rolls-Royce Civil Aerospace website

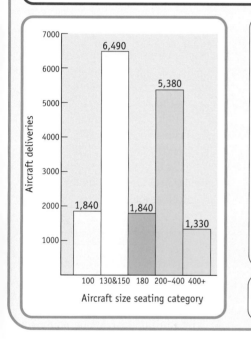

Study points

1. According to Rolls-Royce, how many aircraft will be sold between 1998 and 2017?
2. What percentage will seat more than 400 people?
3. How could Rolls-Royce use these forecasts to plan its research and development?
4. In your view, what developments might make these long-term forecasts inaccurate?

Online link
www.rolls-royce.com

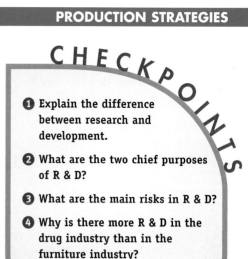

CHECKPOINTS

1. Explain the difference between research and development.
2. What are the two chief purposes of R & D?
3. What are the main risks in R & D?
4. Why is there more R & D in the drug industry than in the furniture industry?

An R & D department has a big part to play in improving and finding new uses for products, finding uses for by-products or secondary items produced as a result of a manufacturing process, and cutting costs by creating new processes.

In the food industry, biotechnologists can provide more flavours in foods by developing potato crisps with different tastes, e.g. prawn cocktail.

Tomato purée, made from genetically modified tomatoes, appeared in British shops in 1996. The tomatoes have modified genes which delay rotting. Because the tomatoes can be left on the plant for a longer time, it is claimed that they have a fuller flavour. Since then, other GM foods and crops have been introduced into Britain. However, public resistance has been so great that many supermarkets have banned GM foods from their shelves.

New products

The development of new products involves the biggest risks. Before work starts, the idea will go through some form of **product evaluation**, usually in a team including marketing, financial and forecasting experts. Work will start if funds are available and approval is given. The basic idea is developed by making a prototype, or model, and possibly samples, before starting full-scale production. Much work is now done by computers (see Unit 51).

While a new product is being developed, decisions are constantly being made about its future. Some products, such as robots or aircraft engines, may take as long as 10 years to develop. A manufacturer of an aircraft engine, therefore, has to forecast what the world will be like then. What will the general economic situation be? How much will fuel cost? How much competition will there be between airlines? These trends are far more difficult to predict. However as the Rolls-Royce case study shows, these predictions have to be made. It is this need to make long-term predictions that makes R&D so risky.

KEY TERMS

Product evaluation Judging whether a new product or process will be practical, marketable and within a company's budget.

Research and development (R & D) Scientific research into present and future products, and materials and production processes, which is then followed by their practical application and development. Development usually takes longer, and costs more, than the research.

Methods of production

The way in which goods are produced depends to a large extent on what they are. An aeroplane, for example, has to be made in a very different way from a car.

For a start, an aeroplane is much bigger and has many more parts. It is made by craftsmen working together as a team. They start with materials, tools and the bare assembly department, which must be big enough to contain the finished product. Gradually, after months of work, they create an aircraft by their individual skills and the aid of outside firms, such as those who make the engines.

Job production

Many goods made in this way, by **job production**, are one-off orders, which may, or may not, be repeated. As each job is different from the last, it presents a great challenge to the workers and provides them with greater satisfaction. Some items, such as ships and railway locomotives, are still produced in this way, but new technologies are gradually taking over (see Unit 51).

The main advantages of job production are that it:
● produces high-quality products
● is extremely flexible
● yields great job satisfaction.

A small bakery

Aluminium manufacturing plant

Car factory

Aircraft plant

Study points

(Read the key terms before you do the study points.)

① Why can't an aircraft be made in the same way as a car?

② Use the definitions in the key terms to suggest which method of production is being used in each of the pictures above.

③ State one other product which might be produced in each of the four different ways.

④ Draw plans showing how a factory might be laid out for two of the methods of production.

⑤ How might each of these four methods affect workers' attitudes towards their jobs?

The main disadvantages are:
- the high labour costs
- few economies of scale
- delays between orders.

Batch production

Most manufactured goods are now produced by either **batch production** or **flow production**. A small bakery is a good example of batch production. The baker mixes the dough – usually in a machine, not by hand – and lets it rise. He or she puts the dough in tins and bakes a batch of loaves in the oven. Chefs in high-class restaurants are another example. Each specializes in one item – meat, sauces, puddings, etc. Their combined efforts produce the complete meal.

Batch production of manufactured goods involves workers who specialize in one job – welding, drilling or painting. The factory is divided into sections so that all the workers of one skill work together. The product passes through each section until it is finished. This is known as layout by process.

The method is most suitable for short to medium production runs, when the number of goods being produced is not very many, and for smaller firms making a variety of parts for bigger manufacturers. It is a flexible system as work can be easily switched from one machine to another. Production is not greatly affected if one machine breaks down. On the other hand, it is costly as materials, parts and subassemblies, or partly finished goods, have to be moved frequently from one section to another.

The main advantages of batch production are that:
- it is more flexible

- wages are lower, as workers are less skilled
- it is cheaper, as there are some economies of scale.

The main disadvantages are that:
- it is difficult to plan production
- time is lost in waiting for new batches
- unfinished goods incur storage costs.

Flow production

In flow production, or mass production, products move continuously by conveyor belt from one group of workers to another group. Each does one job until the whole product is complete. With small items, the assembly work is done by a group of employees working together in a manufacturing cell. This is called layout by product. Standardized parts, made in other factories, are used. The assembly lines – and the speed at which they move – play an important part in the lives of all employees.

Mass consumption goods, or goods bought by many consumers, such as cameras, television sets or cars – are all made by flow production. The main advantage is low costs per unit through economies of scale. Goods are produced more quickly and cheaply because specialized equipment can be used and there are no delays or large material handling costs in moving from one stage of production to the next. Line workers need little training as their work is semiskilled.

On the other hand, the capital cost of setting up lines of production is enormous and a breakdown of one machine can stop the whole line. Many operatives become bored with the repetitive work, which can lead to a high labour turnover or industrial action.

CHECKPOINTS

❶ Which method of production would be used for making: paint, tractors, turbines, handmade shoes, cigarettes and greenhouses?

❷ What is another name for flow production?

❸ Give two examples of when it is used.

❹ What benefits do manufacturers gain by changing to flow production?

The main advantages of flow production are that:
- it provides great economies of scale
- wages are lower
- production is continuous.

The main disadvantages are that:
- capital costs are high
- it is less flexible
- workers are less motivated.

Process production

Process production is a more advanced form of flow production. It is used in the oil, chemical, aluminium and similar industries. The whole process is controlled automatically by computers and only a few workers are needed to supervise it.

The main advantages of process production are that:
- labour costs are low
- work goes on 24-hours a day
- it is easy to control.

The main disadvantages are that:
- capital costs are high
- there is a long wait before plant comes on-stream
- small faults can shut whole plant.

Increasingly, batch production is now also carried out in both process and flow plants. Computers and robots can be reprogrammed to make different versions of a product without halting production. Different working methods have also helped to reduce workers' lack of motivation (see Unit 51).

KEY TERMS

Batch production Producing a large or small quantity of the same item. The process is repeated when there is another order.

Flow production The continuous production of a large quantity of items on a production line, where each worker does the same job time after time as the goods flow past on a conveyor belt or moving platform.

Job production Making a single item, usually according to a customer's specification or detailed description of measurements, design, etc.

Process production The continuous production of large quantities of materials, such as plastics, which undergo a change in physical or chemical form.

New technologies

Robots and robotics

Autotech Robotics are experts in the field of robots and robotic manufacturing systems. We offer a wide range of automated, turn-key manufacturing systems, both new and used. Our systems are suited to a wide variety of industrial applications such as welding, gluing, sealing, routing, drilling and machine-loading.

Existing customers include companies supplying the agricultural, automotive, computer, construction, copier, defence, furniture, health care, horticultural and leisure industries.

Autotech Robotics offer a large variety of robot systems to cater for wide-ranging customer requirements. Standard packages can be configured to suit, or special robot systems can be supplied. A large number of different jobs can be undertaken in the same production run and jobs can be changed without stopping the robot from working. This makes them suitable for a wide variety of work in small batch sizes, or just-in-time production.

Matching the right robot to the right system is essential to obtain optimum performance. Because we are not locked into providing robots from one source we can provide the right robot to suit the requirements of the job. We can supply most makes of industrial robot.

A Fanuc robot, with a 16kg payload, which can be used for arc welding, cutting, handling, deburring, assembling, sealing, cleaning, spraying and glueing

Source: Autotech Robotics website

Study points

1. State three tasks which robots can perform.
2. Why can robots be used for batch production as well as flow production?
3. What is a turn-key system?
4. How do you think robots might be used in a furniture factory?

Online links

www.autotech-robotics.com

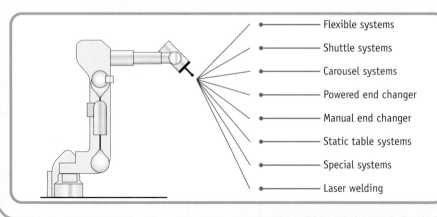

- Flexible systems
- Shuttle systems
- Carousel systems
- Powered end changer
- Manual end changer
- Static table systems
- Special systems
- Laser welding

Robots

Robots, and the computers which control them, have revolutionized the production of many goods. As the case study shows, robots are used in a great variety of industries from agriculture to leisure, but most people associate them with the car industry.

Car manufacturers were the first to use robots on any large scale when they started using them for welding and spray-painting car bodies almost 50 years ago.

Robots have developed greatly since then. 'Sighted' robots, which can recognize components and parts by their shape, are used to load car components into computer-controlled apparatus which machines, or finishes, them. Robots and driverless trucks transport components to teams of workers on the assembly line.

Robots have many advantages. They are cheaper, faster and more efficient than human labour. They can work 24 hours a day. They can also be used in dangerous or unhealthy environments, for example, inside nuclear processing plants.

However, the capital cost of setting up a robotics plant is great. And like all **automation**, it results in a loss of semi-skilled jobs.

Computer-assisted design

Computers are now used in all stages of production from the initial design of products, through their construction or manufacture, and the management of the whole process, to their final delivery.

The invention of small microchips 30 years ago made it possible to produce much smaller, more powerful, computers at much lower costs.

Computer-assisted design (CAD) has completely changed the way in which products are designed. Instead of making expensive models of a bridge, the whole project is designed on a computer screen.

It is possible to simulate what the effects of different loads and wind forces might be. A woman's dress can be designed in the same way. Its shape, composition and colour can be instantly altered or modified onscreen.

Computer-aided manufacturing

Computer-aided manufacturing (CAM) enables the product to be made direct from

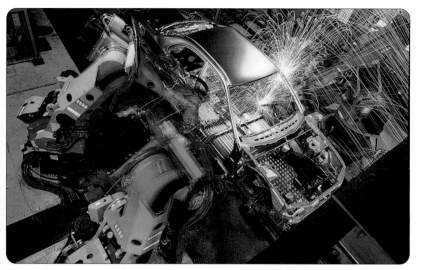

Robots hard at work in a car factory

CHECKPOINTS

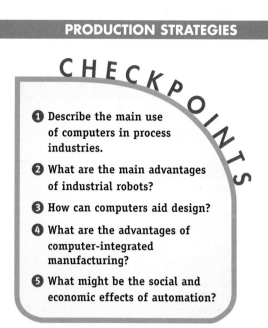

❶ Describe the main use of computers in process industries.

❷ What are the main advantages of industrial robots?

❸ How can computers aid design?

❹ What are the advantages of computer-integrated manufacturing?

❺ What might be the social and economic effects of automation?

the display on the computer screen. For example, a chair could be designed on a computer screen.

The instructions to make it could then be passed to a computer-controlled machine which cuts out the wooden chair frames, to another machine which cuts out the foam rubber for the cushion, and to another machine which cuts the material for the cushion covers. The chairs would then only have to be assembled.

This production method is now used in many industries. For example, in the process industries, such as paint manufacturing, computers control the whole production process including temperature, mixture and rate of flow. As computers can now be reprogrammed so easily, it is possible to produce very small batches of only 25 litres without halting production.

Computer-integrated manufacturing

Computer-integrated manufacturing (CIM) is a combination of all of these methods. Computers are used extensively from the initial design of the product and its components, or parts, through all the different stages of production, including quality control, to the delivery of the finished goods using a computer-controlled system of distribution.

New flexible manufacturing systems (FMS) makes it easier and quicker to produce different versions of the same product, as computer-controlled machines can be reset without stopping production. This **mass customization** is becoming much more common in many industries, including the car industry.

Dealers' orders for a car of a particular model, colour and engine size with any number of optional extras, is fed into a

central computer. This sends instructions to satellite computers at individual workstations on the assembly line.

The machines used in manufacturing are reprogrammed, or given new orders, while they are still operating, to produce the cars required. Furniture factories use a similar process. Chairs are produced in different styles and with different wood veneers.

Just-in-time systems

A constant supply of components needs to be delivered to the factory **just-in-time** if these computer-controlled systems are to work efficiently.

When a production team's supply of parts reaches a critical point, an electronic order is sent to the central computer which automatically orders more parts from the supplier. The parts are delivered to the factory just-in-time.

This system reduces the space needed for storing huge supplies of parts and reduces costs as the firm does not have to hold large quantities of stock.

Computers also manage the whole production process. They control:
- component orders, so that the right quantities are delivered at the right time
- production schedules, so that the work flows smoothly
- quality, so that high-standard goods are produced
- distribution, so that retailers never run out of stocks.

KEY TERMS

Automation A general term used to describe the automatic production of goods by machines using a minimal labour force to supervise production.

Computer-aided manufacturing (CAM) Using computers to control and perform some manufacturing processes.

Computer-assisted design (CAD) A method of design which allows the effects of changes to be seen immediately on a visual display screen.

Computer-integrated manufacturing The latest method of production, in which design, manufacturing and management are all linked electronically and aided, or controlled, by computers.

Just-in-time system Delivering components just before they are required by workers on the assembly line.

Mass customization Using computer-controlled machines to produce different varieties of the same product without stopping production.

Latest production methods

As the case study shows, **total quality management (TQM) systems** involve every person in the firm, both managers and workers alike, in all departments, in providing products of continuously improving quality. The system reaches out to the firm's suppliers, its customers, the environment and society as a whole. It is all-inclusive.

The ten key points in TQM systems are as follows.

1 Customers must always come first, but the firm's suppliers are important too.
2 There should be an unbroken quality chain linking customers, the business and suppliers.
3 Work relationships must be more flexible, with emphasis on sharing, not authority.
4 Relationships should be more people-centred.
5 Status should come from how well a person does his or her job, not from rank in the hierarchy. There should be single-status as much as possible.
6 There should be less emphasis on separate departments, and more on the relationships between teams in the whole firm.
7 There should be greater emphasis on training, not only for employees but also for suppliers' employees.

Dutton Engineering (Woodside) Ltd

Dutton Engineering was founded in 1972 in Luton, in Bedfordshire, and moved to its present purpose-built factory and offices in Sandy in 1980.

Dutton is one of the few companies in the United Kingdom operating annualized hours, where employees are contracted to work a given number of hours over a 12-month period rather than a specific number of hours per week.

Hours of work can be varied from week to week to match employees' hours closer to customer requirements. Employees receive equal instalments of pay throughout the year regardless of the number of hours worked, providing a stable income.

All employees are tasked to build quality into the product: the company has no internal inspectors or goods inwards inspectors.

No job descriptions are issued to employees as this is too restricting for free-thinking people.

One of the cornerstones for a total quality management philosophy is continuous improvement. Dutton has a number of years experience of

developing the **kaizen** approach to continuous improvement. This is seen as further development of the **empowerment** of all personnel.

All employees are able to contact the company's customers direct, if they have any queries regarding the work they are performing.

Where they are partnering with customers on the launch of new products, Dutton operators assist on the customers' production lines, helping with the assembly of the pre-production run.

Dutton has established partnerships with its suppliers since 1991. Goods and services are delivered to the factory on a just-in-time basis.

With annual hours, continuous improvement, team working and partnership sourcing well established, the company is enjoying considerable success in the market place. To continue to improve its performance, the company is using the British Business Excellence Model (see Unit 21).

Dutton won the prestigious Wedgwood Trophy for its pursuit of excellence in 1994. It was recruited into the Inside UK Enterprise scheme as a host company in 1992.

Source: Dutton Engineering website

Inside UK Enterprise

Inside UK Enterprise (IUKE) is a highly successful initiative set up by the Department of Trade & Industry. The aim is to increase the productivity and profitability of UK companies. IUKE recruits companies that have a track record of business excellence. These companies host a series of scheduled visits, at which they share and exchange their expertise with visitor groups – up to 15 each time.

Source: Inside UK Enterprise website

Study points

1 When was Dutton Engineering started?
2 What kind of work does it do?
3 Why doesn't the firm gives its employees job descriptions?
4 What are the main advantages of annualized hours for a) the firm and b) the employees?
5 In your view, how do Dutton's employees benefit compared with other factory workers?

Online links

www.dutton-eng.co.uk
www.iuke.co.uk

Cell manufacturing of fluorescent fittings

8 There should be as much emphasis on personal flexibility as on specialized skills.
9 All employees should be involved in a continual search for improvement and quality.
10 The firm should never lose sight of the main purpose of its core business, which is its customers.

Lean production

One essential part of any TQM system is **lean production**. Lean production is efficient and there is less waste of time, money and human resources. It needs a much higher grade of workforce.

The Japanese were the first to introduce lean production into their car plants in Britain. The main features are as follows.

● Computer integrated engineering (CIE) controls the whole of the production process. Work is carried out by reference to a series of linked computer databases.

KEY TERMS

Empowerment Giving workers power to make some decisions formerly made by supervisors and managers.
Kaizan A system, which started in Japan, involving continual improvement in all aspects of work.
Lean production Using far fewer inputs to make goods than in mass production methods – less human labour, less stock, less space and fewer hours.
Total quality management (TQM) system A system which seeks to build improving quality into all aspects of a business.

● The work is done by multi-functional teams of assembly workers with team leaders who are in charge of the work, performance and training. Members of the team continuously check the quality of the production and reset machines on the spot, which means that there are fewer faults in the goods.
● The use of computer databases streamlines management which makes it possible to get rid of many middle managers.
● Just-in-time stock control systems are used. The workforce sometimes has no more than two hours' amount of stock by the line.
● More parts are bought in and suppliers are integrated into the whole production process.

Effects

Lean production has brought about a great change in the use of the four factors of production. Land is used more economically, as just-in-time systems need much less space for storing stock and warehousing. Labour is reduced, though the workers who remain must be more highly skilled. Capital investment in these highly automated plants has increased greatly. Enterprise is also increased, not only on the shop floor where workers have to cope with many more problems themselves, but also among managers who have to set up and run these complex systems.

As a result, there has been a great change in manufacturing costs. Not long ago, the costs of labour, overheads and purchased goods and services were all about equal. Now, labour is only about 10 per cent, overheads about 20 per cent, and

purchased goods and services about 70 per cent of the total costs in the many modern factories.

Benefits

Lean production has produced great benefits for firms. There have been dramatic reductions in costs as less stock is held and there is less need to rework and repair products at the end of the manufacturing process. As a result, productivity has doubled in some factories. The quality of goods has greatly improved, with far fewer defects.

However, lean production needs a very high investment of capital. A few years ago, Heinz invested £40 million in its new pasta making factory with 150 employees at Harlesden in London.

CHECKPOINTS

1 What is the most important factor in maintaining a TQM system?
2 What is the main aim of the Inside UK Enterprise scheme and how is it achieved?
3 Give one example of your own of how an employee might be empowered.
4 Explain how lean production has affected the use of the four factors of production.

Key skills
Communication and IT

You have been on a visit to Dutton Engineering. Use a word processor to write a report for the chief executive of your company showing how the introduction of a quality management system could improve profits. Use charts showing predicted increases in profits and productivity and any other quantities to illustrate the report.

Revision and exam practice units 48–52

REVIEW POINTS

1 What are the main tasks of a production manager?

2 Describe two methods of quality control.

3 a) Explain what is meant by process production

   b) Give two examples of goods which might be produced in this way.

4 Describe the main purposes of research and development.

5 What types of job might be done by an industrial robot? Give examples in each case.

Extended questions

1 a) Describe what is meant by research and development.

   b) Explain why firms need to spend money on research and development.

   c) Why has research and development become increasingly important in the manufacturing industry?

2 Mr Kiyoshi Sakashita, corporate director of the Japanese electronics firm Sharp, has said: 'We should not let technology become a barrier between humans and their human nature.'

   a) What do you think is meant by this statement?

   b) How do you think that technology comes between humans and their human nature? Give examples.

   c) How might research and development have an effect on this?

Best Factory Awards: Britax Wingard

Manufacturing excellence and the car component industry often go together.

Customers rarely come tougher than Rover, Nissan and Toyota: the penalties for failing to deliver just in time to their assembly tracks are harsh; the expected quality standards are exceptionally tight and the pressure on costs is immense.

This year's winner of the engineering category – and our Factory of the Year – is an extraordinarily accomplished example of manufacturing excellence.

As manufacturing director Howard Emery explains, in 1992 the factory underwent a Nissan benchmarking study and found that it had no single operation that scored higher than 50 per cent of the car manufacturer's assessment of world-class performance.

Equally sobering were the three weeks that Emery and managing director Laurie West spent at the Toyota University in Japan, learning how to put things right.

The assembly operation, for example, is constructed entirely around tightly knit cells, each slickly engineered to be as efficient and error-free as possible and each fed with components by replenishment personnel shuttling between the cells and the equally slick just-in-time component stores.

Many cells operate on the *heijunka* principle, where manufacture is aimed at tightly defined 15-minute slots on the assembly lines – and where a system of differently coloured bar-coded ping-pong balls is used to denote which kind of mirror the cell must build next: left-hand; right-hand; heated; electrically operated and so on.

'We never make anything that hasn't already been sold,' explains West. Each cell's employees produce a specific product for a specific vehicle, with employees' working patterns and holidays tied to the shift pattern of the destination car plant.

'People don't go home until the heijunka board is clear,' says Emery.

Even so, a small catch-up team comes in every night: if there have been no problems that day, the team will produce after-market spares – but if problems have been experienced, they are an invaluable emergency resource.

One of the prime strengths of the plant, however, is the extent to which it has driven manufacturing excellence backwards down the production processes; it's the whole factory that is slick, not just the assembly operation.

Source: adapted from Best Factory Awards : Management Today website

1 What is the name of the company producing the car parts?

2 Who are its customers?

3 Explain the methods of production used.

4 Describe in your own words the responsibilities of each employee and how their work is organised.

Online links

www.bestpractice.haynet.com

Case study 2

The meter monitor

It could be the end of the road for gas meter readers. On trial now is an automatic system which could put them out of a job.

If the huge pilot scheme involving 100,000 homes in London and the North West proves a success, it will soon be extended nationwide. And there will be no further need for estimated readings, which often lead to overcharging and upset customers.

Every home's meter will have a tiny radio transmitter attached. These will beam readings into a network of small relay boxes which will then transmit them to British Gas.

The information they send out into the mobile phone system and on to the gas company's billing department will be updated every 30 minutes.

Mike Alexander, managing director of British Gas Trading said, 'The way people live is changing rapidly. That means it is less likely that you will be at home when the meter reader calls.'

Andrew Hind, spokesman for BCN, its American-owned partner in the venture, said, 'We are hoping this will be the beginning of the world's largest network. British Gas has 14 million gas customers and more than 2.6 million electricity customers. These little units are very unobtrusive. We will be using the existing mobile phone network and we will not be adding to the number of masts.'

Bob Sheldon of the UK Automatic Meter Reading Association said, 'Similar systems already exist for large commercial customers. The benefits for consumers in terms of convenience and accurate billing are huge.'

Source: *Daily Mail*, 1 July 2000

1. Meter in house fitted with tiny transmitter beaming out updated reading every 30 minutes

Meter reading No. 1 High Road 8050.6

2. Signals picked up by relay box fixed to telegraph pole - each box covers around 200 houses

3. Data then transmitted to existing mobile phone mast and relayed to control centre where it is decoded

4. Details sent by digital landline to billing centre and accurate, up-to-date bill sent out

British Gas

Mr M Wyatt
1 High Road
Newtown

GROUP WORK

You are working in a research team in the Royal Mint, which has been asked to help design a new British currency. You have been asked to investigate what people think of the present coinage and to obtain suggestions for improving it.

Divide into groups. Each of you should interview individually one of the following:

- an old person
- a blind person
- a shopkeeper
- a bank worker
- a foreigner
- a very young person.

When you have found out their views, come together as a group again to discuss your findings. Put the results into a database. Write a short report between you, giving your suggestions for changing the coinage and giving reasons for your decisions. Each member of the group should then either design on a computer, draw or make a model of one of the new coins.

1 How many customers does British Gas have currently?

2 State two benefits for the consumer of the new system.

3 In your view, what are two possible disadvantages?

4 Discuss which employees are likely a) to lose b) to gain from the change.

5 What effect does such a development have on the general economic situation in a country?

Case study 3

The Cobra 2000: from only £750 on the road

Built in the UK by hand, each frame is personally inspected by the designer to ensure a high-quality product. The frame is made from high tensile aluminium which produces a very strong and light bicycle.

The seat is made from canvas and being a natural fabric, is extremely comfortable – no more saddle soreness or back aches. It is also removable, so if you are not riding the Cobra 2000, you can take it off to stop it getting wet when it rains.

Because we are a small company and prefer to build relationships with our customers, we can supply the Cobra 2000 with the fixtures and fittings that meet your individual needs and your pocket.

Although the Cobra 2000 has a basic components specification, we are more than happy to fit any specific components you require and will only charge you where the new component exceeds the cost of the replaced one.

All this makes the Cobra 2000 the ideal recumbent for touring, fitness, commuting or just idling away the afternoon round the country lanes.

Ultimate Bikes is a small company based in Berkshire, UK dedicated to designing and building high-quality recumbent bicycles.

Because we are so small, our prices are highly competitive and because we are small, we can offer you unprecedented service.

We can build the Cobra 2000 to your individual needs and provide you with the best after-sales service.

Source: adapted from The Ultimate Recumbent Cycle

1 **What method of production is used by Ultimate Bikes?**

2 **Describe the factors which make it this kind of production.**

3 **What services does the company offer which are not possible for its larger competitors?**

4 **In your opinion, what niche market is Ultimate Bikes catering for?**

Online links
www2.ultimatebikes.com

Donovan's International is a major national company specializing in the design and construction of bridges. In the past, it built expensive models on which to base calculations about specifications such as size, dimensions and weight. Its research was based on conventional means: research papers, telephone enquiries and letters. Today, the company's research laboratories and construction divisions are fully automated. It uses CAD and CAM to carry out its research and manufacturing. It also uses the internet for many different purposes. All its suppliers use computer integrated manufacturing facilities.

Donovan's has just won a contract to build a very long bridge in south-east Asia.

Foundation

1 Explain in your own words what is meant by CAD and CAM.   (4 marks)

2 Describe the uses Donovan's could make of the internet to find suppliers of building materials and long-life paints.   (4 marks)

Higher

1 Describe the uses Donovan's could make of the internet to find suppliers of building materials and long-life paints.   (4 marks)

2 Explain how CAD will enable the company to construct a design for the bridge.   (4 marks)

3 Suggest a) two problems the company may experience in dealing with remote clients in remote parts of the world b) how they can be overcome.

(4 marks)

Section 7

Human resources

Why work?

CASE STUDY

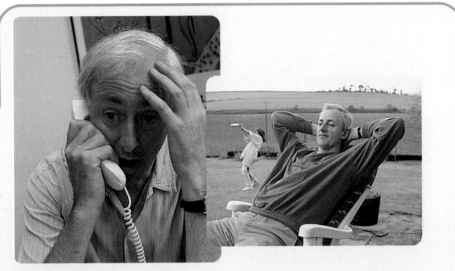

Work-life balance

In a rapidly changing working environment, PricewaterhouseCoopers is fully aware that to produce a contented employee, an effective balance needs to be struck between time spent forging a successful career and time spent enjoying home and personal life.

It's called 'work-life balance', and as if to emphasise our desire to get it right for you, we're actively supporting the National Work-Life Forum, a government-backed initiative, to examine this issue within the business and wider community.

Whether it's a case of reducing hours to enable a working mum to spend more time with young children, or extending leave to allow a would-be David Attenborough to fulfil a lifetime conservation ambition, we're open to suggestion.

We're also aware of the two-way spin-offs of giving up our time to help others. That's why we run an active community affairs programme, utilising the talents of our people in everything from inner city schools to start-up businesses.

Source: PricewaterhouseCoopers website

PricewaterhouseCoopers

Our vision is to be a great place to work – somewhere where talented people want to come and stay.

Corporate profile

18,500 employees in the UK – professional services sector – largest professional services firm in the UK – 55th largest employer in the world.

Key initiatives

Flexible working – job sharing – home-working – enhanced maternity leave – paternity leave – career breaks – sabbaticals – child care support (childcare vouchers – for 12 months after return from maternity leave, employee receives additional 20 per cent of salary in vouchers) – flexible benefits (option to purchase additional holiday and childcare vouchers) – employee support and counselling.

Workforce profile

48 per cent female, 52 per cent male.

Source: adapted from Work-life Balance website

Online links

www.employersforwork-lifebalance.org.uk
www.pwcglobal.com

Money

One of the main reasons for working is to obtain money to satisfy physical needs (see Figure 1). Basically, people work to get enough money to satisfy their primary needs for food, water, shelter, clothes and warmth (see Unit 1). Even when those needs have been met, money still remains a strong motivation, as it buys the luxuries that most people cannot afford – a country mansion, a Rolls-Royce, a diamond necklace.

Affiliation

Money is rarely the only motivation. People want more out of work than that. Some people, but not all, would prefer to do any kind of job rather than sit idly at home. The sense of **affiliation**, of having friends of belonging to a group, is a strong motivation for all kinds of working people. Businesses can use this personal need to motivate the work force by:

- providing company uniforms or overalls
- organizing company entertainments and sports events
- providing free company trips for employees – and sometimes their wives or husbands too

Study points

1. How many people does the accounting firm PricewaterhouseCoopers employ in the United Kingdom?

2. How many of them are women?

3. Which of the firm's work-life balance initiatives would be particularly useful for men?

4. In your view, how would a firm benefit by introducing work-life balance policies?

- producing a company newsletter or magazine
- forming working groups in the factory, so that the members feel part of a team.

Security

A sense of **security** is another basic human need for most people. Until recently, many businesses in both the private and the public sectors provided jobs for life. That kind of security has gone.

The greatest security most people can now obtain is having a job while a million other people do not. Even so, businesses can still increase their employees' sense of security to a certain extent by:
- providing good pension schemes
- providing sick-pay schemes and private healthcare, such as BUPA, for workers
- giving priority to promoting company employees when job vacancies occur
- making sure that the work force knows of any changes in company policy or working conditions.

Self-importance

Another strong motivation for some people is a sense of **self-importance**. Everyone likes to feel important, but these people want to feel much more important than others. Money in the form of large salaries or big expense accounts is one way in which this need can be met (see Unit 57) and another is by offering fringe benefits, such as company cars ranging up to Rolls-Royces and other luxury extras. Businesses exploit this need in many other ways by:
- giving people glorified job titles (e.g. 'police officer' instead of 'policeman' or 'policewoman'; 'rodent operative' instead of 'rat catcher')
- providing status symbols, such as personal assistants or secretaries, thicker carpets, bigger desks, etc.

Figure 1: Abraham Maslow's hierarchy of needs

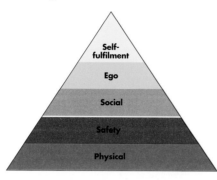

Abraham Maslow (1908–1970), an American psychologist, thought people were motivated by a hierarchy of needs. Physical needs – food, warmth, shelter – had to be satisfied first. Then, safety needs – home, a sense of security, followed by social needs – being part of a group. Ego needs came next – success, being praised – and, finally, self-fulfilment – a sense of achievement.

- arranging first-class travel on planes and trains
- organizing weekend events at stately homes or providing seats in the company box at a theatre.

For some people, this motivation is so strong that they can become almost entirely dependent on company approval. To gain more and more approval they become workaholics, unable to stop themselves working and perhaps putting in 16 hours or more a day.

Job satisfaction

Job satisfaction – a feeling that your work is worthwhile, that you are doing something you really want to do, and that you are using all your skills and creativity – is one of the strongest motivations at work, but not everyone obtains it. It provides a great sense of self-fulfilment – the peak of Abraham Maslow's hierarchy of needs (see Figure 1).

Businesses are becoming increasingly aware of the need to provide some form of job satisfaction for all their employees. For that reason, they have tried to provide manual workers with more interesting and demanding jobs. The are three main job improvement methods.
- *Job rotation.* Workers do one job for a time and are then transferred to another job. For example, a supermarket worker might stack shelves and then help to pack customer's bags at the check-out.
- *Job enlargement.* Workers do more tasks at the same level. For example, a secretary might work for two managers, instead of one.
- *Job enrichment.* Workers perform additional, more demanding, tasks. For example, a railway station porter might be put in charge of a small station, issuing tickets, answering the telephone, etc.

As the case study shows, the best employers now realise that there must also be a satisfactory balance between work and life if employees are to feel contented and fulfilled.

CHECKPOINTS

1. Define job satisfaction. Give two examples of people who obtain it.
2. Explain how a sense of self-importance can motivate people at work.
3. Give one example of job rotation, job enlargement and job enrichment.
4. What do members of your family and other people you know obtain from work apart from money?

KEY TERMS

Affiliation A sense of belonging to a group or an organization.
Job satisfaction Obtaining pleasure from doing work that is satisfying for its own sake.
Security Freedom from worry and fear; knowing that your job and salary are safe.
Self-importance An exaggerated view of one's own worth.

Changes in employment

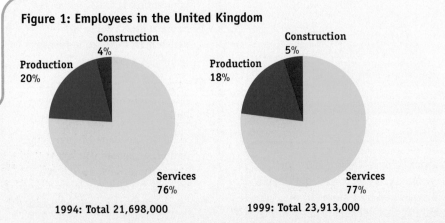

Figure 1: Employees in the United Kingdom

Construction 4%
Production 20%
Services 76%
1994: Total 21,698,000

Construction 5%
Production 18%
Services 77%
1999: Total 23,913,000

Source: based on *Annual Abstract of Statistics 2000*, Office for National Statistics

Job satisfaction

Most UK workers are remarkably satisfied with their jobs (particularly so if they are a 55-year-old woman in a small company) according to new research by Professor Andrew Oswald and Mr Jonathan Gardner of the Economics Department at the University of Warwick.

The researchers have been examining job satisfaction in Britain and other nations. The authors have followed 7,000 randomly selected Britons – tracking and interviewing them in each of the years of the 1990s. Some of the authors' findings are particularly surprising.
The representative British person with extremely low job satisfaction is:
Male, aged in his late 30s, good university degree, low income, works more than 50 hours a week in a private sector job in a large company, commutes for an hour in each direction, lives in the South East.
The representative British person with very high job satisfaction is:
Female, with only O levels, high income, 55 years old, working 30 hours a week, self-employed, or in a public sector job or small firm. Lives close to the workplace, probably in the South West or North.

The authors also show that: firms with incentive pay seem to offer higher job satisfaction, job satisfaction in the public sector fell throughout the 1990s, and that teachers have unusually low job satisfaction.

Overall the message from the economists' work is encouraging. Contrary to some opinion, most workers in the UK appear to be remarkably satisfied with their jobs.

Source: University of Warwick News website

Study points

① **What percentage of employees work in the services sector?**

② **By what percentage did the total number of employees increase in the five years?**

③ **Why do you think that the man in the case study has low job satisfaction?**

④ **In your view, why do many self-employed people obtain great job satisfaction?**

Online links

www.csv.warwick.ac.uk

In recent years, there have been dramatic changes in employment which have affected practically all members of the **working population.**

The old traditional 'smokestack' industries of coalmining, steel-making and shipbuilding have declined, making hundreds of thousands of miners, steelworkers and shipyard workers **redundant.**

New technologies, such as CAD and CIM (see Unit 51) have reduced the number of people employed in **capital intensive** industries, such as vehicle manufacturing. Automation has also caused some office workers to lose their jobs.

There has been a continuing increase in the **labour intensive** services sector which now employs over three-quarters of the working population, as the case study shows.

Global competition

Increasing foreign competition has brought about many other changes. Big companies have been forced to cut their costs so that they can be more competitive. They did this in a number of ways, including:

● **downsizing**, or dismissing employees, which increases profits and productivity as the same amount of work is done by a smaller number of employees

● **outsourcing** the work of whole sections or departments, such as publicity, to outside firms which could do the work more cheaply because of lower overheads and economies of scale

● creating flatter, more efficient, organizational structures which cut the number of middle managers (see Unit 21)

● reducing the size of the company by selling off unprofitable businesses.

To save even more money, many big companies have replaced permanent, full-time jobs with part-time or temporary jobs. They retain a core of key workers with special skills. These employees have full-time jobs with reasonable salaries and chances of promotion.

However, there is much less sense of loyalty between firms and employees than in the past. Employers are ready to dismiss any employee if they need to cut costs. Employees, too, are usually ready to resign if they are head-hunted by a rival firm which offers a better salary or share options.

Flexible workforce

As a result of all these changes, the old idea of a nine to five job with the same firm for the whole of a person's working life has almost disappeared. Instead, there is a **flexible workforce** which works only when the organization wants it to do so.

There is a great range of flexible working arrangements.

- *Short-term contracts*. Employees are given a short-term contract for a year or 18 months instead of a permanent job.
- *Part-time work*. There has been a huge rise in part-time jobs of all kinds, ranging from unskilled office cleaners to highly skilled computer consultants. They have increased four and a half times, to over six million, in the last ten years.
- *Temporary work*. At one time, temporary workers were used mainly to cover for permanent employees who were ill or on holiday. That has changed. In some big companies, up to ten per cent of the work force are temporary workers. This cuts a company's costs, as 'temps' are employed only if there is a special job to be done.

- *Annual hours*. Some firms now employ people for a set number of hours in a year, e.g. 1,976 hours a year instead of 38 hours a week (see Unit 52). They are usually paid a regular monthly wage, with no overtime. This benefits employers whose output peaks at certain times of the year. They can arrange for employees to work three or four long shifts a week followed by a long week-end. Or if the firm is busier in the summer than the winter, employees can work longer hours in summer and shorter hours in winter.

Although these working patterns were introduced for the organizations' benefit, they are useful for some employees, too. Short-term contracts are useful for skilled professionals who want to move from job to job and, often, from country to country. They also suit students who want to obtain some money in their gap year before they go on to university. Part-time work is profitable for mothers of young children and for school and college students. Temporary work is useful for a whole range of people, including students, people returning to work and others who have just retired but want to add to their pension. Annual hours benefit manual workers, as they get regular monthly pay, longer breaks at home and, often, longer holidays.

Flexible hours of work

Some progressive employers look after their employees by offering **flexible hours** of work which fit in with their own way of

CHECKPOINTS

❶ What has caused many employees to be made redundant?

❷ Describe flexible working in your own words.

❸ How do flexible hours benefit employees?

life (see case study in Unit 53). These are some of the main forms of flexible hours.

- *Flexitime*. Employees work every day for an agreed number of hours – core time – but can then do the rest of the work when they choose. This is useful for people who like irregular hours, or who have another job.
- *Term-time working*. Employees work full-time during the term, but have unpaid leave in the school holidays. Useful for mothers with young children.
- *Four-day week*. Employees do five days' work in four days and have an extra day off. Useful for employees with outside interests who like working hard.
- *Teleworking*. Working part of the week at home, using computers to maintain contact with the company. Useful for people who want to spend more time at home.
- *Job sharing*. Two people share the same job and split the salary between them. Useful for mothers with young children, or a couple who are able to live on one salary.
- *Career breaks*. Usually unpaid. Useful for employees who 'want to do their own thing' for a time, or study for a higher qualification, or look after young children or an elderly relative.

Self-employment

Another result of downsizing and redundancy has been a growth in self-employment. Many people started to work for themselves in the 1980s, using their redundancy money to set up their own small businesses. Self-employment reached a peak of more than 3,572,000 million in 1990 and has remained at more than three million ever since.

KEY TERMS

Capital intensive Automated industries which use very expensive machines instead of human beings to do the work, as in process production.

Downsizing Dismissing employees to cut costs.

Flexible hours Allowing employees to choose hours of work which will fit in with the demands of their personal life.

Flexible workforce Employees who do not have permanent full-time jobs but work only when the business needs their labour.

Labour intensive Production which relies more on labour than on capital as in most of the services sector.

Outsourcing Employing outside firms to do specialized work.

Redundant Employees are made redundant if their job is no longer needed. This occurs when a business, or part of it, is closed. If they have worked for the firm for two years, they are given financial compensation.

Working population The total number of people available for employment, including employees, the self-employed and the unemployed.

Women in business

Managing perfectly

Women make the best managers, a workplace survey has found. And it seems their male colleagues are only too ready to agree.

Researchers found that male managers regarded their female counterparts as better with customers and more understanding of their colleagues. They were also seen as more trustworthy, efficient and generous, the survey of 1,000 managers found.

The communication-based management style commonly adopted by women was better suited to the team approach favoured by most modern offices. They were also likely to work hard on establishing positive relationships with staff.

Additional research showed that women scored better than men in 38 out of 47 management attributes.

Sheilah Coules, who chairs the social and employment issues group of the National Council of Women of Great Britain, said women's homemaking skills helped them excel at the office.

'Women have always been good at running the home as well as keeping a job which makes them good at juggling things and dealing with people,' she said.

'They are generally less competitive and just want to get the job done. Also they are much better at working as a team, rather than individually, which brings a certain balance to the workplace.'

Sheilah Coules

The survey results were published in Management Today. Most managers displayed 'gender blindness' when it came to who they preferred to work with. They did not express any particular desire to work with managers of the same sex. Of the men surveyed, only 17 per cent said they would rather work for a male boss. Of this group, many were over 40.

Many of the women managers surveyed listed their male colleague's dominant characteristics as insensitivity and, more positively, decisiveness. Men were generally regarded as not being open-minded enough or considerate.

Source: adapted from the *Daily Mail*, 14 March 2000

Some improvements

In the last few years, there have been some real improvements in women's position in the workplace.

According to the latest analysis of the UK's 3.18 million directors by Experian, the global information solutions company, just over one-third are women. More women than ever before are directors of their own companies. Forty-four per cent of all female directors work in the new, booming service sectors of banking, finance, insurance and leasing.

London has the largest proportion of female directors, with nearly 36 per cent. However, the further north you go, the fewer females directors are found, particularly in regions still dominated by traditional industries. Women also figure more prominently in small businesses, with an annual turnover of less than £5 million, which employ 95 per cent of all female directors. In larger companies, with a turnover of £5 million or more a year, women are just one in ten of the average boardroom, the report says.

There has been some improvement in the number of women managers. Ten years or so ago, only about nine per cent of managers were women. That has now doubled to 18 per cent.

Study points

① **How many managers were surveyed?**

② **According to male managers, what were the main characteristics of women managers?**

③ **What did women managers think were male managers' main characteristics?**

④ **Do you think these opinions are true of men and women managers?**

⑤ **In your view, what effects could a male manager who did not believe in a team approach have on an office?**

Childcare

There has also been some improvement in childcare facilities. The government has introduced a national childcare strategy with a budget of £300 million in England to develop new out-of-school childcare. This will result in many new pre-school and out-of-school clubs, providing many new learning opportunities. Under the government's New Deal programme, 50,000 new childcare workers, including men, will be trained.

The Working Families Tax Credit scheme, which tops up the earnings of low-paid working families, provides some help with childcare. Families with one child can get up to £70 a week and those with two or more children, £105 a week.

Some companies, particularly those with work-life balance policies, have provided more flexible hours of work, including term-time working and job sharing, which are of great assistance to working mothers (see Unit 54). Some also provide their own childcare schemes, like PricewaterhouseCoopers, the accountants, who provide childcare vouchers, equivalent to 20 per cent of their salary, for 12 months after women return from maternity leave (see Unit 53). Other companies now provide nurseries of their own, some of which are run by Kid Unlimited.

Opportunity Now

Opportunity Now, a campaigning organization, recognises that much has been done for women's equality in management and professional jobs, but much still remains to be done in clerical, administrative and sales jobs and in skilled and unskilled manual work, where the vast majority of women are employed. It points out that attitudes and workplace practices still divide 'men's work' and 'women's work'; and that women still receive lower pay than men.

Opportunity Now is chaired by Clara Freeman, Director of UK Stores and Group Personnel at Marks & Spencer. The membership is made up of 350 private, public and education sector employers.

In member organizations, about 35 per cent of managers are women, almost double the national average. Over three-quarters of members offer flexible working options. Over 80 per cent provide extended maternity leave; 19 per cent offer childcare vouchers or nursery places and nearly a quarter have a worked-based crèche.

The organization identifies a number of focus areas of concern. These include:
- the information technology sector where the proportion of women has fallen from 25 per cent to under 19 per cent in ten years

- the construction industry, which has only eight per cent of female employees, but has an estimated 5,000 unfilled training places in colleges
- ethnic minority women who hold more qualifications than their white counterparts, but are severely under-represented in management positions.

Valuing Women

The Equal Opportunities Commission was set up by Parliament in 1976 to end sex discrimination and promote equal opportunities for women and men. Its top priority for the next three years will be its campaign Valuing Women. This aims to persuade the public and employers to get rid of the pay gap between men and women.

The commission points out that women are paid only 80 per cent of men's hourly earnings and that Britain is tenth in the equal pay league of 15 European countries surveyed.

Kids Unlimited

Kids Unlimited is the UK's leading childcare and pre-school education provider. We currently operate 32 nurseries (private and workplace) and two after-school facilities nationally. Our aim is to provide the highest possible standards of nursery facilities and customer service. In 1993–4, we were awarded the first National Training Award to be gained by a childcare company.

Kids Unlimited was founded in 1983 by husband and wife team Jean and Stewart Pickering, who set up their first private nursery in Wilmslow, Cheshire. It now provides a complete range of childcare services for companies. This ranges from advising them on how to assess the

demand for childcare among employees, to providing the most appropriate solution within a given budget.

The business plans to open a further 20 nurseries over the next five years, including nurseries at Cambridge Science Park and Oxford Business Park.

Source: adapted from Kids Unlimited website

Wages

Worst-off shoppers in Europe

British consumers have up to 40 per cent less spending power than those in America and Europe, according to a new study. Even though income taxes and social security contributions are far higher on the Continent, workers are paid more and charged less for most goods and services.

According to the survey, carried out by the William M Mercer consultancy, Britons are 37 per cent poorer than the Dutch, 22 per cent worse off than the French and 15 per cent poorer than the Americans. Even the Spanish, whose net income is far lower, have 23 per cent more disposable income, because the cost of living is dramatically cheaper.

The 'spending power squeeze' is so acute that more than a third of Britons cannot afford a holiday and 26 per cent are living below the poverty line.

The survey, commissioned by *The Sunday Times*, follows national outrage over the soaring cost of petrol. A gallon of unleaded petrol now costs nearly £4 – far dearer than

in Europe and America. More than 80 per cent of the cost is taken up by tax.

Kim Howells, the consumer affairs minister, agreed that British consumers had cause for anger. 'The findings underpin the sense of dissatisfaction felt by many British people about their low disposable income,' he said. 'It is a matter for serious consideration.'

The survey showed that the average German worker is paid £29,921 before tax, and £18,550 after tax. In contrast, the average British worker is paid £21,116 before tax, and £15,819 after. The cost of living in Germany is about 34 per cent cheaper than in this country. These factors taken together mean British spending power is more than 40 per cent lower.

Furthermore, British people work the longest hours in the European Union. The average week is 44 hours, compared with 40 in France and Germany and 38 hours in Italy.

Source: adapted from *The Sunday Times* News website, 9 July 2000

How workers get paid

Most **manual workers** receive **wages** calculated on an hourly basis, e.g. £7.50 an hour. Non-manual, white-collar workers receive **salaries**, calculated for the whole year, e.g. £15,000 per annum.

Although there are still big differences between wages and salaries and the ways in which they are paid, there have been some major changes in the last few years.

There is a national minimum wage, which is currently £3.70 an hour for workers over 22, and £3.20 an hour for workers between 18 and 21 years of age and all new employees on approved training courses.

Although some manual workers are still paid in cash, since the 1986 Wages Act employers have the right to pay all new manual workers by cheque.

Wages used to be lower than salaries, but many manual workers now earn more than office workers.

Unions used to be concerned mainly with negotiating wages. They now also negotiate salaries for many white-collar workers e.g. bank workers or clerical staff.

A few firms have tried to get rid of the

Study points

1. According to the survey, how many Britons are living below the poverty line?
2. On average, how much less is the annual, post-tax pay of a British worker than that of a German worker?
3. What percentage does a) the average German worker and b) the average British worker pay in tax?
4. What might be the main effects on British workers if we had a German-style wage, tax and price structure?

Online links
www.the-times.co.uk

Figure 1: An employee's salary slip

GROSS PAY		DEDUCTIONS			
Scale Pay	1,537.50	Income Tax	270.68	Tax Code 178L	Tax Basics 0
		Nat. Ins	109.77	TAX WK/MTH 02	TAX REFUND HELD
		Pension	44.91	FOR TAXING ONLY	
				CUMULATIVES TO DATE	
				EARNINGS	3,075.00
				TAXABLE PAY	2,985.18
				TAX	541.12
				NIC	219.54
				PENSION	89.82
TOTAL GROSS PAY	1,537.50	Total deductions	425.36	NET PAY	1112.14

'-' after an amount indicates a DEDUCTION 'R' after an amount indicates a REFUND

CHECKPOINTS

❶ Which kinds of employee are usually paid wages?

❷ What is the difference between gross pay and net pay?

❸ Who settles the time rate in some industries?

❹ What is the main drawback of piece rates? Where might they be used as a method of payment?

❺ State three kinds of bonus scheme. What are some of the advantages and disadvantages?

❻ Why can wages of newly employed manual workers be paid by cheque?

distinctions between manual and white-collar workers by paying annual salaries to both. However, most manual workers are still paid by the hour.

National basic wage

The national basic wage, or **time rate**, is agreed once a year in some industries by the employers and unions involved (see Unit 61). The basic wage is decided mainly by the supply and demand for that kind of labour. Generally, wages will be low if a job can be done by almost anyone and high if a job requires qualifications and training. Other factors, such as work conditions or health risks, are also taken into account. The strength of the union involved, the skills of its negotiators and the personality of its leader will also have an influence on the agreed basic wage.

Extra payments

Workers can receive many extra payments on top of their basic pay. Some of these are negotiated nationally and some at the firm where they work. There are many forms of extra payment.

- *Overtime pay* for work done outside normal working hours, such as at weekends or on holidays. Payment can vary from time and a quarter to double time. Increased supervision may be needed to prevent workers deliberately slowing down in working hours so that they can do more of the better-paid overtime.
- *Shift premium payments* for working anti-social hours late at night or early in the morning. About 300,000 people now work at night.
- *Piece rate,* which pays workers a set rate for each article produced. This was popular in the past when more goods were produced individually. Some firms still use it, but it is more usual for homeworkers. One drawback is that low-quality goods may be produced, so careful inspection is required.

- *Bonuses,* which are paid for production beyond an agreed amount. A standard rate of production is fixed for each job by measuring the time taken to do it. A bonus is paid to a worker if more goods are produced in the stated time. Individual bonuses may be replaced by group or team bonuses, but this can cause resentment if there are slow-working members of the team. Company bonus schemes are based on the total output of the whole factory, but the bonus is often too small to motivate individual workers.
- *Profit-sharing schemes* set aside a proportion of a firm's profits for distribution among the work force. A reasonable percentage needs to be set aside to have any motivating effect on the workers.
- *Merit pay* for constant good performance at work. This may cause resentment among other workers who think their work is just as good.

Take-home pay

Employers must make certain deductions under **PAYE** from their employees' **gross pay**. Income tax and national insurance are statutory deductions, which must be made by law. These are shown in Figure 1. Other items, such as union fees, subscriptions or savings, are voluntary deductions. What is left after all deductions is the **net pay**, or take-home pay.

KEY TERMS

Gross pay The total amount an employee earns.

Manual workers People who do mainly physical work, like a carpenter. Sometimes called blue-collar workers.

Net pay The amount an employee receives after deductions for income tax and national insurance and any voluntary deductions have been made.

PAYE (Pay As You Earn) A system under which employers deduct income tax and national insurance from employees' pay before they receive it.

Salaries Pay for non-manual workers, which is based on an annual rate.

Time rate The basic rate for manual workers, based on an hour's work.

Wages Pay for manual workers, which is usually based on an hourly rate plus additional payments for overtime, high productivity, etc.

Salaries and fringe benefits

Fringe benefits for manual workers and managers

Business puts brakes on bosses pay

Executive pay increased by 5.7 per cent in the year to January 2000, the lowest increase in the past four years.

The main constraint on executive pay growth has been a drop in the value of bonuses, according to the National Management Salary Survey 2000, undertaken by the Institute of Management (IM) and Remuneration Economics.

This year the bonus accounted for 8.9 per cent of management pay packets, a drop from 10.5 per cent the year before. Fifty-seven per cent of managers received a bonus last year.

Mary Chapman, director general of the Institute of Management, commented: 'Managers' basic salaries have also moved much more in line with average income increases. This year has seen a significant shift towards linking bonuses to company performance. Taken together, these factors indicate that corporate UK is struggling to deliver high performance and as a result constraining the management pay packet.'

However, for directors, whose bonus is often underpinned by share price, the value of the bonus has remained steadier, at 22 per cent, reflecting the bullish performance of the stockmarket during last year. The number of directors receiving bonuses has dropped from 70 per cent to 66 per cent.

The average manager is 41 years old, earns £37,141 and has been in the organisation for 13 years. The average director is 47 years old, earns £109,192 and has also been with the organisation for 13 years.

The survey shows that the best paid managers are based in London and the South East, those with the lowest pay packets are in the West Midlands.

Region	Earnings £
Inner London	42,107
Outer London	41,070
South East	37,393
East Anglia	37,213
North West	36,622
Scotland	36,536
East Midlands	34,750
Yorkshire	34,719
South West & Wales	34,591
North	33,554
West Midlands	32,742

Source: adapted from the Institute of Management website – press release 23 May 2000

Average executive earnings

Profession	Directors* £	Managers £
Actuarial, insurance and pensions	128,941	28,986
General management and administration	111,261	40,727
Finance	109,157	43,005
Personnel	103,212	37,638
IT and management services	102,205	42,127
Marketing	99,190	40,604
Research and development	88,798	36,176
Sales	87,758	34,063
Manufacturing and production	81,911	35,765
Purchasing and contracting	78,830	38,631

*excluding chief executive officers

Study points

① What is the average annual pay of a) a director b) a manager?

② Which business sector gives the highest pay to a) managers and b) directors?

③ Why was the increase in managerial pay smaller than in the previous four years?

④ In your view, why were managers' earnings highest in inner London and lowest in the West Midlands?

⑤ Explain in your own words why directors' bonuses have not decreased as much as managers' bonuses.

⑥ The average annual wage for manual workers was £15,244. How much bigger was a) the average manager's and b) the average director's annual pay?

⑦ In your view are these differences fair and justified?

Online links
www.inst-mgt.org.uk

White-collar workers – and a few manual workers – receive salaries, which are based on an annual, not an hourly, rate of pay. Payment is made monthly by cheque or electronically into an employee's bank account.

In some of the public sector, there is still an **incremental pay scale** with a minimum and a maximum rate of pay for each kind of job. This means that an employee gets an automatic pay rise each year until the maximum salary is reached. For example, the salary range for a senior manager, or principal officer, in a local council might be: £18,726–£27,987.

These pay scales are negotiated nationally by trade unions and employers (see Unit 61). Public sector employees may also receive an annual cost-of-living increase. Independent pay review bodies recommend what the increase should be for some employees, such as teachers and health workers. The government, however, makes the final decision.

Private sector salaries

Some salaries in the private sector are also decided by national agreement between unions and management. There are national incremental pay scales for various grades of jobs, with extra cost-of-living allowances for employees in particularly expensive areas, such as London.

However, incremental pay scales have drawbacks. Employers are forced to give a pay rise each year whether an employee deserves it or not. Employees may lose motivation when they reach the top of their pay scale.

As a result, most employees in the private sector now have some form of **performance-related pay.** Increases in pay are given only for better work. Performance is often rated against a list of achievements which have been agreed between an employee and his or her line manager, or immediate boss.

Many salaried employees do not receive overtime payments, but their pay may be increased in other ways.

As the case study shows, bonuses are a common method of increasing white-collar pay. Directors, and some managers, are also often given **share options**. This allows them to buy a number of shares in their company for a stated price at any time in the future. If the price of the shares rises, they can take up their option and sell the shares at a profit.

Many companies have profit-related schemes for all employees in which part of their pay is linked to the company's profits. Others run new schemes which allow employees to buy shares in their company without paying income tax on the amount they spend.

In most firms, pay is negotiated by the individual. The salary is usually decided at the interview. Employees may be given pay rises for good work or long service; if not, they have to ask for them.

Fringe benefits

The majority of employees receive some **fringe benefits** in addition to their wages or salaries. These goods or services have one great advantage for employees: either they are not taxed at all or they are taxed at a reduced rate, according to the estimated money value of the benefit. If the employees were given a pay rise instead, they would have to pay more tax.

Most manual workers receive some fringe benefits. Many big firms provide pension and sick-pay schemes, and some also provide private health insurance. In addition, employees may receive free uniforms, discounts on shopping, free travel to work, subsidized meals, free sports facilities and day trips abroad. Fringe benefits for managers include:

- company cars, or a personal contract purchase scheme
- private healthcare
- cheap loans and mortgages
- relocation, or moving expenses
- holidays abroad
- company flats
- big expense accounts
- golden handshakes and hellos (sums of money given on leaving or joining a company)
- payment of school fees.

The higher you rise in a firm, the more fringe benefits you are likely to receive.

CHECKPOINTS

❶ What is a fringe benefit? State two which a manual worker might receive and three that a manager might get.

❷ What is the main advantage of a fringe benefit for an employee?

❸ What is an incremental pay scale? Give three examples of employees who would be paid in that way.

❹ Explain how salaries are determined in the private sector. What are the main advantages and disadvantages of each method for a firm?

❺ What extra payments do some salaried employees receive?

Key skills
Number

A director was given a share option to buy 400,000 shares at a price of 200 pence each. Three years later, the shares had risen to 350 pence. She decided to take up the option for half of the shares and sell them at the new price. Excluding dealing charges, how much would she make?

KEY TERMS

Fringe benefits Goods or services for employees which are provided in addition to wages and salaries.

Incremental pay scale A range of pay with regular increases, or increments, each year. It is used in police forces and in local authorities.

Performance-related pay A system in which pay increases are given for improvements in work.

Share options An opportunity to buy company shares at a stated price at some time in the future.

Revision and exam practice units 53–57

Case study 1

REVIEW POINTS

1 What are the two main kinds of deduction from pay? Give two examples of each.

2 Give three examples of fringe benefits.

3 What is the main purpose of performance-related pay?

4 Describe the various methods of payment for a) manual workers and b) white-collar workers.

5 Describe the main advantages and disadvantages of incremental pay scales for a) employers and b) employees.

6 Describe the main difficulties faced by working women.

Extended questions

1 A firm is trying to reduce the dividing line between manual and white-collar workers. Describe what changes it could make in relation to:
   ● hours of work
   ● fringe benefits
   ● methods of payment
   ● employee car parking
   ● eating arrangements
   ● the wearing of uniforms.

2 What would be the benefit of the change in each case for
   a) employees and
   b) the employer?

3 Describe how work helps to satisfy
   a) basic physical and social needs and
   b) the need for self-fulfilment and creativity.
   In your view, are there any alternative life styles which provide equal, or greater, satisfaction of these needs?

Case study 1

It's a man's world, man's world. Yeah, right!

Carley Childs, 26, realized her childhood dream of being a pilot for British Airways.

'My parents used to take me to air shows every summer. I can vividly remember saying, "When I grow up, I want to be a pilot".

'When I turned 18, I was still obsessed with learning to fly. I had a part-time job and used all the money I'd saved to take a course in learning to fly a light aircraft. At university, I did an aeronautical engineering degree. Then I applied to both the RAF and British Airways to become a trainee pilot.

'I was accepted into the Air Force but failed the medical because I wasn't heavy enough. Apparently, the ejector seats are designed for men so you have to be at least 9st 6lb. It turned out to be a blessing in disguise as I got accepted on to the British Airways training programme. After two years of training, I was made a First Officer.

'There are about 100 female pilots flying with BA and 19 of them are captains. The male captains never take issue with the fact they fly with women; they know we all had the same long, thorough training. It usually takes up to seven years to become a captain and promotions are based on seniority and ability.'

Source: adapted from Spirit of Superdrug June/July 2000

Carley Childs

1 How many female pilots fly with BA?

2 In what ways do you think Carley was unusual?

3 What problems might she have faced in her job?

4 What new legislation will help Carley if she has a family?

5 In your view, what effects do you think equal pay and equal opportunities for men and women will have on
   a) personal relationships
   b) the national economy?

Case study 2

Britain's best boss

An understanding and inspiring boss, committed to encouraging work-life balance and supportive of staff are just some of the tributes that make Lin Arigho the winner of the Parents at Work/Lloyds TSB Best Boss Competition.

Lin (33), managing director of Aricot Vert Design Limited, set up her design business when she was 21. Since then, she has seen Aricot Vert grow into a successful organisation, totally embracing the concept of work-life balance.

Sally Evans, head of equal opportunities at Lloyds TSB, said, 'It wasn't just the formal procedures which impressed us, but also the things which are innovative and fun. For instance, team outings are organized and an Indian head masseur also visits the office to offer hands-on stress relief!'

Aricot Design Ltd is a graphic design company. Lin launched the company in her bedroom of the family home and progressed to a two-person partnership in Farnborough. Today the company has 17 members of staff and new premises in Fleet, Hampshire.

Flexibility is part of Aricot Vert's culture and is open to all staff in the organization. Some staff work nine to five, one works 1pm – 5.30pm, and another person does mornings only. Lin believes it is a system that suits everyone.

Allowing staff to work flexibly ensures a high level of creativity in the organization, a quality it depends on.

Source: adapted from Lloyds TSB News Release, 8 May 2000

1 How many people does Lin employ?

2 How many years has the company been in existence?

3 Why does Lin think that flexibility is so important?

4 From your experience, which other organisations offer flexible working hours?

EXAM PRACTICE

Simon Murray is a married man with two young children and has worked in the retail food industry since he left university at the age of 21.

He has had four years' experience in the marketing department of a large supermarket chain, where he managed and developed one of their major own-product ranges. He then progressed to running the advertising and promotion department of a multinational food retailer in London.

At the age of 35, he now wishes to become a senior manager.

He is considering the following advertisements all of which offer positions at the same managerial level in the advertising, promotions and market research department of well-known multinational organizations. The jobs are in the London area, though one may involve relocating to Brighton, Sussex.

a) Salary: £45,000. Annual pay increase. Annual bonus as percentage of salary. Pension and sick-pay schemes. Sports facilities. Initially one-year contract. School fees.

b) Salary. £40,000 Performance-related increases. Pension and sick-pay schemes. Staff restaurant. Relocation expenses. Travel discounts.

c) Young company, established five years. Salary £25,000 based on a five-year incremental scale to £30,000. Profit-sharing scheme for managerial staff. Company pension and health-care. Company car. Travel commitments part of job. Generous expenses. Possibility of directorship for suitable candidate.

d) Salary £35,000. Share options for management. Company pension, healthcare. Cheap mortgages. School fees. Foreign holidays for employee and family. Possibility of relocation to Brighton.

Foundation

1 What kind of work is carried out in the marketing department of a large company? (4 marks)

2 What would Simon's responsibilities have been in the advertising and promotion department? (4 marks)

3 Which of the four positions advertised do you think would be most suitable for Simon? Explain your reasons. (4 marks)

Higher

1 Describe the responsibilities Simon is likely to have as a senior manager in the advertising, promotions and market research department of a multinational company. (4 marks)

2 Explain and compare the advantages and drawbacks of each of the advertisements he is considering. (8 marks)

3 Which job do you think would be most suitable for Simon? Discuss both financial and non-financial considerations. (4 marks)

Recruitment and selection

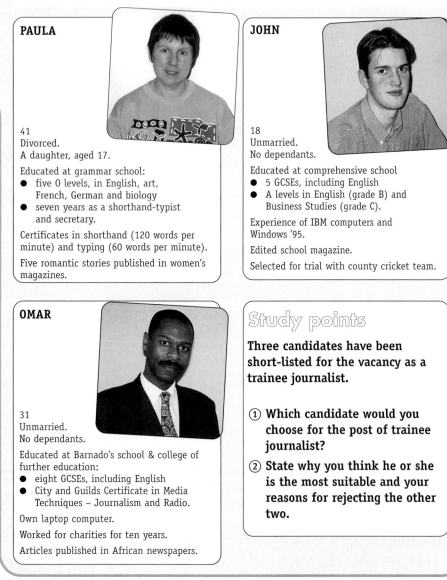

Trainee journalist

Trainee journalist wanted immediately for local weekly newspaper. The ideal candidate will have a minimum of five GCSEs or equivalent, including English, and must be able to demonstrate a good knowledge of current affairs as well as a keen interest in sport. Hands-on experience of computers is essential and an understanding of software including desk-top publishing systems would be an advantage.

If you have the ability to work on your own and as a member of a team and you are prepared to work some evenings and weekends, we would like to hear from you.

In return, we offer two-year training on the job and at a local college, leading to a nationally recognised qualification. Pay and conditions by arrangement.

Box 3342X

PAULA

41
Divorced.
A daughter, aged 17.

Educated at grammar school:
● five O levels, in English, art, French, German and biology
● seven years as a shorthand-typist and secretary.

Certificates in shorthand (120 words per minute) and typing (60 words per minute).

Five romantic stories published in women's magazines.

JOHN

18
Unmarried.
No dependants.

Educated at comprehensive school
● 5 GCSEs, including English
● A levels in English (grade B) and Business Studies (grade C).

Experience of IBM computers and Windows '95.

Edited school magazine.

Selected for trial with county cricket team.

OMAR

31
Unmarried.
No dependants.

Educated at Barnado's school & college of further education:
● eight GCSEs, including English
● City and Guilds Certificate in Media Techniques – Journalism and Radio.

Own laptop computer.

Worked for charities for ten years.

Articles published in African newspapers.

Study points

Three candidates have been short-listed for the vacancy as a trainee journalist.

① **Which candidate would you choose for the post of trainee journalist?**

② **State why you think he or she is the most suitable and your reasons for rejecting the other two.**

Most companies follow the same course of action when they want to take on new employees. First, the personnel, or human resources, department prepares a **job description** (see Figure 1). Although job descriptions vary, they usually contain the following information.

● *Job title*, such as personal assistant.
● *Responsible to*, the person in charge of the employee, such as sales manager.
● *Responsible for*, any person who answers to the new employee, such as one secretary.
● *Duties*, in other words a numbered list of jobs that the employee is required to do.

External recruitment

If new employees are to be obtained outside the organization by **external recruitment**, a number of different methods can be used to recruit them. They include:

● government Jobcentres which help firms recruit mainly manual and office workers free of charge
● private employment agencies which recruit employees of all kinds, including temporary staff, for a fee
● executive employment agencies which use internet websites and newspaper advertisements to recruit managers from all parts of the world
● advertisements in local and national newspapers, magazines, and shop windows, and the firm's own website (see the case study in Unit 59)
● school, college and university careers officers
● personal recommendation by another employee or a business contact
● letters of enquiry from jobseekers.

Selection process

If there is more than one applicant for a job, the firm has to choose which one should be employed. All applicants are usually asked to fill in a printed application form. This asks for details of age, education and training, previous jobs, health, interests and hobbies, and, usually, the reasons for applying for the job. Having information about every applicant listed in the same order makes it easier for the personnel officer to compare the candidates and choose the most suitable.

With some management jobs, candidates are asked to send a letter of application and a *curriculum vitae* (cv) giving full details of their career, instead of filling in an application form.

Interviews

When all the applications have been received, a number of people are put on a shortlist and invited to an interview. In small businesses, there may be just one interviewer, but with most jobs there are two or three, and with senior posts, sometimes many more.

The interview is the main way in which people are selected for jobs, though some big companies also use personality tests, or group tests of leadership qualities. In some jobs, candidates are tested for their skills in the job they will do.

After all the interviews have finished, the successful candidate is told that he or she has been appointed. Sometimes, as the case study shows, no candidate may be really suitable. In that case, the business has to appoint the best person available, or re-advertise the job and start all over again.

If a candidate has been chosen, a formal letter of appointment is sent soon afterwards. A medical examination may be needed, and references from previous employers are usually obtained as well.

Advantages

The main advantages of recruiting new staff externally are:
- biggest possible choice of candidates
- new individuals with new ideas
- wider range of experience.

There are also disadvantages:
- lengthy process
- expensive because of advertisements and/or agency fees
- interviews sometimes give false impressions.

Internal recruitment

Internal recruitment is sometimes used instead of external recruitment. The job is not advertised publicly, but only within the organization. (In some public organizations, all jobs have to be open to outside candidates as well.) The post is advertised on staff notice boards or in the organization's newspaper or house magazine. Line managers often tell suitable candidates about the job and suggest they should apply.

There a number of advantages to internal recruitment. It is much cheaper as there are no expensive newspaper advertisements or employment agency fees. It is much quicker, as no time is wasted processing applications and interviewing unsuitable candidates. It is easier to make the right choice as all the abilities– and faults – of the applicants are already known and recorded in their line manager's annual **appraisals**.

The candidates already have a very good knowledge of the firm and the way in which it works. They are immediately available, so they can start work straight away. It also enables the organization to create a career structure for ambitious employees, by promoting them to higher jobs in the organization.

Disadvantages

However, there are also disadvantages. Internal recruitment limits the number of people who can apply for the job. It introduces no new people or ideas into the organization. It may cause jealousy among candidates who are not appointed. Employees may resent taking orders from their former equals. It creates another vacancy lower down the organization which has to be filled.

Sole proprietors

Sole proprietors normally use the same kind of procedure for external recruitment

CHECKPOINTS

1. What is a job application form? Describe its main purposes.

2. What is a Jobcentre? How does it differ from an employment agency?

3. What are a) the advantages and b) the disadvantages of job advertisements in local newspapers, national newspapers and shop windows?

4. State two advantages of a) internal recruitment and b) external recruitment.

5. What hints would you give to someone writing a job advertisement? Using your own advice, write a classified advertisement for a local newspaper for a part-time care assistant in a residential home for the elderly.

as bigger firms. However, they are more likely to advertise vacancies in local newspapers and shop windows, and to use the Jobcentre and local contacts to find suitable staff. Local people often approach them direct to ask for a job.

Informal interviews

Sole proprietors usually hold some kind of interview, which may be quite informal. Most of them also ask for references from former employers, unless they already know the applicant personally. Not many of them keep a record of what was stated and decided at the interview. However, they need to do so, in case there is a dispute later which could result in the sole proprietor being taken to an employment tribunal (see Unit 63).

KEY TERMS

Appraisal An assessment of an employee's work which is usually made by a superior every year.

External recruitment Finding a suitable recruit outside the organization.

Internal recruitment Finding a suitable recruit inside the organization.

Job description A description of a job and its duties.

Key skills
Communication

Write a job description for any job you have had, or any relative's job, describing in detail all that it involves.

Training

An exciting career with Toys 'R' Us

Toys 'R' Us are Britain's biggest toy and family leisure product megastores, with 63 stores nationwide. To fuel our future success we want first-class managers. Following a rigorous recruitment process and an intensive 12-week training programme, you will be given real responsibility as an assistant manager in charge of one of the three key areas of our multi-million pound megastores. In addition, you will at times assume full responsibility for the store as a duty manager.

These are 12 weeks that could be one of the most challenging and rewarding times of your life.

The training is intense to say the least, but we believe it unnecessary for management trainees to spend endless weeks and months performing the same tasks over and over again. From the very outset, you will be expected to take control of your training. You will be expected to manage your time effectively and to target your training so that YOU extract maximum benefit.

You will receive a full day induction at Geoffrey House in Maidenhead and, following this, a thorough induction at your training store. During your induction you will be issued with your management training programme. Your own performance will be regularly monitored instore by your general store manager and your training manager. You will be given the opportunity to demonstrate your skills and knowledge in management tasks throughout the programme. Your knowledge and understanding will be appraised in the store and regularly throughout your training programme and your knowledge will be tested in our regional training centres.

The support you will receive will be second to none, but will NOT be a substitute for individual effort, good time management and real organization on your behalf.

To supplement your store-based knowledge, we will also complement your training with the following business skill seminars which will be held in our training centres:

● Customer service
● Recruitment and selection
● Sales management
● Employee training
● Loss prevention
● Employment law
● Health and safety
● Management skills.

Your training will culminate in a review panel held by senior management, including members of the training and area management teams. The review panel will ascertain your procedural knowledge and understanding of the job and will also provide us with an insight into your overall management ability.

In the future, you will find us as dedicated to the continual development of all our managers, as we are of our management trainees.

Source: adapted from Toy 'R' Us website

Most business is now so competitive and technical that training has become one of the most important activities in all successful firms. There are many reasons for training, but the main ones are:

● to provide knowledge, for example about the firm, or a new technology, or a new machine
● to increase skills, for example to do better quality work, or a more skilled job
● to change attitudes, for example to improve relations with customers, or other members of staff.

It is also often necessary to retrain people, e.g. the long-term unemployed, mothers returning to work, and workers, such as miners, whose jobs have disappeared.

Internal training

Most big companies have a training manager in the human resources or personnel department to organize all the internal, or on-the-job, training.

One of the most important parts of internal training for all new employees is the **induction** programme. This introduces them to their job, their new colleagues, the premises and the firm.

In a very small business, the induction may be no more than a brief tour of the workplace and a few quick introductions to other people. In a big company, it will be a

Study points

① **How long does the training course last?**

② **What job would you have if you completed the course successfully?**

③ **What is the distinctive feature of the training course?**

④ **Why do you think that Toys 'R' Us continues training and developing managers even after they have passed the course?**

Online links
www.toysrus.co.uk

Figure 1: On the job training

whole-day affair. It usually includes a talk on the company's history, products and policies. The recruit may be given a copy of the staff handbook. This will be followed by an induction at the place of work.

New employees must also be given training in their new job. This may be nothing more than informal advice from a colleague, if they are already experienced and skilled. If they are new to the job, proper training will be needed. Otherwise, present members of the firm may pass on their own bad working methods to new employees.

Own programmes

Most big firms have their own training programmes. The training is usually given by members of the firm, though outside specialists may also be called in. It may include lectures, practical demonstrations, case studies and role-play exercises, in which people act out a real-life business situation to gain experience and confidence. Successful companies, like the one in the case study, provide training throughout employees' working life so that they can develop their abilities to the fullest extent.

Good training benefits both employees and employers. Employees obtain greater skills, knowledge and self-confidence. It improves their chances of promotion, which increases their **motivation** to succeed. Employers also gain, as the quality of products and production both improve. The workforce is also happier. This reduces absenteeism – employees taking time off work without a genuine reason – and **labour turnover**, which reduces costs as fewer new employees have to be recruite.

External training

Some businesses, particularly smaller firms, use external, or off-the-job training, instead. This is provided by public sector colleges which run courses to meet the needs of local businesses or those which lead to recognised qualifications such as National Vocational Qualifications (NVQs). The colleges also provide many other courses in technical and professional subjects, for both full- and part-time students. There are also private sector institutions which provide business training, but their courses are much more expensive.

Government-sponsored bodies also provide training. There are 78 Training and Enterprise Councils (TECs) in England and Wales to give advice on training and to encourage enterprise. Some TECs provide part-time courses in setting up a business and developing it. They also manage the Modern Apprenticeship schemes, which allow employees to take a Level 3 NVQ while they are still working and earning a wage.

Many firms belong to the government-sponsored Investor In People scheme which seeks to increase the training of people at work.

New Deal

Full-time education or training is one of the four options under the government's New Deal programme for people between 18 and 24 who have been unemployed for six months or more. The other options are:

- a subsidised job with an employer for six months
- work with the Environment Task Force
- voluntary work.

Those who choose full-time education receive the equivalent of the Jobseeker's allowance and other benefits. People over 25 who have been unemployed for two years or more can also obtain full-time vocational education or training for a year, though most of their courses are much shorter.

These opportunities are part of the government's welfare-to-work programme which gives special help to the long-term unemployed. It has had a mixed success. A House of Commons committee said that 215,000 people aged 18 to 24 had found jobs since the scheme started in April, 1998. But almost a quarter, 53,000, were dismissed or left within 13 weeks. The official cost of putting an unemployed person into a New Deal job is £4,000, but critics say that each job costs much more than that – up to £11,000.

KEY TERMS

Induction The process of introducing a new employee to the firm and explaining its activities, aims, beliefs and customs.

Labour turnover The rate at which employees leave a firm each year. The number who leave is shown as a percentage of the total workforce.

Motivation The reason, or motive, which makes a person do something.

Revision and exam practice units 58–59

REVIEW POINTS

1 What is a job description?

2 When is induction used? What forms does it usually take?

3 Describe the main stages in selecting staff from the job application form to the final choice.

Extended questions

List the main points that should be included in a job advertisement and comment on the writing and design of the advertisement. State where you would advertise for the following employees, giving the reasons for your choice: a) skilled manual workers b) skilled professionals c) senior managers d) typists.

GROUP WORK

Divide into groups of six. Decide on a job and fix its rate of pay, conditions of service, any fringe benefits, the kinds of work that would be done, the qualifications and experience needed, etc. Decide where the job should be advertised. Three group members should now write and design the advertisement for the specified publication and the other three should plan the interview. The group members who wrote the advertisement should now be interviewed in turn for the job. Finish by discussing whether any improvements could have been made to the advertisement and the interview plan.

Case study 1

Somerset employer survey – recruitment

The hardest-to-fill occupations within Somerset are reported as being personal and protective service (33 per cent), craft (24 per cent) and sales (16 per cent). Skill shortages are blamed for 46 per cent of hard-to-fill vacancies, but 'other factors', such as low pay and unsociable hours, are a close second (40 per cent).

A majority (73 per cent) of businesses report that the main result of skill shortages is longer hours for other staff followed by inefficiency (40 per cent). Whilst 91 per cent of employers try to work around recruitment difficulties, it was encouraging to find that increased training, at 39 per cent, is high on the list of responses to skill shortages.

The six most common skill gaps were:

- basic IT skills (33 per cent)
- use of computer packages (20 per cent)
- sales/marketing (15 per cent)
- technical/specialist (15per cent)
- customer care (14 per cent)
- software/programming (14 per cent)

As can be seen, three of these skill gaps relate to information technology. If firms are to ensure they remain competitive in the modern economy, measures must be taken to develop employees' information and technology (ICT) skills.

Source: adapted from Economic Bulletin 14, Somerset TEC

1 Which occupations are the most difficult to fill?

2 Explain the effect which shortages in skilled occupations have on a) job applicants b) employees c) employers.

3 What government initiative should help to solve the problem?

Case study 2

People management skills top the agenda

Today's managers are increasingly taking responsibility for developing their people, according to research from the Institute of Management (IM) and Venture Marketing Group.

In a time of continual change, top priority is given by managers to developing leadership and teamworking skills in their people (87 per cent). Over three quarters (77 per cent) also see coaching as vital.

The changing nature of work and the 24-hour economy mean that new ways of working are high on the agenda for today's managers. Forty per cent believe that new initiatives on flexible working are likely to be introduced in their organizations over the next year. Initiatives to encourage creativity in the workplace are on the increase.

Source: adapted from Institute of Management website – News Release, 26 April 2000

1 In what ways are management skills changing?

2 What do you think has brought about this change?

3 How will this affect the long-term aims of companies in relation to their employees?

Case study 3

Modern Apprenticeships

Brett Ransley

Michael Harford

Modern Apprenticeships (MAs) are a key part of the government's response to the need to prepare young people for an economy based on high-level skills. MAs now cover over 80 sectors of industry and commerce, with over 500 qualifications available and with more than 136,000 young people currently in training. Many MAs involve some work at a college or other provider of training.

MA profiles

When Brett Ransley joined Phillip Mann estate agents in Peacehaven, East Sussex, three years ago at the age of 20, he knew nothing at all about the work. Starting with little more than endless enthusiasm and good communication skills, he became an MA in Residential Estate Agency. He has now achieved his qualification goal, and is established as a skilled negotiator and has been promoted to a new branch in nearby Newhaven.

Meanwhile, Michael Harford has been following a similar route with Passingham & Co, estate agents in Burgess Hill, West Sussex.

'It has been hard work from the start,' says Michael, 'but also extremely beneficial as I've learned a tremendous amount about the industry and the higher standards now being set.'

Michael now plans to continue his studies for the Certificate of Practice in Estate Agency (CPEA).

NTs (National Traineeships) are now being renamed Foundation Modern Apprenticeships (FMA) while the existing MAs become Advanced Modern Apprenticeships (AMA).

Source: adapted from Careers Adviser Vol: 4 No:2

1 **How many young people are currently in training on apprenticeship schemes?**

2 **What is the difference between an apprenticeship scheme and taking a course at a college or university?**

3 **In what ways is the apprenticeship scheme of benefit to a) an employer b) an apprentice?**

EXAM PRACTICE

Marilyn owns three kitchen shops in a busy industrial town in the Midlands. She sells high-quality cooking utensils of every kind, plus chinaware such as dinner and tea services. Each of the three shops is run by a manager, with three other staff. She now plans to open a fourth shop close to a new housing estate on the outskirts of the city. Marilyn visits each of the shops every day. The stores all have a uniform layout and she places great emphasis on customer care and courtesy. But the managers have complete responsibility for the day-to-day running of their shop.

Marilyn has decided to recruit a manager to run the new shop and one shop assistant.

Foundation

1 Suggest three places where Marilyn might advertise the manager's job.
(3 marks)

2 State two organisations which might help her to find a manager. (4 marks)

3 Design a simple application form suitable for the shop assistant job.
(4 marks)

4 State, with your reasons, the three most important qualities the manager should have. (6 marks)

Higher

1 Design a simple application form for the assistant. (4 marks)

2 Prepare a job description for the manager, which will indicate the kind of qualities necessary to do the job.
(4 marks)

3 a) Write an advertisement for the manager's vacancy. (4 marks)
b) Suggest the three most suitable places in which to place the advertisement. (3 marks)

4 a) State two other possible sources for filling such a vacancy. (4 marks)
b) Which source do you think is most appropriate? (2 marks)

Trade associations and trade unions

CBI chief sends warning to Prime Minister

Sir Clive Thompson, president of the Confederation of British Industry (CBI), warned the Prime Minister against new employment legislation that holds back people from participating in the changing world of work.

He said, 'My two-year CBI presidency has been dominated by the growth in regulation from Whitehall and Brussels. We have had laws on wages, hours and patterns of work – to name but a few. It all adds up to the biggest and most damaging overhaul of labour market regulation for 20 years.

'Everyone understands and sympathises with the call for paid parental leave and a right to part-time work for returning mothers. But the nature of work in the future will be insecure and needs for its very existence to be unprotected.

'Take age discrimination. No one should support such discrimination, but legislating against it is not the answer.

It would only add to company legal bills.

'People seek greater security but to legislate for that will limit the growth of employment.'

Source: adapted from CBI Press Release website, 16 May 2000

An eighty-year-old still doing a full day's work

Darling pledges fight against age prejudice

New measures to tackle prejudice and discrimination against older people were announced today by Alistair Darling, Social Security Secretary. He said a summit of employers and older workers' representatives will be called to examine ways of fighting age discrimination in the workplace. And representatives from TV, advertising and the media will be brought together to discuss how to tackle negative images of older people.

He said, 'Today, a third of the population is aged 50 plus. But in thirty years' time, getting on for half the population will be over 50; and

nearly a quarter over retirement age.

'As employers we need to change our attitudes. There are almost one million vacancies today. In places, people are crying out for workers, not just at 18 or 21, but at 50 and 60. More and more employers are recognising older workers, and plenty of big employers have a good attitude to employing older workers.

The summit would discuss how they could get all employers to follow the lead of the best.

Source: adapted from Department of Social Security website – Press Release, 17 May 2000

The **Confederation of British Industry (CBI)**, is the biggest employers' organization, representing about 250,000 public and private companies, either directly as members, or, indirectly, through 180 employers' organizations and **trade associations**. Its main task is to state the views of British business to the public, the government and the European Commission. As the case study shows, the CBI can state its views; but the government, which also has to consider the views of trade unions and voters, does not always have to agree.

The Federation of Small Businesses, which has 150,000 members, represents owners of small businesses and the self-employed. In addition, there are just over 200 big trade associations representing employers in various industries, and many smaller associations representing employers in smaller sectors.

The main functions of trade associations are to:

- negotiate national rates of pay in some industries (see Unit 61)
- publicize the industry's views
- provide member companies with advice and information
- carry out industrial research for members in some industries.

Study points

1. How many job vacancies are there?
2. What is the CBI's reason for opposing a law on age discrimination?
3. Why does the government believe that we need to change our views about old people?
4. What action is the government proposing to take?
5. In your view, should a law be passed to make it illegal to discriminate against older workers?

Online links

www.cbi.org.uk
www.dss.gov.uk

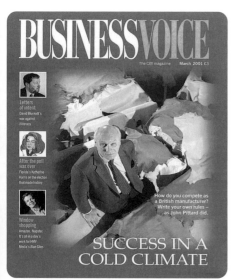

Representing the views of business

Trade unions

Trade unions represent employees. Most of the bigger unions are members of the **Trades Union Congress (TUC)** which was founded in 1868. In the same way that the CBI reflects the views of companies and employers, the TUC reflects the views of more than 70 trade unions and 6.7 million employees.

The main functions of trade unions are to:
- negotiate rates of pay and conditions of work with employers, including health and safety matters (see Unit 61)
- give members legal advice about problems at work and provide lawyers to represent members in courts or at industrial tribunals
- support members financially during strikes and lock-outs by employers and after accidents at work
- provide a range of other services for members, such as mortgages, insurance, personal loans and discounted holidays.

Union changes

There have been many changes in the membership and power of trade unions in the last few years. Trade union members are no longer only manual workers from industrial areas. There are now more white-collar than blue-collar trade unionists. Nearly half of all professional employees are members of trade unions.

However, the total number of trade unionists has fallen. Membership reached a peak of 13.3 million in 1979 and then started to fall. By 1989, membership was just over ten million. It continued to decline until it reached 7.2 million in 1998. In the following year, however, membership increased for the first time, rising by 100,000.

Some reasons for the decline were:
- anti-trade union laws
- the increase in part-time workers, who are far less likely to be union members
- refusal of some employers to negotiate with trade unions
- constant strikes, particularly in the car industry and the public sector, in the past.

The number of unions has also declined, from 330 in 1987 to 219 in 1997. The fall in numbers has been caused mainly by mergers to form bigger unions, which benefit from economies of scale. The biggest union is Unison, a merger of three public service unions, which has nearly 1.3 million members.

Some other big trade unions are the Transport and General Workers Union (TWGU) with over 880,000 members; the Amalgamated Engineering and Electrical Union (AEEU) with nearly 718,000 members; and GMB with 712,000 members. The Manufacturing, Science and Finance Union (MSF), which is very strong in white-collar sectors, has 416,000 members.

KEY TERMS

Confederation of British Industry (CBI) An organization formed in 1965 to represent British employers.

Picketing Trying to persuade employees who are still working to join a strike.

Trade associations Organizations which put employers' views to the government, trade unions and the public.

Trade unions Groups of workers who join together to protect their interests.

Trades Union Congress (TUC) A voluntary association of trade unions which decides the policy of the trade union movement. It also deals with disputes between unions.

CHECKPOINTS

1. Which is the largest trade union?
2. Who belongs to the Confederation of British Industry (CBI)?
3. What are trade associations' main functions?
4. What are the main aims of trade unions?

Protecting the rights of employees

Decrease in power

There was a great decrease in trade union power during the 18 years of Conservative rule from 1979 to 1997. It became much more difficult for unions to use their main weapon of a strike (see Unit 62).

Unofficial strikes were made illegal. Official strikes organized by the unions could be called only after a secret ballot of members. If a strike took place, peaceful **picketing** was allowed, but there could be no more than six people at each entrance to the workplace. Secondary picketing by workers from other plants was banned. And many other restrictions were placed on unions. For example, employers could legally refuse to 'recognize', or deal with, unions, if they wished.

However, trade unions have regained a little of their former power under the Employment Relations Act of 1999, which came into force in 2000. In businesses with more than 20 employees, a union must be recognized if a majority of the workforce are members, or if there is a majority vote for recognition in a ballot. As a result, more firms are having to have negotiate with trade unions over pay, and other matters (see case study in Unit 61).

Collective bargaining

Union recognition at Airtours set for take off

Sir Ken Jackson

Cabin crew at Airtours have voted overwhelmingly in favour of union recognition of Cabin Crew 89 (now part of the AEEU union). Of the 1,166 ballot papers issued, 961 were returned and 955 voted in favour. The vote clears the way for detailed negotiations between the company and the union to establish negotiating procedures.

Airtours agreed to the vote on the basis that the AEEU already has 60 per cent of the workforce signed up. Preliminary negotiations were friendly and non-confrontational.

Commenting on the result, AEEU general secretary Sir Ken Jackson said: 'It's an excellent start to a positive partnership with Airtours.'

Steve Hayes, Airtours' general manager, personnel, added: 'All of us were delighted by the high turnout, and clear result in the ballot. The next step will be for us to sit down together to formalize the negotiating procedures. We believe that Cabin Crew 89 have a modern approach to trade unionism which will make negotiations more positive.'

Source: AEEU White Collar Membership website – Latest campaigns

Airtours plc and its associates carry passengers from 18 countries, with
- **45 aircraft**
- **ten cruise ships**
- **and employ over 23,000 people worldwide.**

Source: adapted from Welcome to Airtours plc website

Study points

(Read the unit before you do the study points.)

① **What percentage of Airtours cabin crew were members of Cabin Crew 89?**

② **What percentage voted for union recognition?**

③ **Why did Airtours agree to the vote taking place?**

④ **Why do some employers not want to recognize unions?**

⑤ **In your view, 'what is 'a modern approach to trade unionism'?**

Online links

www.airtours.com
www.aeeu.org.uk

National bargaining

In almost half of all workplaces, rates of pay are decided nationally by **collective bargaining** between employers and trade unions.

The employers are represented by their trade associations and the trade unions by representatives of all the unions involved.

These representatives decide a minimum rate of pay for workers in the industry. In a few industries, they decide the actual rates of pay.

In addition, they usually decide the length of the working week, overtime rates and the minimum length of holiday.

There may also be talks on working conditions and other matters, including:
- sick pay
- maternity leave
- fringe benefits
- changes in working practices
- training
- recruitment
- health and safety
- pensions.

National bargaining is also used in much of the public sector to set salary scales and other working conditions for employees throughout the country.

Local bargaining

In the private sector, the working conditions in firms vary so much that it has long been common to hold local talks on pay and conditions in addition to the national discussions.

This collective bargaining between management and unions goes on at both company and factory level.

For example, the managers and unions at plant level might agree that shop-floor workers should be paid £2 an hour extra for working evening shifts and £3 an hour extra for night shifts. Extra payments for white-collar workers might also be decided at the local level.

For example, managers and unions might agree to give a cost-of-living allowance of £1,800 a year to office staff as the factory is in Greater London, where homes and other things cost more. There can be a lot of hard bargaining over pay at local level.

Other matters that might be decided locally include:

- redundancy policies
- productivity agreements
- appraisal systems.

Advantages

Collective bargaining has big advantages for employees. The trade union has much greater bargaining power than individual workers.

It represents thousands of workers, it can speak with one voice and it has trained, highly-skilled negotiators.

Collective bargaining also has some advantages for employers, which is why is used by many big manufacturing companies. It:

- provides pay stability for a year at least
- increases co-operation with the unions
- gives an opportunity to discuss any problems or possible conflicts of interest with the union.

Disadvantages

However, there are also some disadvantages for employers. It:

- gives great power to the union
- reduces managers' choices
- can increase labour costs
- may reduce workers' motivation.

There are still some companies and many small firms where collective bargaining does not apply.

Many firms now have personal contracts of employment with their white-collar employees.

Pay rises may be given as a result of an annual appraisal or employees may be given pay rises for achieving certain targets. For example, a bank employee may have to sell a certain number of insurance policies to bank customers to get a pay rise.

In the public sector, too, there has also been a trend towards performance-related pay. It has been introduced in parts of the Civil Service and in some National Health Service trusts.

'New style' agreements

Some Far Eastern companies with factories in Britain and trade unions have introduced 'new style' agreements which depend on much closer co-operation between managers and unions. Some of the main features of these 'new style' agreements are as follows.

- *Recognition of only one union*. It is easier for management to make deals with only one union than with a number of unions. It also strengthens the union if no other union is allowed to join in the talks.
- *Single-status employment*. The traditional differences between managers and workers, between 'them' and 'us', is ended. Manual workers have the same hours of work, holidays, canteens and car parking as white-collar workers.
- *Labour flexibility*. All workers do any job which they are capable of doing.
- *Teamwork*. There is a greater emphasis on teamwork and co-operation between all grades of employees.
- *No-strike agreements*. The union agrees not to strike. Both management and union agree to accept the decision of an arbitrator, or independent judge, in any dispute. Pendulum arbitration is often used.

Pendulum arbitration

In pendulum arbitration, the arbitrator makes a straight choice between the views of the management and the union.

For example, if the management has offered a pay rise of £1 an hour and the union wants £2 an hour, the arbitrator cannot say that the rise should be £1.50 or £1.75. The arbitrator has to say 'yes' to either the managers or the unions: the pay rise has to be set at either £1 an hour or £2 an hour.

This kind of arbitration encourages both sides to be moderate in their demands. They know that if their case is extreme it is likely to be rejected outright.

Many trade unionists see these 'new style' agreements as the way forward into a new era of co-operation between management and workers.

More reforms

The Employment Relations Act of 1999 (see Unit 60) also introduced other reforms.

These apply to all employees whether they are members of trade unions or not, and in all firms, including those which do not recognize unions.

The reforms include:

- maximum payment for unfair dismissal increased from £12,000 to £50,000
- maternity leave increased from four to 18 weeks
- up to three months' unpaid leave for both mothers and fathers during the first five years of a baby's life
- reasonable time off work for family emergencies.

Works council

Another reform was introduced in 2000 under European law. Big firms with more than 1,000 employees, which operate in two or more European Union countries, now have to set up European-style **works councils**. The works councils have the right to be informed and consulted on all matters that affect the interests of the workers.

CHECKPOINTS

1. What is collective bargaining?
2. What are the main matters that are usually decided at the national level?
3. What has replaced collective bargaining in much of the private sector?
4. Describe the main features of 'new style' agreements.

KEY TERMS

Collective bargaining Talks between representatives of employers and trade unions to decide pay rates and other terms and conditions of employment.

Works councils Committees of workers (and sometimes managers) which participate, or have a share, in the running of a business.

Industrial conflict

Unions turn to ballots

Unions are increasingly using industrial action ballots as a successful means of negotiating with employers, according to a TUC report. Although balloting for industrial action has doubled in the last year, the proportion that result in action – strikes or other action such as overtime bans – has fallen.

Unions organized 983 ballots compared to 464 last year. Yet industrial action resulted in only 32 per cent of cases, compared to 40 per cent in 1998.

TUC general secretary, John Monks, said, 'This survey shows that unions can win for their members without taking industrial action. It shows unions are acting responsibly where employers bargain responsibly.'

Source: adapted from TUC website – News, 22 June 2000

Strike called off

Transport and General Workers' Union bus workers at Yorkshire Traction have voted by a margin of just over two to one to accept a revised pay deal and call off industrial action. The deal was negotiated after the dispute was referred to the Advisory Conciliation and Arbitration Service (ACAS).

The T&G shop stewards were informed of the revised offer earlier this week with a recommendation to accept the new deal. In a ballot of members, the voting was 291 to accept and 134 to reject the revised offer. Approximately two-thirds of T&G members voted.

A union spokesman said: 'This long-running dispute has now ended. The general public have been very supportive of our members and we thank them for that support.'

Source: T&G website – News Releases, 27 May 2000

Figure 1: Working days lost through industrial action

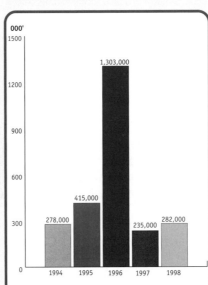

Source: adapted from *Annual Abstract of Statistics, 2000*

Study points

1. How many working days were lost through strikes in 1996?
2. What was the average number of working days lost annually through industrial action during the five-year period?
3. According to the TUC report, how many industrial actions were there in 1999?
4. In your view, how do trade unions benefit by using industrial action ballots in negotiations with employers?

Online links

www.twgu.org.uk
www. tuc.org.uk

In recent years, the number of strikes in Britain has fallen dramatically. The number of working days lost through strikes was the lowest in 1997 since records began in 1891. In 1999, there were still only 205 strikes, involving a loss of 242,000 days. Just over 20 years ago, it was a very different story. In 1979, 21 million working days were lost through major strikes alone, and millions more days were lost during the long, bitter miners' strike of 1984–5.

Strikes are still the workers' most powerful, and final, weapon. A strike creates great losses for an employer.

- Revenue falls as it cannot produce any goods or services.
- It still has to pay all its fixed costs, such as rent and business rates.
- Orders are lost during the time it is unable to supply its products.
- It may cause longer-lasting harm as the firm's reputation may be damaged and customers may not want to order its products again.
- Even after the strike is over, relations between the employer and employees are likely to be poor, which may have a harmful effect on production.

However, the employees also suffer during a strike – and afterwards.

- They lose their income and receive only a few pounds a week in strike pay from their union.
- The company's losses may force it to make some workers redundant after the strike is over, or even to close the factory.

Other industrial action

Conservative laws made it much more difficult for workers to strike (see Unit 60). However, as the case study shows, unions have recently started to use the threat of a strike – a strike ballot – instead of going on strike.

In addition to strikes, there are also other kinds of **industrial action**.

- *Non-co-operation*. The workers may boycott, or refuse to have anything to do with a new working practice of which they do not approve. For example, a new method of keeping records may have been introduced without prior talks with the unions. The workers may refuse to operate the new system.

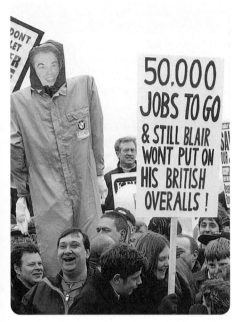

- *Working to rule*. There are official rules in workplaces about the conditions and terms of employment. For example, they may specify all the parts that should be checked before a machine is used or all the protective clothing that should be worn for a particular job. In practice, some of these rules are often ignored in the interests of greater speed and efficiency. However, when there is a **work to rule**, or go-slow, all the rules will be strictly observed. As a result, the jobs take much longer and productivity falls. Shop stewards may take every single complaint and grievance to management, which he or she would previously have settled on the spot. As a result, management time is wasted.

- *Overtime ban*. Workers may refuse to work beyond the normal hours. Firms that rely heavily on overtime working to keep to their production schedules will be affected. The workers are also affected as they lose valuable overtime pay.

Employers' action

Employers can also take industrial action against the work force. Some of their main actions are as follows.

- *Closer work supervision*. Managers can supervise, or examine, employees' work more closely and point out the faults.
- *Pay freeze*. Employers can say that costs have to be cut and, therefore, wages and/or salaries will have to be frozen at their present level for a period of six months or a year.
- *Lock-outs*. Employers lock the workplace gates or doors to prevent employees entering and to stop paying them wages. **A lock-out** also harms employers as they have to go on paying their overheads and may lose orders and damage the image of the firm.
- *Factory or office closure*. The employers' final weapon is to close a factory or an office with a long record of conflict. However, the employers may then face a large redundancy bill.

ACAS

Many disputes are settled peacefully by management and unions. If they cannot settle the dispute themselves, they may call in the **Advisory, Conciliation and Arbitration Service (ACAS)**. This

CHECKPOINTS

1. What effects do strikes have on a) employees and b) employers?
2. Describe two other kinds of industrial action workers can take.
3. What is a lock-out?
4. What is the employers' final weapon?
5. Describe the work of ACAS.

independent body was set up during the great industrial disputes of the 1970s. Some of its main functions are:

- to settle disputes between unions and employers by **conciliation**
- to refer unsettled disputes to **arbitration** with the agreement of all the parties involved
- to advise both sides of industry on ways of improving industrial relations.

In recent years, it has not had to deal with so many industrial conflicts, owing to the great decline in both collective bargaining and trade union actions.

However, ACAS still has an excellent record in settling collective disputes, as the case study shows. It also helps to settle many disputes between individual employees and their employer.

More employee rights

The Employment Relations Act of 1999 not only made it easier for trade unions to gain recognition, it also increased individual employees' rights.

- Employees cannot be dismissed for taking part in legal industrial action. (If they are, they can bring a case for unfair dismissal and receive up to £50,000 in compensation).
- Employees can be accompanied by a trade union representative at any disciplinary hearing (see Unit 63).
- Consultations must take place when any redundancies are planned, or when the firm is involved in a takeover or merger which may involve loss of jobs.

KEY TERMS

Advisory, Conciliation and Arbitration Service (ACAS) An independent body which helps to settle industrial disputes peacefully, to improve industrial relations and to investigate alleged breaches of employees' rights.

Arbitration A voluntary settlement of a dispute by an independent person, an arbitrator, whose decisions both sides have agreed to accept.

Conciliation Talking to both sides in an industrial dispute and trying to bring them together before attitudes have had time to harden.

Industrial action Action taken by trade unions or employers to harm the other party.

Lock-out Employers shutting employees out of the workplace and stopping their pay.

Work to rule Obeying every official rule so that work is slowed down.

Employees' rights

There are dozens of laws affecting employees. The most important are:

- *Equal Pay Act 1970*. Men and women doing equal work or work of equal value must receive the same pay.
- *Health and Safety at Work Act 1974*. Employers must provide safe premises, machinery and working conditions. Under new regulations of 1993, employers must estimate all health and safety risks and take suitable action.
- *Race Relations Act 1976*. People must not be discriminated against because of their colour, race, nationality or ethnic origins.
- *Employment Protection Act 1978*. Employees must be given a written **contract of employment**. They must not be dismissed unfairly, i.e. without a reasonable cause. They must receive redundancy pay if they have been working for the firm for two years or more and their job is abolished.
- *Trade Union Reform and Employment Rights Act, 1993*. Restated the principle that employees have the right to belong, or not to belong, to a trade union.
- *Disability Discrimination Act, 1995*. Disabled people must be treated no less favourably than other workers. (Only applies to firms with over 20 employees.)
- *Employment Relations Act, 1999*. Employers must recognize unions when a majority of employees are members; improved parental rights (see Unit 61); increased employee rights in disputes (see Unit 62).

In July 2000, new government regulations gave Britain's six million part-time workers the same rights as full-time employees in rates of pay, pensions, and

Study points

(Read the unit before you do the study points.)

① **Which laws do you think the café owner has broken?**

② **What action would you advise the waitress to take?**

annual paid leave (four weeks for full-time employees and *pro rata*, or proportionately, for part-time workers.)

First tasks

One of the personnel department's first tasks after an employee has been taken on is to make arrangements for them to be paid, either by cheque or direct to a bank account. All employees must be provided with an itemized pay statement showing gross and net pay, deductions for income tax and national insurance, and any pension and voluntary deductions (see Figure 1, Unit 56).

Within two months of starting work, all employees must also be provided with a written statement of employment. This contract of employment should contain the following information:

- the employer's name
- the employee's name
- the date employment began
- the amount of pay and the intervals between payments
- hours of work
- holiday entitlement
- sick leave arrangements
- pension arrangements
- length of notice for ending employment
- job title or brief description
- if not a permanent job, the period for which employment is expected to last
- the place of work
- details of disciplinary and grievance procedures.

Discipline

All employees must be treated fairly at work. That is why the statement of employment includes details of the disciplinary and grievance code. The first part of the code shows what will happen if the employer is dissatisfied with the

Figure 1: An employer's responsibilities

MUST GIVE ✔
Equal pay
Written statement of employment
Redundancy pay

MUST NOT ✗
Dismiss an employee unfairly
Discriminate because of race
Stop employees joining union

employee. The second part tells employees how they can make a complaint if they think they are being treated unfairly and whom they should tell.

The disciplinary code, which has to be fair and reasonable, usually states:

- how a first offence will be treated
- the number of warnings to be given for later offences
- which warnings will be oral and which written
- who will dismiss employees
- how to appeal, and to whom.

Dismissals

Employees can only be dismissed without notice for some crimes, such as theft. They can also be dismissed with notice for persistent misconduct, inability to do the job, or because their kind of work is no longer required.

If they are dismissed for misconduct, the employer must be able to show that the disciplinary code has been used. For inability to do the job, the employer must show that adequate training and supervision were provided, and that a more suitable job was offered instead. In redundancy cases, the employer must show that as much notice was given as possible, and that the method of selection was fair.

CHECKPOINTS

1. What is an employment tribunal?
2. What special employment rights are provided for women?
3. When is it legal to make deductions from pay?
4. Explain what is meant by unfair dismissal and give possible examples.

Otherwise, any employees, who have been in the job for at least a year, can claim that they have been dismissed unfairly and take the case to an **employment tribunal**. These tribunals have a legally-qualified chairperson plus one trade union and one employers' organization representative. They can award up to £50,000 in compensation for unfair dismissal, and much more for sexual or racial discrimination.

Personnel department

Making sure that no employment laws are broken is just one the many duties of the **personnel, or human resources department**, which is one of the busiest in all companies. Its other duties include looking after:

- employee welfare
- pay and fringe benefits
- working conditions
- recruitment and selection
- training
- collective bargaining
- industrial relations.

These have all been covered in Units 54–62 of this section.

Key skills
IT and communication

STATEMENTS OF EMPLOYMENT
Using a computer, write a statement of employment for the waitress in the case study, covering all the items in the text, making up the individual details. Print a hard copy and save the file with an appropriate name.

KEY TERMS

Employment tribunal An independent body dealing with alleged breaches of employees' rights, such as unfair dismissal, equal pay, trade union rights, etc. The tribunal can award compensation to employees.

Contract of employment A legal agreement covering an employee's terms and conditions of employment.

Personnel, or human resources, department The department which is responsible for all relations between the employer and employees.

Revision and exam practice units 60–63

REVIEW POINTS

1 What is the CBI? What is its full name? Describe its main objectives.

2 What are the functions of trade associations?

3 What are the main functions of trade unions?

4 What is collective bargaining? What does it deal with?

5 Describe the different kinds of industrial action and state their objectives.

6 How does ACAS help in settling industrial conflicts?

7 Describe the work of employment tribunals. What is their importance in protecting employees' rights?

8 What are the main grounds on which employees can be fairly dismissed? Give an example of each.

Extended questions

1 The workers in your firm are threatening to go on strike for higher pay. Describe in detail the steps you would take to resolve the problem.

2 A new computer unit has been set up in your firm staffed by members from the company's headquarters. State what actions you would take in relation to
a) the new staff and
b) the existing staff to ensure that they worked together peacefully.

Case study 1

Work/life balance tipped against British workers

An EOC (Equal Opportunities Commission) survey conducted over 12 months has revealed workers' problems in trying to achieve a work-life balance.

Chair Julie Mellor said employers were not applying family friendly policies and did not appreciate the benefits of flexible working for their businesses.

'Unfortunately, in over half of cases, requests for changes in working arrangements were rejected or the arrangements offered were unacceptable.

'But most disturbing was the fact that one in five of those refused changes were either dismissed, made redundant or forced to resign.

'The remaining unsuccessful employees did not fare much better – 25 per cent left their employment whether or not they had another job to go to and 34 per cent lodged a complaint with the employment tribunal.

'Sadly only two per cent who used their company's grievance procedure succeeded in getting working arrangements that were acceptable,' Ms Mellor said.

'How can we ever hope to be a clever country when people with other commitments, be they children or other family responsibilities, are treated in such a way?'

Most individuals wanted to move from full-time to part-time hours and/or to job share. Other applicants wanted to work from home or to negotiate changes in working hours. Ms Mellor said only one in five employees said their employer had a policy which provided for flexible working arrangements.

Complainants came from all sectors of employment, from large and small workplaces from the public and private sectors. The survey included nurses, air cabin crew, architects, police officers, solicitors, teachers, secretaries, lecturers and managers from banking, arts, human resources and other fields.

Source: adapted from EOC online information, 9 March 2000

1 How many employees failed to obtain changes in their working arrangements?

2 What is meant by work/life balance?

3 What changes did employees want in their working arrangements?

4 Why do you think employers from all sectors of employment are opposed to these changes?

5 With the changes in employment (see case study 2) are the employees' requests likely to be fulfilled in the future?

Online links
www.eoc.org.uk

Case study 2

Loyalty 'does not bring rewards'

In an age of freelancers and short-term contracts does it pay to be loyal to a boss? According to a survey by the Institute of Management (IM), two-thirds of managers feel increasingly less loyal to their companies.

Mark Hastings, the IM's head of policy says: 'Employers, particularly in new industry sectors, compete for employees and have to reward them well to get them. Employment flexibility has shifted the balance of power to the employee.'

Employees no longer feel they have to work for the local company, but are nationally and even internationally mobile. The victims have been those with redundant or outmoded skills.

Angela Baron of the Institute says: 'It is no longer a matter of a formal contract that says you have 20 days paid holiday a year. What is important is whether you, the employee, feel that you will be rewarded if you work harder and give more.'

Increasingly, employees are setting a price for their loyalty when in the past the mere offer of a job would have been enough.

Hastings adds: 'Employees want their work to fit in with the demands of home life. They want to have the flexibility of working part of the time from home.'

Source: adapted from *Financial Mail on Sunday*, 9 July 2000

1 What proportion of managers feel less loyal to their companies?

2 How have employees' working conditions changed?

3 How have they a) gained and b) lost by the changes?

4 What do you think are the priorities now for
   a) employers
   b) employees?

Case study 3

Work beats a rest

Holidays are just too much for some workers – a third do not take their full entitlement, a survey revealed yesterday. And women are twice as likely as men to remain at their post.

Computer staff are the worst workaholics, with more than half giving up some holiday. Four in ten bank workers also end up with days owing. Up to 50 per cent of those who don't take their full provision work HALF their holiday time.

Four in ten are aged 25–35, said an NOP poll for travel firm Airtours Holidays. The keen workers either simply enjoy the job or do not want the odd day off once they have had breaks abroad. Others know they will only come back to a mountain of paperwork.

The Family Holiday Association backed the survey. Now it and Airtours want firms to use the money saved to back an FHA charity providing holidays for children in residential care.

Source: adapted from *The Mirror*, 29 May 2000

1 What proportion of employees do not take their full holiday?

2 Who are the worst workaholics?

3 Suggest two reasons why people may not wish to take all their holiday entitlement.

Case study 4

OH, DOC, I FEEL REALLY ROUGH. IT'S MONDAY AGAIN.

Absent trends

According to a survey by the Institute of Personnel and Development (IDP), one third of all sickness absence has nothing to do with genuine ill health. This might explain why so much of it takes place on Mondays and Fridays.

When quizzed about why workers took so much time off, managers thought boredom was four times more important a reason than hangovers.

The IPD research found that once organizations reached over 100 employees in size, their absentee rates rose dramatically.

With full employment, it has been noted that absenteeism usually rises. Forty per cent of employers are saying that the problem is once more on the increase and one company in five has identified absenteeism as a major current problem.

Tesco's Midland region recently halved its absenteeism rate. Regional manager Maggie Pedder says: 'We got the message out to all our staff that we cared and wanted to help those with problems. If they didn't report to the right person, then disciplinary action was taken.

'We halved absenteeism in a few months and improved morale as those who are conscientious realized they were not being taken for a ride.'

Source: adapted from *Business Age*, July/August 2000

Workers' health checks 'will lead to skiving'

Trade union leaders are encouraging workers to monitor their health closely. Union representatives are being trained to teach 'body mapping', which involves workers marking on a map of the body where they are experiencing pain and identifying links with work.

The TUC, which is behind the scheme, claims it will makes workers' lives safer and could lead to a cut in compensation claims from sick employees.

The CBI, the employers' body, estimates that British workers take an average of eight and a half sick days off work a year, costing employers more than £10 billion a year.

Richard Baron, deputy head of the policy unit at the Institute of Directors said: 'This idea of body-mapping is very unscientific. It could easily lead to people attributing to work illnesses and conditions which have nothing to do with the workplace at all.'

But TUC general secretary John Monks said: 'This isn't scare-mongering. It's about finding out what's hurting and killing people at work and stopping it before more lives are needlessly put in danger.'

Source: *Daily Mail*, 16 August 2000

1 **What reasons are employers giving for high absenteeism?**
2 **Do you think body-mapping is a legitimate method of assessing illness?**
3 **In your view, what steps could be taken to decrease absenteeism by a) employers b) employees c) trades unions?**

EXAM PRACTICE

John Barlow runs a small newsagent and confectionery business in the suburbs of a large town in the South of England. He decided to take on one full-time woman employee to work in the shop and one part-time female worker. They have now worked for him for over two years.

Foundation

1 Did John need to provide a written statement of employment for both of his employees?   (2 marks)
2 If a) the part-time worker and b) the full-time worker become pregnant, will John have to pay their wages?   (4 marks)
3 What effect could this have on his business?   (4 marks)

Higher

1 What are John Barlow's statutory obligations relating to maternity leave?   (4 marks)
2 What legitimate grounds would he have for dismissing the full-time employee?   (2 marks)
3 In your view, what effects has employee legislation had on a) employees b) employers c) society?   (6 marks)

Section 8

Communications

Traditional communications

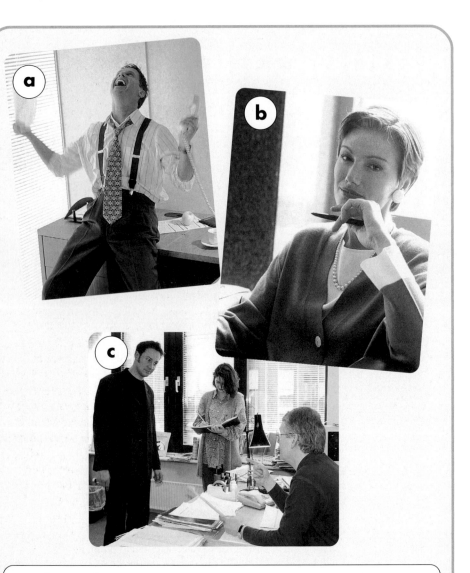

a

b

c

Study points

We communicate with other people not only with words but also with our gestures, our expressions and our posture, or the way we hold ourselves. This body language often says just as much as words.

① What does the man's gesture in photograph A mean?

② Describe the body language of the two men in C. What is going on between them?

③ In photograph C, what does the woman's posture show about her feelings?

④ In photograph B, what is the woman's attitude towards what she is hearing?

⑤ Give one example from your own life of how someone's body language has shown his or her feelings.

⑥ Why is it important for managers to be aware of body language?

There are three main types of traditional communications:
- body language
- spoken communications
- written communications.

Visual aids, such as charts, graphs, diagrams, photographs and videos are often used to give, or support, messages. They summarize information and present it in a striking way.

Body language

As the case study shows, we can say a lot without speaking a word. However, we are not always aware of our **body language** or its effects on others. Usually, it is quite clear what body language means but sometimes it is a little more difficult to decide.

Figure 1: Two-way communication

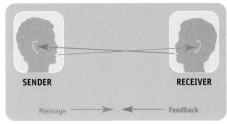

SENDER　　　　　　　　　RECEIVER

Message ⟶　　⟵ Feedback

Some communications, such as body language, are one-way as no reply is expected. Many communications, however, are two-way, where some **feedback**, or response, is required (see Figure 1).

Spoken messages

The main advantage of spoken messages is that you get instant feedback from the other person: you know immediately what they think and if they have understood. There are also disadvantages. Sometimes, there is no permanent record, such as a tape recording, which makes it impossible to check what was said. Face-to-face communications can also cost time and money. For example, if a meeting is held, those involved cannot be doing their own work. Moreover, some of them may have had to travel a long way to attend the meeting.

Figure 2: Layout of a business letter

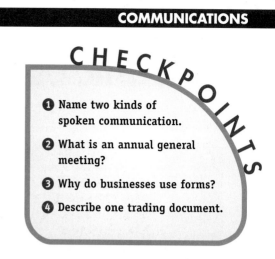

Letterhead includes writer's address

Lovely Moves
12 Wilton Way
Worrall
Southshire
Telephone: 01234 667459

Reference — WP/WH

Date — Today's date

Inside address — Mrs J Brown
11 High Road
Worrall
Southshire

Salutation — Dear Mrs Brown

Text of letter —

Close — Yours sincerely

Winston Powell

Some of the main methods of spoken communication are as follows.

- *Face-to-face meetings.* It is estimated that company managers spend up to 60 per cent of their day in meetings. At large formal meetings, there is often a written agenda, or a list of items to be discussed.
- *Interviews.* Used for external recruitment and internal promotions (see Unit 58); and by the press, television and the rest of the media to obtain information.

- *Presentations.* Business people often use this method to explain a project or a plan to a group of colleagues or to a possible client. The talk is often accompanied by visual aids, such as a video.
- *Annual general meetings (AGMs).* Companies have to hold a general meeting for their shareholders every year to tell them of their past performance and plans for the future. Small investors have a right to attend, but few of them usually do.

- *Conferences.* Experts provide information for large groups of business people.

Written communications

The main advantage of written communications is that there is a permanent record which can be referred to for ever, if necessary; the main disadvantage is that there is slow feedback, or sometimes, none at all.

These are some of the main written communication methods used by business.

- *Letters.* Even in this new electronic age, all businesses still use letters for a variety of purposes, including formal communications, direct mail, offers of services, etc. They are written on letterheaded paper and set out in a standard way (see Figure 2).
- *Reports.* **Reports** are used for informing colleagues of investigations or plans. A report usually has a title, a brief introduction, headings or subheadings for each section, a conclusion, a list of recommendations and the name of the author(s) and the date.
- *Memoranda.* Managers use a **memorandum** or memo to make arrangements or requests and to send confirmations to other managers.
- *Notices.* These provide a cheap way of communicating the same information to a large number of people but they may not be read, or may be ignored.
- *Business forms.* Printed forms, such as market research questionnaires, save time and effort as all essential points are covered. Many business forms are trading documents, such as quotations, or an estimate of the total cost of a job.

KEY TERMS

Body language Showing feelings and attitudes through usually unconscious gestures, expressions and posture.

Feedback The response to a message which is transmitted back to the sender. It indicates whether the message has been received and understood and gives the sender the opportunity to modify the original message if necessary.

Memorandum A written message between members of the same firm, usually on a standard form.

Report A written account in a standard format of what has been investigated, discussed or done.

Visual aids Pictorial means of communication, such as charts and videos.

Electronic communications

More than mobile

The mobile world is set to enter cyberspace. **Wireless application protocol**, or Wap, is a technology which links the internet to wireless portable devices, such as mobile phones. This heralds the birth of m-commerce, a new way of doing business that will change the way we live.

What will consumers do with **m-commerce**? Everything from buying goods and services to downloading music and books and asking for stock quotes and geographic information. Online banking is a typical application.

According to some estimates, the growth of mobile commerce will outstrip electronic commerce within three years.

These new WAP handsets will need to have special capabilities. The content providers will know where their users are geographically and will be able to direct them to specific destinations – restaurants or theatres, for example. They will be able to carry out secure transactions.

So the leading operators, including the world's largest mobile telephone group, Vodafone AirTouch, are doing deals with content providers to ensure they have a rich menu of goods and services to offer consumers in the new m-world.

Wap is one of a number of curiously named new technologies. General packet radio service (GPRS) will deliver internet information to mobile phones many times faster than conventional technology.

Most experts believe that the introduction of GPRS later this year will be the turning point for mobile commerce.

Source: adapted from FT.Com website – Understanding WAP

Offices: assets or liabilities?

Office space, especially in city centre locations, is hugely expensive. The average occupancy of an office desk is 11 per cent, taking account of standard working hours, five-day weeks, holidays, sickness and – most significantly – the fact that many staff with desks are usually somewhere else!

Radical changes have been brought about by information and communication technologies. These enable business working practices to be streamlined.

The following options are now available to support more productive working and lower facilities costs:

- private space and support services (that is, personal offices and secretaries) can be reduced dramatically

- some of the savings from reduced private space can be used to increase shared space and services (that is, **hot-desks**, meeting rooms, studies, cafés, etc.)
- large, central facilities can be replaced by networks of smaller facilities, including third party telecentres, that are closer to employee's homes and to customers
- home workers can be fully integrated with the computer and telephone systems
- mobile workers – salespeople, travelling professionals, field support staff, etc. – can work effectively from any location and use their homes or local offices as bases.

Source: adapted from Home Office Partnership website – Offices White Paper

Study points

1. Which is the biggest mobile telephone group?
2. What is GPRS and what are its main advantages?
3. Which sorts of goods and services is m-commerce likely to provide?
4. What effects do you think mobile communications will have on the conventional office?

Online links

www.ft.com
www.hop.co.uk

Electronic communications had their origins in the nineteenth century; the first practical telegraph system was tried out in 1837; the telephone was invented in the United States by the Scotsman, Alexander Graham Bell, in 1876; and wireless telegraphy began before the close of the nineteenth century.

Now, at the dawn of twenty-first century, we are at the beginning of an even bigger revolution in the way we communicate with each other. This does not mean that all older forms of communication will disappear.

The book survived the arrival of the telephone, wireless and television and will, doubtless, continue into the new electronic age.

However, just as the telephone had a huge effect on personal and business life, so the present electronic revolution will have an even bigger impact on both.

As the case study shows, it is now introducing a completely new form of business – **m-commerce** – and may bring about revolutionary changes in the old-style offices which have been at the heart of business for the past century.

It is still too early to predict how successful and widespread m-commerce will be. A few years ago, some experts were predicting that e-commerce would be much bigger than it is.

It has been much slower to take off than some experts predicted. M-commerce may have an equally slow start, particularly as the companies which provide the service have had to pay the government billions of pounds for licences. If they try to pass on all these costs to customers, m-commerce may also get off to a slow start.

Mobile phones

However, the new electronic age has already had a big impact on communications. The majority of people in Britain – over 50 per cent of the total population – own a mobile phone. This was expected to reach 60 per cent by the end of 2000.

The mobile phone boom in Britain was caused to a large extent by the pay-as-you-go service. Users have to buy only a minimum of £10 worth of calls in advance, instead of taking out a more expensive annual contract. Britain has a much higher proportion of mobile phone users than the United States. There, only about one-third of the population has a mobile phone, although they are catching up fast. In Italy and Finland, almost three-quarters of the population are mobile phone users.

This rapid expansion in the use of mobile phones, plus growth in the use of the internet, has already brought about great changes in the ways we communicate with each other.

Free speech

For the first time ever, the internet provides an opportunity for millions of people to communicate with other people in all parts of the world. Hundreds of thousands of people, organizations and businesses, both large and small, have taken advantage of this opportunity and set up their own websites.

This has introduced real democracy into communication for the first time. Everyone has a voice. There are no editors, no publishers (only neutral **Internet Service Providers, ISPs**), no government intervention, though some governments want the right to intercept and read e-mails to fight crime and terrorism.

This freedom has had a great effect on communication. People can say exactly what they like – at any length – on their own website, even though some of it may lack much sense or interest. There is no

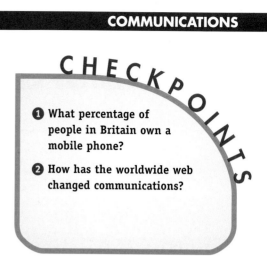

CHECKPOINTS

❶ What percentage of people in Britain own a mobile phone?

❷ How has the worldwide web changed communications?

guarantee that the message is true, unless the sender is a well-known company or organization which already has an honest reputation in the real world. It is also easy to communicate illegal information, such as how to make a bomb.

Despite these drawbacks, the internet has made it possible to create worldwide groups of people with similar tastes or needs, from fan clubs to support groups for sick people.

Pressure groups have able to get their message across to millions more people (see Unit 75).

Information of all kinds on every imaginable topic is freely available on the internet. However, there is so much information that it is sometimes difficult to find exactly what you want, unless you can find a well-edited specialist site.

Effects of e-mail

The other main component of the internet – e-mail – has had an equally big impact on communications. There is no strict layout for e-mail – no formal salutation or close – as there is with business letters (see Unit 64). Business e-mails tend to be brief, to the point and relaxed in style.

There is one big advantage to this. At present, businesses usually reply much more promptly to e-mails than they do to letters.

Another big advantage is that e-mails are much quicker and cheaper to send, particularly to foreign countries.

Some senior managers receive as many as 200 e-mails in a single day.

WAP communications will produce further changes. Messages will need to be even more succinct and brief because of the small size of the mobile screen.

KEY TERMS

Hot-desks Office desks which are used by more than one person.
Internet Service Providers (ISPs) Organizations which connect computers to the internet through a modem.
M-commerce Business transactions which are made by electronic means while people are on the move.
Wireless application protocol (WAP) A technology which allows mobile phones to receive internet communications.

Successful communications

CASE STUDY

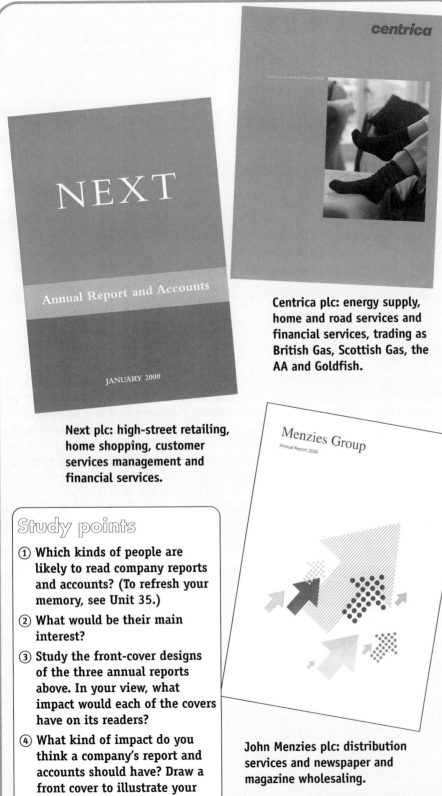

Next plc: high-street retailing, home shopping, customer services management and financial services.

Centrica plc: energy supply, home and road services and financial services, trading as British Gas, Scottish Gas, the AA and Goldfish.

John Menzies plc: distribution services and newspaper and magazine wholesaling.

Study points

① **Which kinds of people are likely to read company reports and accounts? (To refresh your memory, see Unit 35.)**

② **What would be their main interest?**

③ **Study the front-cover designs of the three annual reports above. In your view, what impact would each of the covers have on its readers?**

④ **What kind of impact do you think a company's report and accounts should have? Draw a front cover to illustrate your answer.**

> 'Remember that you have two ears and one mouth. Try to use them in roughly that proportion.'
>
> Source: Lifeplan, *The Sunday Times*, 7 June 1987

The main aim of all communications is to get your message across – and to receive the kind of response you want.

Basic skills

There are four basic communication skills.

- *Accuracy* is vital. In both face-to-face and telephone conversations it is essential to listen carefully to what other people are saying to gain an accurate idea of their views. Accuracy is just as important in writing. Check everything that you write to make sure it is accurate. If you don't know how to spell a word, use a dictionary. If you are not sure where a place is, look it up in an atlas. Don't make guesses.

- *Clarity* is also necessary. People must understand immediately what you are saying or what you have written. Before you write a word or open your mouth, make sure that you know the exact message you want to get across. Then make the message as clear and as simple as possible.

- *Simplicity* in speech or writing is also desirable. Short words are usually more effective than long ones. Being brief saves time and money. Sometimes, as with mobile phone messages, brevity is essential.

- *Completeness* is another important factor. To check that you have covered all the essential points make sure that you have answered the five key questions: Who? What? Why? When? How?

For example, if you were writing an e-mail or a memorandum to inform your line manager about a meeting with a supplier, you would need to answer all the following questions. *Who* was involved? *What* did

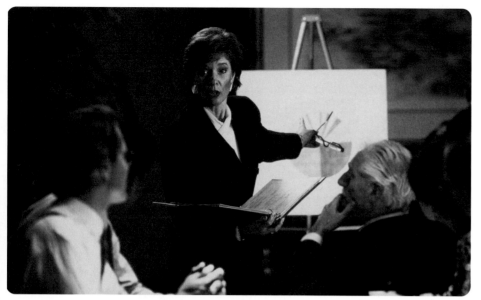

Presentations enable complex information to be communicated to many people at the same time

CHECKPOINTS

❶ Name four qualities in good communications.

❷ Explain in your own words why it is important to think of the receiver when you are communicating.

❸ Give two examples of how speed and timing could be important in communications.

they say? *Why* did they say it? *When* will they be able to deliver? *How* will they send it? And any other relevant information. If your communication leaves out one vital piece of information, it will fail.

Different responses

The kind of response you expect to your communication will differ according to whether the message is going downwards, upwards, or sideways in your organization. The main uses of downwards communication are:

● to give orders or instructions
● to provide, or ask for, information.

For example, your communication might be an announcement on a staff notice board telling employees to make sure all windows are locked before they leave at night. The message should be strong, clear and decisive. The expected response would be that employees would obey the order.

Upward communications are mainly used:

● to describe the results of actions
● to provide information which has been requested
● to make requests or appeals.

The message will tend to be more polite and persuasive. The hoped-for response might be agreement or gratitude.

The main uses of sideways communication are:

● to keep equals informed of actions taken, or results achieved
● to discuss means of tackling problems together.

For example, a manager might be making a presentation about a new product to her colleagues in other departments. She would hope that her colleagues would understand the complex information she was presenting. To make it easier to understand she is using visual aids. She would hope that her colleagues would be supportive and enthusiastic and come up with some useful suggestions.

Failed communications

There are many reasons why communications fail. The message may not be clear and simple enough to be understood by the receiver. Or, it may be so badly presented, or so boring, that it fails to hold the receiver's attention. A message should be designed for the person or organization it is being sent to.

The receiver of the message is just as important as the message itself. When you are talking to people, study their reactions. Watch what makes them annoyed, pleased, interested etc. Use these reactions to shape your message so that it will appeal to what they like to hear.

Receivers may be the main cause of the failure. They may be unwilling to take in the message because they are too busy,

or because they have made up their mind already, or because they are too prejudiced to hear the message clearly. In such cases, there is very little that the sender can do to get the message across.

The chosen channel may be wrong. For example, it would be no good trying to discuss a very complex contract with a colleague who had not seen a written copy of the contract. Therefore, always make sure that the receiver has been given some information in advance if there is a complex matter to discuss.

Or the timing may be wrong. If you want to interview a shopkeeper about her work, it is not a good idea to try to interview her when she is trying to serve a large number of customers. Always try to pick the right time for the communication – just ask the person you want to interview for a convenient date and time.

Key skills –
IT and communication

'IT'S THE WAY THAT YOU SAY IT.'
A florist imported some rare houseplants from Australia which proved so popular that the initial batch sold out on the first day. Using this information, write:

● a notice for the shop window
● a press release for the local newspaper
● a press release for a trade magazine
● a letter to the Australian supplier.

Save the files in an appropriate folder.

Revision and exam practice units 64–66

REVIEW POINTS

1 Give examples of situations when you would use:
- a memo
- a report
- a notice
- a circular letter
- a presentation.

2 Explain why communications are not always effective and how they can be improved.

3 State when you would use:
- a modem
- the web
- e-mail.

4 What are the most important factors in verbal communications?

5 Why is it important to be aware of the other person when you are trying to communicate?

Extended questions

1 You have been asked to re-equip a building company in Windsor with the latest information technology. The firm specializes in converting large houses into residential homes for the elderly and in designing and building new residential homes. It is now expanding into France. The firm does not have a large permanent staff, but employs many freelance professionals and subcontractors. Write a detailed report for the chief executive stating the information technology system you would recommend and its main purposes and advantages.

2 'Information technology produces more communication, but less sense.' Discuss.

Case study 1

St Lukes Communications

St Lukes is an employee-owned company operating within the communications/advertising sector. St Lukes was founded in 1995 and claims to be the world's first ethical, stakeholding advertising agency. Every employee is a shareholder in the company.

There are no job descriptions within St Lukes and everyone is encouraged to work outside their remit. Starting and finishing times are left up to the individual employee.

Employees work in project teams which are very much self-managed, although there is also a line manager for the purpose of appraisal and day-to-day resource decisions.

There is a review system of everyone's performance. This is a forward-looking exercise at which an employee's performance is discussed and planned and performance targets are agreed.

Personal development is discretionary, in that employees can define their own learning needs and targets with the proviso that staff share their knowledge with colleagues.

There are no office or dedicated meeting rooms in St Lukes. Instead there are Brand Rooms which are devoted to and used by clients.

They are decorated and fitted out to the client's taste. The Clark's room for example is like a shoe shop. The room can also reflect the product that the Brand Room exists to promote; the Boots No 17 room is furnished like a teenager's bedroom.

No employee has their own desk. Employees work anywhere they find it convenient to do so, as there are PCs available throughout the building, including the restaurant.

There are no fixed telephones as everyone has a mobile phone which works both inside and outside the building. Employees can choose to work at home if they wish to and the company has the internet and IT facilities to allow anyone to do so.

St Lukes attempts to communicate openly, transparently and directly. Staff are fully informed on all matters relating directly to the business, including such issues as major capital investment, new products, new services and the introduction of new technology.

Every Monday everyone in the company gets together to discuss pressing issues. Once every month, there is a creative review called the Flag Meeting at which everyone is brought together to talk about their work.

Every year employees choose two other employees to review their wages. The level of labour turnover within St Lukes is phenomenally low. Since the company started, only one person has left to join another company.

Absenteeism is also negligible within the company.

The value of its billed work in 1998 was £85 million. St Lukes achieved Agency of the Year award for 1997.

Source: adapted from DTI's Partnership at Work

1 When was the company started?

2 What is the main means of communication in the firm?

3 What special benefits does St Lukes provide for its clients?

4 Describe the working conditions of a St Lukes employee

5 Why do you think the labour turnover is so low?

Online links
www.dti.gov.uk

Case study 2

UK websites a turn-off for virtual shoppers

Britain's reputation as a nation of shopkeepers is under threat because while many retailers' high street operations continue to attract customers, their virtual stores on the internet are proving a turn-off.

The survey, by consultants from Shelley Taylor & Associates, found that websites of British online retailers, or e-tailers, typically trailed their US counterparts.

The survey of consumers' experiences at 100 e-tailers in the US and UK will present another blow for Britain's online retail sector. Jungle.com. which sells computer equipment and CDs was the only British company in the survey's top five. However, four of the bottom five were British.

Shelley Taylor said that the latest survey compared functions such as a retail website's ease of navigation,

Webpage from jungle.com

home page, links, browsing, ordering and customer service and support.

Ms Taylor added that more than three quarters of online shoppers were abandoning their virtual 'shopping carts' without completing their transactions.

Ms Taylor said that online retailers had to offer the same level of service as traditional stores, including the best delivery of goods and services and

consumer value.

'Contrary to media hype, web commerce represents a selling evolution rather than a revolution,' she said. 'The web is simply a new technology that can be used to facilitate an age-old process.'

Source: adapted from *The Times*, 22 May 2000

1 How many e-tailors did the survey cover?

2 Which two online functions do you think are most important for shoppers? Give your reasons.

3 In your opinion, what advantages could online shopping have over conventional methods for a) the consumer b) the retailer?

Case study 3

Satellite to create jobs and find cats

A new European satellite system that can track lost pets, sort out traffic jams, direct trawlers to fish, and bombs to their targets is being proposed by a consortium of Europe's main space companies. It would create thousands of jobs in Britain, but could also generate conflict with America.

'This system will have benefits beyond space,' said Eduert Dudok, Dutch chairman of Galileo Industries. 'It will go into mobile phones, banking systems, ground transport, you name it. Everyone will have a receiver.'

The Galileo satellites are being heavily backed by industry, which is putting up at least 50 per cent of the estimated £2 billion cost.

What is now driving the companies, led by Stevenage-based Astrium, is the potential for 120,000 new jobs and business opportunities – in traffic control, the emergency services and aviation – estimated to be worth at least £30 billion when the system starts up in 2008.

Source: adapted from *Evening Standard*, 5 June 2000

1 How much will the new system cost?

2 How many new jobs will it create?

3 Name what you think will be two of its greatest benefits.

Case study 4

Auction yourself online

The UK's first online people auction – enabling candidates to auction themselves to the highest-paying potential employer – has been launched by interviewme.co.uk. It follows last year's introduction of Talent Market, the world's first employment auction, which allows individuals to put personal profiles on to the web describing experience, skills and education, along with ideal assignments, fees and scope of work. Interested companies then bid for those they want to hire.

'It won't work here,' says Alannah Hunt, head of the executive search and selection group at PricewaterhouseCoopers. 'It's ridiculous to expect companies to hire people whom they haven't even met. Anyway, we all know some people embellish their CVs, so what exactly is it that companies will be bidding for?'

Source: adapted from *Independent on Sunday*, 25 June 2000

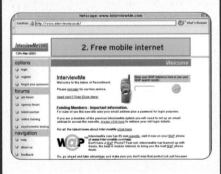

1 **What do you think are the advantages and disadvantages of this method of recruitment a) for the employer b) for the employee?**

2 **How might the disadvantages be overcome?**

3 **Suggest two kinds of employment where this method of recruitment might be appropriate.**

EXAM PRACTICE

A large company located in Surrey manufactures perfumes and cosmetics. For economic reasons, it has been decided to move the company to a new greenfield site in the Midlands. There are 800 employees but the company hopes, with more space and the introduction of new products, to expand its workforce to 1,000.

A number of the employees have been with the firm for many years, some are near retirement age, but others are highly skilled personnel in their thirties and forties.

Employees had been aware for the past year that changes were being discussed but the decision was reached only a month ago. There had been many rumours about the company – from fears of complete closure, to bankruptcy and take-overs by foreign firms.

The information was given by an announcement on the staff notice boards in each department. This indicated that most staff would be invited to move to the Midlands, that there would be relocation payments but some redundancy payments were anticipated.

At the end of August, in three months' time, the factory and administration is to close for a month while everything is moved. This time scale will also provide the opportunity for staff to find accommodation in the new area and to sell their homes.

The notice concluded with the notification of a meeting on the following Monday with the management of the company and the whole workforce, when further information would be given about future plans.

Up to the present time, industrial relations have been satisfactory and there have been no complaints relating to unfair dismissal or other areas of dispute.

Foundation

1 When was the decision to relocate made? (2 marks)

2 When should the workforce have been told about the possibility of relocation? (2 marks)

3 What methods of communication do you think should have been used to inform employees? (4 marks)

4 What necessary procedures do you think were not carried out? (4 marks)

5 What problems are a) the company b) the employees likely to face? (4 marks)

Higher

1 When was the decision to relocate made? (2 marks)

2 In what ways do you think the workforce should have been involved? (4 marks)

3 Make out a plan of the procedures which should have been followed. (4 marks)

4 Explain how the problems which have been created can now be resolved. (4 marks)

Section 9

Business in its environment

Government help

£180 billion investment plan

A £180 billion investment package to modernize the nation's transport system, cut congestion and deliver real choice, was unveiled in July 2000 by the Deputy Prime Minister, John Prescott.

Presenting Transport 2010 – The Ten-Year Plan, Mr Prescott said the government was working with business to deliver the long-term investment needed to rebuild our infrastructure, cut congestion, improve public transport and give people choice.

The plan sets out investment and spending plans of:

- £60 billion to improve the national rail network with new track, signalling, stations and rolling stock
- £21 billion for national roads to tackle congestion hotspots and safety through widening schemes, bypasses, junction improvements
- £59 billion to improve local transport, including up to 25 new light rail projects in our major cities, guided bus schemes, park and ride, priority routes and funding to improve rural transport
- £25 billion for London
- £15 billion held in reserve for future schemes.

Mr Prescott said: 'Private and public investment over ten years will be £180 billion: almost three-quarters – £132 billion – will come from the public purse.

'We will secure that investment through long-term partnership with the private sector: new rail franchises lasting up to 20 years, 30-year contracts for roads and a 30-year public private partnership for London Underground.'

Source: adapted from Department of the Environment, Transport and the Regions website news release, 20 July 2000

Online links
www.detr.gov.uk

Study points

① On average, what will be the annual cost of the transport investment package?
② How much will be provided by the private sector?
③ What is a public private partnership?
④ What are the main benefits that business will receive through the ten-year transport plan?
⑤ Do you foresee any difficulties in carrying out the ten-year plan?

In providing financial aid, the government tries to satisfy the needs of as many sections of the population as possible.

The government's ten-year plan for transport, described in the case study, is a good example. It is designed to bring many benefits to practically all sectors of business through easier and quicker transport of goods, and also to benefit millions of commuters.

It will be of particular assistance to firms in the road-building and construction sectors. Other firms which provide

transport services, such as rail companies, will also gain. Practically the whole of the population is supposed to benefit, too, through easier, quicker travel.

The plan may also encourage foreign firms to invest in Britain by setting up factories and offices here. Under European Union rules, the government is not allowed to offer foreign firms large sums of money to invest in Britain; but providing a good transport system and general infrastructure may encourage them to locate factories in Britain.

Assisted areas

Some people and areas of the country also need special help. By agreement with the European Commission, the government is allowed to give **regional selective assistance (RSA)** to firms in **assisted areas**. These areas suffer from high rates of unemployment, lack of opportunity and general neglect. Their decline has been caused mainly by the closing of the old traditional 'smoke-stack' industries of coal mining, steel-making and shipbuilding.

There are two kinds of assisted area:

development areas which need most help and intermediate areas which need somewhat less.

Northern Ireland has its own aid scheme. The aid is usually given for some large-scale project, such as opening a new factory, or modernizing or extending an existing plant. The grant usually covers five to 15 per cent of the total costs. The grants are designed to help **job creation**, to retain existing jobs, or to attract foreign companies, or businesses from other parts of the country, to the area.

Inner cities

Inner cities, with their widespread poverty and lack of businesses, are an even bigger problem. Governments have tried various ways of helping them.

In the 1980s, the government set up 12 urban development corporations (UDCs) to improve inner-city areas. The infrastructure – roads, public buildings, leisure facilities, etc. – was modernized in the hope that the private sector would open businesses.

The government also set up 24 **enterprise zones** to attract firms to inner-city areas.

Firms get valuable benefits, including not having to pay business rates, 100 per cent tax allowances for new buildings and easier planning permission. An enterprise zone designation lasts for ten years, but it can be extended. There are still a few enterprise zones, but there are no plans to create new ones.

New Deal

The present government has adopted a somewhat different approach to poverty by trying to help people to escape from their deprived lives through their own efforts.

They have been encouraged to find jobs through the government's New Deal welfare-to-work programme.

The working families' tax credit guarantees an income of £200 for families with a full-time earner. Inner city organizations which help the disadvantaged into work have been subsidized.

In all, £30 million has been provided to encourage enterprise in deprived areas.

Small businesses

One of the most successful and long-lasting aid programmes is the Small Firms Loan Guarantee Scheme.

It has helped thousands of small businesses, which do not have sufficient security, to obtain bank loans. The government guarantees 70 per cent of the loan, or 85 per cent for businesses which have been trading for two years or more. Loans range from £5,000 to £250,000 and can last from two to ten years. A new Enterprise Fund has now become responsible for this scheme.

The vast majority of firms are small businesses. They play a vital part in the economy as they create far more jobs than large companies.

The government recognized their importance by setting up a Small Business Service (SBS) in April 2000. The chief executive is David Irwin, former CEO of the enterprise agency Project North East.

The SBS is designed to create an enterprise society in which small firms can succeed. Its main objectives are to:

- provide a voice for small firms at the heart of government
- simplify and improve support for small firms
- help small firms to deal with rules and regulations.

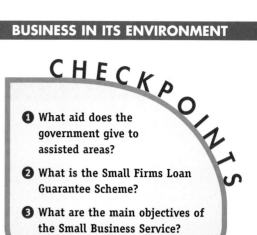

CHECKPOINTS

❶ What aid does the government give to assisted areas?

❷ What is the Small Firms Loan Guarantee Scheme?

❸ What are the main objectives of the Small Business Service?

It is too early yet to judge how successful the SBS will be in reducing red tape, which is one of small businesses' constant complaints.

Another long-standing grievance of small firms was the late payment of bills by big firms. Small businesses often waited months before big firms paid them and some went into liquidation in the meanwhile.

Small firms hoped that the government would make late payment illegal. Instead, in 1998, the government gave them the right to charge interest on unpaid bills.

The vast majority of small businesses have seen no real improvement in big firms' payments. Although they can now sue big firms, very few do so, Some fear they might lose future orders while others think it costs too much time and money.

Business Link

One of the first tasks of SBS was to restructure the **Business Link** organization. This provides support and advice for both small- and medium-sized companies. It provides:

- personal business advisers with general and specialized business skills, who will draw up plans to put businesses on the path to success
- an information service covering all aspects of business, including finance and exporting
- training programmes and conferences.

The existing 81 Business Link areas will be slimmed down to 45 in 2001. At the same time, 72 Training and Enterprise Councils, most of which are run by local business people, will lose some of their powers. Their training function will be taken over by new Learning and Skills Councils.

KEY TERMS

Assisted areas Areas where the decline of traditional industries, such as coal, steel and shipbuilding, has created high unemployment.

Business Links Government-sponsored agencies providing advice and information for small- and medium-sized businesses.

Enterprise zones Inner-city areas with tax and business rate concessions and easier planning permission.

Job creation Creating new jobs through investment or enterprise.

Regional selective assistance (RSA) Government aid for creating jobs in poorer areas of the country.

The European Union and its effects

Eurobarometer 53

Eurobarometer No 53 involved a survey of more than 16,000 people in April and May 2000.

Of those surveyed, 49 per cent (end of 1999, 51 per cent) took a favourable view of their country's membership of the EU, with 14 per cent opposed to membership and 28 per cent regarding it as neither a good nor a bad thing. The member states in which support is strongest are Ireland, Luxembourg and the Netherlands. The lowest levels of support were found in the United Kingdom, Austria and Sweden. There is a general downward trend in levels of support for the EU in most member states, including Germany and Austria.

The level of confidence in the Commission remains the same: 45 per cent of Europeans expressing trust in the Commission, with 30 per cent expressing mistrust. The Commission enjoys the confidence of only 25 per cent of the UK population.

Fifty-eight per cent (end of 1999, 60 per cent) of Europeans support the introduction of the single currency, the euro, whilst 33 per cent are against it.

Figure 1: The 15 members of the European Union.

For the first time, Eurobarometer surveyed the level of support for a European constitution, which was defined as a 'fundamental document combining the various treaties currently in place'. Seven out of 10 of those surveyed were in favour, with levels of support ranging from 88 per cent in the Netherlands to 47 per cent in the United Kingdom.

Source: adapted from European Union website, Eurobarometer 53

Figure 2: How the European Union works

European Court of Justice
Thirteen judges, assisted by six advocate-generals, from member states. Interprets European Union (EU) law and decides cases brought by governments, the European Commission, companies and individuals. Can impose fines. No right of appeal.

European Parliament
Voters in 15 member states elect 626 members of European Parliament (MEPs). Checks work of European Commission; approves budget; suggests changes in laws and can veto some.

Council of Ministers
Government ministers from the 15 member countries. Makes laws.

European Council
Heads of government of the 15 countries and their foreign ministers, plus the president of the European Commission. Meets three or four times a year to discuss major problems and policies.

European Commission
Twenty commissioners, including a president, chosen by governments of member states. Suggests laws; makes sure EU laws and treaties are applied; manages day-to-day running of the EU.

Study points

① **Which countries are members of the European Union?**

② **Which countries have the lowest level of support?**

③ **Explain in your own words the work of the European Commission.**

Fifteen countries, with a total population of 370 million, now belong to the European Union (EU), which started in 1957 as the European Economic Community (EEC).

The EEC's first aim was to create a common market by abolishing all **tariffs** between member countries and putting a **common external tariff** on all imported goods. That was achieved by 1968.

The next stage was to create a **single market** by removing all barriers to trade and the movement of capital and people between member countries. To a large extent, that has already been achieved.

The euro

In 1991, under the Maastricht Treaty, it was decided to replace national currencies with a single European currency, the euro. The euro notes and coins come into use on 1 January 2002.

Only 11 countries joined the euro zone. Greece did not join because it failed the economic tests, but it is now expected to join in 2001. Britain, Sweden and Denmark preferred not to join. In 2000, Denmark decided in a referendum, or vote of the whole people, not to join the euro. Britain may also hold a referendum, though the date has not yet been fixed.

Over 60 per cent of the British people are currently opposed to joining the euro zone, particularly since its value has fallen so sharply on foreign exchanges since its launch in 1999.

However, many businesses will have to be involved with the euro whether Britain joins the euro zone or not. Many companies will be forced to deal in euros, and foreign firms operating in Britain will do the same. Exporters will be forced to quote their prices in euros, and so, probably, will the Stock Exchange.

Enlargement

The second big change that is being made is to increase the membership of the European Union. Most national governments support this plan, although the policy does not enjoy popular support. In the Eurobarometer survey (see case study), only 27 per cent of people surveyed regarded it as a priority. Those most in favour of enlargement are the Danes (57 per cent) and the Greeks (53 per cent).

In December 1999, the EU invited six countries – Latvia, Lithuania, Romania, Bulgaria, Slovakia and Malta – to apply for membership. It also extended the same invitation to Turkey which has wanted to join for 36 years, but which had always been rejected (partly because of its human rights record).

There are already another six applicants in the queue – Hungary, Poland, the Czech Republic, Slovenia, Estonia and Cyprus. All these countries have to put their economic house in order before they join.

The first country may be admitted in 2002. If all eventually succeed, there will be 28 member states, with a combined population of over 500 million people.

Effects on Britain

The EU has had a great impact on business and many other aspects of life since Britain became a member in 1973.

Trade

Before Britain joined the European Union, about 40 per cent of its exports and imports were with EU countries. Now, its EU trade is 56 per cent.

Free competition

The European Commission can ban government subsidies or hand-outs to firms and can stop mergers between big firms if they would reduce European competition.

CHECKPOINTS

❶ Which countries did not join the euro zone when it started?

❷ How many countries want to join the European Union?

❸ When do euronotes and coins come into use?

Agriculture

The EU decides the number of animals British farmers can keep, and the basic prices they receive for some of their products. Its strict control over British farming was dramatically shown in 1996 when the EU banned all exports of British beef because of BSE, or mad cow disease.

Fisheries

To preserve fish stocks, the EU tells each country how many fish it can catch.

Environmental protection

The EU has introduced a wide range of laws to protect the environment. These include higher standards for drinking water and bathing beaches; a reduction in air pollution, particularly by cars; stricter controls over the disposal of poisonous materials and other harmful waste; encouragement to recycle and reuse paper and cardboard.

Social chapter

The social chapter of the Maastricht Treaty guarantees workers a minimum wage, a maximum working week of 48 hours and a minimum annual holiday of four weeks. Britain opted out of the social chapter. However, some of the reforms are being introduced.

VAT harmonization

Value added tax is now imposed in all member countries. As a first step to harmonizing VAT rates, or making them all the same, a minimum rate of 15 per cent has been set for most goods and services throughout the EU.

KEY TERMS

Common external tariff The common, or equal, tax which all EU countries put on goods from non-member countries.

Single market A single market guarantees free movement of goods, services, persons and capital in the EU.

Tariffs Customs duties, or taxes, on imported goods.

International trade

Trading into the future

Dover is a major trading port

The World Trade Organization (WTO) is the only international body dealing with the rules of trade between nations. WTO agreements have three main objectives: to help trade flow as freely as possible, to achieve further liberalization gradually through negotiation, and to set up an impartial means of settling disputes.

A number of simple, fundamental principles run throughout all the WTO agreements. They include: non-discrimination, freer trade, predictable policies, encouraging competition, and extra provisions for less developed countries.

The economic case for an open trading system, based on agreed rules, is simple enough and rests largely on commercial common sense. But it is also supported by evidence. **Protectionism** leads to bloated, inefficient companies and can in the end lead to factory closures and job losses. One of the WTO's objectives is to reduce protectionism.

Source: adapted from WTO website – Trading into the Future

'Why the world trade system is bad for people and the planet'

The world trade system pursues growth at all costs. It sees economic growth and increasing consumption as ends in themselves.

It ignores the fact that increasing consumption is depleting natural capital (the environment) on which the global economy is based. Increased trade also means more transport, leading to a loss of natural habitats and biodiversity and negative impacts on local communities.

It does little to promote development and environmental protection. The world trade system is increasing inequality between the 'haves' and the 'have nots'. It is also increasing employment insecurity. It

has not advanced human development, or relieved poverty, as more than a quarter of the developing world still live in poverty and more than 100 million people in the developed world live below the income poverty line.

Source: adapted from Friends of the Earth International website – Campaigns: the World Trade System

A trading nation

Membership of the European Union has changed the focus of British trade (see Unit 68) but trade with the rest of the world is still very important. For many centuries, Britain has lived on its overseas trade. It is currently the world's fourth biggest trading nation.

Every country's trade is divided into two parts: visible and invisible.

- **Visible trade** consists of imports and exports of physical goods, such as raw materials, components and manufactured goods.
- **Invisible trade** consists of imports and exports of services such as banking and insurance.

The difference between the value of visible imports and visible exports gives the balance of trade. For a number of years, Britain has usually had a deficit on its **balance of trade** because it imports more goods than it exports.

The difference in the value of the trade in both visibles (goods) and invisibles (services) gives the **current balance**. In the past, there was usually a surplus on invisible trade (services) which made up for the deficit on the balance trade (goods), creating a surplus.

Study points

① Which organization manages international trade?

② What are its three main aims?

③ What are the drawbacks of protectionism

④ Do you think Friends of the Earth International makes a good case against the world trade system? State your reasons.

Online links
www.wto.org
www.foei.org

However, in 1986, the invisible surplus was not big enough to make up for the deficit on visible trade. Therefore, Britain was in the red, or had a deficit, on its current balance. This continued until 1997 when the current balance was brought back into surplus again.

The **balance of payments** shows the total results of all Britain's financial dealings with the rest of the world, including visible and invisible trade and flows of capital, or investments by British companies abroad or investments by foreign companies in this country.

If there were to be a continuing deficit in the balance of payments, Britain would get more and more into debt with other countries.

It would have to borrow more money to make up the difference, or sell some of the assets its owns abroad.

Foreign firms might start to take out their investments in Britain and ask for repayment of current debts.

As a result, the value of the pound would start to fall, which would make imports dearer. Inflation might start to increase, which would result in a rise in interest rates. After a few years, the whole economy could start to spiral out of control.

Exchange rates changes

Changes in exchange rates cause some of the biggest problems in foreign trade. The **exchange rate** is the rate at which one currency can be exchanged for another.

For example, there might be a small decrease in the value of the pound against the United States dollar, from £1 = $1.41

to £1 = $1.39. That difference of a couple of cents would make very little difference to a family which was having a holiday in Florida; but it would make an enormous difference to a British exporter with a multi-million pound contract with an American firm. It would mean that the firm would receive far fewer dollars than it had expected. The difference might be large enough to wipe out a large part of its profit.

A high pound can also cause trouble for exporters.

In 1999–2000, the pound was high in relation to the euro. This meant that it became increasingly difficult for British manufacturers to sell their goods on the Continent. High interest rates in Britain were one of the main causes of the high value of the pound (see Unit 71).

One big advantage of the euro zone is that member states do not have that kind of problem, as the relative values of their currencies are already fixed. (In July 2002, their national currencies will be replaced by the euro.)

Help for exporters

Exporting is so important to Britain that the government makes a continuous effort to encourage British firms to export more, and to provide help for those businesses that do.

The Exports Credits Guarantee Department (ECGD) is a government department which guarantees British exporters against the risk of foreign importers not being able to pay their bills. It issues policies worth over £3 billion a year, some for as little as £25,000.

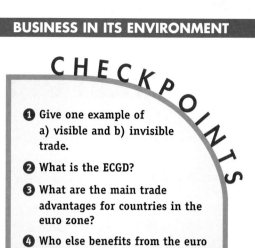

CHECKPOINTS

❶ Give one example of a) visible and b) invisible trade.

❷ What is the ECGD?

❸ What are the main trade advantages for countries in the euro zone?

❹ Who else benefits from the euro zone?

Government agencies

There are many more government agencies to help exporters. In 2000, they were all put under one brand name, Trade Partners UK. It is led by British Trade International (BTI) which has over 2,000 staff across Britain and throughout the world.

There is also a network of other organizations such as more than 100 chambers of commerce, over 100 export clubs and 45 Business Links to help exporters.

Another government agency, the Invest in Britain Bureau, has a different task. Its function is to encourage overseas companies to set up businesses in Britain (inward investment). This helps in job creation and is particularly important in assisted areas.

Inward investment

There has been a remarkable increase in inward investment by foreign firms in Britain in the last few years. The number of foreign investment projects increased to 757 in 1999–2000, a rise of nearly 75 per cent in five years. Almost half of the investments are in the services sector.

Britain is now the second most popular country in the world for foreign investment. Some of the main reasons are:
- no tariffs on exports to other EU countries
- relatively low wages
- flexible working
- less job protection than in some other EU countries
- the English language
- first-rate research facilities
- economic stability.

Location of business

Burroughs & Jackson, imaginary magazine printers, have had an excellent year with profits increasing 35 per cent to a record £1.68 million. Since the beginning of the financial year, they have won five new magazine contracts, all of them with publishers in London.

There is no room to expand on their present site in Crouch End, North London, so they have decided to relocate to new premises in either Milton Keynes, Buckinghamshire, or Brighton, Sussex.

Brighton & Hove

- Just over 50 miles south of central London, and the M25 London Orbital within 30 minutes drive time.
- Thirty-three direct train services per day to London Victoria, and 49 direct services to the City at London Bridge.
- London Gatwick International airport is 25 minutes by road and 30 minutes by train.
- Brighton attracts and retains a highly skilled, well-educated workforce with the lowest average earnings on the South East mainland.
- Brighton & Hove boasts over four million square feet of high-quality business accommodation.
- You can choose to live in an elegant Regency terrace, or a charming country residence just out of town.
- To relax, you can water-ski, windsurf or scuba dive, sail from the UK's largest marina, play 18 holes on one of our six golf courses and eat in a different restaurant every night of the year.

Source: adapted from Brighton & Hove website – Making Waves in Business

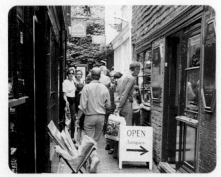

The Lanes in Brighton

Milton Keynes

- A congestion-free grid road network and excellent communication links. The M1 motorway runs through the area.
- Milton Keynes Central provides rapid rail access to London and is due to join the Eurostar network.
- Heathrow and Birmingham International airports are within 75 minutes drive.
- Working population estimated at 115,000 and expected to grow to 132,000 by 2001.
- New industrial and warehouse developments underway at Bradwell Abbey and Kingston, and 800 more acres of greenfield sites for industrial or commercial use.
- A wide range of housing, from modern executive homes to established townhouses.
- The area has numerous parks, lakes, traditional towns and villages and, in Milton Keynes City, over 180 miles of dedicated bridleways, footpaths and cycletracks.
- Sports Village is a new sports and entertainment complex with shops and restaurants and Europe's largest indoor real snow ski slope.

Source: adapted from Invest in Milton Keynes website

Online links

www.imk.co.uk
www.brighton-hove.gov.uk

Study points

① How long would it take to drive
   a) from Milton Keynes to Heathrow airport and
   b) from Brighton to London Gatwick airport?

② Why is the surrounding countryside important in choosing a business location?

③ In your view, which town would be the most suitable for Burroughs & Jackson? Give your reasons.

④ What else would the firm need to know before it came to a final decision?

The Sports Village in Milton Keynes

As the case study shows, it is not always easy to choose the best site for a business, because so many factors are involved. Some of the most important are:

- transport links
- nearness to main markets
- suitability of premises for business and homes for employees
- work force, particularly availability, age, skills and wages
- local environment and infrastructure
- possibility of grants from local council, government and the EU
- **external economies of scale.**

Transport links

At one time, many industries, such as steel and textiles, which relied on coal for power and raw materials from overseas, had to be near coal mines and ports. Improved transport has given businesses a much greater choice of location.

About 80 per cent of goods are delivered by road. Motorways make it easy to deliver raw materials or goods door-to-door, even to remote regions.

Nearness to motorways is therefore one of the most important factors in choosing a location.

Until recently, most exports to Europe also went by road. However, the Channel Tunnel has speeded up journeys to the Continent so much that railways may regain a bigger share of the market. Businesses that trade with more distant countries need easy access to ports and airports.

Nearness to markets

Improved transport has given manufacturers a freer choice of locations, though there are a few exceptions.

For example, firms that use heavy, bulky raw materials may find it easier to be near the source of their supplies. Other manufacturers can move out of cramped, old-fashioned, expensive inner-city factories into purpose-built premises on **greenfield sites** or **industrial estates**.

Retailers have a smaller choice. They have to choose locations that are convenient for their customers.

Workforce

The supply of labour is another important factor. Are the right kinds of skilled and graduate employees available? Are the local wage and salary levels reasonable? Is the work force adaptable? Are there similar industries in the area?

Local environment

The local environment is also important. If the location is pleasant and has good facilities, it will be easier to attract and retain employees and their families.

Again, employers must ask a number of questions. Is there plenty of good housing at reasonable prices and of different grades, from 'semis' to executive homes? Are there good schools, both State and private, and colleges that might provide training courses? Are there good entertainment facilities, such as golf courses, swimming pools, fitness centres, cinemas, theatres and clubs? Is the surrounding countryside attractive and easy to access?

Grants

It would not be wise to move to a location simply to get a grant, but it can be useful if a large investment is involved.

As Unit 67 has shown, it is not always easy to get government grants, even in assisted areas.

Some foreign firms which invest in Britain receive government grants, but the amount and the conditions are controlled by the EU which has to make sure that competition between countries remains fair.

The EU also provides some grants for various regions of member states.

Under Agenda 2000, these are now concentrated on regions whose development is lagging behind that of other regions (Objective 1) and regions with economic structural difficulties (Objective 2). These are areas where a long-established industry, such as coal mining, has ended, creating large numbers of unemployed people.

The EU also gives other grants for modernizing education and training (Objective 3).

CHECKPOINTS

❶ Why are transport links important in choosing a business location?

❷ What are the advantages of greenfield sites?

❸ Where would you site a) a flower stall b) a fruit and vegetable import firm and c) a nuclear power plant? State your reasons.

Planning permission

The attitudes of local authorities towards business are still important. Most of them are now far more sympathetic about planning permission than they used to be. They are more willing to give permission for new buildings or necessary alterations to existing premises.

It is often much easier for a business to obtain planning permission if it can show that the development will create new jobs. In some assisted areas, local authorities offer financial inducements for businesses to move to the area.

It is not always necessary to get planning permission from the local authority if the premises have previously been used for the same sort of business.

Permission would be needed, however, if there was to be a change of use from, say, a jeweller's to a fish-and-chip shop. Some businesses, such as child minding, pet shops and scrap-metal dealing, also require licences.

Economies of scale

Firms in the same line of business often set up near each other.

For example, lawyers may be found in the same street, or restaurants in the same area of a city. This can bring great benefits through external economies of scale.

For example, a restaurant will be able to obtain supplies of food, staff and customers more easily as there are similar firms nearby. Banks, too, may be more willing to help as they will understand the special problems of the industry.

KEY TERMS

External economies of scale Cost-saving benefits which arise when similar firms are located near each other or when a whole industry sets up an organization to take common action, such as providing training courses.

Greenfield sites Farm or waste land used for building new towns, industrial estates or retail parks.

Industrial estates Factory sites in selected areas of towns and cities which provide new industrial buildings and all necessary services, such as roads and power supplies.

Revision and exam practice units 67–70

REVIEW POINTS

1 What kinds of help does the government provide for small businesses?

2 What is an enterprise zone? State two benefits businesses receive.

3 What are the benefits and drawbacks of Britain's membership of the European Union?

Extended question

1 Show, using examples, how the choice of a location for a business might depend on
a) transport links
b) government aid
c) opportunity cost.

Case study 1

Offices into homes as firms move out of town

Firms moving out of inner cities have been a growing headache for local authorities and property agents alike. As companies pull out they leave behind a wasteland of unused office blocks. This in turn has a knock-on effect on secondary businesses and the whole city economy.

Filling the hole left by departing firms has been a tricky task; but in Bristol many industry players lay the credit firmly at the door of one group – city-based Unite. The company, which builds and manages student and key worker accommodation, is widely seen as the catalyst of the city centre's revival.

Philip Hillman, partner at King Sturge, said Unite has played a fundamental role in the revival of the centre. It was the first to recognize the demand for student accommodation as well as the potential of unwanted office buildings.

'Nobody could find a use for 1970s office buildings standing empty and unlettable in the early 1990s,' said Mr Hillman.

'Along came Unite, the first company in Bristol and at least one of the earliest nationally to recognize the potential of city centre living.'

The company has acquired around 20 properties in Bristol, including three former BT offices which it converted to student accommodation. A former Mecca building has been levelled and a 392-room student accommodation block and several retail outlets built in its place.

Source: adapted from *Bristol Evening Post*, 24 May 2000

1 Why are companies moving out of city centres?

2 Why is it a headache for
a) local authorities and
b) property agents?

3 In what way does it have a knock-on effect on secondary businesses?

4 What effect is the new student accommodation likely to have on the city?

Case study 2

Shoeshop.com

Steven Cochrane, 41, and co-director Stuart Paver set up their internet site Shoeshop.com in York five months ago, but they've already had thousands of pounds in grants.

'I've just been on an online retailing course which costs £1,000 but £500 was paid by a grant from Teesside Training and Enterprise Council,' says Mr Cochrane. 'When we put virtual reality graphics on our website, three-quarters of the £4,500 cost was paid by the EU Regional Development Fund. Now we are talking to Business Link Teesside about IT training for some of our five staff – we may be able to get a 100 per cent grant for that.'

The company is applying for a grant to help meet the cost of translating the website into other languages and are seeking grants to help them set up a distribution centre in the Netherlands.

Source: adapted from *Daily Mail*, 23 August 2000

1 Why have Steven and Stuart been awarded so many grants?

Case study 3

Why the money tree is unpicked

There are millions of pounds in grants lying around waiting for small firms to take them up, but many small businesses never do, simply because they don't know about them. There is no central government-run hotline where you can find out about grants for small businesses.

Your chances of getting grants are better if you are in business in a depressed area or area of high unemployment. But some grants are far more widely available. IT and exporting are considered to be the easiest areas in which to get grants.

You will have to show how the grant will benefit not only your own firm, but also the local economy or the economy as a whole, by providing more jobs for instance.

- Enterprise grants are aimed especially at small firms in selected areas.
- Smart awards are grants to help you improve your use of technology.
- Regional Development Agencies offer grants for converting rural buildings for commercial use.
- Export market research grants from the DTI can pay up to half your costs for research, travel etc. in connection with starting to export.

Source: adapted from *Daily Mail*, 23 August 2000

1 Which business people are most likely to get grants?

2 Why do you think the government is offering grants for IT and exporting companies?

3 What conditions does the government impose on its grants?

4 What are the drawbacks of government aid?

Case study 4

Flood of investment from abroad as UK booms outside euro

The Invest in Britain Bureau said foreign investment has soared to new heights in the first full year since the launch of the single currency.

There were 757 new inward investment projects from 30 countries in the year up to March, creating 52,783 jobs.

The UK continues to outstrip the rest of Europe, taking the lion's share of American and Japanese investment in the EU.

There was also a dramatic rise in the level of money flowing in from Germany, with an increase of more than 50 per cent in the number of projects to 63.

Why Britain?

Harry Wagner, co-owner of the internet service provider Net-Thing, said the reason he came here was because Britain is 'buzzing with high-tech innovation and know-how.

'I regard the East Anglia and Cambridge area as the Silicon Valley of Europe. There is a window of opportunity for firms like mine. Things are really moving there and I have great confidence in Britain.'

Confidence in the UK economy was the main reason why French giant Saint Gobain poured £65 million into a new glass factory near Selby, North Yorkshire.

Spokesman Steve Watkinson said, 'We definitely see this country as having major business potential.' Another plus point was the 'aptitude and attitude' of UK workers who can rapidly pick up the required skills.

The skill of British workers was also a factor in the decision by Japanese firm Mitsui Kinsoku to open a car components plant at Capel Hendre, South Wales.

Source: adapted from *Daily Mail*, 6 July 2000

EXAM PRACTICE

Pete Brooklyn deals in antiques and collectables from his home in Norfolk. He obtains most of his stock from early-morning visits to car boot sales, local auctions and by knocking at doors of houses in surrounding villages. Most of his goods are sold on to bigger dealers in cities for a reasonable profit. He has decided to expand his business by exporting some of his goods to dealers on the Continent.

Foundation

1 State the kind of production Pete is involved in. (2 marks)

2 How could the internet help in the expansion of his business? (4 marks)

3 What would be the main advantages of exporting some of Pete's goods? (4 marks)

Higher

1 What would be the main advantages of exporting some of his goods? (4 marks)

2 The value of the pound has dropped against the euro. What effects would this have on Pete's business? (2 marks)

3 What help could Pete obtain from the government to expand his business? (4 marks)

1 What was the number of inward investment projects last year?

2 On average, how many new jobs did each project create?

3 Why are foreign firms choosing to invest in Britain?

Government controls

Halifax house price index

The Halifax house price index has been published since 1983. It therefore indicates how average house prices within each UK region have moved during the last few years.

The indices are based on the detailed records of the prices, physical characteristics and the regional location of all the houses on which the organization has made a mortgage offer in each time period.

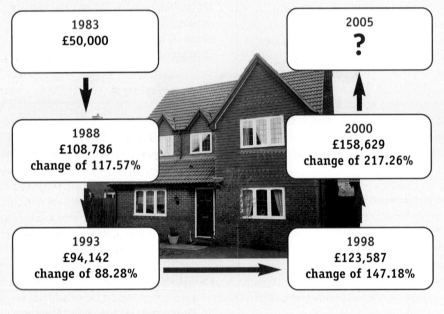

1983
£50,000

2005
?

1988
£108,786
change of 117.57%

2000
£158,629
change of 217.26%

1993
£94,142
change of 88.28%

1998
£123,587
change of 147.18%

Source: adapted from Halifax house price index website

Study points

① How much did the price of an average house in the South East increase between 1983 and 2000?

② What was the average annual increase in price?

③ What was the average annual percentage increase in the two years between 1998 and 2000?

④ In your view, what is the price of the average house in the South East likely to be in 2005?

Online links
www.halifax.co.uk

Inflation

Inflation is a rise in the general level of prices. As the case study shows, there was a general upwards trend in the price of houses in the South East throughout the whole period, but not at an even rate.

In fact, prices actually fell in the early 1990s, when there was a slump, or a decline in the economy, with falling prices, rising unemployment, and declining trade.

The rate of inflation in the cost of certain goods, particularly houses, also varies greatly in different parts of the country.

The highest rises are usually in London and the South East. The lowest are usually in the north of the country.

Inflation is greatly affected by the general state of the economy. When a country's economy is booming, demand increases and prices rise. This results in bigger pay demands by workers. Firms are forced to put up their own prices to pay for the higher wages.

And so it goes on, with increasing wages and rising prices, until the government puts up taxes, or the central bank increases interest rates, so that the economy starts to slow down again.

Inflation creates a general uncertainty, which practically all businesses dislike. It is difficult to plan or to invest, as it is impossible to predict prices or what will happen to the economy.

The businesses that benefit most are those that want to make a quick profit in any way they can, but many other firms and people suffer greatly.

Pensioners are usually the first to be affected, as they often have a low fixed income and few savings to fall back on. With inflation, or the general rise in prices, their pensions buy less and less each year.

Exporters are also affected. Wage increases and other costs force up the prices of their products in both British and foreign markets. Their products become uncompetitive abroad, so their customers refuse to buy them.

Savers suffer for a similar reason to pensioners. With inflation, their savings buy less and less each year.

However, companies and individuals who have borrowed large sums of money benefit. Their burden of debt declines in the same way as the value of savings, because all money is affected whether it is saved or borrowed.

For instance, at an annual inflation rate of ten per cent, both debts and savings would halve in real money terms in less than seven years. A firm which owed £100,000 would owe the equivalent of only £50,000 at the end of that period.

Taxation

Because inflation has such harmful effects on the economy, all governments try to control it. One of their main weapons is **fiscal policy**, which deals with taxation and public spending. An increase in any tax will slow down business activity in various ways.

- An increase in income tax will reduce the amount that consumers have to spend as they will have to pay more tax to the government.
- An increase in VAT will also reduce consumer demand as goods and services will become more expensive. However, it increases prices and may therefore lead to bigger wage claims.
- An increase in fuel duty will put up the cost of motoring and bus fares. It will also make most goods dearer as there is a transport cost built into their prices.
- A rise in corporation tax, which is paid by businesses, will force them to reduce investment, pay lower dividends or cut costs.
- An increase in national insurance contributions will reduce consumer spending as employees will have less to spend. It will also increase firms' costs – and cut their other spending – as they will have to pay more money to the government to cover their share of the national insurance contributions.

Public spending

The amount the government spends also has an effect on inflation. Sometimes, the government spends more money than it receives in taxes. The difference is made up by borrowing money – the **public sector borrowing requirement (PSBR)**. However, the government may decide to reduce its spending. For example, it might decide to cut spending on defence. This will have two main effects. It will reduce demand, as the firms which supply the armed forces with goods and services will have fewer orders. It will also help to cut the supply of money, as the government will have to borrow less money.

Monetary policy

Another way of controlling inflation is through **monetary policy**. This has two main components: **money supply** and **interest rates**.

Money supply is the total amount of money available in the economy, including coins and notes, and bank and building society deposits. Some economists believe that reducing the money supply is the most effective means of controlling inflation.

However, it now generally accepted that interest rates are a better weapon. High interest rates raise the cost of all borrowed money, such as mortgages and credit card debts, so that consumers have less money to spend on other goods and services.

Businesses will also think twice about new investments because it will cost them more to borrow money. This all helps to cool the economy.

Until 1997, the government controlled interest rates. Very often, decisions about changing interest rates were made on political, not economic, grounds. No government was likely to raise interest rates in the year before a general election, as millions of voters would be affected.

One of the first acts of the Labour government, when it came to power in 1997, was to hand control of interest rates to the Bank of England, so that totally independent decisions could be made on purely economic grounds. If Britain joined the euro zone, the Bank of England would have to hand over control of interest rates to the European Central Bank.

Exchange rates

Another important effect of changes in interest rates (in the short term, at least) is on exchange rates. The exchange rate is the price you have to pay to buy another currency. At any one time, the pound buys so many American dollars, so many euros etc. If Britain raised its interest rates, foreign investors and currency dealers would tend to buy the pound, or keep it if they have it already, as they will get a bigger return on their money. This would keep the value of the pound high in relation to other currencies.

However, if Britain cut its interest rates, foreign investors would tend to sell the currency, as the return on their money would drop. This would lower the value of the pound. It is important to keep exchange rates at a steady level. Otherwise, it is difficult for businesses to plan, as they do not know how much they will receive for their exports or how much they will have to pay for their imports.

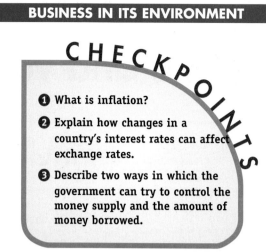

CHECKPOINTS

1. What is inflation?
2. Explain how changes in a country's interest rates can affect exchange rates.
3. Describe two ways in which the government can try to control the money supply and the amount of money borrowed.

KEY TERMS

Fiscal policy Government decisions about taxes and public spending.

Inflation A continuing rise in the general level of prices. For example, with an inflation rate of 10 per cent a year, a £100 suit would cost £110 the next year, £121 the following year, and so on.

Interest rate The price paid for borrowing money, stated as a percentage.

Monetary policy Controlling interest rates and the money supply, or the total amount of money in the economy.

Money supply The amount of money of all kinds circulating in an economy.

Public sector borrowing requirement (PSBR) The amount of money the government borrows to balance its books.

Key skills
Number

INTEREST RATE CHANGES
You borrowed £50,000 at an interest rate of nine per cent which was later increased to 10.5 per cent. How much more would you have to pay in interest each month?

Laws and voluntary codes

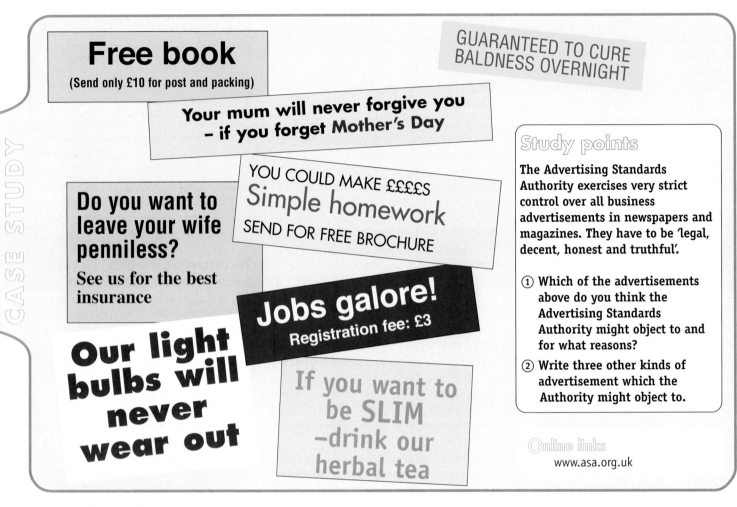

Free book
(Send only £10 for post and packing)

GUARANTEED TO CURE BALDNESS OVERNIGHT

Your mum will never forgive you – if you forget Mother's Day

Do you want to leave your wife penniless?
See us for the best insurance

YOU COULD MAKE £££££ Simple homework SEND FOR FREE BROCHURE

Jobs galore! Registration fee: £3

Our light bulbs will never wear out

If you want to be SLIM –drink our herbal tea

Study points

The Advertising Standards Authority exercises very strict control over all business advertisements in newspapers and magazines. They have to be 'legal, decent, honest and truthful'.

① Which of the advertisements above do you think the Advertising Standards Authority might object to and for what reasons?

② Write three other kinds of advertisement which the Authority might object to.

Online links
www.asa.org.uk

Business and the law

There are thousands of laws relating to business. Every year, the government and the EU make many more. Some of their main aims are to:

- protect employees (see Units 61, 62 and 63)
- protect consumers (see Unit 73)
- protect the environment (see Unit 74)
- increase competition by ending monopolies (see below).

Monopolies

A total monopoly exists when one firm has complete control over the production of one kind of good or service. It can then set any price it chooses for its products because there is no competition.

Before privatization there were a number of monopolies in Britain, such as railways (see Unit 13). These have now been split up so that they are no longer controlled by one firm. Twenty-three companies have a franchise to operate rail services on different sections of the rail network.

The Monopolies and Mergers Commission was set up in 1948 to investigate takeovers and mergers which might be against the public interest. Mergers were usually investigated if they would create a market share of more than 25 per cent, or if they involved acquiring assets over a certain amount.

In 1973, the Fair Trading Act set up an Office of Fair Trading with wider powers and a director general who had greater independence and the power to investigate anti-competitive actions by single firms or even individuals.

Then in 1998, a new Competition Act was passed which prohibited many more anti-competitive practices. The Act, which came into force in 2000, applies to businesses of all kinds, including sole proprietors. It makes illegal all **cartels** and any abuse by one firm of it dominant position in a market. For example, price-fixing between firms, where they agree to keep prices at a high level, or agreements to restrict output to keep up prices, are both illegal.

Under the Act, the director general of fair trading is given much greater powers. His or her officials can enter premises and demand to see relevant documents.

Penalties are very heavy. A business can be fined up to ten per cent of its UK turnover, which could be millions of pounds.

At the same time, the old Monopolies and Mergers Commission was replaced by a new Competition Commission.

Figure 1: Major laws affecting business

1968 **Trade Description Act** stops businesses giving a false or misleading description of goods or services.

1970 **Equal Pay Act** says men and women should receive the same pay for the same work or work of equal value.

1973 **Fair Trading Act** sets up Office of Fair Trading.

1974 **Consumer Credit Act** protects people who buy on credit.

1974 **Health and Safety at Work Act** requires employers to provide safe premises and healthy working conditions.

1975 **Sex Discrimination Act** makes sex discrimination illegal.

1976 **Race Relations Act** make it illegal to discriminate on grounds of race, or colour, or ethnic origins.

1987 **Consumer Protection Act** makes businesses liable for any damage caused by defective goods.

1994 **Sale and Supply of Goods Act** says all goods must be safe, durable and free from defects.

1995 **Disability Discrimination Act** makes big firms treat disabled people no less favourably than other employees.

1995 **Environment Act** controls pollution of land, air and water.

1998 **Competition Act** makes anti-competitive agreements between firms illegal.

1999 **Employment Relations Act** makes trade union recognition easier and improves parents' rights.

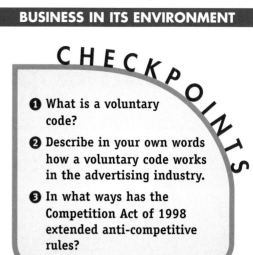

CHECKPOINTS

❶ What is a voluntary code?

❷ Describe in your own words how a voluntary code works in the advertising industry.

❸ In what ways has the Competition Act of 1998 extended anti-competitive rules?

The ASA supervises the rules which were written by the industry. The code's basic principles are that advertisements should be:

● legal, decent, honest and truthful
● written with a sense of responsibility to consumers and to society
● in line with the principles of fair competition.

If the advertisement breaks the code the ASA can ask the advertiser to withdraw it – a request which is rarely refused.

It is doubtful if any of the advertisements in the case study would find much favour with the ASA. Goods cannot be described as 'free' if consumers have to pay more than the current postal rates with no extra charge for packing. There are strict rules about advertisements dealing with baldness and slimming. No claims can be made unless they can be scientifically proved! The same condition applies to electric light bulbs. Children should not feel inferior if they do not buy something and no advertisement should prey upon fear without good reason. Job advertisements should not include a request for money and homeworkers should be told what they might earn.

This has two main functions. It investigates mergers to see if they are against the public interest. It also hears any appeals against decisions of the director general of fair trading.

Industry regulators

Before privatization, many of the public utilities, which supply essential services, such as water, were monopolies.

Although some competition has been introduced since the public utilities were privatized, the companies which provide essential services are still very powerful. The government has created **industry regulators**, or watchdogs, to make sure that the companies do not exploit their customers or make excessive profits.

Under the new Competition Act, the regulators have been given the same powers as the director general of fair trading.

Voluntary codes

Many businesses are subject not only to the law, but also to **voluntary codes**. Some of the businesses which have their own codes are travel agents, dry cleaners and garages.

One of the most successful is the British Code of Advertising and Sales Promotion, which covers all business advertisements except those on television and radio. One of the main reasons for its success is that it is run by an independent body – the Advertising Standards Authority (ASA) – which was set up in 1962.

Cartel A small number of firms which agree to share out a market between themselves.
Industry regulators Officials who make sure that privatized public utilities do not charge excessive prices and do not restrict competition.
Voluntary codes Standards of business behaviour which are established freely by trade associations for all their members to follow.

Key skills
Communication

Write a voluntary code for a football club of your choice, suggesting ways of behaviour for fans that will help to prevent trouble both inside and outside the ground.

Consumer protection

You buy a jacket in a sale, but find that it has a dirty mark on the sleeve. When you take it back, the shop assistant refuses to give you your money back.

You order some fresh broccoli in a restaurant, but you are sure that it is frozen. The waiter denies this and says that it was freshly cooked that evening.

A woman signs an agreement at home to buy some double glazing on credit terms. Three weeks later she goes back to the shop and says she's changed her mind. The firm refuses to cancel the order.

A man asks a broker to get him a mortgage and pays a deposit of £100. Eventually, he gets a mortgage on better terms elsewhere. Six months later, he asks the broker for his money back, but she refuses to give it to him.

Study points

(Read the Unit before you attempt the study points.)

① Who was right – the business or the customer? Explain your reasons.

② If the customer was right, what further action could be taken?

Consumer rights

Consumers need laws to protect them because they are much weaker than the big, powerful companies which sell them goods and services. The government has made many laws to protect consumers.

Trade Descriptions Acts, 1968 and 1972, stop businesses giving false or misleading descriptions of goods or services.

Consumer Credit Act, 1974, protects consumers when they buy on credit. It:

- makes firms which give credit have a licence
- forces firms to state the annual percentage rate of interest, or APR (see Unit 26)
- prevents firms inviting people under 18 to buy on credit or to borrow money
- gives people who sign credit agreements at home time several days to change their mind
- allows mortgage brokers to charge only £3 if a mortgage offer is not taken up within six months.

Consumer Safety Act, 1978, prevents firms selling goods which might be harmful or dangerous, especially toys, electrical goods, and cosmetics.

Consumer Protection Act, 1987, makes firms liable for any injury caused by defective goods and prevents misleading pricing.

Sale and Supply of Goods Act, 1994, states that all goods, including sales goods, must be:

- safe
- durable, or not likely to wear out quickly
- fit for all purposes for which they are normally used
- free from even minor defects, including appearance, unless they are pointed out at the time.

Effects of laws

Consumer protection laws have had a great impact on business. Before manufacturers launch a new product, they have to take into account all the relevant laws. When it is being made, they must have strict quality control to make sure that all the goods are up to the legal standard. If there is a faulty batch, the manufacturers must order retailers to clear their shelves or publish recall notices in the newspapers, or both. Most big businesses now have a customer service department to deal with any complaints.

Trading standards

Trading standards officers, employed by 200 local authorities in the UK, try to make sure that the 50 Acts of Parliament and 500 sets of regulations which control the buying and selling of goods and services, are carried out. They visit shops regularly to see that:

- their scales and other measuring equipment are accurate
- goods are being sold at the advertised price
- the goods comply with laws relating to quality.

Officers also visit farms to inspect how food is produced and to check on the welfare of animals, particularly when they are transported. They also investigate complaints from members of the public and give advice to both shopkeepers and consumers.

If they find a trader is breaking the law, trading standards officers will usually give a warning. If the trader does not stop breaking the law, they will prosecute. But they are so badly underfunded that they cannot always carry out all the work they would like to do.

Watchdogs

There are many other official and unofficial watchdogs to protect consumers. The Director General of Fair Trading has wide powers to investigate and ban any business practices that are against consumers' interests. There are official regulators with powers to control prices for the privatized utilities, such as water and gas. There is an **ombudsman** for the National Health Service (NHS) and one for

local government. Banks, building societies and insurance companies have all set up their own ombudsman schemes.

One of the strongest defenders of consumer rights is the Consumers' Association. It investigates all kinds of goods and services, and many other consumer issues, and publishes the results in the Which? series of magazines. There are articles in newspapers and magazines dealing with consumer topics, while radio and television programmes, such as Watchdog, carry out in-depth investigations. Citizens' Advice Bureaux provide general help and advice for consumers.

Small claims cases

If all else fails, consumers can sue firms for damages. If the claim is for £5,000 or less, the consumer can use the small claims procedure in a county court, which costs much less than going to a higher court. The hearing is informal and is usually presided over by a district judge. Most people do not employ a solicitor but state their own case. One big advantage is that the costs payable by people who lose are very strictly limited, which means that they do not have to pay the other side's large legal bills.

Which? magazine, produced by the Consumers' Association

Revision and exam practice units 71–73

Case study 1

Small firms rage at red-tape tide

The government is coming under increasing fire from small businesses for its failure to tackle red tape. It follows last month's damning report from the Better Regulation Task Force, which said government departments ignored their own guidelines on cutting red tape.

The British Chambers of Commerce estimates the total cost of red-tape burdens over the five-year parliamentary term at £10 billion.

Among the burdens cited by small-business people are:

- *Working Time Directive*: limits the working week to 48 hours. Owners have to spend time doing paperwork to show they comply.
- *Working Families Tax Credit*: one of the growing number of taxes small businesses are supposed to administer – without compensation. Others include PAYE, student loans and, in the future, housing benefit. Each time one is introduced, the firm's pay-roll systems must be changed.
- *Other regulations* such as health and safety, environmental and fire regulations. Each has a separate inspector – small firms have called for one to complete all the tasks.

The government has taken steps to stem the red-tape tide. But the Better Regulation Task Force says only a major change in Whitehall culture can eliminate it.

Source: adapted from *Daily Express*, 23 May 2000

1 What is the estimated cost of red tape to business?

2 In what ways does it place a burden on small employers?

3 How does the government benefit from red tape?

4 Which regulations do you think are of most benefit to employees?

Case study 2

EU says all food vendors need a licence

Every food outlet in the country, including ice-cream sellers, sandwich bars and hot dog stands, must prove they adhere to strict hygiene standards or lose a licence to trade under new Brussels rules.

Outlet operators will not be able to handle money and food at the same time – unless they wear gloves and remove them to accept cash.

The move is likely to affect more than 500,000 food businesses in Britain, including farms, supermarkets, manufacturing companies, corner cafés and street kebab vendors.

A Food Standards Agency spokesman said that even charity event organisers may have to consult local environmental health officers.

All food premises will have to display a licence number, just like London taxis, so that people can complain or report an outlet for poor hygiene.

Owners will also have to draw up a risk analysis for their business and their controls, and safeguards will be checked by food inspectors before they are allowed to trade.

It could cost each trader from £200 to £1,000 to comply with the new standards. Critics last night condemned the increase of red tape from Brussels, but EC Health and Consumer Protection Commissioner, David Byrne, insisted: 'This has got to be done for the protection of the consumer. Public health is very important.'

Source: adapted from *The Times*, 22 July 2000

1 How many businesses will be affected by the new regulations?

2 What problems will it create for a) the government b) employers?

3 What benefits could it provide for the consumer?

4 What do you think would be the hygiene risks and safeguards needed with a road-side tea-bar?

Case study 3

Petrol prices 'crippling industry'

The rising cost of petrol is doing more damage to business than staying outside the euro, hauliers claimed last night.

The Freight Transport Association (FTA), with 11,000 member firms operating more than 200,000 goods vehicles – half the UK fleet, said the 'ultra-high' cost of fuel was crippling British industry. The FTA has written to the Chancellor of the Exchequer demanding an immediate cut in fuel tax, which accounts for 75 per cent of the cost of petrol.

The fact that British industry faces the highest fuel tax burden in Europe means that fuel costs represented one-third of the operating costs of a truck, with the largest vehicles paying more than £20,000 a year in fuel duty. FTA director general David Green said other European countries were reducing tax to counteract rising crude oil prices.

The vice chairman of the Road Haulage Association, Bob Russett, who runs Birmingham-based Palletline PLC with 3,000 vehicles and 2,200 employees across the UK said: 'Fuel duty is hurting us more than the effect of the weak euro.

'We've seen our fuel costs increase by £8 million this year. It is absolutely horrendous. Fuel used to account for up to 28 per cent of our operating costs, but now it is 40 per cent.'

Sir Tom Blundell, chairman of the Royal Commission on Environmental Pollution, said traffic exhaust fumes are growing and increasing the peril posed by greenhouse gases.

Source: adapted from *Daily Mail*, 6 July 2000

1 Why are petrol prices high in the UK?

2 What effect does the high fuel tax have on a) British industry b) the consumer c) the government?

3 Do you think the high taxes help to reduce the effects of exhaust fumes and greenhouse gases? Give your reasons.

4 What other steps could the government take to reduce environmental pollution, apart from raising petrol taxes?

EXAM PRACTICE

Paula and Rodney had just bought their first flat on the second floor of a large Victorian house, converted into four apartments.

They decided to buy a blue three-piece suite and found just what they wanted in one of the large out-of-town stores. The company said they could deliver it in a week and Paula and Rodney paid with a cheque. They were disappointed when the salesman later phoned to say it would take a month, but they decided to wait and it finally arrived.

After the departure of the delivery men, they examined the settee and found that one of the feet had been broken off and was missing. They promptly complained to the company, who said that they should have checked before the men left and that perhaps they had done it themselves. They also observed that it was a large object to carry up two flights of stairs.

Paula and Rodney later also noticed, to their consternation, that the material on the side of one of the chairs was torn. When they examined it, they realised that the chairs and settee were stuffed with sponge rubber and not with the special material as advertised. There was even an illustration of the material in the pamphlet the store had given them.

They contacted the firm again. They were told that they could have torn the chair themselves, that the company could not repair the foot for the same reason and that they had been unable to send the exact model as advertised in the pamphlet as these were now out of stock. They said they had sent the substitute model in good faith.

Foundation

1 Which consumer protection Acts has the company failed to observe?
(2 marks)

2 What steps might Paula and Rodney have taken earlier to avoid some of the problems? (4 marks)

3 Write a letter that Paula and Rodney might send to the company, stating all the problems and the course of action they expect them to pursue.
(6 marks)

4 If they fail to act on those instructions, what further steps can Paula and Rodney take? (6 marks)

Higher

1 Which consumer protection Acts has the company failed to observe?
(2 marks)

2 Enumerate the various clauses of the Acts which are relevant to their situation. (6 marks)

3 Explain the steps that Paula and Rodney can take to deal with the situation. (4 marks)

4 What other methods of purchase for durable goods could Paul and Rodney have used? Give your views about what would have been the best method. (6 marks)

Environmental issues

CASE STUDY

Kyoto climate treaty heading for the rocks

Leading industrialized nations are working to undermine the effectiveness of the world's only agreement to combat global warming, according to a global coalition of environmental organisations, including Friends Of The Earth, Greenpeace and WWF.

The Kyoto treaty that is supposed to reduce emissions of global warming pollution by five per cent over the coming decade could be twisted to allow some country's emissions to increase by 15 to 20 per cent.

One of the largest loopholes concerns rules for forestry activities. Canada, Japan, Australia, the United States, New Zealand, Sweden and France favour rules which would give incentives to chop down old-growth forests and replace them with new plantations from which they can claim pollution credits.

The treaty offers enormous flexibility for countries to meet their targets by trading pollution 'rights' through projects in each other's countries, and by relying on forests to soak up carbon pollution from the air.

'If governments don't pull the helm over, the Kyoto Protocol is headed for the rocks,' said Jennifer Morgan of WWF International.

Environmental groups are also pressing to prevent Canada, Japan, France, Australia, the USA, New Zealand and the UK from having nuclear power accepted under Kyoto's 'Clean Development Mechanism'.

'The Kyoto Protocol is slowly but surely being destroyed as governments seek to open up loophole after loophole. It would allow them to avoid doing anything to reduce emissions from burning fossil fuels, which is the primary cause of climate change,' warned Karla Schoeters of Climate Network Europe.

'Just as surely as we are seeing the world warm, and the first signs of climate disasters ahead, like the floods in Mozambique and the big storms in Europe at the end of 1999, the main polluters are trying to escape putting their own house in order,' said Mie Asaoka of Kiko Network, Japan.

Source adapted from Greenpeace website, Climate press releases, 13 June 2000

Study points

1. State one recent sign of global warming.
2. What is the main cause of global warming?
3. How are some developed countries trying to evade their obligations under the Kyoto treaty?
4. Describe one other big environmental problem apart from global warming.

Online links

www.greenpeace.org

Green issues

Global warming, acid rain, water **pollution** and similar issues have become of great concern to business, the government and the public in recent years. Everyone, it seems, is interested in protecting the **environment** now. What has brought about this dramatic shift in attitudes? Environmental pressure groups are mainly responsible. Three of the most important pressure groups are:

- *Worldwide Fund For Nature (WWF)*, which was originally set up as the World Wildlife Fund in 1961. It now has offices in many countries and is concerned not only with wildlife but also with many other issues.
- *Friends Of The Earth*, which was started in the United States in 1970. A British branch was set up a year later. It has made the public – and governments – aware of many environmental problems, such as the cost of nuclear power, the dangers of air pollution, etc.
- *Greenpeace*, which was founded in 1971 in the United States and now has branches in many countries, including Britain. It is best known for its small boat protests against nuclear tests. It also carries out educational and research work.

These three groups, and others, have campaigned for many other measures to protect the environment, such as lead-free petrol, animal rights, etc. It is an almost endless list, as independent scientists and researchers go on discovering the harmful effects of so many industrial 'advances' of the last 20 or 30 years.

Some of the main environmental concerns are global warming, acid rain, the hole in the ozone layer, pollution, waste disposal, loss of wildlife and GM food.

Global warming

Global warming is caused mainly by carbon dioxide (CO_2) emissions. In the United Kingdom these are caused mainly by industry (28 per cent), domestic (27 per cent), transport (26 per cent) and other (19 per cent). During the last 30 years, industry has been most successful in cutting its emissions by over one-third, while emissions from cars and lorries and other forms of transport have more than doubled.

Developed countries agreed to reduce emissions of carbon dioxide and the five other main 'global warming' gases, by an average of 5.2 per cent in a treaty (protocol) signed at Kyoto, Japan, in 1997. Britain is committed to reducing its CO_2 emissions by 12.5 per cent below 1990 levels by 2012. However, the government wants to achieve a bigger reduction of 20 per cent. An annual six per cent increase in duty on fuel was one of the ways in which the government hoped to achieve its target but this caused such great protests from the transport industry and ordinary motorists that it has now been dropped.

If CO_2 emissions are not checked, it is calculated that the average global temperature will rise by about 0.3°C and the sea level by about 4 cm every ten years. This would result in more extremes of drought and floods in different areas and violent winds and hurricanes. There would be an increase in desert areas, more coastal and river flooding and great climatic changes.

Acid rain

The main cause is sulphur dioxide (SO_2) and other gases from power stations and vehicle exhausts. Acid rain kills trees and fish, and damages the stonework of buildings. The government has decided that SO_2 emissions should be reduced to 80 per cent of the 1980 level by 2010!

Ozone layer

The ozone layer is a thin layer of bluish gas 20 to 40 km above the Earth. It protects the Earth from ultraviolet radiation, which can cause skin cancer. Some chemicals, such as CFCs (chlorofluorocarbons) in aerosols, refrigerators and plastic foam can deplete, or thin, the ozone layer and let through dangerous radiation. There is now a huge hole in the ozone layer, the size of the United States. The use of CFCs was ended in the European Union and Britain in 1994, though their use is still permitted for a few

medical purposes; but they will not be phased out in developing countries until 2010. It is hoped that the ozone layer will eventually thicken up again.

Air pollution

Air pollution is of various kinds and comes from a variety of sources. Motor vehicles are one of the main sources. New cars now have to be fitted with catalytic converters, which reduce harmful emissions by over 75 per cent. All vehicles are now tested annually for black and harmful smoke emissions. Leaded petrol has now been phased out for general use in Britain. Old cars, which cannot be converted, use lead replacement petrol instead.

Some cities have banned all cars, or restricted them from entering central areas, to reduce atmospheric pollution, traffic noise and congestion. Roadside tracks have been built to encourage commuters and shoppers to use bicycles instead of cars. Car manufacturers have produced new gasoline direct injection (gdi) engines, which reduce petrol consumption by a fifth, and reduce harmful exhaust emissions; while others have made eco-friendly electric cars and vans. But car ownership and use is still soaring.

Water pollution

Some progress has been made in cleaning up seas and rivers. Sea dumping of liquid and solid industrial waste, including metals and ash from power stations, was banned in 1993. Some experts are concerned that pesticides and other chemicals used in farming may seep down through the earth and pollute water supplies.

Waste disposal

Elaborate packaging of goods causes litter and waste disposal problems. The EU plans to convert all member states from throwaway to recycling societies, by reusing such materials as paper, glass and steel cans. The disposal of dangerous wastes, such as poisonous chemicals and radioactive materials from nuclear plants and hospitals, presents special problems.

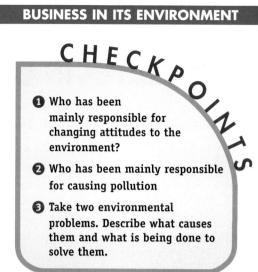

Wildlife

Many British songbirds are under threat. In all, there are 116 endangered species of animals, including the red squirrel and otter, and many endangered wild plants. The main reason is the loss of their natural habitat, or home, such as hedges, heaths, woods and moorland. These have been destroyed by new farming methods and by new housing estates, factories and roads.

GM food

Genetically modified (GM) food is produced by taking a gene from one species of plant or animal and putting it in another, so that it gains some of the characteristics of the other species. For example, genetically modified tomatoes contain a gene which delays rotting and allows them to remain firm even when they are ripe.

Organic farmers fear that GM crops will pollute their own crops by pollination. Doctors are unsure what effects GM foods might have on health as insufficient independent tests have been carried out. There are also concerns about the long-term effects on other plants and animals and the whole environment.

Key skills
Communication and IT

REPORT WRITING
Take a factory, an airport, a club or any other business you know and write an environmental report stating how it affects the environment and what improvements could be made. Print a hard copy.

KEY TERMS

Environment The physical surroundings necessary to support life.
Pollution Doing something which makes the environment unhealthy or dangerous.

The effects of pressure groups

Live animal transport

Every year millions of animals destined for slaughter suffer appalling journeys across Europe. The Royal Society for the Prevention of Cruelty to Animals (RSPCA) is fighting for their welfare.

After intense pressure from the RSPCA and other animal welfare groups, a maximum journey limit was agreed in June 1995 under a European Union Directive.

No animal – from cattle and sheep to horses and pigs – should travel in the EU for more than eight hours in 'basic' vehicles without being unloaded, fed, watered and rested for 24 hours. However, in vehicles that meet certain additional standards, animals can travel for much longer periods, depending on species and age.

The RSPCA believes that the Directive has not been properly put into effect in all member states. For example, France has excluded the eight-hour journey limit from its legislation, meaning that animals can travel through France for up to 24 hours.

The Directive has also been interpreted differently by member states. Germany and Italy, for example, do not believe that the EU can stop imports from countries outside the EU which break EU standards. Other countries, such as the UK, disagree.

Ultimately, the RSPCA wants to see a carcass-only trade where animals are slaughtered close to the point of production and the carcasses transported in refrigerated lorries. In the meantime the society wants:

- proper enforcement of the permitted journey times
- financial encouragement from the EU and national governments to develop local abattoirs, or slaughterhouses

- clarification of the obligations of authorities which maintain border controls
- France to immediately implement the EU Directive's eight-hour maximum journey time.

Source: adapted from RSPCA website: Campaigns – Live animal transport

Online links
www.rspca.org.uk

Study points

1. **Under EU rules, what is the maximum time live animals can be transported in a day?**
2. **Which EU country does not obey this rule?**
3. **Explain the loophole that Germany and Italy have found in the rule.**
4. **What reforms does the RSPCA want?**
5. **What actions do you think the RSPCA could ask its supporters to take to help in the campaign?**

Businesses are affected not only by laws, but also by **pressure group** campaigns.

Pressure groups try to change attitudes and persuade the government or other organizations to ban activities they oppose, such as testing the safety of cosmetics on live animals.

If that method of protest fails, another group may take direct action by picketing shops which sell goods that have been tested on animals.

It is much easier for a company to deal with a complaint by an individual than a campaign by a pressure group.

In the same way that a trade union has greater strength than isolated workers, a pressure group has greater power than its individual members.

Unlike trade unions, however, most pressure groups usually concentrate on just one issue – such as stopping cruelty to animals.

Long history

Some pressure groups have a long history. The oldest animal welfare organization in the world is the Royal Society for the Prevention of Cruelty to Animals (RSPCA) which was started in 1824.

Among the society's founders were William Wilberforce, who helped to end slavery in the British colonies, and Richard Martin MP, who sponsored the Animal Protection Act of 1822. This was the first law in the world to ban cruelty to cattle, horses and sheep. In 1840, Queen Victoria gave the society the right to use 'Royal' in its name.

Since then, the society has grown into a nationwide organization with a budget of £60 million a year and a network of nearly 200 volunteer branches in England and Wales. It is supported entirely by voluntary contributions.

Every year, its 328 inspectors investigate more than 100,000 complaints about cruelty to animals. RSPCA animal hospitals and clinics care for over a quarter of a million animals a year, including some wild animals.

In addition to the campaign described in the case study, the RSPCA is opposed to keeping hens in battery cages, fur farming and hunting.

In recent years, the number of pressure groups has increased greatly. Some are international, like Greenpeace (see Unit 74). Others are national, like the anti-smoking group ASH (Action on Smoking and Health). There are also many local pressure groups.

A minority of these local groups are concerned more with selfish interests – the NIMBY ('not in my back yard') principle – than genuine principles.

For example, rich residents may oppose a housing association building rented homes in their area as it might reduce the value of their houses; or small shopkeepers may campaign against a supermarket opening on the edge of town to save their own businesses.

Pressure groups can also campaign against government or official policies.

For example, the campaign in the early 1990s against the Thatcher government's poll tax, or community charge, was one of the most widespread and violent in recent times. Millions of people refused to pay the tax, and there were many marches and demonstrations.

The government had replaced local rates by a standard tax of a set amount which practically all people over 18 had to pay to the local council, regardless of their income.

After a few years, the government abolished the poll tax and the present system of a local rate on the value of the home was introduced.

Campaign methods

Whether they are large or small, pressure groups use similar means to achieve their objectives. They try to contact the chairperson of the company or companies against which they are campaigning. They lobby (or meet) MPs or government ministers to get their support. Local pressure groups also contact local councillors to see if they can help.

Pressure groups also use many kinds of publicity to achieve their aims. These include:

- writing letters to newspapers and magazines
- holding public meetings
- publishing advertisements
- distributing leaflets
- organizing marches and demonstrations.

The internet has provided pressure groups with a far more powerful means of communication. They can now make their views known 24 hours a day to any interested persons in any part of the world at very small cost. The internet has also been used for organizing direct action through e-mails.

Direct action

If these constitutional methods fail, some groups may use **direct action** instead, which is designed to have an immediate impact on the organization itself. For example:

- protesters have occupied trees to prevent a bypass being built
- workers have staged sit-ins to stop a factory being closed
- animals used to test drugs or cosmetics have been released from their cages
- GM crops have been pulled up
- fuel refineries and distribution centres have been picketed by lorry drivers and farmers.

Effects on business

Pressure groups have had some dramatic effects on businesses by reducing their turnover or forcing them to change the way they make their products.

Pressure group campaigns against smoking, fur coats and testing cosmetics on animals have all had a great impact on the businesses involved.

Business reactions

Some companies respond positively to the action of pressure groups by discussing the matter with them and either agreeing to their demands or coming to some compromise.

Companies may also use campaigns as a guide to public thinking and shape their policy accordingly to give consumers more of what they want.

Other companies oppose the activities of pressure groups through a public relations campaign of their own.

Key skills
Communication and IT

You are working for a pressure group which is opposed to the government's welfare to work policy and wants to obtain increased support and benefits for single parents who wish to stay at home and bring up their children. You have been asked to produce a small pamphlet setting out the group's aims and appealing for support. Print hard copies of the cover, including an image, and the introduction to the pamphlet which gives a summary of the group's case.

KEY TERMS

Direct action Campaigns designed to have a direct effect on an organization, e.g. by not buying its products. This method is used when normal means of persuasion appear to have failed.

Pressure group People who band together to try to change the attitudes of politicians, business people and the public to a particular issue, such as experiments on animals.

Social responsibilities of business

The Body Shop: company profile

Anita Roddick, founder of the Body Shop

The Body Shop International plc is a values-driven, high-quality skin and hair-care manufacturer and retailer operating in 49 countries with over 1,800 outlets.

The Body Shop has always believed that business is primarily about human relationships. We take the view that the more we listen to our stakeholders, and the more we involve them in decision-making, the better our business will run.

The company's campaigns against human rights abuses and in favour of animal protection have won support from a generation of consumers. The company continues to lead the way for other businesses to use their voice for social and environmental change.

How we do 'business as unusual'
The company retains its trademark emphasis on natural-based products using traditional recipes. The Body Shop has also developed a Community Trade programme which creates sustainable trading relationships with communities in need around the world.

What we believe in
The Body Shop is a stakeholding company. It believes its success is dependent upon its relationships with all its stakeholders: employees, franchisees, customers, communities, suppliers, shareholders and NGOs (non-governmental organizations). In 1995, the company put that belief to the test. It introduced an independently-verified audit of its own performance promises on social and environmental issues – The Values Report.

The report, three independently verified statements on the company's environmental, animal protection and social/stakeholder performance, was hailed as trailblazing by the United Nations Environmental Programme.

The Body Shop approach to ethical business operates on three levels.
Compliance: opening up to defined standards of human rights, social welfare and worker safety, environmental protection and, where relevant, wider ethical issues like animal protection.
Disclosure: only through public disclosure can a real process of dialogue and discussion with stakeholders be achieved and the right direction charted for the future.
Campaigning: to play an active part in agitating and campaigning for positive change in the way the business world works, with the ultimate aim of making a positive impact on the world at large.

Source: adapted from The Body Shop website – About Us

Online links

www.the-body-shop.com

Study points

① In how many countries does The Body Shop operate?

② Who are the company's stakeholders?

③ What type of production is the company involved in?

④ In your view, which are the three most important ethical business principles of The Body Shop?

Businesses do not exist separately from the rest of society. Think what might happen if a company decided to close a big factory and transfer the work to other sites for the sake of greater efficiency and productivity.

If the factory provided most of the work in the town, the effects could be terrible. Not only would many people lose their jobs, but smaller firms which provided the factory with goods and services would also suffer. Shops, pubs, cafés, banks, transport, leisure facilities and much more would also be affected. There would be an effect on the whole of society as social security payments would increase, though these might be balanced by the firm's greater profits and productivity.

Nevertheless, the costs to society could be great: a 'ghost' town of unemployed might result.

Social responsibilities

A company's first responsibility may be to its shareholders to increase profits so that they are happy and the company survives.

But, as the case study shows, some companies now believe that they have **social responsibilities** to all their stakeholders – their employees, franchisees (if any), customers, communities, suppliers, shareholders and charitable organizations (see Unit 22).

In the past, business decisions were made almost entirely on the basis of **private costs and private benefits.** For example, if an airport was being extended, some of the private costs would be:

- the cost of the land
- building costs
- interest charges
- running costs.

Some of the private benefits would be:

- greater turnover
- bigger profits
- lower unit costs.

External costs

The private costs and benefits would all be itemized in a firm's accounts, but they would not include the **external costs and benefits.** Some of the external costs might be:

- greater noise
- more traffic congestion
- reduction in business at other airports.

Some of the external benefits might be:

- greater British share of air traffic
- more employment
- cheaper air fares.

When the private costs and benefits and the external costs and benefits are combined, or joined together, they produce the **social costs and benefits.**

- private costs + external costs = social costs
- private benefits + external benefits = social benefits.

Environmental effects

Environmentalists have made us far more conscious of the external costs and benefits of business decisions. Sometimes these are not easy to measure in financial terms, but this is not always the case.

Let's look at the issue of acid rain (see Unit 74). It is fairly easy to assess how much it would cost to stop emissions from factories, power stations and car exhausts that result in acid rain.

It is not much more difficult to calculate the external costs of this in the destruction of forests, fisheries and crops.

If it cost a billion pounds to stop acid rain for good and it resulted in a saving every year of £500 million in trees, fish and crops, it would be a great bargain.

Human safety

The argument about external costs becomes most heated when human life is involved.

All forms of transport involve some risk. None of them can ever be made completely safe. Sometimes, however, improvements could be made if enough money were spent.

For example, many experts believe that roll-on roll-off ferries could be made safer by fitting bulkheads. These are huge metal partitions which can be closed to divide the ship into watertight compartments. If one part of the ship is holed and starts to let in water, the other compartments would keep the ship afloat.

This would delay the sinking of the ship, giving passengers and crew much more time to escape.

Would it be worthwhile spending millions of pounds to put bulkheads in all ferries, if human lives might be saved? Or should we continue to take the risk that a few lives might be lost?

And if bulkheads were to be installed, who should pay?

Different groups in society might give very different answers to these questions.

KEY TERMS

External costs and benefits The consequences for the rest of society of a business decision.

Private costs and benefits The effects of a business decision on the business itself.

Social benefits The benefits of a business decision on both the firm concerned and the rest of society.

Social costs The costs of a business decision on both the firm concerned and the rest of society.

Social responsibilities The obligations that one group, e.g. a business, a trade union, or a government, has to other groups in society.

Key skills
Communication and IT

A big manufacturing company, which provides most of the jobs in a town, announced it is to close. This has provoked many critical letters in the local newspaper. You are the company's public relations officer. Compose a letter to the newspaper explaining the reasons for the closure, and print a hard copy.

Population and change

The changing face of Britain

IT DOESN'T MEAN YOU'RE SOFT.
IT MEANS YOU WON'T HAVE DRY SKIN.

A booming sector for the next 10 years

By the year 2010, there will be more people in this country aged over 55 than under 25. Although young people in general are in decline, this new decade will see a nine per cent recovery among 15-24s. Coming directly after Generation X, this group of young adults has been called Generation Y.

However, they are very different in outlook from their more pessimistic and anti-establishment predecessors. Generation Y are a more optimistic group, highly technology- and media-literate.

In real terms this group is more well off than any youth generation since the 1960s. The growth of this age group is good news for the fashion and personal care sectors, although with this notoriously fickle segment it is still just as hard to predict exactly which fashions will be in vogue from one season to the next.

The most dramatic fall in Britain's demographic landscape is amongst late twentysomethings and thirtysomethings. Growing wealth and conspicuous spending during the 1980s and late 1990s made this the main target segment for many retail brands.

Smaller segment

By 2010, the 25–39-year-old segment will have lost a total of two million adults, equivalent to 15 per cent of their 2000 population. This is bad news for the many 'mainstream' retail brands targeting this segment, and also for household or DIY-related products, as there will be fewer people in this generation settling down and buying their first home.

While thirtysomethings are declining, the number of fortysomethings is charging ahead. There will be a million more people between 40 and 49 in the next five years, and a further half-million by the end of the decade – an increase of 19 per cent over the ten-year period.

Value for money

In the past, reaching 40 has seen a change in people's spending priorities: fashion, convenience and out-of-home pursuits have traditionally begun to take a back seat to value for money, investing in the home and saving for the future. However, these fortysomethings will have grown up in a brand-conscious environment. They are unlikely to want to give up this lifestyle as they reach middle age.

There will be over a million more 55–69-year-olds (a 12 per increase) in the next five years, and then a further 600,000 before the decade is out – representing a total population increase of 19 per cent in the ten years.

This will be the first generation to benefit significantly from private pensions. Advances in health and living standards will make them much more energetic, actively looking for products, services and activities to spend their disposable income on.

Retailing changes

These shifts are all helping to change the nature of the retail economy. According to Verdict, the whole idea of the mass market is now defunct. What is emerging to take its place is a far more fragmented marketplace in which each fragment wants to be spoken to separately.

Source: adapted from Verdict on Retail Demographics website

Study points

① Which population group will decrease most in the next ten years

② Explain what effects this decline is likely to have on retailers.

③ How are the new generation of people, aged 55 to 69, likely to be different from previous generations of that age group?

④ If you were the owner of a three-star hotel in the Cotswolds, how would you try to take advantage of these changes in population?

Online links
www.verdict.co.uk

As the case study shows, changes in the population can have a dramatic impact on all businesses, including retailing – the biggest sector in the whole economy. These changes can also have a great effect on the public sector.

National census

The main official source of information about the population is the Office for National Statistics. Every ten years, it carries out a national **census** of all the people and households in Great Britain.

The census held in April 2001, will provide valuable information on the age, sex and ethnic composition of the population, family structure, types of housing, vehicles and work. It will help the government and local authorities to plan local services and make it easy to discover regional differences and variations.

The census also provides a useful mine of information for the private sector and for researchers.

The science which studies the population and its changes is called **demography**. Some of the most important aspects for the public sector are:

- total size of population
- proportions in various age groups
- the working population
- the retired
- geographical distribution.

Population size

The population of the United Kingdom is 59 million and still growing. Unlike most other EU countries, where the population is static or falling, Britain's population is expected to keep on growing until 2023, when it will reach 61.5 million. Then it will start to fall again until, in time, it reaches a figure of 54 million.

The size of various age groups in the total population is of no less importance than the overall size. If there are a large number of people below school-leaving age for example, the government and local

authorities will have to spend more on education. If, on the other hand, there is a decline in the number of children under 16, the costs to the public sector will fall.

However, when that generation starts working, there might be a new problem – a fall in the total working population. This might be partly balanced by cutting unemployment, by persuading older people to go on working, or by making it easier for mothers to work. But a decline in the working population means that there are fewer people to support those who are either too young, or too old to work. This creates more problems for the public authorities.

Senior citizens

Better living conditions and improved medical care have increased expectation of life.

In 1911, a man's expectation of life was 50 and a woman's 54. In 2021, it will be 79 and 83 respectively. However, this puts an increasing burden on the National Health Service as older people are the main users.

There are also problems with long-term care. At one time, old people did not have to pay to live in public sector nursing homes. However, the cost became so great that the government started to make a charge. Some old people had to sell their homes to pay the charges. There was such a public outcry, that the government has decided that nursing care in nursing homes will be free. But, except for the very poorest, people will have to pay for living there.

Pensions

Over 11 million people now receive a State retirement pension. Just over one-tenth of them also receive income support.

The British pension is much smaller than the pension in most other EU countries, but governments have been unwilling to pay old people a reasonable

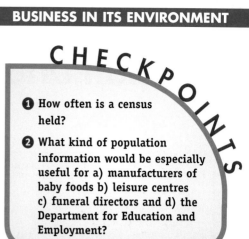

pension. Instead, successive governments have gradually reduced their obligations to the elderly.

The last Conservative government broke the link between pensions and wages so that pensioners no longer share in the rises in general prosperity. Instead, increases in the State pension were linked to the retail price index.

In spite of protests from their supporters, the present Labour government has failed to restore the wages link.

The government is also encouraging people to provide their own pension. Over half of the working population are now in occupational pension schemes.

Distribution

Movement of the population between different regions creates more problems for the public authorities.

The number of people in central London is currently growing again, partly reversing the previous trend for Londoners to move out to the suburbs.

At the same time, thousands of people are moving from the North of the country to the South East in search of better jobs.

The public sector has to provide more general facilities for people in London and the South East and deal with increasing road congestion, crime and stress.

At the same time, the public authorities may need to provide more aid for the North which is being deprived of some of its most skilled, and ambitious, workers who have moved South.

KEY TERMS

Census An official count of the population, including such data as sex, age, occupation etc., which is carried out at regular intervals.
Demography The scientific study of population.

Revision and exam practice units 74–77

REVIEW POINTS

1 Explain how pressure groups operate. Describe the objectives and methods of one pressure group.

2 What are social costs and benefits? State what the social costs and benefits might be of opening a) a supermarket b) a club and c) a police station.

3 State the effects that recent environmental laws and regulations have had on business.

Extended questions

1 You have been put in charge of local community relations at a 20-year-old nuclear plant which has been getting some bad publicity lately. Explain in full how you would try to gain the goodwill of the public by
a) conducting tours of the plant
b) local sponsorship schemes
c) newspaper publicity.

2 What is demography?

3 Explain how a demographic study might be of use to a business, giving examples and illustrating your answer with charts or graphs.

Case study 1

Supermarket's probe to restore our faith in food

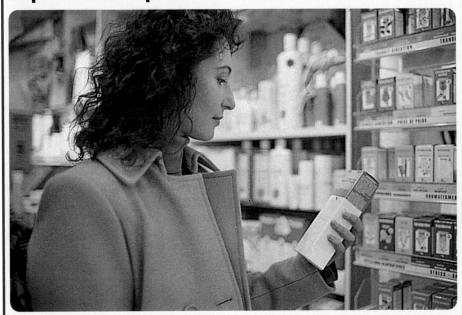

The Co-op has launched an investigation into concerns over how Britain's food is produced.

A survey by the supermarket chain found that more than three-quarters of shoppers believe the food industry does not act in the public interest and is preoccupied with profits.

The inquiry will focus on the ethics of supermarkets and their food sources. It will name and shame companies guilty of failed safety promises, unnatural farming methods and unsubstantiated health claims on packaging.

The report found that 78 per cent of shoppers do not trust the food industry to tell them the truth. Eight in ten are worried that animals are not being treated properly and almost nine in ten believe multinational manufacturers have too much power over what people eat.

The findings also betrayed a lack of trust in the government's food safety regulation. Last month officials admitted that 'agricultural cannibalism' was still allowed, with feed containing blood products, tallow and gelatin from cows regularly fed back to cows.

A spokeswoman for the Co-op said, 'We cannot ignore the overwhelming sense of unease among shoppers towards the food industry. The way the world rears animals, grows crops and markets food is beginning to sicken the public.'

Sheila McKechnie, director of the Consumers' Association, said: 'This research shows that consumers' views have been ignored for far too long by the industry and government.'

Source: adapted from *Daily Express*, 23 May 2000

1 According to the report, what percentage of shoppers do not trust the food industry?

2 Why is the public concerned about methods of food production?

3 Suggest three steps which, in your opinion, could be taken to ensure that the consumer has more control over what he eats.

Case study 2

Recycling target set at 33 per cent to end 'dustbin culture'

A range of legally binding recycling targets for local authorities was announced by the government yesterday in an attempt to reduce the amount of household waste.

Councils will be required to recycle or compost 25 per cent of household rubbish by 2005; 30 per cent by 2010 and 33 per cent by 2015.

Michael Meacher, Environment Minister, said: 'In many cases, people will, in three to five years, have different coloured dustbins and different coloured sacks.'

Some of the money to pay for the scheme would come from the landfill tax. The lion's share, estimated by environment groups and industry at £200 million or £10 a household annually, will come from government.

Only nine per cent of household rubbish is recycled and eight per cent is processed in waste-to-energy schemes.

New European Union directives

require member states to reduce the percentage of household waste going to tips from a current average of 85 per cent to no more than 35 per cent by 2016. Britain has been given a four-year breathing space to meet the target by 2020.

New packaging regulations require industry and retailers to recover 52 per cent of packaging, at least half of which must be recycled by 2001 with new targets likely to be set for 2006.

Source: *The Times*, 26 May 2000

1 Why will people have different coloured dustbins and sacks?

2 Why is it necessary
a) to reduce the amount of household waste going to tips
b) to recycle it?

3 In your opinion, is there any alternative to recycling waste?

4 What do you think is the effect of the dustbin culture on a) the consumer
b) the environment
c) Third World countries?

Case study 3

Escape from city causes homes boom

Migration from the North to the South is not to blame for the majority of new homes needed in the South East, a report by the Joseph Rowntree Foundation said yesterday.

Instead it shows that movement from London, a bigger than expected increase in the population and incomers from abroad have brought regions nearest the capital under pressure to expand.

The report's authors found that fewer than one in ten of the homes built in the South East of England between 1991 and 1998 was to house people moving from Scotland, Northern Ireland, Wales, the Midlands or the North.

Half of the homes built accommodated people moving out of London, whether to escape the poor schools, crime and grime of the city or to find more space because family houses had become unaffordable.

A quarter of the homes needed in the South East were the result of people living longer, thus boosting the population.

A fifth was the result of immigration at both ends of the spectrum, high income migrants going to work in the City and poor refugees.

The report used the latest 1998 projections of population growth for England which show an increase in population of more than 1.2 million by 2021.

Dr Alan Holmans of Cambridge University has forecast that 4.3 million households will be in need of accommodation by 2021. This is 500,000 more than estimated by the Department of the Environment, Transport and the Regions. He predicted that the biggest impact would be in the South East, where the population was expected to grow by 50,000 a year. He said an extra 150,000 homes than

previously expected would be needed outside London.

Source: adapted from *Daily Telegraph*, 24 August 2000

1 By how much is the population expected to increase by 2021?

2 What are the three main causes of the demand for more housing in the South East?

3 What are the reasons given for people moving out of London?

4 What other factors are increasing housing demand in the South East?

5 Discuss the possible effects of the projected increase of population in the South East on a) that region
b) government plans
c) the national economy.

Case study 4

Pollution watchdog accused of leadership failure

The future of the Environment Agency was called into question yesterday after MPs published a damning report accusing the pollution watchdog of 'a failure of leadership'.

The agency, set up more than three years ago, spends £600 million of public money each year and acts as independent regulator of companies in the waste, nuclear, chemicals, water and agricultural industries.

The Commons environment, transport and regional affairs committee said it had become sluggish, mired by bureaucracy and inadequate training.

MPs said there were 'serious concerns' that the agency was failing to perform its waste management function. It was not making requirements clear to those it regulated with inspectors enforcing rules that had not been made available to affected groups.

They were concerned that the agency was not providing adequate guidance on radioactive waste management and discharge regulation. Inspectors had been made responsible for all aspects of environmental pollution, making them 'jacks of all trades and masters of none'.

Sir John Harman, chairman of the Environment Agency, shrugged off suggestions that the agency's future was at risk. 'Our task is enormous and we recognize the comments of the committee about the need for clear aims. But in its first few years the agency has delivered real improvements.'

Source: adapted from *Financial Times*, 20/21 May 2000

1 **What is the job of the Environment Agency?**

2 **In what way is it alleged to have failed?**

3 **Make out a schedule of actions it could take to improve the situation.**

4 **Explain in your own words the difficulties the Environment Agency faces.**

EXAM PRACTICE

Permission has been given for the erection of a thousand bungalows for retired people two miles outside a small country town.

Foundation

1 State three businesses which are likely to benefit as a result of the development. (3 marks)

2 What effect is the development likely to have on the local hospital waiting lists? (3 marks)

Higher

1 Suggest three retail outlets you might expect to be included on the estate. Give your reasons. (6 marks)

2 Discuss two sectors of the local economy which are likely to be affected as a result of the development. (6 marks)

Final exam practice 1

Case study

Matthew worked for five years in the garden department of a large DIY store in a shopping complex on the outskirts of a city. When it was taken over by another superstore, he was given the choice of working in another branch forty miles away or accepting a redundancy settlement.

Matthew had developed an interest in cacti and hothouse plants. He had just inherited a house with a large garden and two large heated greenhouses from his father, so he thought he could set up his own business. He accepted the redundancy payment and obtained a loan from his bank manager. After he had obtained planning permission from the local council, he started the business in the two large greenhouses.

That was eight years ago. Since then, Matthew has bought an acre of unused land adjoining the garden. The heated greenhouses have been converted into a tea-room. There are another four large greenhouses on the site – now named Exotica Homes And Gardens. Three years ago, Matthew decided to install plastic tunnels where he grows herbs and fruit such as strawberries and raspberries.

The business became a private company two years ago. Matthew has eight permanent employees in the nursery garden and three in the cafe. He uses casual labour in the summer for picking the fruit. He has a good reputation for the quality of his cacti and exotic plants. He is now considering whether to expand his range of products or to sell his products abroad.

Foundation

1 Complete the sentences below.

- When selling cacti, Exotica Homes And Gardens are operating in the ....sector.

  tertiary

  private

  secondary

  public

- People who buy cacti and exotic plants are ....

  market orientated

  executives

  a niche market

  entrepreneurs

- A private limited company is owned by ....

  the government

  relatives

  public

  shareholders.

- Dividends are sums of money paid to ....

  creditors

  directors

  shareholder

  producers

- A contract of employment must be given to a new employee within .... of starting work.

  five years

  one year

  two months

  two days

- A gardening business is ....

  job sharing

  labour intensive

  flow production

  expensive

- An opportunity cost is a ....

  trading expense

  net loss

  owner's drawings

  sacrificed alternative

- A merger of two identical businesses is an example of........ integration.

  lateral

  vertical

  horizontal

  conglomerate

- Stock is ....

  gross profit

  an asset

  depreciation

  the cost of sales

- VAT is an example of ....

  an indirect tax

  marketing mix

  social cost

  chain of production   (10 marks)

2 For each of the following questions, write the letter A B C or D to show the correct answer in the box provided.

- The assets in Matthew's balance sheet show:

  A what the company owns

  B his profit for the year

  C total sales

  D tax owing.

- One advantage to Matthew of forming a private company is:

  A shares can be sold on the Stock Exchange

  B gives limited liability

  C improves cash flow

  D increases turnover.

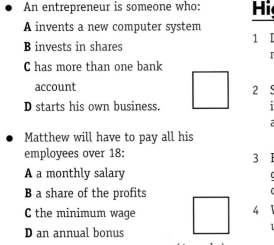

- An entrepreneur is someone who:
  A invents a new computer system
  B invests in shares
  C has more than one bank account
  D starts his own business.

- Matthew will have to pay all his employees over 18:
  A a monthly salary
  B a share of the profits
  C the minimum wage
  D an annual bonus

  (4 marks)

3 When Matthew left the DIY store, he was given a 'redundancy payment'.

a) State what is meant by redundancy payment. (2 marks)

b) Give two reasons why he decided to become a sole proprietor. (2 marks)

c) Describe three advantages to Matthew of starting his own business. (3 marks)

4 Matthew submitted a business plan to his bank manager to obtain a loan. Give details of what he would have included in his business plan.
(4 marks)

5 Describe Matthew's main methods of production. (5 marks)

6 a) Suggest two methods of advertising Matthew might employ. (2 marks)

b) What would be his two main sources of recruitment for staff? (4 marks)

c) State four laws he must observe in employing staff. (4 marks)

7 a) Describe two ways in which Matthew has diversified since starting his business. (4 marks)

b) What problems might this diversification cause? (4 marks)

Total 48 marks

Higher

1 Describe three decisions Matthew made to expand his business.
(6 marks)

2 State the details Matthew might have included in his business plan to obtain a loan from his bank manager.
(4 marks)

3 Explain three benefits he would have gained from becoming a private company. (6 marks)

4 What are two disadvantages of setting up a private company?
(4 marks)

5 Give examples of three assets and three liabilities which will appear in the balance sheet of Exotica Homes And Gardens. (6 marks)

6 In view of the information you have been given, do you think it would be a good idea for Matthew to introduce new products? Explain your reasons.
(4 marks)

7 What problems is Matthew likely to face if the company decides to export?
(4 marks)

8 Describe three ways in which the government may be of assistance to a company expanding into the export market. (6 marks)

9 At a board meeting, it is suggested by one of the directors that instead of exporting, they should expand by acquiring another garden centre. Identify two factors which may influence their decision. (4 marks)

10 Explain how these two factors will affect that decision. (4 marks)

Total 48 marks

FINAL TOTAL

48
marks

Final exam practice 2

Case study 1

Clare Boston has qualifications in health and beauty. She has worked at a health farm and therapy centre for five years and is now employed in the research department of a large firm producing perfumes and make-up. She is well-paid and enjoys fringe benefits such as a company pension fund, six weeks' holidays and a company car. She and her friend, Julie, have decided to start their own business so that they can make and sell health and beauty products which contain only organic, non-animal products. Julie will be responsible for marketing the products.

Foundation

1 Explain the opportunity costs which are involved in Clare's decision to start her own business. (8 marks)

2 Clare will need a loan to obtain a mortgage for a suitable property, to obtain equipment and materials, and to buy a car. Describe the various sources of short- and medium-term finance which may be available to her for these requirements. (8 marks)

3 As well as a business plan, Clare and Julie have worked out a detailed cash-flow forecast for the business.
a) What is a cash-flow forecast?
b) Why is it important?
c) Give two examples of receipts and payments it may contain.
(10 marks)

Total 26 marks

Higher

1 Describe three opportunity costs which Clare has foregone in order to start her business.
(6 marks)

2 Describe the market research she should have carried out before leaving her current job.
(4 marks)

3 Suggest two kinds of advertising and two promotions Julie could use in order to sell their products. In each case, explain their purpose.
(8 marks)

4 What business problems could Clare and Julie face in starting a business together? (8 marks)

Total 26 marks

Case study 2

Charles Baker started out twenty years ago with a small shop in a country town selling vacuum cleaners. Over the years he opened further branches, and today has a large business making an annual profit of £1 million, with branches all over the country. He has always ensured that all the shops have the same appearance, with identical interior layout and furnishings. All the shops' activities are controlled by headquarters, with staff in four departments under a marketing director, finance director, personnel manager and administrative manager. The branch managers are responsible for the general running of their own branch. Charles Baker is the chairman and chief executive of the company.

Foundation

1 Draw an organization chart showing the main staff at company headquarters. (4 marks)

2 How has Charles Baker introduced a brand element into his shops?
(4 marks)

3 Explain the purpose of branding and brand recognition. (4 marks)

4 What are the four main elements in marketing a product? (4 marks)

5 Select one of these elements and describe how Charles Baker could use this in selling his vacuum cleaners.
(8 marks)

Total 24 marks

Higher

1 Draw an organization chart, showing the main staff at company headquarters. (4 marks)

2 Describe the work of the personnel department in a large company.
(6 marks)

3 Explain what is meant by the marketing mix. (4 marks)

4 Explain which elements of marketing you think have been of most importance to Charles Baker.
(4 marks)

5 Why did he have a centralized organization structure? (6 marks)

Total 24 marks

Case study 3

James and Paula Mansell met when they both worked in the film development, printing and photocopying department of a large department store. When they married two years later, they were earning £27,000 gross between them. They decided they would like to start their own business.

They had read that a franchise business has a much greater chance of success than an independent business. After studying the franchise market, they saw a large company's advertisement offering franchises to a few promising candidates in their photocopying business. This is the information they received.

Year company established: 1990

Number of franchised outlets: 10

Number of franchises planned: 50

Total cost of franchise: £10,000

Royalties payable : 9 per cent on turnover

Projected turnover: 1st year £40,000, 2nd year £65,000

Projected profit: 1st year £30,000 2nd year £45,000

Training provided: three-day residential training course and two-monthly refresher courses.

Support services: Legal advice, national marketing.

After a number of interviews and discussions with the company, they were offered a franchise.

Foundation

1   Explain what is meant by a franchise.
(4 marks)

2   Give three advantages to James and Paula of taking a franchise rather than operating as a partnership.
(6 marks)

3   Do you think it would be a good idea to become a franchisee with this company? Give your reasons for your answer.
(4 marks)

4   If James and Paula had been given a choice of locating their business in the centre of a small town or on an out-of-town retail estate, which do you think would be most suitable? Give three reasons for your choice.
(8 marks)

Total 22 marks

Higher

1   Do you think it would be a good business decision for James and Paula to become franchisees rather than setting up a partnership? Give your reasons.
(4 marks)

2   What are the disadvantages of being a franchisee?
(6 marks)

3   What further information might James and Paula seek from the franchiser before making a decision?
(4 marks)

4   James and Paula have a choice of locations – a high street lock-up shop, a unit in the out-of-town industrial estate, a unit in a large department store and a shop with accommodation on the outskirts of the city. State the advantages and disadvantages of each and suggest which you think would be most suitable.
(8 marks)

Total 22 marks

FINAL TOTAL

72 marks

Final exam practice 3

Case study

Thirty years ago, Anthony Foster started his own business making specialized metal domestic items for the home, such as fire baskets and ornamental iron and kettle stands for customers placing individual orders. He enjoyed the personal nature of his business, but as demand grew, he needed to take on staff. He decided to expand by producing simple garden gates and balcony balustrades. From a small workshop, he moved to a larger factory. By advertising his products regionally, he gradually extended his business to the adjacent counties.

With the great expansion in the housing market, Anthony realised it would be a good idea to diversify into other domestic markets such as ornamental gates, garage doors, fire escapes, and electric driveway and garage gates. He decided to form a private company with ten other shareholders. It was given a new brand name, Iron Safety. The increase in capital meant that the company could move to larger premises, where it employed 50 people. Some automated equipment and machinery was installed which increased production greatly. Another factory was soon opened in the South of the country.

The factories now started to make products for the commercial market, concentrating first on hotels. That side of their business grew when insurance companies started to demand that commercial firms should install security equipment in their premises. Iron Safety's R & D department designed new security grilles, window and security bars and shop grilles. The company also decided to diversify into safes, both domestic and commercial.

To finance the expansion, Iron Safety became a public limited company. Another factory was opened in the North of the country. Automated production, using computers and robots, was installed in all three factories.

The company then started to produce goods for the public sector. Its first local government order involved designing and manufacturing security gates and surveillance equipment for car parks. Later, the company started to manufacture special, made-to-order equipment for government departments.

The board of directors is now discussing the takeover of a smaller company which specialises in distribution. This would give Iron Safety an entry to export markets.

Foundation

1 What were Anthony Foster's original business objectives? (4 marks)

2 Explain the reasons why he decided to become a) a private company b) a plc. (4 marks)

3 In what ways has the company diversified over the years? (8 marks)

4 What market research might have been carried out before the business a) expanded its domestic products b) diversified into the commercial and public sector markets? (8 marks)

5 Describe the three kinds of production the company would use in fulfilling contracts for a) a garden gate for a stately home b) ten fire escapes for a large hotel c) an internal security system which would be sold to many other commercial and official organizations. (10 marks)

6 Where would the firm be likely to advertise a) domestic items when it was a small business b) commercial products when it was a large company? (4 marks)

7 What is meant by 'automated equipment and machinery'? (4 marks)

8 State a) three variable costs and b) three fixed costs involved in operating the company. (6 marks)

9 What effect would the installation of computer equipment and robots have on a) production b) manpower? (6 marks)

10 Explain the external costs and benefits of the automation revolution. (6 marks)

Total 60 marks

Higher

1 Explain how Anthony Foster's business objectives changed over the years.
(4 marks)

2 In what ways would his decision to form a) a private company and b) a plc have affected his financial situation?
(4 marks)

3 In what other ways would his business have been changed?
(4 marks)

4 Describe the three significant decisions Andrew Foster made to diversify.
(6 marks)

5 What market research might have been carried out before the business
a) expanded its domestic products
b) diversified into the commercial and public sector markets?
(8 marks)

6 Describe the three kinds of production the company would use in fulfilling contracts for a) a garden gate for a stately home b) ten fire escapes for a large hotel c) an internal security system which would be sold to many other commercial and official organizations.
(10 marks)

7 The company accounts for the past two years, included the following figures.

	2000	2001
Current assets	£80 million	£98 million
Current liabilities	£64 million	£70 million
Sales	£30 million	£42 million
Net profit	£8 million	£12 million

a) Calculate the current ratio and net profit ratio.
(4 marks)

b) Do you think the directors of the company would find these figures satisfactory? Explain your reasons.
(4 marks)

8 How will the technological changes which have been introduced affect
a) the company's workforce
b) profitability
c) the national economy?
(6 marks)

9 a) What kind of integration would be involved in the takeover of the distribution company?
b) Do you think it would be a good business decision?
(4 marks)

10 Explain the external costs and benefits of the automation revolution.
(6 marks)

Total 60 marks

FINAL TOTAL

60 marks

Index

Acknowledgements

Published by Collins Educational
An imprint of HarperCollins*Publishers*
77–85 Fulham Palace Road
London W6 8JB

www.**Collins**Education.com
On-line Support for Schools and Colleges

© HarperCollins*Publishers* 2001

First published 1988
Second edition 1993, Third edition 1997
This edition first published 2001
10 9 8

ISBN-13 978 0 00 711513 6
ISBN-10 0 00 711513 X

British cataloguing-in-publication data
A catalogue record for this book is available from the
British Library.

Commissioned by Mary James
Design, layout and editing by DSM Partnership
Cover design by DSM Partnership
Cover pictures by Stone (left) The Stock Market (right)
Project management by Paul Stirner and Kay Wright
Original artwork by Barking Dog Art pp. 119, 131, 134, 139
Gay Galsworthy pp. 6, 7, 11, 36, 66, 166, 167
Cartoons by Martin Shovel pp. 49, 196
Illustrations by Alan Fraser, Pennant Inc pp. 10, 18, 56,
148, 168, 169, 170, 179, 198, 199
Production by James Graves
Printed and bound by Printing Express, Hong Kong

Acknowledgements

The Publishers would like to thank the following for
permission to reproduce photographs and artwork in this
book:

Abbey National, p. 125; ACE/Kevin Phillips, p. 69, pp. 89, 160; ADtranz,
p. 12; Advertising Archives, p. 206; AEEU, p. 162; AFP, p. 60; Ainsworth
Finishing, p. 128; Airtours, p. 162; Asda, p. 126; Aston Martin, p. 40; BP
Amoco, p. 42; Autotech Robotics, p. 134; Boots plc, p. 90; Patricia
Briggs, pp. 3, 25, 172; British Aerospace, p. 52; Business Post, p. 116;
Justin Canning, p. 152 ; Cardline, p. 32; Caterpillar (uk), p. 136; CBI,
p. 161; Centrica plc, p. 176; Collections, pp. 74,186, 188; Gaynor Cornell,
p. 68; Sheila Coules, p. 146; *Daily Mail*, p. 190; Dixons plc, p. 4; Ducati,
p. 14; Dyson Press Office, p. 130; EAT/Niall MacArthur, p. 38;
Environmental Images, p. 15; Helen Evans, p. 99; *Financial Times*, p. 26;
First Choice, pp. 46, 48; Gillian Goode, pp. 4, 90, 98, 162; Gold Major,
p. 26; Sally & Richard Greenhill, pp. 120, 142; Halifax Property Services,
p. 192; Michael Harford, p. 159; Hypatia Trust, p. 70; Impact, pp. 132,
186; Infoplan Ltd., p. 102; Johnson & Johnson, p. 54; John Lewis
Partnership, p. 20; Kids Unlimited, p. 147; McCarthy & Stone plc, p. 86;
Marks & Spencer, p. 100; John Menzies plc, p. 176; National Packaging
Group plc, p. 110; Next plc, p. 176; Nokia, p. 180; Norton and Townsend,
p. 108; Nike, p. 115; Pictor International Ltd., p. 2; Popperfoto, pp. 29,
40, 80, 161, 165, 200; QA Photos, pp. 76; Primetime Petfoods, p 70;
Pronuptia, p. 24; Psion, p. 180; Brett Ransley, p. 159; Rockwood, p. 64;
Rex Features, p 8; RSPCA, p. 202; J Sainsbury plc p. 16; Tim Scrivener/
Farmers Weekly, p. 79; Scottish Daily Mail/Stan Hunter, p. 44; Roger
Scruton, pp. 96, 156; Shell LiveWire Award, p. 98; Shout Pictures, p. 113;
Smile.com, p. 9; Spectrum Colour Library, pp. 4, 72, 209; Sturgess Van
Damme PR, p. 118; The British Quality Foundation, p. 52; Telegraph
Colour Library/ A Tilley, p. 2, Michael Bussey, p. 172, C Ryan, pp. 96,
128, 172,182, 208; Tesco, p. 92; The Body Shop, p. 204; The Prince's
Youth Trust, p. 62; Times Newspapers Limited, p. 106, p. 122;Trevor
Peters Design, p. 180; Stone/Jay Ward, p. 2, Jon Riley, pp. 2, 180, Paul
Chesley, p. 30, Bruce Ayres, pp. 157, 177; Ultimate Bikes, p. 140; John
Walmsley, p. 112; Welsh Dragon Coal Limited, p. 22; Williams
Photographers, p. 122; Kay Wright, p. 104; Xscape, p. 188; Yell.com, p. 8.

The Publishers also wish to acknowledge the following
sources of articles and data:

Barclays Bank plc, p. 77; *Bristol Evening Post*, p. 190; *Business Age*, p. 170;
Daily Express, pp. 198, 208; *Daily Mail*, pp. 45, 58, 119, 139, 146, 170,
190, 191; 199; *Daily Telegraph*, pp. 125, 209; DTI, p. 178; Express Dairies,
p. 129; *Evening Standard*, p. 179; *Farmers Weekly*, p. 79; *Financial Mail on
Sunday*, pp. 56, 106, 169; *Financial Times*, p. 210; First Choice Holidays,
pp. 46, 48, 50; Hypatia Trust, p. 70; *Investors Chronicle*, p. 82; Lloyds TSB
plc, p. 78; Office for National Statistics, pp. 2, 26, 42, 94; *Somerset
Business*, p. 118; Superdrug, p. 152; *The Independent*, p. 124; *The
Independent on Sunday*, p. 180; *The Mirror*, p. 169; *The Times*, pp. 60, 80,
106, 122, 126, 179, 198, 209.

www.**fireandwater**.com
Visit the book lover's website